THE

PUBLICATIONS

OF THE

SURTEES SOCIETY

VOL. CXII.

THE

PUBLICATIONS

OF THE

SURTEES SOCIETY

ESTABLISHED IN THE YEAR

M.DCCC.XXXIV.

VOL. CXII.

FOR THE YEAR M.CM.VI.

WILLS

AND

INVENTORIES

FROM THE

REGISTRY AT DURHAM

PART III.

𝔓𝔲𝔟𝔩𝔦𝔰𝔥𝔢𝔡 𝔣𝔬𝔯 𝔱𝔥𝔢 𝔖𝔬𝔠𝔦𝔢𝔱𝔶

BY ANDREWS & CO., DURHAM
WHITTAKER & CO., 2 WHITE HART STREET
PATERNOSTER SQUARE
BERNARD QUARITCH, 15 PICCADILLY
BLACKWOOD & SONS, EDINBURGH

1906

Reprinted 1967 for
Wm. DAWSON & SONS LTD., LONDON
with the permission of
THE SURTEES SOCIETY

At a Meeting of the COUNCIL OF THE SURTEES SOCIETY, held in Durham Castle on Tuesday, March 7th, 1899, the REV. WILLIAM GREENWELL in the chair,

It was ordered that a third volume of Wills and Inventories be edited by Mr. J. C. HODGSON.

WILLIAM BROWN,
Secretary.

ORIGINALLY PRINTED IN GREAT BRITAIN BY
ANDREW REID AND COMPANY, LIMITED
LONDON AND NEWCASTLE-UPON-TYNE

PRINTED IN GREAT BRITAIN
BY PHOTOLITHOGRAPHY
UNWIN BROTHERS LIMITED
WOKING AND LONDON

PREFACE.

OF the ever increasing number of volumes issued by the
Surtees Society, perhaps none have possessed more general
interest and popularity than the two volumes of Wills and
Inventories selected from the Registry at Durham, and edited
respectively by the Rev. James Raine and the Rev. William
Greenwell. Although the choicest of the wills of the spacious
Tudor period were taken for the second volume of the series,
published forty-seven years ago, there remains a very large
number belonging to the smaller gentry, clergy, yeomen and
merchants. Some of them were indeed transcribed or abstracted
for, but were crowded out of, that volume. These have been
handed over to the present editor by Mr. Greenwell and form
the nucleus of the following selection.

The union of the two Crowns, in 1603, in the person of
James I., ushered in a period of peaceful development and
extended to the country parishes of Northumberland and
Durham the security which previously had been enjoyed only
by the inhabitants of the walled towns, and, to some extent, by
the owners of the greater castles. Wills of a later period,
therefore, lose a considerable part of their historical interest
and for that reason it is considered desirable not to extend the
present collection beyond the reign of Elizabeth.

Specimens of nuncupative wills are given on pp. 35, 97,
100, 114, 157, 164 and 165. The will of 'the lady of Kenton'
(p. 10) and the will of Gawen Hoppen (p. 66) supply
additional details to the pedigrees of Bennet and Hoppen.
Bertram Anderson (p. 60) gives to his sister, Marion Chapman,
three 'tennes of coals'; Simon Wellbury (p. 87) gives legacies to his 'cosins,' the children of his son; Margaret
Middleton (p. 122) bequeathes a 'garnyshe,'—that is, a set of 12
platters, 12 dishes, 12 saucers, and 12 porringers,—of pewter;

and on pp. 99, 123, are preserved some of the names which the farmers and breeders of the day gave to their cattle. An innkeeper's will may be found on p. 52, while the inventory (p. 178) of the goods of Sir William Hilton affords particulars of the disposition of the rooms and of their contents at Hilton Castle in 1600.

The Editor desires to acknowledge with gratitude the help he has received from the Rev. William Greenwell, D.C.L., F.R.S., who, as noticed above, gave his transcripts of a great number of wills; to Mr. J. J. Howe, for collating proofs with the original documents in the Registry; to Mr. Richard Welford, M.A., for reading the proofs; and to Mr. Herbert M. Wood, B.A., for proving the burial of several of the testators by extracts from parish registers.

DURHAM

WILLS AND INVENTORIES.

WILL OF EDWARD SURTEES.

Dec. 14, 15... Edwarde Surteis of Newcastell, draper.[1] To be buried in the churche of Sainct Ny[cholas] on the southe syde of the queyr over against . . . . doore. I give for my laierstall, 6s. 8d. To the vicar of the towne for my forgotton tyethes, 3s. 4d. To Andrewe Surteis, my soonne, my howes in the Close upon condicion that he and his heirs shall case yereyle sowlle masse and dirige to be song within the churche of Sainct Nicholas for the sowlles of me, Isabell, my wyffe, and all christian sowlles for ever. To Isabell, my wyffe, my howes in the Syde in which I [dwell], my fyve tenements in the . . . . gate nigh unto the dissolved ho[ouse] . . . . my daughter Jane: residue to Isabell, my wyffe. Witnesses, Robert Wood, my curatt, Andrew Surtees. [Pr. 1543.]

WILL OF ROBERT BIDDIC.

Feb. 20, 1543/4. Robert Bedyke of Duresme, tanner. To be buryed in the chapell of Saynt Margarett ny unto my wyiffe laytly buryed. To the hy alter for my forgotton tithes, 12d. To 30 preasts the daye of my buryall for masse and dirige to every one of them, 6d. To the clarks and chyldren the said daye, 3s. 4d. In almesse to poure folks in breid aill, 5s. I wolle that my executors the daye of my buryall maike on denar to my nebours. To Mawld, my wyffe, in gowld and sylver, 20l. To Robert Bedyke, my elder soon, in gowld and sylver, 23l. 6s. 8d. To William Bedyke, my

---

[1] A member of the wide-spreading Derwentside family of Surtees and a draper in the Side, then one of the chief streets of Newcastle. Many members of this family are buried in St. Nicholas's church.

On April 13, 1517, the mayor and community of Newcastle granted to Edward Surtees, bowmaker, a tenement in the Side, extending from the highway on the east to the castle moat on the west, he paying a free rent of 16s. to the use of the Tyne bridge. Welford, *Newcastle and Gateshead*, vol. ii. p. 51.

younger soon, 20*l*. and my emptie barke fatts in parte of payment, and if they will nott soo fare extend I wolle he have my barke to arraise the rest upon. To Sir John Foster, preast,[1] for the many-ffold kyndnes that I have found in hym bothe toward my selffe and my soon Robert, trustyng that he wolle continewe them, one ryall in gowld for a token.

WILL OF GEORGE SMITH.

Feb. 24, 1544/5. I, George Smythe of Nonstaynton, in the countie of Duresme, esq., being hole of mynd and perfite remem-braunce, dothe order and make thys my last will and testament in maner and forme following : That is to say, first, I bequethe my soule to Almighty God and to the most blissid Virgin, his mother our Lady Saint Marye, and to all the blissid companye of hevin, besicheyng thame all to pray for me ; and my body to be beried where it shall please God to call me to his mercye. Also I will that Anne, my wyffe, after my dethe imediatly enter into all my howses and two parts of all my grounde in Nonstaynton, that is to say these parcells following : First the East-feylde, two Est-closes, Bradmier, the Crokehills, Haverclose, Freermedow, th'orchard, the Dovecoyte-close, Robinson-close, Goldisburgh, Darlyng, the Cowper-carre, Jonkett-carre, Close-carre, Horse-carre, Cow-carre, Scurton-carre, Milne-carre, and 24 Acre-carre, the Corne-croks, which, as I think, is skarce the two parts, and if the law will not suffer, that she may have thes grounds whiche I have appointed for terme of her lyffe, and after hir deathe to the right hirs of me, the said George Smythe. And if my son Cuthbert,[2] when he comes to the full age of 21 years, make hir assurance that he will not trobill hir duryng hir lyffe of the howse and two parts of the foresaid grounds, then I will that my said wyffe shall geve hym on hundrethe marks towards his levying or ells nott.

WILL OF BARTHOLOMEW PAGE.

May 6, 1544. I, Barthe Paige of Aislebie, within the parishe of Egglisclife, within the countie of Duresme, syke in my bodie but of perfecte remembrance, maketh this my last will and testament as

---

[1] The Mr. Foster whose kindly offices are so gratefully acknowledged by the testator does not appear in the list of curates of St. Margaret's as given in Surtees, *Durham*, vol. iv. p. 131.

[2] From the *Inq. p.m.* held at Durham Jan. 15, 37 Hen. VIII., it appears that the testator died Sept. 5, 36 Hen. VIII., leaving Cuthbert Smyth, his son, 16 years and 40 weeks old.

The Smiths of Esh were tenants of Nun Stainton under the nuns of Monketon, and after the dissolution of religious houses they acquired the fee simple. *Cf.* Surtees, *Durham*, vol. iii. p. 335, *note* q.

followeth. First, I bequyth my sowll to Almightie God and my bodie to be buried within the church-yarde of Egglisclife aforesaid. I gyve to the blissed Sacrament 12*d*. I gyve to Martayn Paige my iron bounde wayne, the hedyocke and the oxen cleare . . . . of parten. I gyve to my six doughters, unto every one of them one ewe and a lambe owt of parte. To everye childe of Roland Burdon's a pecke of wheat. To my syster, Esabell Burdon, one bushell of wheat. To my syster Elsabith one bushell of wheat. To my bretherene, Richard Paige and Jamys Paige, two bushels of wheat. The rest of my goods, boith moveable and unmoveable, I give to my wife and seven children, whom I make all jointlie together my holl executors, and thay to pay my debts and funerall expences. Records, John Semer and Richerde Bell, and Sir William Burdon my curate.

INVENTORY. 4 oxen, 53*s*. 4*d*. 3 kyne, 30*s*. 5 horses and mears, 53*s*. 4*d*. 2 foils, 6*s*. 20 sheep, 20*s*. 4 lamis, 2*s*. 4 young beasts, 15*s*. 1 swyne, 2*s*. 4 swarmes, 10*s*. 1 bounde wayne, 26*s*. 8*d*. A woyne wayine, a cowpe pleighe with certayne teames and yocks, 24*s*. 8*d*. 8 acres of corne, 53*s*. 4*d*. 1 cowell and one ambrie, 4*s*. A table, a chair with stoles, 12*d*. 4 potts, a caidrene, a ketle, 2 panis, 10*s*. 10 pecis of pewder, 4*s*. 4*d*. Tubbes, skeils, bowils and 3 dishes, 2*s*. Tongs, rackencrooke and pott and kytles, 8*d*. 3 coverletts, 2 blanketts, 4 pair of sheitts and 2 skeils, 16*s*. 4*d*. Total, 17*l*. 4*s*. 8*d*.

WILL OF THOMAS BERTRAM.

May 31, 1544. Thomas Bartram, late sone of William Bartram, marchaunte, of Newcastell. To be bured in Alhalloes chyrche besyd my mother. To my uncle, Georg Bartram, the tenement that lyes in the hed of the Syde. To my brother, Christofer Wylkeson, the best of my 3 sylver peces and a dosen silver spones. The resydew to my brethren, Robert and Christofer Wylkeson, they executors.

WILL OF ROBERT SHADFORTH.

Aug. 7, 1545. Robert Shaldeforthe of Newcastle, baker. To be buryed within the churche yarde of All Sancts. To Thomas Shaldeforthe[1] of Newcastle, maryner, my two tenements in the Keysyde, paying to my pouer mother 10*s*. yerlye during hir lyfe. To Peter, son of John Chator, marchaunte, all my tenement in Pilgrime-strete in the teanor of Edwarde Davynson, mynstrell; remainder to Thomas Shaldeforthe, he executor.

---

[1] Amongst 'the namys off the maryners that promysyd to provyde them harnez . . . . alle goode men, and able to do the kynge servyce,' is that of Thomas Schawdfforth, Newcastle. Muster Roll, 1539; Welford, *Newcastle and Gateshead*, vol. ii. p. 192. He was one of the elder brethren of the Trinity House in 1541, 1547, etc. *Ibid*. pp. 208, 251, etc.

WILL OF JOHN SWINBURNE.

Sept. 26, 1545. John Swynborne of Newcastle, tayllor. To be buryed within my paryche churche off Alhallowis so nye the fonte and my brother as may be. I wyll that ther shalbe celebrat for my sowlle the day of my buryall sallmes and derge after the most laudable custom. To John Raw of Hawkwell, for a tokene, an angell noble. To the reparacions of Stannerdell churche, 5s. To the tow pore womene in the Masyngdew, 12d. To my brother Robert's sone in the sowthe parts, 12d. To every servante of George Swynborne, 12d. to pray for me. Residue to my sone Patryke Swynborne and my cossing George Swynborne. [Pr. 1549.]

WILL OF JOHN HEDLEY.

Oct. 18, 1545. Johne Hedley, carischman, of Newcastell.[1] To be buryit in Saunt Andro churche. To Esabeth, my wyffe, my seate-housse duryng hir lyffe, then to my dogther Alysone Gray and hir ears, then to my doghter Annes Dunne. To my doghters the silver beads that was their mother's. My house in Sedgaytte to Annes Dunne. To my sister, Elsebell Whetston, 10s. To Rychard Musgrave, my greyne jakkett. To Robert Colynwood, my jak. To Robert Colynwod sone, my bowe and schayfts. To William Dekesone, my best bonet with the George.

WILL OF NICHOLAS CARR.

Oct. 20, 1545. Nycoles Carr, tanner, of the parish of Sainct John's, Newcastle. To be buryed in my pariche churche yarde nie my wyffe. To my sone Robert Carr all my howses and landes to him and his heirs, then to my two daughters Alison and Jane Carr. To Wylliam Carr wyffe, marchand in the Syde, 6s. 8d. To George Carr wyffe, sadlere, in the Syde, 6s. 8d. To Cuthbert Elyson, taylyor, 6s. 8d. To Esabell Carr, my brother's daughter, 6s. 8d. The rest to my three children. Maister Galpinge and Roger Carre, my sonne, supervysors. I wyll that Maister Gelpinge have thre angels in gold and the gryssinge of 3 oxinge yerelye in my close so longe as it is unlawfude [sic]. My son Roger Rawe and Elizabeth, his wife, and his five children ; to my daughter Mauglen Camber, 20s. To my syster Isabell Taylor, in Belsawe, 6s. 8d. Witnesses, William Salkeld, clarke, Roger Rawe, William Carr, merchant, etc.

---

[1] 'Jhon Hedley,' furnished with ' a jak-stell bonnett, a bowe and a schayff of arrays,' appeared at the Newcastle muster of 1539. Welford, *Newcastle and Gateshead*, vol ii. p. 190.

WILL OF EDWARD GREY.

Nov. 2, 1545.   Edward Gray.   To be buryed in Lowyk churche yarde.   To Sir George Archer and Sir Lawrens Myll, 3s. 4d. to pray for me and my wyff.   My brother William Gray exsector, and levys to him my doughter Elsapeth and all my goods.

WILL OF THOMAS SURTEES.

Nov. 20, 1545.   Thomas Surttes (parish of Ovingham).   My wyfe and Wyllm Surttes, my son, executors; Agnes Surttees; the children of my son John Surttees.   Supervisors, Rauffe Surttees, my cosynge, and John Surttees, my son.   Witnesses, William Norton, vicar, etc.

WILL OF CUTHBERT ROGERLY.

Dec. 3, 1545.   Cuthberte Rogerlie of Westow, yoman.   To be buried within the chapell of Sanct Hilde at Sheles.   To the hight alter, one alter clothe and one towell, and to our Ladie alter, one towell.   For my layrston, 3s. 4d.   To my curat, Sir Edward Yonger,[1] 3s. 4d., to pray for me.   To my sone, George Rogerlie, my velvett dublett, one stele bonnett with a cott of olepye.   I will that a bowle of wheit be bakett in brede and dalt for my soule to pore folks at Sheles.

WILL OF JOHN WATSON.

Jhesus, Mari.   Oct., 1547.   John Watson of Holy Iland, yoman.[2] To be burred in the churche garthe of Holy Ilande with soull messes and dirge.   Remainder to Agnes, my wyffe, and my childer, Thomas, Robert and Rauffe Watson.

Debts.   To Agnes Neylson for to com to me and my wyff when we war infect, 10s. for clensynge my hous and beryng of my husband, my father and three childer, 13s. 4d.   For costes in tyme of my vysytacione, 3l.   To Herre Ogle for farme, 2s.

INVENTORY OF THOMAS STANTONE OF THE PARISH OF ALL SAINTS, NEWCASTLE.

1548.   13 capps, 13s. 4d.   17 yards wurstett, 17s.   On quarter and halfe of welwet, 3s.   7 yerds whitt fustyon, 6s.   14 yards of lynnynge clothe, 11s.   4 reide nightt capps, 16d.   18 yards syndall, 6s.

---

[1] Edward Younger's will is printed in *Wills and Inventories*, vol. i. p. 141.

[2] This will of a member of the family of Watson, for many generations settled at Holy Island, has a pathetic interest from the list of debts exhibited by the widow, from which it would appear that she lost her husband, her father and three of her children struck down one after the other by some epidemic.

7 dosen yerds brode sylke, 14s. 6 rounde sylke gyrdlls, 2s. A grose and a halfe sylk pontts, 3s. Bobbyng sylke, 3s. 13 semys, 4s. On quartrone of lasing sylke, 3s. 4d. On quartrone of suyng sylke, 3s. 3 dosen layse, 12s. 3 dosen perchmentt lase, 2s. Lasing croolls, 3s. Ponde blake thrid, 16d. Skeine threide, 16d. 3 ponde whit ynkle, 3s. 4d. 6 purssas, 8d. Layse, 2s. Pynns, 16d. On foxe skyne and a fowmeartt, 6d. Daker shethes, 8d. 4 dosen knyffes, 3s. 2 ponde pouder, 16d. On dosen sark colers, 18d. 8 payre playing cards, 16d. Playte and whissylls, 12d. Safrone, 12s. Spycys, 13s. 4d. Bottons, 2s. 3 dosen stryngs, 6d. 5 quare paper, 10d. Daker chaypps, 8d. 5 bronsts (?) 4d. On almery, one chimnay, on borde, 6s. A dosen graytts, halfe a ferkyng sope, 3s 4d. On mayre, 8s. Sewger candy, 20d. All his rayment with a woode knyffe, 31s. 8d. *Summa totalis*, 11l. 20d.

WILL OF WILLIAM REED.

April 15, 1549. William Rede of Newcastle, draper. To be buried within the chyrche of Saynt Nicolas. My lannds and tenements in Newcastle to George Rede, my sone, and his heirs, then to Richard Rede, Johan and Ann Rede my children, then to Water and John Rede my brothers. To Richard Rede, my sone, my lease of the parsonages and tyethes cornes of Emylton and Ponte Ilond of the demission and graunte of the Maister and Fellowes of Marton College in Oxforde, providet that Margaret, my wyf, have the glebe lound and the tyeth cornes of Pontiland and Johannet Rede my daughter, the half of the tyethe corne of Kyrkley, and Anne Rede, my daughter, half the tiethes cornes of Highe Calleton. To Anthonye Mytford, my brother-in-law, my gown fased with womes of foxes, one sleiveles jacket of silke camlet and one velvet dublet. To Jasper Mytford my gown fased with coney. The rest to my wife and children ; my brother in law, Anthony Mytford, and my wife to bring them up.

WILL OF GERARD SELBY.

June 30, 1549. Gerard Selby of Pauston, gentleman.[1] To be buried in the church of Norham. To John Selby, 3l. 6s. 8d. To Gawen Ourd and Margaret Selby, 6l. 13s. 4d. To . . . . s Selbie's children, 6l. 13s. 4d. To Leonard Selbie's children, 6l. 13s. 4d. To Katerine Selbie, 3l. 6s. 8d. To my godsonne Gerard Selbie, 6l. 13s. 4d. My daughter to have 40 marks. William my sonne ; Fortune my daughter ; William my brother ; Robert Selby, clerke,

---

[1] The testator had purchased the township of Pawston and built the tower there, 'without a barmekyn,' which was not quite finished when Sir Robert Bowes made his survey of the Marches in 1541. Bates, *Border Holds*, p. 31.

vicar of Norham [1] (my brother) my executors, and my said two brothers to be guardians of my two children. Supervisors, George my brother and . . . . of Twicell and Gilberte Swynnho.

INVENTORY. In the handes of Sir Francise Leake, knight, to be paid for goodes of Sir Richard Maners, knight, taken, 49*l*. 10*s*. Mony owid of Newcastell, 28*l*. Sir Robert Selby, vicar of Norham, oweth 60*l*.

WILL OF MARION ERRINGTON.

Aug. 31, 1549. Marion Eryngton of Littylle Whetton,[2] wedo. To be bured in the quere of Corbryge besyde my husband. I geve my place to Cuthbert and Jarard Eryngton my sons. My sons George and Geaspar. To Margaret Eryngton one dune brokytt wye. Cuthbert's chylder. Randell Fennyk's chylder, 3 yowes. To Robert Eryngtons daughter and Marion Carnaby, a yow and a lamb. My sons, George and Jerard, executors. Witnesses, Harther and Robert Eryngton, Rundall Fennyke and Odnall Carnabye.

INVENTORY, 11*l*. 13*s*.

WILL OF HENRY SANDERSON.

Jan. 23, 1549/50. Henry Sanderson of Newcastell, marchaunte.[3] My hooll ramente that longed to my bodye to be canted and solde, and of the money to be given to 13 poore naked children, 13 white cotes and 13 shertes and the reste shalbe putt in one pourse severall 'and my wif to have the custodeye of it, and at all tymes when as she shall chanshe for to see any indecente or naked bretheren or baubes, otherwise called poure naked folkes, men, women or children, that then shee shall releyve the sayd mesterfull and neadye with coote, sherte, hoos, dublett or shone, so longe as any of the money is remanente to the sayde use. To my vykker for my forgotte tethe, 3*s*. To three old men to praye for my soull, 3*s*. To Peter Sanderson, my sone, this house I dwell in in the Syde (the white rent payed) to paye for his bringinge upe to he bee 18, and a payre of gylte sautes dowble with a cover, and a standinge persell gilte pese with a cover, and a dosson spunes gylte with lyones, and 300 marks. To Essabell Sanderson, my doughter, the house in the Clothe Market for her brenginge upe and 200 markes. To Jayne Sanderson, my dowghter, a house in the Syde, to bring her up, unto

---

[1] Robert Selby was vicar of Norham from 1537 to 1565 ; and also vicar of Berwick from 1541 to 1565.

[2] Probably Little Whittington, in the parish of Corbridge.

[3] Probably a member of the family of Sanderson of Brancepeth and Hedleyhope, whose pedigree was entered at the Heralds' Visitations of Durham in 1615 and 1666.

God proyde a oneste marige for her, and 200 markes.   To my
brother Nycholas Baxter.[1]   To eache of my four sisters one angell for
a token.   To Ellynor Sanderson my wyf all my laundes, etc., and
she to make a sure and sufficyent stayt of on house in the Clothe
Market, or of the lease of Heghton to be taken to Essabell Sanderson,
my dowghter.   To my unkle, Roberte Lewen, 3 angells ; the same to
William Dente, they supervisors.   My wife, executrix.

WILL OF THOMAS CRAMLINGTON.

July 7, 1550.   I, Thomas Cra[m]lington of Newishame,[2] maikes
this my laste will and testamete in this mannor followinge : Firste
I geve my sowle to God and our Ladie Saincte Marie et cetera.   Also
I geve my wif, Agnes Cramlington, the thriddes of all my landes
and howses in Newishame.   Also I geve unto my sonn, Lancelot
Cramlyngton, my farmolde in Slekeburne and 26s. 8d. of rente out
of Blythesnooke, for terme of his lif.   Also I geve unto my sonn,
Lamwell Cramlyngton, all my towne of Blythesnooke, landes, and
pastures, and all other commodities thereto belongeinge, and he to
pay his brother Lancelotte 26s. 8d.   Also I geve unto my said
sonne Lamwell all my fysheinges and coblegates in Blythesenooke
together with the northe ende of my lynke frome Fullage apon the
sowthe to Blythesenooke apon the northe, and frome the dyke on the
west unto the see apon the este, for terme of his lyf.   Also I geve
unto my twoo sonnes Lancelotte and Lamwell a coblegate and fowre
howses in Blythesenooke duringe thare lyves.   Also I geve my sonn
Lamwell my best horsse.   And to my dowghter Elizabeth 20 kyee,
40 yeowes and lames, and 40 fleeses of woolle.   Also I geve unto
Ales Balif 40s. and twoo kyee.   The reste of my goodes I geve unto
my wyf and my twoo sonnes whoo I make my executores et cetera.[3]

WILL OF WILLIAM BEWICK.

Nov. 16, 1551.   William Bewyke of Newcastell, merchant.[4]
To be buriede within Sainte Nicholas churche before Saynte Katheren
alter as nigh my mother's grave as maye be convenientle.   I make
Cuthbert and William Bewyke my executors and I bequeth them my
take or lease belonginge to the house of Carlyle, paying everye yeare

[1] The will of Nicholas Baxter of Newcastle, merchant, is printed in *Wills
and Inventories*, vol. i. p. 298.

[2] An account of the family of Cramlington of Newsham, with a pedigree,
is given in *Arch. Ael.* 2nd series, vol. xix. p. 1, and a revised account may be
found in the new *History of Northumberland*, vol. viii.

[3] This will is obtained from *P.R.O. Chancery inq. p.m.* vol. 142, No. 95.

[4] A collateral ancestor of the family of Bewick of Close-house, who seems
to have been admitted free of the Merchant Adventurers' Company *circa* 1520.
Dendy, *Merchant Adventurers*, vol. ii. p. 194.

11*l.* to the deanery of Carlyle; my house, barne and foure leises in Sydegate and thre free tenaments in Felton. To Percyvall, sone to Peires Bewyke, my brother, my house in the Meal-market to him and his heirs male; then to Cuthbert Bewyke and his heirs male (it never to be sold nor wedsett); then to Thomas Bewyke, sone to my brother John Bewyke, and his heirs male. To every brother's child and syster's child, 6*s.* 8*d.* To every one of Bartrame Bewyke's children, 3*s.* 4*d.* To Thomas Bewyk, my brother's sone, my best furyd gowne. To Robert Scott, smith, my next best furred gowne. To my brother Thomas Bewyke's chylde which my syster is with, when God sends it, the furryd gowne wich my brother Thomas did give me. To Peter, my brother Peares Bewyke's sone, my velvett dublet. To Percyvall, my brother Peter Bewyke's sone, my best chamlott jackott garded with velvet. To Thomas Johnson my damaske dublet and to every one of his children, 3*s.* 4*d.* To Henry Dallayhay my bright tauny gowne and my best clock and 3*l.* 6*s.* 8*d.*, and I chardge my executors to put him to a good crafte. To John Mowell my gowne lyned with black lambs skine and to his daughter, Agnes Mowell, 3*l.* 6*s.* 8*d.* To Richard Benson, for a token, my velvett hatt and syx years of worsete. To my brother Thomas's wyf my best gold rynge and to Janet hir daughter a pair of crokes, also I will that my syster, Thomas Bewyk's wyf, has the quarter of Kynton and the quarter of Fenham tythes during hir wedowehead. To Cuthbert Bewike's wyf my second gold rynge. To Sir George Connyngham, my son, for a token, my third gold rynge. To my syster, Pyers Bewyke's wyf, a gown lyned with black shanks. To Leonard Whit, my hart lether dublet and my elder clocke. To my executors a sylver salt parcell gylt with a cover, and syx sylver spones with the madenheads of other syx sylver spones. The rest to Cuthbert and John Bewyk and they to dispone for my soule and all christen soules as theie think best to the honer of the Holy Trynity and the well of my soull. Amen. Witnesses, Symond Braccenbe, etc. I will to John Mowl the half tythe corne of West Bronton.

WILL OF ELLEN MUSCHAMP.

Jesus. December 15, 1551. Helyng Muschaunce.[1] To be berryd in the chappell of Beforthe. My chylderyng, executors; my sonne in law Th . . . . ; my dowghter Elsabethe. I gyffe to Sir Harry a sckyp. Witnesses, Francis Armorer,[2] George Carr, etc.

INVENTORY. To me . . . . Armorer for poste money . . . . James Bednell, 6*s.* 8*d.* Wyliam Beadnell, 10*s.* Post mony awyng to me in the kyng's hands, 6*l.* I gyff to Roger Armorer, 3*l.* To Agnes Horsley if schey mane with frends, 3*l.* I awe to my sonn John Carr . . . . To Maystrys Bednell . . . .

---

[1] Apparently the postmistress, or the widow of the postmaster, of Belford.

[2] Francis Armorer's will is printed in *Wills and Inventories*, vol. i. p. 404.

WILL OF AGNES CRAMER.

Dec. 7, 1552. Agnes Cramer, widowe, lat wyffe of Robert Cramer of Newcastle, merchaunte. To be burede within the churche of All Sayntes. To Cuthbert Rukebye, 20*l.*, a sylver goblett and thre sylver spones. To Robert Rukebye, 20*l.*, a sylver goblett and thre sylver spones. To John and James Rukebye, the same. To my sone, John Taylor of Londone, an olde angell of golde and to his sone, George Taylor, an olde angell of golde. To my sone-in-lawe, Laurence Rukbye one olde angell and one sylver salte with the cooverynge. To his wyffe, a sylver potte. To Laurence Rukebye and Robert Ellysone, either of them, an olde ryall of gold, whome I make my supervisors. The rest to Cuthbert, Robert, John and James Rukeby, chyldren of my sone-in-lawe, Laurence Rukeby, falinge them to Laurence Rukeby, my sone-in-law and Elsabethe, his wyff. Witnesses, John Collyngwode, cordyner, Andro Surties, merchaunte, etc.

'THE TESTAMENT OF ISABELL BENETT THE LAYDYE OF KENTON.'

. . . . 1553. I, Isabell Benett,[1] wedow, hole off mynde and will although I be sycke in my bodye maketh my last will and testament in manner and forme followinge. Firste, I bequieth my soule to Almightie God, to our blessed Ladye and to all the sancts in heavon and my bodye to be buried in the churche of Gosforth within the quere besydes my husband. I gyve to John Heron of Symoborne 10 yowes and 10 lambs, 2 oxen that I bought at Mydsomar, —one redd and another blakhawked—and one graye meire. I gyve to my brother John's dowghter, Beill, one pott, 3 dublers and 3 dishes, 10 yowes and 10 lambes. I gyve to Agnes Eden one cowe, and also to Besse Gack, one other cowe. I gyve to my fyve servants 5 yowes. I gyve to Antonye Erington, my brother Georg sonne, 10*s.* and one cowe that he haith here within, and one oxe and one qwye. I will that Sir Hewgh Erington shall have one fetherbed off the best that ther as, one pair of sheitts, 2 pillowes and one coverlett off the best. I gyve to little Rauff Erington one whye. The reste off my goods moveable and unmoveable I gyve to Robert Fenwick, Lamwell Marche and Rauff Walles, whome I make myne executors all as one to dispose my goodds for the weill off my soule, and also I make Robert Wythrington and John Wythrington supervisors off this my will to se itt fulfylled in all poynts and degreis. Thes wyttnes, John Fenwick, Thomas Erington, Jarret Erington, Sir Hewgh Herington, Robrt Tompson, Robert Welche.

[1] Michaelmas Term, 29 Hen. VIII. (1537). Hugh Heryngton, chaplain, plaintiff, and William Benett of Keynton and Isabella, his wife, deforciants. Twelve messuages in Keynton, Heddon-super-murum, West Hedwyn and Cowpen, and one messuage in Keynton in the tenure of Robert Thompson, of the yearly value of 20*s.*, to hold to the said William and Isabella for their lives, and after their decease to remain wholly to Isabella and Margaret Benett and their heirs for ever. *Feet of Fines*, Northumberland.

WILL OF MARTIN TURPIN.

April 1, 1554. Martine Turping of Langley.[1] To be buried in the parishe churche of Hadenbrighe. To my moither, Margaret Turpyng, the farmhold of Howghton and my elder whytt horsse. To my brother, a gray gellott, etc. To Elizabeth Turping, my dowghter, all the yong notte I have at Morpeth. To my unkell, Arthure Fenwyk, a bay horsse wiche was Percevell Pawston, and all raknings betwene hym and me, and a yong cowe for remembrans. To Georg Fenwik, my servand, a lod off otts and ten lames. To my servand, Gilbert Crage, all raknings betwene hym and me and 20s. in corne to by hym a nag. To my son, John Turping, mye cheyne of goold, with the implements of Witchester howsse, who I mak my hayre and he to be ordret by my Lord Dacre, who he is ward unto during his noneage. To my yong master, Sir Thomas Dacre, a payre of gloves of maille. To Mr. Henry Percye, my sword. To Mr. Lanard Dacre, my bow and my quyver. To Robert Erington, my servand, all raknyngs betwene hym and me. I give my best whyt horsse unto my brother, Mr. Parson Dacre. To my curat, John Oliver, prest, 20s. To Janet Shaiftoo of Stanfurham, a yong cowe. I will that such leces, etc., as I had with my wyff, Agnes Turping, to returne to her seylff agane. To George Turping, my son, all such raknyngs as is betwene my Ladye Elsabeth Dacre and me, beseching her ladyship to implowe the same to his usse and prefarment and to be good ladye unto him. The rest to Agnes, my wyff, George, Thomas, Elsabeth and Agnes Turping, my children, they executors. The right worshipfull Mr. John Dacre, parson of Morpath, Georg Fenwik of Brenkburne, John Shaiftoo of Bevington, esquires, and my son, John Turping, supervisors. Witnesses, Mr. John Dacre, etc.

WILL OF RALPH HARDING.

April 28, 1555. Rauffe Hardynge of Newcastell, maryner, hoole of mynde, etc. To be buryed in the church of All Hallowes. To Edward Johnson suche goods as I left in the house which he now dwelleth in. To Thomas Shawdfurthe, a damaske dublet. To Christopher Shawdfurthe, my silver qwystle and my chyne. To Nicholas Tomson, on courslet jaket gardyd, and a clothe jakit, and a blew worslet doublet. To Jane Smorquet, two brasse potts and six pece pewder wissell. To my servant, Lawrence Mylborne, all my see clothes. My wife, Elizabeth Hardynge, executrix. Witnesses, William Wylkynsone, George Swynborne, Edward Tynmothe, Robert . . . . , Edmunde Fyeffe, Robert Harle, curat, with others more.

[1] Martin Turpyn headed the Whitchester muster roll in 1538, and in 1552 he was an Enclosures Commissioner. The family owned Houghton in the parish of Heddon during the thirteenth, fourteenth and fifteenth centuries, and after that estate passed by marriage to Thomas Read of the Close, a cadet line continued to hold Whitchester. *Cf. Arch. Ael.* vol. xi. p. 256.

INVENTORY. 7 brasse potts and a posnet, 14s. 4d. 14 pore pewder vessell, 5 pottyndgers and 5 sawsers, 20s. 14 pewder potts, small and grey[t] on bassynge and 2 . . . : , 12s. 9 candylstyks, 7 bassynges, a morter, a pestyll and one fyshe spone, 10s. 5 lavers, 3 candylstyks, 3 borsyngs, 10s. 4 chysts, 20s. 4 conters, 10s. 12 cussyngs, 8s. 3 federbeds, 3l. 5 coverynge for bedds, 10s. 5 coverletts, 7 blanketts, 20s. 11 payre sheytts with other nappery wayre, 30s. 2 paynted clothes, 5s. 1 copper ketyll, 10s. On lancettle, 2s. On riall and on old angell nobill, on payr say courtyngs, 10s. 21l. 6s. 4d. [sic].

WILL OF AMBROSE MIDDLETON.

Aug. 4, 1555. I, Ambrose Midelton of . . . . Cumberlande, esquier. My wretched and sinful bodye to be buried in the parishe churche of Kyrkland[1] if I dye within twenty myles thereof ; and if I dye nere to Barnard-castle, then to be buryed in the churche or chapell there, emonge my poore auncestors, or ellis in christian buriall, where it shall happen the bodye to dye, with the oblacons and mortuaryes there due, and such divine service to be songe or said in the daye of my buriall as shall appertain to the order and custome of the churche and christian buriall, and the ministers thereof to be rewarded for there paynes by the discretion of my executors. Also I will there be distributed in the parishe or congregacon of the said churche or chappell of Barnard-castle and in the parishe of Kyrklande, in either of the same places, within twenty dayes next after my buriall, 40s. and at the yere's ende, in the weke byfore Easter so moche, and so yerly duringe thre yeres next after my decease, to be distributed and paid by my executors, after the rate, to the [poore] aged, crased or impotente people, 4d. or 6d. the pece. And to poore crased or impot[ent] children, 2d. or 1d. the pece, by the advise and discrection of the curate and church-wardons of either of the same parishes. Also I geve and bequithe to the amending of [the] highewaye or tram frome the west ende of Bridgegait in Barnard-castle [afore]said . . . . brydge-ende there, 20s. To the amendinge of the cawsy. . . . chair, 6s. 8d. And to the amendinge of the rofe of the . . . . next to the quere ende, 20s. And to the churche work . . . . 8d., to be paid by my said executors, the one halfe thereof . . . . end entered unto the same wor . . . . the other halfe . . . . Also I geve . . . . to everye of my said sons, 20 . . . . con of my goods and cattalles and to be . . . . them by myne executors after they shall come to there severall ages of 21 yeres . . . . 8d. by yere or more for there preferment by there discrectione if they will . . . . e the

[1] The parish of Kirkland is situated on the river Eden and is about nine miles east of Penrith.

same in full recompence and satissfaction of the younger childes parte or porcon of my goods . . . . unto them or any of them after my decease. Also I will geve and bequithe to Cycill [my] enterly welbeloved wife th . . [full] half of . . . . my holl launds and tenements charged as is . . . . said at hir own election, to have duringe hir lyfe in full recompence and satisfaction of all hir wynter and dower to hir belonginge of all my holl laundes and tenements. Also I will that Thomas, my son and heyre apparante, shall have the other half of my said laundes and tenements, with the revertion of the other half after the decease of my said wife, his mother, to hym and his heyres mayle of his bodye lawfully bigotten, and in defaulte of suche issue to the heyres mailes of my bodye lawfully bigotten, and in defaulte of suche issue to remayn to my right heyres for ever. And all other my goodes, catalles and leases not byfore gevn or bequithed, I geve and bequithe to my said enterly welbeloved wife, and son Thomas, whome I make and ordeyne executors of this my presente testamente and last will, therewith to paye my debts and legacies, and to performe this my will, and to bring up my said son Rycherd unto the complete age of 21 yeres. Requiringe my said son, Thomas, of my blessinge to be good, naturall and favorable to his said mother and bretheren as apperteanithe. And also I make and ordeyn my most trustie and welbeloved frendes, Thomas Sandefurthe of Ascoyn, esquier, and Anthonye Middleton of Kepyer, gentleman, to be supervisors of the same and do bequithe to either of them for there paynes to be sustened in this byhalf, 40s. In witnes wherof I, the said Ambrose, to this presente wrytinge have set to my seale and subscribed my name the daye and yere abovesaid, per me Ambrosium Middelton. More witness hereof : Thomas Sandfurthe, esquire, Anthony Middleton and Thomas Myddleton, gentlemen, with others.

WILL OF ROBERT LASSE.

April 10, 1557. Robert Lasse of Alnewicke, yeoman. To be buried in the churche yard of Sanct Myhell. To my nephew, Edmond, sonne of Rynyone Maxsone of Shipley, my house on Alnewicke, one the northe side of Bailigait. To my nephew, John, sonne of Thomas Atkinsone of Lerchild, 4s. of rent of my house in Alnewicke on the north syd of Bongait, and 8d. rent of my house in the tenure of Henry Herone, one the northe sid of the Marketplaice. My daughter, Jenatt Stampfurthe. To Rawfe Collingwood of Titlington, gent., and Thomas Lygthone of Alnewick, yeoman, my house in Alnewicke that Cuthbert Strother dwelleth in.

WILL OF THOMAS CRASTER.

May 19, 1557. Thomas Craster of Allnwick. I geve my sowle to Allmyghtie God and to all the holly company, leaving my body to be buryed in my parishe churche of Sainte Mychaell th'archangell of Allnewik with my mortuary accustomed by the lawe. I geve my howse unto Margret Craster, my wyff, during hir lyff naturall and after hyr to my sonne, William Craster. The residewe of all my goodes I geve unto my wyff and my childer to be distributyd amonge them equally, whome I make my solle executors conjoyntly, etc., to pay my detts, as they shall think to be to the honor of God, and to the well of my solle. Witnesses, Edward Thompson of Allnick, the elder, James Yong and Robert Tailyer of the same.

WILL OF JOHN GASCOIGNE.

Dec. 8, 1557. John Gucyne of . . . . to be buried in the church-yard of Darnton, nighe the corps of . . . . To William Robynson, my daughter's sonne, thre sylver spones, etc. To Barberie Robynson, his syster, fower sylver spones, my wyfe's best sylver girdle, one paire of . . . . my best sylver tache. To my brother, Foreman, my foxe-furde gowne, one cote of plaite, one sallet, one paire of . . . . stafe ; and to his wyfe, my sister, 6s. 8d., and to aither of his sonnes, 5s. For my brother, Somersyde, my sister, his wife, and his children, etc. ; my brother, George Robynson, his wyfe and children, etc. To Lyones Claxton, halfe of my workinge instruments or tooles and fyve noble of money. My sonne in lawe Richard Johnson. I give my lease of Hawghton mylne to William and Barberie Robynson and Cecilie Robynson, their mother, and they to fyne my house at the next court for my good lord and master my lorde of Durham. William Robynson to be kept at schoole for eight years. Mr. Rauffe Dalton, supervisor.

WILL OF RALPH SURTEES.

July 3, 1558. Raff Surtes of Duresme, marchaunte. To Janet, my wyfe, and to John Surtes, my son, the lease of the Bishop mylnes and the Myln close that I bought of the kynge and the lease of the Collfelde close I have of Mr. Myddleton. To Raff Surtes, my son, my house in Geligate duringe his lyfe and then to John Surtes, my son. To William and Christopher Surtes, my sons, the Shawe close. To Phillis, my doughter, 3s. 4d. of a close called the Well-bancke for lyfe. To Elisabethe, my doughter, 3s. 4d. of the little house in Fleshergayt duringe hir lyfe. To Jayn, my doughter, 3s. 4d. furthe of the chapell of the bridge. To Janet, my wyfe, the lease of my house I dwell in, and then to William Surtes, my son. To my wyfe a goblet of silver parcell gilt. To John Surtes, my son, a silver pece weyng eight unces. To Raffe Surtes, my son, a salt of silver with a coveringe weinge eight unces. To William, my son, a maser of silver and gylt and two silver spones. To Christopher, my son, six silver spoones. To Phillis, my doughter, and Elesabeth and Janet, my daughters, two silver spoones each. To Isabell

Marche, my suster s doughter, 20s. To Myles, my brother, 5s. To
Jayn, my suster, 5s. The rest to my wyfe and children and they
executors. Witnesses, Christopher Chaytor, Christopher Surtes, etc.

WILL OF PETER RIDDELL.

Nov. 5, 1558. Peter Riddell of Newcastle, merchant. To be
buried in the church of Saint Nicholas where my father doth lye,
with sowle masse and dirge. Alsoe I give unto the vicar of the
said churche the some of 10s. in recompance of forgotten tythes.
Also I will that there be given to the poore peoplle twentye pounds in
monie soe shortly after my deceasing as it reasonable can, that is
to saie, eight poundes of that to be bestowed in victualling the
priseners in the high castle and in the Newe-gaite (?) soe much until
the said eight pounds be runn out, the other twelfe pounds to be
given to poore householders and other poore people as my supervisors shall see right, meit and neid. To my sonne, William Riddell,
and his heires males, my house with all the implements thereto
belonging nowe in the tenor of John Ellison, merchaunt, and 2
sellers in the Broad Garth with the lofts and little house att the
head of the same garth, and he to pay yerely out of the said house
26s. 8d. to the wardes of almes house or to any other poore people
he pleaseth. To my sonne, Peter Riddell and his heires males, my
house in the Cloth Markitt nowe in the tenore of Umfrye Parker,
merchaunt, provided . alwaies that God of his grace call my
sonne, Thomas Riddell, to the office of preisthood . . . . then
I will that my sonne, William Riddell and his heires mayles, shall
have all my landes unbequeathed . . . . painge yearely out of the
said lands to my said sonne, Thomas Riddell, dureing his life the
soumme of 13l. 6s. 8d. towardes his exhibicon. To Peter Riddell, my
sonne . . . . paing out of the said lands yearely to my said sonne,
Thomas Riddell, during his life 13l. 6s. 8d. provided alwayes that if
my said sonne, Thomas, be a preist, soe that the house wherein I
dwell and all other my lands come to my sonne, William, as aforesaid, then I will that my sonn, Peter and his heires, shall have the
said house and implements in which John Ellison dwelleth, with
two sellers, etc., and my former bequest to my sons, William and
Peter in that counte concerning my house aforesaid be void. To
my daughter, Elizabeth Riddell, 100l. for her childes portion and
the same some to my daughters, Elinor, Mary and Katherine
Riddell, if they follow the advice of my supervisors. To John
Ellison, marchaunt, my violet gowne and 5l., and to every one of
his children one angell. To George Bee, 6s. 8d. To my cosine,
Edward Anderson, 20s., and to every one of my sister Shaftoe
children one angell. To my servant, William, my horse, and 3s. 4d.
To Agnes Paker, nowe wife to Umfray Parker, merchaunt, 3l. 6s. 8d.
To Janet Swynborne widdowe, 20s., by yeare, for life out of my

house in the tennor of John Whitfeild, smith. To her eldest
daughter, 20s. All the rest of my goods to my sonns, Thomas,
William and Peter Riddell, whome I make my executors, provided
they shall be ordered during their minority by my trustie frends,
Sir Robert Brandelinge, knight, William Claxton of Wynyerde, and
Richard Hodgson, merchaunte, whome I make supervisors of this
my will. Wittnesses, Edward Shaftoe, merchant, John Ellison,
merchaunt, and Edward Anderson, merchaunt, Richard Hodgson,
marchaunt, alderman.[1]

WILL OF ROGER ERRINGTON.

Jhesus. Nov. 29, 1558. Roger Eryngton of Wallyke, gent.
To be buryed within the parysche churche of Wardon. I gyve all
my fyrmynges and landes purchased in Wallyk or ellyswhere to my
suster's soon, John Carr; my wyff, Margaret Eryngton, to enjoye the
same duryng hyr wydowhead. My nephew, John Carr, my heyr.
My wife and my sister Jane Carr executors. Lyonell Fenyk of
Blakden, Randell Fenyke of Kirkharll, Rauf Eryngton of Hexame and
Alexander Basnett of Heddon, supervisors. To Isabell, my dowghter,
6 nott and 20 shep. To Kateryne Eryngton, my brother's doghter,
2 nott. To Wardon churche, 6s. 8d. Witnesses, John Olyver, vyccar
of Wardon, etc.

WILL OF RALPH HUTTON.

Dec. 8, 1558. Raphe Hewton of Walworthe, co. Durham, gent.,
being visit with sicknes but off hole mynde and perfect remembrane
doo contitut and make this my last will.[2] Firste, I gyve and
bequieth my soule to Almightie God my Creator and Redemer, to
our blessed ladye, St. Marye and all the hollye compenye of Heavon,
my bodye to be buried within the parish churche off Heighington
with my mortuaryes dewe and accustomed according to the lawes
of this realme. Also I gyve and bequieth to every one off my thre
doughters fortye marks off my goodes over and besydes their childes'
porcons, also whereas I have thre rings of golde, not off equal valew,
I will that my eldest doughter shalhave the best, my second
doughter the next best and my youngest doughter the third. I will

---

[1] Jan. 10, 1618/9. William Riddell of Newcastle, merchant, appeared in
person in the Durham Consistory Court and begged that the original of the
will printed above should be given to him. It was delivered to him the
same day on an oath for its safe restoration being made by Lancelot S[h]afto
and Thomas Swan.

The testator was ancestor of the family of Riddell of Swinburn castle and
Felton park, whose pedigree is printed in the new History of Northumberland, vol. iv. p. 284.

[2] The inventory of the testator's goods is printed in Wills and Inventories,
vol. i. p. 209.

that my thre doughters aforesaid shalhave equally divided amongst theim all such apparell and rayment as dyd belonge to ther mother. I will that my sonne, Georg, shalhave one sylver salt, eight sylver spoones and one sylver peic. I bequieth to my servant, Raph Coltman, 40s., and to my servant, Margaret Bainbrig, 10s. If my sonne, Robert, when he shall accomplish the full aidg of 21 yeres shall pay or cause to be payd to my said three doughters yff they lyve so long, or to such of them as shalbe lyving at the same tyme, the somme of 20l. of good and lawfull money of England upon reasonable request to hym maid for the same, then I will and bequieth that my said sonne, Robert, shall have all my burgage landes in Darlington and Bushop-awkland for terme of his liff naturall, and yff my said sonne, Robert, hapen to decease bifore he accomplish the said aidg, or refuse at the said aidg off 21 yeres to pay the said somme off 20l., then I will my sonne Georg, shalle have the said burgaig lands if he wyll pay the said somme of 20l. to my thre dowghters in manor and forme aforsaid, and yf neither off my said sonnes will pay the said somme of 20l. to my doughters as ys aforesaid, then I will that the said burgag launds in Darlington and Bushop-awkland shalbe solde by the supervisors off this my will and testament, or so many off theim as shalbe then lyving, and the money theroff to be equallye devyded amongest my thre doughters aforesaid. And in the mean tyme during the none aidg off my said sonne, Robert, I will that the profetts yerely proceding and comying of and upon the said lands to be equallye devided bitwixt my said two sonns, George and Robert. The resydewe off all my goods and cattals, over and besydes this my will performed, to be equallye devided bitwixt my said two sonns. And I make Robert Hewton, my younger sonne, my sole executor off this my last will and testament. Moreover I constitut and make my welbeloved cosyns and freinds, Robert Tempest of Holmesyd, John Hewton of Hunwick, William Smithe off Esh, Edward Parkinson off Bemount-hill, Francs Parkinson, the younger, and Nicholas Young of Heighington, the supervisors of this my last will and testament, and they to have the hole order off all my childrein, ther launds, goods and cattalls during ther none aidg. Provided alwaye that yf any off my said dowghters [die] before mariadg and bifore she accomplish th' aidg off 21 yeres, then I will that hir or ther porcons, soo deceasing, shall remane to thother dowghters or dowghter then lyving. I gyve to my landlord, Sir Francs Askew, knight, and to my ladye, his wiffe, and to Mr. William Askew, her eldest sonne, to every off theim, one olde riall for a token to the intent to be good to my childrein. In wytness hereoff, etc.[1]

---

[1] The following is the will of a clergyman of the same surname :—June 1, 1561 : William Huton, clerke :—To be buried in the church yard of our Lady at Chester. To John Huton, my brother, 6l. 13s. 4d., with my wages. To the five childer of my m[aste]r, to every of them 5s. To Christopher Huton, my brother's son, 20s. To my m[aste]r and my ladye and every one of them one old riall. Rest to Richard Harbottle, etc.

WILL OF LANCELOT HODGSON.

Feb. 23, 1558-9. Lanclott Hodschon of the parish of Lanchester. To be buried in the peasche churche of Lanchester. To
the reparasyons for all forgottyn tythes, 20s. To the mendyng off
the ornaments, etc., 3l. 6s. 8d. To my kurett, the preiste, to pray
for me, 6s. 8d. To the mendyng off thee bryggs, Lanchester greyn,
and the kawsey, the gayt from my howse to the churche, 6l. 13s. 4d.
To the poore of the peaschyng of Lanchester, Esche and Medomsley,
6l. 13s. 4d. To Mr. Sayr, Mr. Crathorne, Mr. Tempest and my brother
Rycherde Hodshon, every on of theme a ryall, and I make them
supervysors. To my lord of Westmorland on old sovarayn of gold.
To every on off my wyff's chylder a ryall. To my wyff's two brether
off Durham, ether off them a ryall. To my brother Robertt Hodschon
and his wyff, and to my brother Rychard Hodshon's wyffe, a ryall
each. To my cosyng, Thomas . . . . To my syster, Issabell
Hodgson, 10l. To my cosyn, Wylliam Wylle, 40s. To my cosyng,
Nycolas . . . . 3l. 6s. 8d. To my cosyng, Issabell Tempest, a new
calffed cowe. To my suster (?) Dorrathy Wylley, 8l. 13s. 4d. To
my cosyng, Rawff Wylley, all my apperrell, savyng my best gowne,
which I gyve to my brother, William Hodshon. To my cosyng,
Jhon Wylley, 6l. 13s. 4d. To my cosyngs, Elsabythe, Anne,
Kathcryn, and Margery Wylley, every on off theme, 3l. 6s. 8d.
To Lanclot Hodschon, my brother Rychard's son, whom I crystyned,
3l. 6s. 8d.; and to the rest of his bretther and sisters, 20s. To my
brother, Robertt Hodshon chylder, 20s. To every on off my syster,
Oggell's chylder . . . . To my servantt, Umpay Mayre, 40s. and
my lyttyll bawsen meyre. To Nycoles Tempest, Thomas Tempest's
eldest son, 40s. to by hym a nagge. To my brother, William
Hodschon all my leesys of Hedlehope and a closse called the Wall
and my partt of the lees of the churche off Lanchester. To my wyffe,
Annes, all my leesys off Edmondsley and the tythe of the prebend
of Newbygyne duryng hyr life, and then to William Hodschon my
brother. As I have a silver salte and halffe a dossyng sylver spoyns,
the wich, Deane Claxton, my master, gave me, I wyll that my
wyffe have the same durynge hyr lyffe, and then to William
Hodschon. To my brother, Robert Hodschon, 30l. in just
recompenssyn off my fyne called the Meralees, the which I meyn
to gyve to Rychard Hodschon my brother. My wyfe and brother,
William, executors. Witnesses, Robert Tempest and William
Hodshon.[1]

WILL OF ISABELLA WILKINSON.

March 23, 1558/9. Isabell Wilkeson, widowe. To be buryed in
Alhallows church [Newcastle] beside my husband, William
Wilkinson. To my sonne, Christopher, and to my daughter, his

---

[1] This will makes additions to the pedigrees of Hodgson printed in
Surtees, *Durham*, vol. ii. pp. 77, 319.

wiffe, a ryall a pece. To my sonne, John Chaitor, and his wiffe, eyther of them, a ryall. To my daughter, Jane Kirkehouse, a riall, a silver peice, my best beids and a reade belt. To Andrew Wilkinson, a riall. To Margaret Hicson, my second beids, my least morter, a windoe-cloth and the sacks. To Jane Baitman, my best gowne and my cowe. To John Baitman, a black bonett. To Margaret Chaitor, a chamlett kirtle. To Alison Burrell, a paire of currell beids. To Agnes Chaitor, my gowne lyned with worsett. To Elizabeth Chaitor, daughter to my sonne John, two silver spones and my best brasse pott. To Janett Sharpe, a paire of silver croks and ten furre sparras (?). To my sister . . . . To my servant, Janett Gray, her hole waigs and fower yerds of my best white . . . . a little almerye and a little counter. To John Wilkinson of Herte, a feder bed. To John Wilkinson's daughter, my best cappe. To his sonne, a dagger. The rest to my sonne, Christopher Chaitor, accordinge to my husband's will.

WILL OF GEORGE ERRINGTON.[1]

March 25, 1559. George Eringtonn of Denton, gentleman. To be buryede in Sancte Myghel's churche in Nuberen so nye my father as cane be. To my wyff Barberaye Eringtonn the proffet of the collpett. To my son, Robarte Eringtonn, the farmolde in Butterlaye, savinge onlye the haye on Edward Eringtonn's felde. The rest to my wyf, Robert, Nycholas, Martyn and Lanslet Eringtonn, my sonnes; Jan, Anne, Kusteris [sic] and Belteres Eringtonn, my doughters; they executors. My welbilovede brother, Gylbert Eringtonn, Cuthbert Musgrave and Lanslett Eringtou suppervisers. Witnesses, Roger Eringtonn, William Nycholson, clarke.

WILL OF CUTHBERT BLOUNT.

Nov. 18, 1559. Cuthbert Blownt of Newcastle, merchant. To my uncle, Morlande, the tuisshion of my sonne, Edward Blunt, and his goods. To my awnt of Gateside, callid Agnes Lawson, dwelling at Saint Edmonds in Gaytesid, the tuishon of my daughter. Anne Blownt and her goods. To my brother Henry Lawson. the tuishon of my son, Mark Blownt, and his goods, and I give him a bay yong gelding for a token. To my brother, Mr. Hodshon, the tuishon of my sons, Jaymes and Robert Blownt, and their goods. To my wife, Barbare Blount, the rule of my yongest son, William Blownt, and his goods. I gyve to Sir James Croft, knight, for

---

[1] The testator, George Errington, was the second son of Roger Errington of Denton by his wife Catherine, daughter of Robert Cresswell of Cresswell. His wife Barbara was a Shafto of Bavington. The will makes additions to the pedigree of Errington of Denton printed by Foster in *Visitation Pedigrees of Northumberland*, p. 46.

a token [blank]. To my Ladye Croft . . . . for a token . . . . To Mr.
Doctor . . . . for a token. To my forenamed aunt of Gatisid for
a token, a hope of gold. To my welbelloved mother for a token
[blank]. To my aunt, Morland, for a token [blank]. To my sister,
Rawe, for a token [blank]. To my sister, Wilkinson, for a token
[blank]. To my brother, Hodshon, for a token my best gowne
faced with velvett. To my brother, Georg Lawson, for a token,
a newe furyd coot and a cloke. To John Butter, a cassock
of mockarde furrid, for a token. To Christofer Blunt, a black
satten doblett. To William Coockeson, my best spanyshe jerkin
and a newe worsett cassok furrid. To my man, John Sclater, 4*l.*
To my man, Thomas Broune, 20*s.* To every woman servant at
my howse at home 6*s.* 8*d.* a pece. To every servant in Doctor
MacFyne's (?) howse, 5*s.* a pece. The rest to my wife and children,
James, Robert, Anne, Edward, Mark and William Blount. Supervisors, Christopher Morland, Henry Lawson, Georg Lawson and my
father, Brymley. [Pr. 16 Oct., 1569.]

WILL OF HUMPHREY CARR.

Nov. 28, 1559. Humphrey Carr of Newcastle, yeoman. To be
buried at Saincte Andrewes besides the bones of my father and
mother. My wyfe, Margerie, to have her parte of my goods. To
Cuthbert Carr, late sonne of John Carre, deceasid, begotten of my
dawghter Isabell, late also deceased, all my leases in Newcastle
and in the rectorie or parsonage of Mychell Benton, with the lettinge,
settynge and 'mannred' of the same, to him and his heirs, and then
to Margerie Wilkinson, sister to the said Cuthbert, and wyfe to John
Wilkenson of Newcastle, marchaunt. Whereas John Carr, father
unto the said Cuthbert, did leve to me for his use two tenements in
Benwell, he to enter upon them. My sister, Alleson Stampe, late
wife to Robert Stampe, deceeased, to have the halfe of the tynde
of corne in Northe Weteslond, paying 23*s.* 4*d.* to the said Cuthbert
per annum. My sister, Elyoner, now wife to John Ollevar, to have
the other moytie. To Margerie Carr, dowghter to my brother,
William Carr, 40*s.* To Christopher Carr, her brother, 20*s.* To my
brother, Robert Carr, my best gowne. To Margerie Carr, my wyfe,
my second gowne. To Alleson Stampe, my sister, my foxefurred
gowne. To John Ollever, my blake gowne furred with lambe. To
John Wilkinson, one duble ducket of gowlde, and to Margerie, his
wyf, one owlde angell of gowlde. The rest to Cuthbert Carr, he
my executor, and I make Mr. Cuthbert Elleson of Newcastle and alderman and my brother, Robert Carr, supervisors. Witnesses, Robert
Anderson, sherif of Newcastle, Cuthbert Elleson, clarke, etc.[1]

---

[1] *Cf.* Welford, *Newcastle and Gateshead,* vol. ii. p. 349.

WILL OF JOHN RACKETT.

March 6, 1559/60. John Rackett of the parish of Saynt Oswaldes in Duresme, etc. To be buried in Sanct Oswoldes churche [1] as nighe my mother and wiffe as may be. To my sonne, William Rackett, over and besides his filiall porcon of my goodes, a geldinge and a som . . . . nag suche as myne executors with th' advise of my supervisors shall seeme good att ther discretions. To my doughter's sonne, Thomas Forster, 10*l.* To Robert Rackett, 10*l.* I gyve to Anthonye Barton, my doughter's sone, 3*l.* 6*s.* 8*d.* I gyve to my sonne, Cuthbert, my house here in Elvett which I dwell in, with thre leands, the great iron chymney, two racks and tonges, one ambre, the morter stone, the house in Framwellgait and all my tytle and lease of yeres in Quarrington. I bequiethe to my sone George, the 20*s.* by yere in Awckland, to hym and to his heres for ever, yf the law will so suffer, yff not I doo requier my sonne, Cuthbert, as I ame good to hyme, for my blissinge to lett hym fyne for the same. To Ambrose Pele, Christofor Pele and to their two systers, my nephewes and neices, to every of them 26*s.* a peic. Also I had of my nephew, Anthony Rackett childer parcel (?) off goodes so moche as came to 24*l.* or ther about, whereoff I have paid him 20*l.* I gyve to every of my servants, as well women as men, a lambe. I bequieth to my sonne, Cuthbert, my litle goblett and a dosen sylver spones. I woll have the day of my buriall thre yerds of brode blake [cloth] bought to be laid above my corps; and when it is buried, the clothe to be solde and the money gyevon to my god-children whome I have christened. I gyve to my baisgotten sonne, [William] 40*s.* I gyve to my sone Cuthbert's two sonnes 20*s.* a peic, and to his daughter, Elizabeth, 40*s.* I gyve to my sonne William's basterd doughter, 40*s.* The resydewe off all my goodes I bequieth to my two sonnes, Cuthbert and George Rackett, whome I make my executors off this my last will and testament to dispose the same to the pleasor of God and for my soule's health. And I make supervisors hereoff to se this my last will accomplished and fullfylled my worshipfull cosyn and trustye friend, Mr. John Sayer and my gossope, Christopher Chaitor, and I gyve to Mr. Sayer for his paynes, two olde rialls and to my gossopp, Chaytor, other two olde rialls. And moreover I will that yff any off my said childeren will not be rewilled as my supervisors shall think good that they and ther children shalhave no such legacies as I have gyven to them. But thir legacies shalbe continued to suche of my children as my supervisors thinke most meit. Also I gyve to my cosyn, Thomas Sayer, for a token, one olde angell of good. Moreover I gyve to Christopher Barton, 40*s.* Witnesses, John Taylffer, Christofor Chaitor, notarye, Heugh Teddcastell and Hewe Freind.

[1] 1562, Dec. 11. John Rawkket buried. *Reg. St. Oswald's*, Durham.

WILL OF EDMUND HODGSON.

June 13, 1560. Edmund Hodgeson of Derlingtone, merchaunt. To be buried in the parishe churche of Darlington so nighe the corps of my wyffe as may be. I bequiethe to George Claxton, Elizabeth Claxton, Margaret Claxton, Jane Claxton, Margerye Claxton and John Claxton, childrein of John Claxton of Hurworth, my sonne in lawe, to every one of them 20*l.*, and yf yt happen enye of the foresaid six childrein to decease before they receyve this my bequest I will then that his or hir part of theim so deceased be gyvon to the survivors. I gyve to Edwarde Hodgeson, my brother's sonne, my servant, all my interest and lease off Denams howses and lands lyinge and being within the towne and feildes of the foresaid towne of Darlington, and I will that he shall paye furthe yerelye of the same unto my doughter Elizabeth Claxton during hir naturall lyffe, 40*s.* But yf yt happen the said Edwarde to decease furthe of this worlde bifore the yeres of the said lease be expired, having no children or childe of his owne to whome he may assigne and gyve the said lease, then I will that the said lease shall remaine and be to John Claxton aforesaid. I bequieth to Elynor Hodegson, my dowghter in lawe, 40*s.* and to Gabriell Hodgeson, hir sone, 40*s.*, and to George Hodgeson, hir sone, 40*s.*, and to Barberye Hodgeson, hir doughter, 40*s.* And yf yt happen eny of the foresaid thre children to decease before they come to lawfull yeres of age then I will that his or hir part so deceasing be delyvered unto the other of them survyving. I bequieth to the foresaid Edwarde Hodgeson, his heires and assignes for ever, two burgaigies called the Lampflat and two other burgaiges lying in Marthergarthes, and the other of my burgageis lying in the same place I gyve to my kinsman John Nesam and his heires. I gyve to Janet, his wife, my syster's doughter, 6*l.* I bequieth to the right worshipfull Mr. Sergiant Menell, my speciall good freind, one olde ryall. I bequiethe to William Thewe and his children, 20*s.* I bequieth to Michaell Hodgeson and his children, 20*s.* I bequieth to Gyeles Hodgeson, brother to the foresaid Edwarde Hodgeson, 5*l.* I bequieth to Isabell Wilberforth, lait doughter of Robert Wilberfurthe, 3*l.* 6*s.* 8*d.* I gyve to ytche off my god-childrein, 6*d.* I bequieth to Sir John Clapam, vicar of Derlington, 26*s.* 8*d.* And to Robert Hall, scholemaster, I bequieth 13*s.* 4*d.* And to Isabell Toller, 6*s.* 8*d.* I bequiethe to the reparacons of the heigh-waies of this towne, 4*l.* And to the poore people that shalbe at my buriall, fower marke. I bequieth to Christophor Hodgeson of Yerme, 6*s.* 8*d.*, and to every one of his sisters being alyve, 6*s.* 8*d.* I forgyve my kynswoman, Thomas Warde's wyff, all suche debts as she owith unto me to thintend she shall the better bring up hir childrein. I bequieth to every one of Marmaduke Fairbarne's children, which is in number nine, thate he haith nowe with this (*sic*) wyff, Hewe Macame's doughter, 6*s.* 8*d.* I bequieth to my sonne, John Claxton, halff of all my debts as they shalbe receyved. I bequieth to Edmunde Thewe, the sonne of Thomas Thewe, 20s. The rest of all my goodes, my debts paid and my funerall expensis discharged, I gyve unto Edwarde Hodgeson aforesaid, my . . . . brother's sonne, whome I make myne wholl executor. And the supervisiors of this my [last will] I make Mr. Sergaant Menell, Mr. Francis Wicklif, Nycholas Yonge and Marmaduke Fairrebairne to each of them I bequeth 40s.

WILL OF ROBERT DALTON.

Oct. 3, 1560. Robert Dalton [1] of West-awkland in the ,countie of Duresme, gentleman. I bequithe my sowle into the hands of Almightie God emongst the holie companye of heaven and my bodie to be beryed where it shall please my executors, and I geve and bequithe unto my uncle, Sir Robert Dalton, all the tymber tres beinge upone the greyne in West-awkland and myne interest and lease of the tithe Saynt [Helen] Auckland and my interest of the tythe corne of West-awkland with my reversion and my lease of Gordym and all my interest and terme thereon and also my leace of Saltmas and Cowpland and my lease and interest of Lymesyke. Also I geve and bequith unto my uncle, Mr. George Readman, the moyte, or one full half, of my two partes of all my leases interest

[1] Robert Dalton, only surviving son and heir of Ralph Dalton of West Auckland, surveyor of works to Bishop Tunstall, by his second marriage with . . . Redman, married Dorothy, daughter of William Hilton of Biddic, and died *s.p.* Feb. 10, 1567/8. His widow remarried Michael Constable. Robert Dalton, B.D., prebendary of the seventh stall, was found by *Inq. p.m.*, July 27, 10 Eliz., to be uncle, and heir of the whole blood, of the testator. He died July 10, 12 Eliz., and by *Inq. p.m.* taken Oct. 13, 14 Eliz., his coheirs were found to be Margaret, wife of Christopher Athy of Aldernage ; Jane, wife of Robert Eden of West Auckland ; Margary, wife of Matthew Crathorne of West Auckland ; Elizabeth, wife of George Tocketts of Tocketts ; Constance, wife of John Thomson of Newcastle, and Anne, wife of . . . Cragges, being the six daughters of Elizabeth, wife of John Hoton of Hunwyke, sister of the half-blood of Robert Dalton the testator, and daughter and, in her issue, sole heiress of Ralph Dalton of West Auckland, by his first wife, . . . Strangeways.

The following is an abstract of the will of the above-mentioned Elizabeth Hooton, widow :—

1566. To be buried in the hollowed grounde (of St. Andrew Auckland). My late husbande, Johne Hooton, esquier, deceised (whose sowle God pardon), dyd bequieth all his land, etc., in Hunweake, Whitehall and Mansforth, etc., to me for thirty yeres for the payment of his debts and the preferment of his children, I give the order of the saide lands to my derely beloved uncle, Mr. Robert Dalton, my son-in-lawe Christopher Aththe and my dowghter Margaret, his wyfe. To my verie good ladie Ewerie, a golde ring, besechin hir to be good ladie unto Margerie, hir maid and servaunte. To my sister Tunstall, 10s. for a token. To my dowghter Margreate Aththe, of my portion of my husbande goods, 66l. 13s. 4d. I will that Johne Stephenson shall have to hym and to his wyfe, my yongest childe's nurce, for nursing my said childe, the remander of the leise of the fermeholde in Hunweake which my late husbande had of the Deane and Chapiter of Durham. The rest to my six dowghters, Margaret Aththe, Jane, Margerie, Elyzabeth, Custance and Anne Hooton, whom I make my executors.

and term of yeres that I have in and of Holm, and of all the tythe corne of Billingham, upon condicione that he shall neither demand nor clam one houndrethe marks that I owe him. Also I gyve and bequithe unto Dorothe, my wif, the other moyte of the said my two pertes of such leases, and the other moyte or one half of all my estaite, interest, and terme of yeres, that I have in the said tythe corne of Billingham and Holm, upon condicion that after my deathe she shall not demande nor claime any parte of my lands and tenements for hir wedowe righte, savinge onlye 20*l.* by yere, provided alway that if my said wif do dye duringe the yeres, and before the yeres be endid and expired, then I will that hir moyte shall hollye cum and remayne unto my said uncle, Sir Robert Daltone, or to any suche as he shall nayme and apointe; and whereas my father-in-lawe, Mr. William Hiltone, haithe covenaynted to paye me or my assignes, in parte of paymente of my marige money, 20*s.* yerly, till 40*l.* be paid, I will and bequithe unto my servant, John Thirkeld, the said 40*l.* to be yerlie receyved at the hands of the said William Hiltone, his executors or assignes, and all the resydewe of my goodes and cattalls, my debts payd and will performed, I geve unto my wif Dorothe, myne uncle, Sir Robert Daltone, and my uncle, George Readman, whom I make the executors of this my last will and testament. In witnes wherof, etc.

Jesus, 1560. A sedell to be sett to Mr. Robert Dalton his will.

Imprimis: I geve unto my syster, Frauncis Daltone, 40*l.* I geve unto my cosen, Marmaduke Lamptone, 40*l.* I geve five of my systere Holton's chylderen, 66*l.* 13*s.* 4*d.* I geve unto my aunte, Allys Allanson, 40*s.* I geve unto my aunte, Custance Grenebank, 40*s.* I geve unto my servant, John Thirkelt, a graye horse that he rode . . . . to Cambrige and fower marks, 53*s.* 4*d.* I geve unto Thomas Thirkeld fower marks besyds the anuete of 26*s.* 8*d.* . . . . father did wyll unto him, 53*s.* 4*d.* [erased]. I geve unto [   ]er Charltone, 40*s.* I geve unto [   ]d Dalton, 40*s.* I geve unto [   ] Hodgeson a lease that I promised hym, 40*s.* I geve unto [   ] 4 kye-gayte in Copland duringe his lif, 40*s.* I geve unto [   ]dly, 40*s.* I geve unto [   ] the 20*s.* I geve unto [   ] kynsman and kynswomen that shall fortune . . . . shall have one blake gowne, and my . . . . theyre founralls blacke cootts . . . . my executors with that thaye se theme . . . . well as if thaye were wretten . . . . th . . . . wyll aunswere. I geve unto . . . . an . . . . John Thirkelle, Richard . . . . 17*l.*

WILL OF ROBERT LEWEN.

Nov. 26, 1562. Robert Lewen [1] of the towne of Newcastell upon Tyne, esquire. First, I will that my wiffe Jeahne shall have all those

[1] A shorter abstract of this will is printed in the first volume of this series, p. 210. The testator, the son of William Lewen by his wife Alice, daughter of Lancelot Heslerigg of Swarland, was apprenticed in 1519 to

lands in Hetton in the Holl, as well off ancient eneritanc as of thos which I have purchased, during her liff naturall, paying unto Georg Lewen, my sonne and aire, and to his aires during her naturall liffe, 2*l.* 6*s.* 8*d.* yerelie, which was the onlie rent before I dyd purchas these other lands. And I will the foresaid Georg Lewen immediatlye after my deathe shall have, to him and his aires, owte of the manor of Sylksworth, yerelye, for ever 6*l.* 13*s.* 4*d.* and all other rights and heriditaments which I have in Sylksworth, Grindon-more and the feildes of Tunstail, and all my lands, rents and tenements in the citie of Durhm and suburbes of the same. To Robert Lewen, my youngest sonne, all my lands, rents and heredita- ments in Newcastle in Pillgram streit, parcell of the lait Graý Frears, which amounteth yerelye 8*l.* 13*s.* 4*d.* ; the medowe of the Castle-feild, which is 20*s.* yerelye ; the out-rent paid and two tenements of the Over Dene Brige, whereof one in the tenor of Georg Twissill, the other of wedoo Swadill, the rent is 21*s.* yerelye ; and 3*l.* of yerelye rent goyng owte of the leat White Frears in the tenor of Henrye Whycliff, gentleman ; and a lytle close without Panden-yeat in the tenor of Thomas Scott, the rent is 3*s.* 4*d.* yerely, to have to him and his haires ; then to Christopher Lewen ; then to Edward Lewen ; then to my right aires for ever. And also I will that all the proffitts of my lease of the deanrye of Chester and parsonaig of the same, the prebens of Chester, Lumlye, Urpith, Tamfild, Lamsley, Burtley and Peltone, shalbe yerelye resaived by Christofor Mitfourthe of Newcastle, marchaunt, William Sherewood of the same towne, gentle- man, and John Hagthropp of Chester-in-the-Streat, gentleman, according to certon indenturs maid betwene me, the said Robert Lewen of the one part and the said John Haggthropp of the other parte, except the tieth corne of Ravinsworthe, which proffetts, over and above the rents and reprises, is cleare to me *communibuz annis* above 40*s.*, which sommes of monie I will shall remayne in the hands of the said Christofer, William and John, to suche use and uses as in a sedoull hereunto annexed shalbe specified, etc. Allso I will that all the profetts growing and rysing of suche colles as shalbe wone or gotten for me, my executors or assynes, in thre cole pitts whereof

<hr>

Gilbert Middleton of Newcastle, merchant adventurer,—whose daughter Margaret he subsequently married,—and was admitted free of the Merchants' Company *circa* 1525. He became sheriff of Newcastle in 1541 and mayor in 1544 and 1552 ; he was elected to represent the borough in parliament in 1553, 1558 and 1559. His second wife was Jane, daughter of Christopher Brigham of Newcastle, and her will is printed in the first volume of this series, p. 305. A pedigree of Lewen may be found in the new *History of Northumberland*, vol. vi. p. 148.

The arms upon the testator's ring were : *argent, a bend bretessé gules, over all a portcullis in chief azure.*

In the 'cassocks' of damask and worsted, given by the testator to his sons George and Edward, is an interesting example of the word used as a long loose coat or gown, a sense in which it replaced the original meaning of a soldier's or horseman's coat.

two is of the Crose-mor and on neare Fugfild, after the rents, wurk-
manshipp and caryaig, etc., be expendyd, be deducted, the residew to
remayne in the custodie of the said three men to suche use and uses as
in the sedill is assigned, which some, over the reprise, haithe bein
affore this abowt on hundreth pound yerelye.   And I will that
Nicholas Byerley, my trustie servant, shall have the oversight of my
said coles and to have for his paines 8*l*. yerelye, so long as there is no
default proved against him in the use of that office.   And I will that
the said three, yerelye, when they shall take the adyt of the same coles
and deanrye, etc., shall alowe to every one of themselves 10*s*.   I will
that suche moitie as ys comed to my hand, as aperithe by indenturs
betwene Mr. William Dent and me, wherein is declared how muche
remayneth in his hand and howe muche in myne, be well, thankfullie,
and favorablye paid to Henrye Sanderson's children according to
there father's will, and the monie that remaynethe in other mennes
hands be called for by order of lawe, for assuranc whereoff I have
obligacons remayning in my hands.   To my son Edward and his
heires, my sellers and lofts in Plumer chare.   I give to my wiffe a
standing cupp with a cover gilt, a dosen spoynes, a payre of gilt saltes,
and the teand corne of Ravinswourthe duryng my yeres.   I give to my
sonne, George Lewen, iff he be lyving, a gowne furred with black
taunye, a cassack of dammaske, a velvett bonnett.   I give to
Christofor Lewen, my sonne, what gownc he lykith best, a jackett of
velvitt, a dublett of satton, my sworde and dagger.   I give to
Edward Lewen, my sonne, another gowne, jackett or cassack of
worsted and my best gowne, my shoutinge bowes and shafts.   I give
to Robert Lewen, my sonne, the resydewe of my apperell at my wiff's
discretion.   I give my ring with the seall of my armes to Georg
Lewen, and, iff he be departed, then I give the same ring to my sonne,
Christofor Lewen.   I give to Robert Bell and his wife aither ten
shillings.   I give to Richard Boys and his wiffe aither ten shillings.
I give to my cosen, Mr. John Hagthropp of Chester-in-the-Street, my
dagg with the caise and all things thereto belonging; and to my
cosyng, his wiffe, my gray staige.   I give to Christofor Maire
of Durham, one old ryall for a token.   I give to my cosing,
Christofor Mytfourthe, my best paire of marturs [*sic*].   I will that
Christofor Mytfourthe, William Sherewood and John Hagthorpe
shall yerelye resaive 6*l*. 13*s*. 4*d*. rent-charge goinge owte of a howss
wherein Umfraye Brigham dwellithe for terme of the lyffe of Nicholas
Baxter, to suche use as in the said sedall is declared.   The resydew
of all my goods not legated, commonlye called the dead's porcon,
I will to the use of the said three, as declared in the sedall.   Executor,
my youngest son, Robert Lewen.   Supervisors, the above three.
Witnesses, Christofor Midfourth, William Salkeld, William Sherwood.
[Pr. 1563.]

A further declaration of my last will in this sedall, A.D. 1562.

I will that iff Christofor Lewen do followe the advise of my
trustye freinds **Christofor Mitforth, William Sherwood** and **John**

Hagthropp, that they shall paye for thre years to finde him at
tuicons, in three score pounde, and more toward the finding of his
wiffe during thos thre yeres, 5l. yearelye. Allso I will of all suche
monye as shalbe come into there hands they shall paye thre
hundrethe marks, or more at there discretion, toward the purchaes of
some office to the same Christofor Lewen yff the Master of the Roules,
Sir William Cordall[1] be a helpe in the same. And I will that the
rest of suche monye as shall come to the hands of Christofor Mitt-
fourthe, William Sherwood and John Hagthrope shalbe disposed by
theme even so by there discrecian, to be bestowe monye of theme
or for there preferment. And I wyll that Nicholas Byerlaye shall
come upp with my ostes to my wiffe, as the custome is, to taike there
meat and drink at there incoming and payment of there monie, and
she to have of everie chalder of coles 1d. of evrye shype that is loden.
Further, I will that allthoffe my sonne, Gilbert Lewen, be preferred
by my meane to the Hospitall of the Marie Madlens, which is worthe
tenn pownde on the yere, besyde a great deall of other chargs which
I have bestowed of him, yet that not withstanding iff the same
Gilbert do obedientlye observe, etc., my last will and maike suche
releases and estaits, as my said three freinds shall devise, that the said
Gilbert shall maik no further claime to anye goods or lands as his
childes porcion, then I will he shalbe maid sure of 4l. in the yere
during his liffe. My will is that Jeahnie, my wiffe, shall have all
suche intereste, etc., as I have, or aught to have, by leasse made unto
me by Gilbert Lewen, my sonne, master of the Hospitall of the
Marye Maglens withowte the towne of Newcastle, bering dait 2 Feb.,
3 and 4 Phillip and Mary. And I will that yff Sir Robert Brandling,
knight, doo suffer my said wiffe to enjoye quitlye the tyeth of
Jesmonte, in suche maner as before this tyme I have doyne, that then
and so longe he shall quietlye have and occupye the abovesaid Marye
Maglens with suche proffetts as is thereto belonging. And all such
goods, etc., as come to the hands of the said three shall be paid to the
use of my children before the expiracion of eight yeres next after
the dait of the said will.

Witnesses, Christofor Metfford, William Sherwood, William
Salkeld, John Haggthroppe, Peter Fairbarne, Mathewe Armestrong,
Nicholas Byerlaye, Robert Bell, Richard Bois, Peter Dawton, William
Haull.

WILL OF CUTHBERT BURRELL.

Jan. 17, 1562/3. Cuthbert Burrell of Headlam, in the parishe
of Gaynfourthe. I commende my soule unto Almightie God
and my bodie to be buried within the churche of Gaynforthe.
I bequieth to Gainforth churche for forgotten tiethes, 3s. 4d.
I give to the same churche workes, 3s. 4d. I give to the

[1] Sir William Cordell was Master of the Rolls, 1557-1581.

poore man's boxe, 12*d*. I bequiethe to John Burrell, my eldest sonne, an yrone bounde wayne with a turne teame and a waine head shakle. I bequiethe to the said John Burrell, my eldest sonne, one fether-bedde with all that belongeth unto it, which fetherbedde I will that Margaret, my wife, have it duringe hir wedowe head and if she marie againe then the said fetherbedd to remaine to John Burrell with all that belongethe it. I will that my sonne, John Burrell, have all my harnes to serve the quene for defence of the realme, that is to saye, a jacke, a stelecappe, a stuffed cote, a sworde, a buckeler, a bowe and a quiver. I bequieth to the said John Burrell one maskinge tube with a worte stone, one of the best chaires, the best paire of tonges with a scumer. I bequieth to my two sonnes, John Burrell and Percivell Burrell, all my apparell, that is to saye, my jackats, dublets, jirkins, hoise and cappes. I bequieth to my wife duringe hir wedowe head and my two sones, John Burrell and Percivell Burrell, all my leases within Diance. I will that my wife and my children shall nether lett nor sell no parte nor parcell of the said leases or grounde of Diance but one to an other in paine of forfitinge 20*l*. one to another. I give to my sonne, John Burrell, my good will of my fermehoulde in Headlame, with the licence of the queines grace and the officers, with all other fermolds ; and in defaulte of my sonne John Burrell, I will that all the said fermehoulds or anye thinge or thinges bequested to the said John shall remayne unto Percivell. I bequieth to Anthonie Morton and his wife eyther of them, 10*s*. I bequieth to George Dode and his wife, eyther of them, 10*s*. I bequieth to Henrie Carter, Marmaduke Carter and to George Carter, everye one of them, one ewe. The rest of all my goods boethe moveable and unmoveable, my debts beinge paid and legaces fulfilled, I give unto my wife and my two sonnes, John Burrell and Percivell Burrell, whome I make my full executors of this my last will and testament, and therefore to give and dispounde to the honer of God. Also I bequieth to my brother, John Burrell, one cowe, or els 20*s*. in monye, and I give to George Carter and his wife, 10*s*. Recordes of this my last will and testament, Anthonye Rutter, Christofer Burrell, William Clerke, Christofer Rutter, Christofer Robinson, clerke, William Kinge. Sent unto Mr. Dode, my sonne in lawe, twenty nobles by Rowland Herrisone ; sent by John Richardson, 8*l*. 16*s*. 4*d*. ; and now in full consideracione of hir dowrie and porcion I give the some of 3*l*. 6*s*. 8*d*. Witnesses heareof nowe at his departure, Ambrose Lancaster, Richard Garthe, Richarde Crawforthe. [Pr. Jan. 14, 1580.] [1]

WILL OF JOHN ALLAN.

Aug. 21, 1564. John Allen of Bernard-castell. To be buryed in the chappell or churche of our Ladye of Barnard-castell aforsayde, with the dewties of holy churche nowe accustomed by the lawes.

[1] This will is noticed in a footnote to the will of his son, John Burrell of Headlam, printed in *Wills and Inventories*, vol. ii. p. 110.

I will that my funerall expenses be maid at the dyscrecon of my executors within named. I geve to Peter Allen, my son, my burgage in Newgate lying upon the south syde of the strete with all th' appurtenances to ytt belonging, after my deth, to remayne to hym and hys heires for ever. I geve to my son, Thomas Allen, my burgage upon Barkeman-dike with 5 roodes of londe lieng in the feildes of Barnard-castell, with the appurtenances therto belonging, and also all my lands lately purchased called the Byrketre chauntrye, to remayne to hym and his heires for ever, saving that I geve and bequiethe to my sayd son Peter all my londs in Barnard-castell lately purchased, to have and to hold to hym and hys assignes for the terme of fyve yeres next folowing after my death upon thys condicion :— that my sayd son Peter and his assignes shall discharg and pay the sum of 9*l.* 6*s.* 8*d.* in maner and forme folowing, that is to saye :—To Thomas Allen, my son, 40*s.*, to Elyzabeth Allen, my dowghter, 3*l.* 6*s.* 8*d.* ; and 4*l.* for the dyscharing for my debts which my goods will not extend unto, provyded alwayes that if my sayd son, Thomas Allen, can fynd the meanes to pay and discharg the sayd sum of 9*l.* 6*s.* 8*d.* at any tyme after my sayd death, within the said fyve yeres, that then he the sayd Thomas to have and to enjoye the sayd londes in Barnard-castell not otherwyse geven and bequiethed to hym and to his heires for ever. I will that my son, Peter Allen, shall have my fermeholde belonging to the chauntry of the Apostles. I will, that if the sayd Peter and Thomas have no yshew of ther bodies lawfully begotten that neyther of them shall sell or morgage from other, but all the sayd burgags, londs and tenements clere to discend to the other and to his heires for ever, and if thei both dye without yshewe of chyldren, then I will that the sayd burgags and londs dyscend to the next heyres. The resydewe of all my goods and cattalls above not bequithed, my debtes paid and my expenses funerall discharged, I geve to my son, Peter Allen, whom I maike and ordeine sole executor of this my sayd will, to dispose as he shall thinke best to the plesor of God and profett of my soull ; also I ordeine and maik James Philloppe and Thomas Rolandson super-visors of this my laste will and testament to se that it be executed and fulfilled as my trust is in them. Thes being records : Marke Bedall, John Dennyson, Thomas Rolandsone, yonger, with others.

WILL OF MICHAEL SPENCE.

Jan. 3, 1564/5. Michell Spence of Derlinton. To be buryed in the churche of Derlinton aforsaid with my mortuarye dewe and accustomed. I bequithe to my son Rowlande all myn intereste, lease and terme of yeares that I have in Raker. I bequithe to my son, Lawrence Spence, all my intereste, lease and tearme of yeres that I have in Stapleton, as well of Sir Thomas Metham as of James Belmbye [? Bellamye] ; and my son in lawe, Roberte Jeffrason, to have the guyding and governmente of the saide Lawrence, and his porcion and his bequests, untill he be of lawfull yeres of discretion to occupie the same hymselfe, puttyng in suirtyes to thordinarye. I geve and bequithe to my doughters, Isabell, Barbara, Jayn and Cecill Spence and to every of them, 40 shepe, that is to saye, 20 ewes and hoggs. I geve to Alyce Pacoke one hawket whye wiche I bought of my brother William at Bedall, and one ewe. I geve and bequithe to my sons, George and John Spence jointlye, my intereste, lease and terme of yeres that I have in Hereh'm tiethe. I geve and bequithe to Rauffe Spence, my eldest son, one burgage in Richemonde that Thomas Ubancke nowe dwellithe in, to hym and hys heyres for ever. The residue of all my goods unbequithed, my debtes paide and my funerale expensis discharged, I geve to my sonns, Rowlande, George and John Spence, whome I maike my executors, and will desyre Mr. Myghall Wandisforde and Mr. Bryane Palmes to be supervisors of this my last will. In witnesse hereof, John Hogerde, Robert Jeffrason, Rowland Semer and Rauffe Spence.

WILL OF WILLIAM EGGLESTON

March 23, 1565/6. William Egleston of Haswell Grainge, parish of Easington, yeoman. To be buried in Esington church. To my brother, Christofer Egleston of Hunstanworth, a fermhold held by Steven Egleston, his brother, and the gifte of the parsonage of Hunstanworth.[1] To Steven Egleston and Thomas Egleston, my brother Christofer's son, after the death of Margaret, my wife, a peace of ground called Sleyde-medows. To my brother Steven, the farmhold of Knewkton, occupied by Nycholas Dyxon. To Phillippe Genninge, the lease of a fermhold lying in the sayd Knewkton, now in his owne occupation. To my brother's son, William Egleston, the ferm which the said William has now in his own occupation. To Steven Egleston, my brother, the fermehold now held by George Dunne, and I will that his brother Christofer shall help him to make a new stone hows. To Rychard Egleston, my brother, a peace of grasse ground called Towne-grene and a house he lyveth in. To the poore of Esington parish, 20s. To the poore of Hunstanworth parish, 20s. To the poore of Pyttington parish, 5s. Supervisor, my welbeloved frend, Mr. Doctor Bennet. Witnesses, Rowland Shaftoo, John Swalwell, Phillippe Parkinson, etc.

INVENTORY. April 3, 1567.

INVENTORY OF RICHARD BAYNE.

INVENTORY. May 2, 1565. Richard Bayne of Gatisheid, tanner.[2] Praised by Thomas Potts, Richard Rand, William Wilkinson and Robert Readshawe.

---

[1] There is a pedigree of Eggleston of Hunstanworth in Surtees, *Durham*, vol. ii. p. 367. The grave-covers of two members of this family still exist in Blanchland Abbey-church. *Cf.* new *History of Northumberland*, vol. vi. p. 337.

[2] Buried at Gateshead, May 1, 1565. An abstract of his will is printed in Welford, *Newcastle and Gateshead*, vol. ii. p. 398.

Imprimis: 2 dacres and a half of sooles, 14*l.*   A daker of ou'lethers, 3 roulues and a stike lether, 4*l.* ; all the barke to go with the lether.   10 fatts, 3 tubbs, 2 soes, 4 byves, with all other geare that perteyns to the tanne howse, 4*l.* 4*s.*   One yron chymney with a rekkin croke.   2 rost yrons, a paire of tonges, a speite, 13*s.* 4*d.*   One almerie, 14*s.*   A table, 3*s.*   A counter, 2*s.*   A Danske chist, 8*s.* Formes, 6*d.*   6 dublers, 8*s.*   6 puder disshes, 2 saucers, and 2 plaits, 6*s.*   A pottle pott, a gyle pott, 2 salts, 4*s.*   A bason, a laver, 3 candlesticks, and a latten salt, 3*s.*   2 potts and a pann, 7*s.*   Another kettle panne, 8*d.*   2 bucketts, one skeile, 2 tubs, 16*d.*   A cann, a pire of qucarns, a douson trenchers, a chaffen dishe, 6*d.*   A table clothe and 4 quisshens, 2 aulings and other 2 old aulings, 5*s.* 6*d.*   2 coverletts, a happing, a old mattresse, 2 bedstocks, 9*s.*   21 yeards strakins, 8*s.* 8*d.*   24 yerds lynn clothe, 12*s.*   3 strakin sheits, a bordclothe of strakins, 4 towells of lynn, 6*s.*   A cowe, 26*s.* 8*d.*

WILL OF JOHN WALL.

June 20, 1565.   John Wall of the cytye of Dureham, th' elder, marchaunt and draper.   To be buryed in the churche of Saynt Nycholas [1] in the northe side, nere my sonne Edward.   To the poure folkes the day of my buryall, 40*s.*   To John Wall, my son, a burgage in Flesshergate now in his tenure, a close in Gelygate nowe in the tenure of Thomas Layton, esquier, and a close nere Magdelyn-close. To my sons, John and Robert Wall, my burgage in the Market-place. To Robert, my son, a burgage in Flesshergate and two closes in Gelygate.   To Elynor Wall, my daughter, 8 leases or riggys in the brod close on Gelygate and a close in the said stret.   To Jennat, my doughter, nowe wyffe of George Cuthbert, my messuage or fermeholde in Kybblesworthe and a rent of 4*s.* 8*d.* per annum out of Porter-close ; an annual rent of 20*s.* out of a house nowe in the tenure of Christopher Adthe, and a yerelye rent of 4*d.* out of a house in the tenure of Christopher Morland.   To Elizabeth Wall, my daughter, my burgage in Sylverstrete.   To Katherine Wall, my daughter, the burgage I dwell in.   To Dorothy Wall, my daughter, one acre of ground on Gelygate and 2 rygges of medowe.   To William Wall, sone of William Wall, layt of Barwycke, marchant, deceased, 6*l.* 13*s.* 4*d.*   To Elizabeth and Katherine, my daughters, the right of my fermeholde called Whytes-close, and my goods at Ile and Myddleham.   To Elynor and Dorothy Wall, my rent of 30*l.* 11*s.* by yere out of the towne chamber in Newcastle whiche I have of the grant of Henry, layt erle of Westmerland.   To Agnes Emerson and hir syster Mgarett Emerson each a goune.   To William Clerke, my servant, 6*s.* 8*d.*   To Agnes Wall, one kowe.   To Robert Emerson, 5*s.* To every one of my doughters, one gyrdle with a head and pendessa

[1] 1565, Dec. 12.   John Wall, the elder, buried.   *Reg. St. Nicholas',* Durham.

of sylver and 6*l.* 13*s.* 4*d.* The rest to John and Robert Wall, my sons,
they executors. Supervisors, Christopher 'Chaytor and Antony
Myddleton, esquires. John Crosbye, gent., Thomas Knyghton and
Edward Huddispethe, yeomen. [Pr., 1568.]

WILL OF MARGERY OGLE.

June 25, 1565. Margerye Ogle.[1] To be buried in Bedlington
queere. I gyve all my children to Dame Dorethy Fenwicke, and Johan
Fenwicke my mother, in Brenkburn. The thirde parte of my lease
to my 2 dowghters, whyles eyther of them have 40*l.* to there
mariagge, and then yt to come to Cuthbert, Robert and Thomas Ogle.
To Robert Hull, 40*s.* To Isabelle Hull one loid of rye. I will,
yf Johan Fenwicke dye, my brother, Thomas Ogle, have the
charge she had. To Thomas Oggle, the bastarde, the halfe teithe
corne of Benley when yt comes to my hands. To myne eldeste
sonne, Cuthbert Ogle, my horse that George Heron haithe in hands.
My children, Cuthbert, Robert and Thomas Oggle, executors. My
two brethren, my lord Oogle and Thomas Oggle, supervisors. Witnesses, Cuthbert Watson, clerke, Lyonell and Thomas Ogle, Mar-
meduke Fenwycke and Thomas Harle. [Pr., May 22, 1566.]

WILL OF SIR ROBERT ELLERKER.

[Sept. 6, 1565.] Sir Robert Ellikar of Hulle parke, knight.[2]
To be buried in the church of Alnwick. To [my son], William Elliker,
the house of Hulne, and I beseach the right honorable [Henry] erle
of Northumberland to receyve [him] into his service and goverment.
To my sonne, William Elliker, my lease of the tithe cornes and
shaves of . . . . Lilburne and Eworth and Nesbet as doth appare-
by the lease in the custody of Sir Rauff Graye's executors, and certain
landes in Felkington. To my sonne, Robert Elliker, my interest
to the land in Ryveley, ... Chillingham and the Newtowne,
To . . . . Thomas Elliker, my horse called Gray Perci. To John
Elliker, my servaund . . . . yong blak stage of 3 yeres old by past,
wich I gave hym three dayes befor the making hereof. To my servant,
Robert Stanlay, a whet strake, or shearyng, growing on the ground.
Robert and John Selby . . . . To my neveue, Edward Ellikar, one
horse, etc. Residue to William and Robert Elliker, my sons. Robert
Horsley of Acklington park and Rauff Collinwood of Wittingham,
supervisors.

---

[1] Margery, widow of Gregory Ogle of Choppington and daughter of Robert,
fifth Lord Ogle. *Cf.* Sir Henry Ogle, *Ogle and Bothal,* p. 182.

[2] Sir Robert Ellerker enjoyed Huln priory by a lease granted Feb. 16,
1539/40. *Cal. Letters and Papers Foreign and Domestic,* Hen. VIII. vol. xv.
p. 564.

Debts owing to testator: John Shafto of Bavington, 78s. 8d.
Wedowe Shafto of Bavington, his mother, 15s. 1d. The Quenes
Majesty for my half-year's annuity, 20l. Robert Horsley of Ackling-
ton parke, 5l. 13s. 4d.

Debts owing by the testator: To Thomas Gray of Alnewyk,
13s. 4d. To my prest, Sir George, 5s. 6d. To a woman that
company's with me, 2s. 8d. To my Lord Warden, 20s., etc.

WILL OF REGINALD FORSTER.

Nov. 18, 1565. Ranolde Forster of Captheton, gent.[1] Whereas
Dorothye Ladye Carnabye, wedowe, my sister, hath a graunte from
me of all the tyth cornes of Hexham, Fallofeelde, Fowrestones, the
Newborough and Keepyck, she to have it during my yeres by vertue
of the graunte to me made from Sir Rafe Sadler, knight, and yf
she dye, then it to come to my children, Margaret and Dorothye
Forster. To Clare, nowe my wife, my tyth cornes of Chollerton,
Gunnerton, Colwell and Allerweshe during my yeres, and if she dye,
to my said children. To my said two daughters, my tythe cornes
of the barrenrye of Langlie. Whereas at the request of my brother
in lawe, Cuthbert Carnabye, I have graunted 40 bowles of otes, 40
bowles of beare and 20 bowles of wheate and rye of the said tyth
cornes to John Carnaby—it to remain to my two daughters. To
my nevewe, John Forster, sonne of my brother Thomas Forster, my
terme of yeres in my lands, etc., in Burton, Northumberland, which I
had of Sir Reginolde Carnabye, knight, deceased. To my sister
Dorothye, Ladye Carnabye, my terme of yeres in Harwood Sheele in
the libertie of Hexham duringe her life. I will that the covenants of
maryage made for the uniteinge in maryage of my sonne in lawe,
Thomas Swynborn, and Margaret, daughter of my said brother,
Thomas Forster, remayne in effect, and the mariage allredye begun
betwene William Lawson, sonne to Robert Lawson late of Rock, esq.,
and my owne daughter remain in effect. To William Lawson of
Wesshynton, gent., my terme of yeres in my tythe cornes in Anewyck
in the liberties of Hexham, in the tenure of Roland Lawson, gent. The
rest to my wife and two daughters : they executors. My lovinge
bretheren, Sir John Forster, knt., Thomas Forster of Ederston,
esquier, Roland Forster of Warke, gent., George Heron or Chypchace,
esquire, and the said William Lawson of Wesshyngton, gent., supervisors. Witnesses, John and Rowland Forster, George Heron,
William and Rowland Lawson, etc.

INVENTORY. Jan. 28, 1565/6.

[1] The name of the testator's first wife is unknown, but she may have been
the mother of his two daughters. His second wife was Clare, widow of
[William] Swinburne of Capheaton ; her will is dated July 21, 1579.

WILL OF SIR GEORGE CONYERS, KNIGHT.

July 13, 1566. George Conyers of Harpeley, in the countie of Durham, knight.[1] To be buried where it shall please him [God]. I geve and bequithe to the vicare of Morton for teythes forgotten, 20s. I geve and bequithe to my sonne, Robert Conyers, my lands in Carleton in Lyncolneshire as followithe, viz., one close there called the oxe pasture in the holdinge of James Hutcheson, of the yerely valewe of 6l., and lands called Greate Cracowe in the holdinge of Thomas Blantcharde, and other lands in his holdinge, value 4l. 18s. 8d., and one tenement there lait in the holding of Humfrey Collingwoode, yerlye value 47s. 4d., and 8d. of fre rent to be paid by Sir Henry Baston for one acre of grounde in the west fennes. To William, my son, all these my lands in Carleton in Lyncolnshier— one close next the southe bancke in the holdinge of James Hutcheson, yerlye value 3l., and one other close there, held by the said James, lienge next the Northe Bancke, yerlye value 3l., and one tenement, there held by Christofor White, yerlye value 13s. 6d., and also my lands in Wellom in the countie of Yorke, yerlye value, 6l. 13s. 2d. to be paid him yerlye out of my launds in Sutton nere adjoninge upon the said Wellom. To Thomas, my son, my lands in Ayton, in Pikeringe lithe, which I purchesed of Edwarde Ellecar, esquier, yerly value 5l. 13s., and one tenement there held by Roger Leasley, yerly value, 36s., and one tenement there held by John . . . . emoke, yerly value 36s., and one tenement held by John Harwode, yerly value 36s., and on tenement held by Henry Harwode, yerly value 36s., and one cottage held by John Applegarthe, yerly value 3s. 10d., and one cotage held of Sir Thomas Bradeley, clarcke, yerly value 3s. 10d., and 2s. of fre rent to be paid to him out of the lands of [blank] Hodshon lienge in Ayton of the easte syde of the rever Darwin. To Roger, my son, these my landes in Hooton Busshell, in Pickeringe lithe, first, one tenement held of William Nicolls, yerly value 30s. ½d., one tenement held of Robert Keathe, yerly value 8s. 8d., one tenement held of John Kethe, yerly value, 33s. 1½d., one tenement held of Roger Lighton, yerly value 30s., one tenement held of Water Undrell, yerly value 30s. 9d., one tenement held of Richarde Keathe, yerly value 27s., one tenement held of Hearye Pacocke, yerly value 16s., one tenement held of Thomas Claxtone called the wode howse, yerly value 20s., and also 3l. 11s. ½d. to be paid him in rent yerelye out of my lands in Malton and Halton. I will that Robert Aske of Aughton, John Dawney of Seassey, and John Saier of Worsall, esquiers, shall restreyne and take the fines and profyts of my lands and tenements in Girsbey, Dinsdell, Hornebey,

---

[1] Sir George Conyers of Sockburn and Harperley married Anne, daughter of Sir John Dawney of Sessay, by whom he had a numerous family, and dying Oct. 15, 1567, was buried at Witton-le-Wear. The inventory of his goods and chattels at Harperley, taken on Oct. 22, 1567, is printed in Wills and Inventories, vol. i p. 266.

and Worsall, yerly value 19*l* 11*s*. 4*d*., and lands in Bishopton, yerly value 26*l*. 4*s*. 5*d*., and my lands in Wintringham, co. Yorke, yerly value 21*l*. 22*d*., and my lands in Newbigginge and Litle Stainton, yerly value 18*l*. 19*s*. 6*d*. My lands in Sockbourne, yerly value 8*l*. 17*s*. 10*d*., and my lands in Harperley and Blacke Hall, yerely value 4*l*. 4*s*. 5*d*., to have the said lands till they receyve from them fyve hundrethe markes to th'use of Elinor Conyers, my doughter, for hir preferment in mariage, or when she reaches twenty-one ; and the same sum to Mary Conyers, my doughter. I will that all my manors, etc., be, discend and come to John Conyers, my sonne and heire apparent, and I give to him all my leaces and teithes that I have. To Francis, my doughter, 20*l*. Supervisors, John Dawney and John Sayer, the elder, esquires. Executors, John Conyers, my son, John Sayer, my sonne in lawe, and my uncle, Bryan Palmes. Witnesses, Anthony Martindall, William Robinson, etc.

NUNCUPATIVE WILL OF ROBERT CONYERS.

Robert Conyers of Cotom. To be buried in the parish church of Longnewton.[1] To my sonne, Rauffe Conyers, my maner and lordshippe of Cotome. The profits of the third parte of Cotom to be reserved to the use of my daughters, Anne, Cicell and Margat, untill suche tyme as ther be, fore everye one of them, 100*l*. a peice raysed towards ther dowre. To James, George and Richard, my sons, the rent of my land in Elton of the valew of 6*l*. 16*d*. between them. To Edward and John, my sons, the profites of my lands in Longnewton towne and feilds and they to pay yerely to my unckle, Edward Conyers, during his life 13 nobles, 20*d*. To my son, William, 40*l*. My daughters to have 20 nobles yerely for their porcons out of Cotome. To my son James, who is base begotten, all my leases in Hartlepoole. To my mother, 4 markes yerelye for life. 40*l*. worthe of stock to John Conyers, my brother. The guyding, etc., of my children to John and Edward Conyers, my brethren. Witnesses, Edward Conyers th' elder, gent., George Conyers, gent., Richard Morey, Edward Bankes. [Pr. *circa*, 1566.]

WILL OF JOHN WOLDHAVE.

Oct. 21, 1566. John Woldhave of Elswicke. To be buried in St. John's church-yard, Newcastle, as nigh as my father and wife as may be. To Edward Woldhave, my son, my burgage in Westgaitt, Newcastle. To Christofer Woldhave, my son, 3*l*. 6*s*. 8*d*. which Edward, my son, shall pay him. To Edward Woldhave, all the lyme and stonnes within the said tenement in Newcastle, with certain wood

---

[1] 1566, April 13. Mr. Robert Conyers, buried. *Longnewton Register*. A shorter abstract of this will is printed in the first volume of this series, p. 261.

that lyes without the falde gate of my farmold in Elswicke. To George, my son, my gardeyne that lyeth in Newcastle in Sainct John's church chare which lyeth in morgage to me of the some of 40s., and 10l. for his child's portion. I will my son Edward shall take George, my son, to be his apprentyce to the tanner craft seven yeares and he to have 5l. for it, and after the seven yeres to give 5l. to the said George. To my son, Bartram Woldhave, for his portion, 13l. 6s. 8d., and I desire Cuthbert Carre to take him as apprentice to the trayde and art of merchandrie. To Jenet, my daughter, 12l. and one counter. To Alice, my daughter, the same. To my brother, William Woldhave of Gatsyde, one read whye that goith at Walker and the said William to make a chist to bury me in. To Richard Woldhave, my brother's son, one black rigged whye that goith at Walker. To Agnes Dalton and Agnes Baites one quye each. To John Woldhave, maryner, one gimmer. To my syster, Elizabeth Woldhave, two yowes. To Mr. Lanclote Erington of Denton, gent., 10s., to be good master to my children. To George Delavell, Oswald Delavell, Henry Woldhave, James Woldhave and Thomas Rey, a yowe lambe each. To William, my son, my farme at Elswicke; my son John to remayne on it with him. Supervisors, John Dalton of Elswicke, William Rey of Horton Grainge, yeoman. Witnesses, Henry Eden, smyth, Edward Woldhave, tanner, Christofer Woldhave, surgeon, and George Walles.

WILL OF RICHARD NORMAN.

Nov. 13, 1566. Richard Norman of Chester. To be buried in the church of Chester. To Sir William Whowler [sic], 3s. 4d. To Sir Raufe Crawe, my best bonnett. To Thomas Mathew, my best sarcenett tippet, a book of the New Testament boith in Latine and Englishe; a booke named Postolans, to Francis Trolopp; one booke named Tresdem Sermones, one other Joh[an]es vider [sic], and one booke of Ambros, in parts, to Mr. Chayter. To Sir William Hardwik, my worsted jackett. To Sir Roland Blenkinshop, my best worset jacket. To Sir William Blenkenshope, one new fosyen dublett. To the church of Chester, 2 Englishe salters. To John Marshall, one Testament in Latine. To the poore, 10s. The pencion of Yorke, due to be payd att Martinmas last past, 4s. My hole pencion for Chester, 5l. To John Becke, 1 silver tache. To George Midleton, 1 silver ringe. To the children of Richard Rand equallye, 3s. 4d. To Agnes Clarke, 1 brod clothe jackett with a cape. To Christopher Norman, 1 new mattrass. To George Browne, 1 girkin. To Richard Wales, 20d. To Richard Smith, surgeon, 20s. To Leonard Sands, 10l. To Robert Lester, 2s. To Thomas Wedeston, 10s. To Thomas Davison, 10s. Residue to Allison Sands, Leonard Sands, Christopher Norman and make them my executors.

WILL OF ANTHONY TROLLOPE.

Feb. 2, 1566/7. Anthony Trollope. First I geve and bequith my soull to Almightie God, my Creator and Redemer, trusting in his grace and mercye to be one of his elect childring. Also I geve and bequieth to Esable Jackson one yewe with one lame. I geve and bequieth to Elysabeth, my wyf, to Mychell Troulope, Georg Troullope, Andrew Trowlope, Roger Troulope, Thomas Troullope and Margrett Troullope, Elling Troulope and Anne Troulope, my childring, all my goods that I have, with my detts and legaces paid, whome I mak to be my trew and lawfull executors. Supervisors of this my last will and testament, Mr. Robert Tempest, Mr. John Troullope, Mr. Mychell Tempest, Mr. Mychell Fetterstonehought. Witness of this my last will and testament, Mr. Michell Fetterstonehought, and one of them to have 10s. for panes, Georg Chappman, Lanclott Chappman, Richard Morgaine, Rowland Woller, and Thomas Benson, the curat of Stannhope in Wardell, with others. [Pr., Aug. 4, 1567.]

INVENTORY. *Summa bonorum*, 53*l*. 18*s*. He owes : To Mr. William Brick, the parson of Stannop in Wardell, 26s. 8d. To Oswold Care of the Newcastell, 14s. 4d. To Mr. Bartram Anderson, 10s. To Sir Thomas Benson, 6s. 6d. To Mr. John Trowlope, 5s. To Jaine Hayslaybe, 3s. 4d. To Clemett Ogyll of the Newcastell, 3s. 4d. To Thomas Tempest, 3s. 4d. To Mr. Robert Tempast, 11s. 6d. To Mr. Thomas Tempest, 10s. To Mistress Hall, the wyf of Christofer Hall of Wendgat Grayng, 7s. To Raufe Wall, 8s. To Thomas Whytfeld, 8s. To Robert Garthwatt, 1s. 8d. To James Raye, 6s. 8d. To Thomas Wilson, 3s. To George Chapman, 4s. To Rauf Mason, 11s. To Christofer Whytfield, 11s. To John Chapman, 2s. 4d. To Ricard Mowbray, 11d. To John Crook, 1s. 6d. To Thomas Wall, 10d. To Thomas Thompson, 5s.

WILL OF EDWARD PARKINSON.

July 2, 1567. Edward Parkinson of Beamont-hill,[1] in the countie of Durham, gentilman, etc. To be buryed within the parishe churche of Howghton yff I shall forton to dye within the same parishe, or suche other place nere there unto as my bodye maye be convenientlye caried thither. And I will and bequithe 6*l*. 13*s*. 4*d*. to be givven

---

[1] Edward Parkinson of Beaumont-hill, co. Durham, son of Richard Parkinson of the same place, married first a daughter of Crathorn of Crathorn, co. York, who died *s.p.*, and second, Anne, daughter of Sir Ralph Hedworth of Harraton, knight, daughter of Sir William Hilton, baron of Hilton, by whom he had a numerous issue. This will makes many additions to the pedigree of Parkinson of Beaumont-hill entered at Flower's *Visitation of Durham* in 1575 by the testator's grand-nephew, Francis Parkinson of Whessey.

The inventory of testator's goods is printed in *Wills and Inventories*, vol. i. p. 271.

and distributed amonge the most poore and nedie people within the parishe of Howghtou, the parishes of Heighinton, Ayclife and Derlington in the said countie of Durham, imediatlye and so sone after my deathe as convenientlye it maie be done. Also I geve and bequithe to the churche works of Howghton churche aforsaid, 13s. 4d. Also I will, etc., that Anne, now my wyffe, shall have the occupacion of one tenement and farmhould in Sadburye, now in the tenor of Richerd Allen, of all my lands and tenements in Whessoe and Dringefeld during her widowheade, and if she fortune to marye or dye, the said lands, etc., to come to my sonne, Henrye Parkinson, for the remainder of the yeres. Also I geve and bequithe to my doughter Esabell one anuitie or annuall rent of 20l., issuing from all the lands, tenements, meadowes and pasturs in Nesbett, which I have in lease of the graunt of one, Edward Walgrauve, and Jane his wife, for terme of nyne yers yett induringe. I will that my wife shall have the occupacion of my said fermhould in Nesbett for the 8 yeres, payinge the said some of 20l. to my doughter Esabell, and if my wife marie, then it to come to the hands of my supervisors, etc. The resydewe of my interest, etc., in the same farme of Nesbett to my said sonne Henrye. Also I geve and bequithe unto my dowghter Elinor all that annuitie or annuall rent of 10l. issuinge forthe of all the lands, etc., in Hurdishouse, near Durham, and of all the lands, etc., of one Christofor Maire of Durham, or ells wher in the countye of Durham (with clause of distresse) which one, James Lasinbye, had of the graunte of the said Christophor Maire for the terme of 27 yeres yett enduringe as by a deade therof maid between the said two, bearinge daitt 12 Nov., 3rd of Phillip and Mary. And I will that Anne, my wyfe, shall receave the said rent of 10l. yerlye during the said 17 yeres for the use of the said Elinor. Also I geve and bequiethe to my sonne, Cuthbert Parkinson and his assignes, all thes my messuags, lands, tenements and hereditaments, etc., liinge in Blacwell for the terme of his lyfe. And Anne, my wife, to have the order of my said son Cuthbert and his lands till he come to lawfull aige. And if she dye, then I will that Bryan Palmes of Morton, gentilman, shall have the order of him and his part of goods and also the occupacion of the said lands in Blackwell to th' use of my said sonne. Also I geve and bequithe to Henry Parkinson, my son, my best silver salte and 13 silver spones whiche haithe the image of Christ and the 12 appostels upon them, and a gilted goblett with the coveringe upon it, and my best maire. Also I geve to my said sonne Henrye two brewe leads and one coolinge leade whiche stands in the new backhouse at Beamonte-hill withe a trough ston, and they to remayne and be as aireloomes unto the said house withe all suche things as my mother did geve as airelomes. And further I geve also to my said sonne Henrye one pair of bed-stocks that is turned, standinge in the chamber over the kitchen, and another paire of bedstocks standing in the chamber over the hall, withe a portall in the said chamber, to be as airelomes in the

said house at Beamont-hill. Also I will that Anne, my wyfe, shall
have the occupacion of my silver peac whiche is punsed, with a dosen
silver spones, so longe as she levithe, and after hir decease I geve and
bequithe the said peace and spones unto my sonne, Cuthbert Parkinson ; (and if he die before 21, to Henry Parkinson). Also I will
that my suster Killinghall shall have 20*l*. of my goods and she to
bestowe it at her discretion amongst my brother Killinghall children
and hers. Also I geve to Henrye Killinghall, 6*l*. I geve to my suster
Killinghall for a token of remembrance, my silver beeds. Also
I will that Dorithe Hodgeson shall have 10*l*. of my goods if she
follow the advise of my wyfe and my supervisors in hir mariadge.
I geve to everye one of my suster Mallett's children, 6*s*. 8*d*.
I geve to my cosinge, William Morden, one blacke cloke and my
blacke satten jerkin. I geve to my onkell, James Parkinson, 20*s*.,
and to everye one of his sones, 6*s*. 8*d*. I geve to Edward Wren, my
godson, my gresald maire, and to everye one of his brether, 6*s*. 8*d*.
I geve to my aunt Salvin an angell, and to every one of hir children
6*s*. 8*d*. I geve to Francis Parkinson the yonger, an angell. I geve
to my cosinge, William Wiclife of Wiclife, an old aungell. I geve to
Robert Tempest of Holmsyd, an angell. I geve to William Wren
the yonger, an angell. I geve to William Kendell an angell.
I geve to Sir Robert Richeson an angell. I geve to my suster
Hedworthe an angell. I geve to my brother Tomlinson an angell.
I geve to my suster Tomlinson an angell. I geve to my godsonne,
Edward Tomlinson, an angell. I geve to my suster Lawson an
angell. I geve to my brother Mydfurthe an angell and to my
sister, his wyfe, another angell. I geve to my cosinge, William
Jennyngson, an angell. I geve to William Strangwishe an
angell. I geve to Sir George Conyers, 5*s*. I geve to Sir George
Vayne, 5*s*. I geve to Sir John Sótheron, 5*s*. I geve to Sir Robert
Barber, 6*s*. 8*d*. I geve to Raufe Cowtman, 10*s*. I geve to John
Aykrigg, 20*s*. I geve to Thomas Tulby, 6*s*. 8*d*. I geve to
Nycholas Yong and his wife, 3*l*. 6*s*. 8*d*., which Raufe Huton, lait of
Walworthe, deceased, gentilman, was indetted to me, which some of
3*l*. 6*s*. 8*d*. is in the hands of William Smythe of Eshe, esquier.
I geve to Anthony Appelbye one annual or yearely rent of 20*s*. yerly
issuing furthe of all my lands, etc., in Cottom Mundvell, nowe in
the teanore of Bartilmew Addye. Also I will 20*s*. yerely to Richard
Akrigg, my servant, out of the said lands. I geve to Robert Browen,
5*s*. I geve to every of my houshould servants, beinge men servants
havinge nothinge before bequest, 2*s*., and to every of my women
servants, 12*d*. I give to Mr. Robert Dalton an angell. Also I geve
to my brother, John Hedworthe, 40*s*., and to my uncle, Jarerd
Salvin, 5*l*., to my brother, John Killinghall, 40*s*., and to Brian
Palmes of Morton, gentilman, 40*s*., to be supervisors of this my will.
I geve to Francis Parkinson, th' elder, 10*s*. I geve to Robert Thorpe,
6*s*. 8*d*. I geve to Robert Younge, 5*s*. I geve to Jeffraye Trotter,
3*s*. 4*d*. The rest to my wife. Witnesses, Jarrerd Salvin, th' elder
John Killinghall and Richard Akrigge.

WILL OF CHRISTOPHER HALL.

Dec. 10, 1567.   Christopher Hall of Wyngait Graung, gentylman. To be buryed in the quere of Kellowe nighe unto my mother.   To my wyffe, all my right, title, etc., upon my farmehold of Wingayt Grange where now I dwell, which I have by the force of two severall leases, th'one frome the Quein's majestie and th'other by the layt Prior and Convent of the laite monasterie of Durham, for her life; then to Philope, my sonn.   To Philope Hall, 30*l.*   To Cuthbert Hall, his sonne, 6*l.* 13*s.* 4*d.*   To Margret Hall, 3*l.* 6*s.* 8*d.*   To Margere Warde, 13*l.* 6*s.* 8*d.*   To James Ward, 3*l.* 6*s.* 8*d.*   I forgyve Rycherd Ward, his father, 3*l.* 6*s.* 8*d.* he was owinge to me.   To Cecile Trotter, 10*l.*, and to the said Cecile, in consyderacon that she had not to her marige so much as her syster Margery had, 10*l.*   To Thomas Trotter, 3*l.* 6*s.* 8*d.*   I desire my wife to have the guyde goverment of the said Thomas (?) at schole and in learing during his nonag.   To Rauffe, Walter and Helen Trotter, 3*l.* 6*s.* 8*d.* each.   To Edmond Grene, 1 qwye and 2 ewes.   To Godfrey Bailey, one Frenche crowne of gold.   To William Benet, doctor, 6*s.* 8*d.*   To Jane Eislybe, one yowe and one lame.   To William Thomson, my curat, 5*s.*   To Thomas Lytlefayre, the clerke, 2*s.* 6*d.*   Supervisors, Mr. John Troloppe of Thornlye and Mr. Francis Bainbrigg of Wheatley-hyll, esquire.   To each of them for their paines, a ryall of gold of 15*s.*   The rest to Betresse Hall, my wife.   Witness, William Tompson, curat.   Edmond Grene, Thomas Shawe, Brian Trotter, John Trollop, Fransis Bainbrige, supervisors.

WILL OF RICHARD WOODIFIELD.

Jan. 25, 1567/8.   Richard Weddefeld of Fyshburne.   To be buryed in Shedfeld church yard.   To Esable Weddefeld, my wyf, 1 read cowe, one acre and a half of land in hav'rfeld during her lyf; in the west feld, 4 riggs one the poyll lands; in the south feld, one acre one the baring lands besyde the baring bawpe (?) healf, 1 acre one the alt lands; in the est feld one the warrell flatt, 2 riggs, one acre and 2 buts; 1 half acre one the same flatt and all the hay in the gyells raks, and one howse to sett in, etc.   To Richard and William Weddefeld, my sons, my wayne gere, etc., etc.   To Richard Weddefeld, my son, my leses of my farmold.   To Essabell Weddefeld, the daughter of Roland Weddefeld, 40*s.*   To Thomas Weddefeld, Roland Weddefeld's son, one wedder.   Alyson Johnson, ... my daughter Elisbeth Weddefeld.[1]

---

[1] The following is the will of another member of the same family, perhaps a son of the testator:—

Nov. 20, 1568.   William Widdefeld of Ferry-hill.   To be buried in the churchyard of Merinton.   To the poore man's boxe, 12*d.*   To Robert Widdefeld, my son, the right, etc., of my farmhold, my mother to govern him. Katherine, my daughter.   My wife, Issabell Widdefeld.

Inventory exhibited Jan. 20, 1568/9, by Robert Darneton, Christopher Widdefeld.

WILL OF SAMPSON WYVILL.

April 12, 1568. Sampson Wyvell of Walworth [1] in the parishe of Heighinton. I frelye committ and give my soul to God Allmightye and his onlye sonne, my Saviour and Redemer, Jesus Christ, and my bodye to be buryed within the parishe churche of Heighinton afor-sayd, or else yf itt do please God to call me to his mercye att any other place then Walworthe, my bodye to be buryed wheras my frends shall thinke most convenient. I give to the mainteining of the stocke of my parishe church of Heighinton, 10s. I give to Christofor Wivell, my eldest sonne, in full consideration of his child's porcion, to be payd furthe of my farmhold at Walworth yearlye duringe all the holl terme of my lease which I have of the sayd ferminge, the some of 5l. of good and lawfull currant Englishe monye. Also I give to my sayd sonne, Christofor Wivall, furth of the rectorye of Lanfurth within the countye of Notingham, duringe all the terme which I have in the sayd rectorye, the some of 4l. I give unto Thomas Wivell, my younger sonne, in full consideration of his child's porcion, furth of my sayd fermold att Walworth yerlye duringe the terme of my sayd lease, the some of 3l. And I give unto my sayd sonne, Thomas Wivall, in consideration aforsayd furth of the rectorye of Lanforth duringe the terme of my sayd lease which I have of the sayd rectorye, the sum of 3l. I give unto Margarett Wivell, my daughter, the third parte of all my goods, moveable and unmoveable, all my leases excepted, in full consideracion of hir child's porcion, and yf that itt please God that Fayth Wivell, my wiffe, have an other sonne or dowghter, then I will that the sayd sonne or doughter, wheather itt shall please God to send, shall have in full consideration of ther child's porcion, furth of my sayd fermold of Walworth yerlye duringe all the hole terme of my lease which I have in the sayd fermold, the some of 3l. Yf itt please God to take unto his mercye anye of these, my children, during the tyme of ther younge age, that is to say, Christopher Wivell, Thomas Wivell or the other child which my wiffe is with, then I will that the same annuytye or annuytyes which I have, by vertue of this presente will, geven unto my sayd childe or children shall remaine to the use of my children which is then livinge and be equallye devided amongst them, and yf itt shall please God to take to his mercye my doughter, Margaret Wyvell, duringe the terme of hir noneage, then I will that the thirde parte of all my goods which I have by this present will geven unto the sayd Margarete, shall be equallye devided and given unto my other children which ys then livinge. Whereas I have covenaunted and graunted by indenture beringe date 24 Feb., 1560/1, my hole

---

[1] Sampson Wyvill, a younger son of Sir Marmaduke Wyvill of Burton Constable, married Faith, daughter of Nicholas Girlington of Hackforth. Testator's widow remarried George Pudsay of Stapleton-on-Tees. A short pedigree of the family may be found in Surtees, *Durham*, vol. iii. p. 263. *Cf.* Surtees, *Durham*, vol. i. p. 105.

right and title that I have in the moytye and one halfe of the rectorye
of Sadbar, Garsdaylle and Dente, with all and singuler commodites
and profitts thereto belonginge, to the use and profitt of Fayth Wivell,
my wiffe, duringe the terme of thirtye yeares then next after followinge, etc., my will is that my wife shall enjoye the sayd yeres and
occupye the same quietlye duringe the same terme. And all the
residue of yeres which I have in the moytye of the sayd rectorye of
Garsdayle, Sadbar and Dente (except thos that I have before graunted
and covenanted unto my sayd wiffe), I give unto my eldest sonne,
Christofor Wivell, so that he the sayd Christofor pay yerlye unto my
sonne, Thomas Wivell, his brother, 3*l.*, furth of the sayd moytye of
the rectorye of Sedbar, yerlye duringe all the yeres that he shall
have in the moytye of the rectorye of Sedbar. And yf it please God
that my wiffe have an other sonne, the said Christofor Wivell shall
pay yerlye all the sayd yeres that he shall have in the moytye of
the sayd rectorye of Sedbar unto him 3*l.*, furth of the sayd moytye
of the sayd rectorye of Sedbar. And yf itt shall please God that my
sayd wiffe have a doughter, then the sayd Christofor Wivel shall pay
unto hir and my dowghter, Margaret Wivell, 3*l.*, furth of the moietye
of the sayd rectorye of Sedbar, duringe all the yeares that he shall
have in the same, as is aforsayd. And yf it please God to take my
sonne, Christofor, to his mercye before that he entre in the sayd
yeres in revercion of the moietye of the rectorye of Garsdayll and
Sedbar, then I give all my right of the sayd revercion of the sayd
moietye of the rectorye of Sedbar, unto my sonne, Thomas Wivell,
during all those yeres that I have in the same, to begin after the
expiration of those yeres that I have graunted to my wiffe, so that
he pay yerlye duringe the sayd yeres furth of the moietye of the
sayd rectorye unto his brother, yf it please God that he have one,
3*l.*, and yf it please God that my wiffe have a doughter, then my
sonne, Thomas Wivell, shall pay yerlye unto hir and my doughter,
Margaret Wivel, hir sister, 4*l.*, that is to say, eyther of them 40*s.*,
furth of the moietye of the rectorye of Sedbar, duringe all thos years
as he haith by vertue herof in the same. And yf it please God to
take my sonne, Thomas Wivell, to his mercye, he havinge no ishew
male before the entringe of the sayd yeres of the moietye of the
rectorye of Sedbar, then I give itt to the other child my wiffe is
with, yf itt be a sonne, so that he pay yerlye out of the same moytye
of the rectorye to my dowghter, Margaret Wivell, 3*l.*, and yf itt
please God that the sayd child which my wiffe is with be a doughter,
then yf boith my sonnes be as I have declared before (gone to the
mercye of God) I will that Fayth Wivell, my wiffe, shall have the
residue of yeres in the same moietye of the rectorye of Sedbar, so
that she pay yerly out of the same to my doughter, Margaret Wivel,
and hir sister, 4*l.*, that is, eyther of them 40*s.*, dureinge the terme
of the sayd yeres. All my leasses, rents and revercions and all
other my goods, moveable and unmoveable, my debts, rents, legaces

and funerall expences discharged and payd, I give unto Faith
Wivell, my wiffe, whom I make my holle executrixe of this my last
will and testament. Also I constitute and appoint supervisors of
this my last will and testament, Christofor Wivell of Burton and
Nicholas Girlington of Hackforth, esquiers, Marmaduke Wivell,
Nicholas Girlington, younger, gent. And unto my brother, Christofor
Wivell, I give and putt my sonne, Christofor Wivell, and his yearlye
rent or porcion to bringe up him and his discretion. Also I would
require my father-in-law, Nicholas Girlington of Hackforth, to
receive all such yerlye rent and porcions as I have bequithed to
Thomas Wivell and suche child as itt shall please God that my wiffe
shall have that she is now with, be itt sonne or doughter, painge
yerlye unto my sayd wiffe, Fayth Wivell, suche reasonable allowans
during the infancye of my sayd two children for ther necessarye
findinge as shall seme reasonable unto my sayd supervisors. And
after my sayd children shall come to such age as they shalbe able
to goo forward to the schoole, then I committ my sayd children to
be brought upp with ther yerlye porcion of rentt att the discretion
of my sayd father in law, and he to make accompt unto my sayd
children when they shall accomplisshe the full age of 21 yeres,
having reasonable allowanns for ther bringing upp, and yf my father-
in-law refuse to take the charge upon him, then I appoint my brother,
Nicholas Girlington, to take the mattir in hande and charge of him
in suche ordre as I have appointed my sayd father in law to do in
the same. I give to the poore folks of this parishinge and of Denton
towne and Somerous, 20s. Thes being witnesses of this my last will
Richard Bilton, Thomas Smith, Thomas Robinson and William
Temple.

INVENTORYE praysed att Walworth, Sept. 16, 1568. Hard corne
in the barne, by estimacon, 180 threaves at 30*l*.   Oots and
pease by estimacon, 8 threaves at 10*l*.   Hay contayning by
estimation, 48 lode at 12*l*.   80 yowes at 15*l*.   76 hoggs,
price 9*l*. 10*s*.   17 draffe yowes, price 56*s*. 8*d*.   17 oxen, price
30*l*. 1*d*.   25 stirks, price 14*l*.   22 kye, price thereof, 26*l*. 13*s*. 4*d*.
One bull and 9 calves, price 3*l*. 6*s*. 8*d*.   6 stotts, price . . . .   One
bay horse and one fillye stagge, price 9*l*.   One white stagg, price 5*l*.
One meare and hir fool, price 40*s*.   One bay fillye, price 20*s*.   One
gray fillye, price 20*s*.   One stoned stagge, price 40*s*.   One old bay
horse, price 40*s*.   One litle blacke nagg, price 20*s*.   One bull at
Awkland, price 20*s*.   2 meares and one nagge, price 3*l*.   27 swine,
the price 50*s*.   Wheat and malte in the garners, price 4*l*.   Waines,
plewes, with yoks, temes and all other geare thereto belonging, with
culter, socke and shakell, price thereof, 53*s*. 4*d*.   2 sestrons, one
brewlead with potts, pannes, spets, rost yron, yron toings, and all
implements of the kitchin, 8*l*.   The butterye with the stuffe
therein, 4*l*.   Fedder bedds and bedstocks, takells, buffett stoolls,
forms, chists and other implements in the parler, price 8*l*.   2 bedds

in the mayds chambér, 20s. The furniture of the hall, price 13s. 4d. One windoclothe, with sexes and pooks, 7s. Gese and hennes, price 6s. In woll, 20l.

Debts owing by the testator :—

Imprimis: To my brother Frances, 12l. To my father-in-law, Nicholas Girlington, 10l. In servants' wages, 40s. In rents of Walworth and Sedbar, 25l. To the smith for a stone of yron, 14d. To my brother Francis, for malt, 12d. In funerall expences, 7l.

INVENTORY OF ANNE HEBBURN.

INVENTORY of the goods of Maystres Anne Hebborne [1] of Shotton, *vidua*, layt disceased. [1568.]

Imprimis: 44 kye and 3 calves, at 53l. 3s. 4d. 35 oxen, at 85l. 16 stotts, at 24l. 21 stotts and whies, att 16l. 16s. 2 bulles, at 46s. 8d. 21 stirks, at 12l. 21 calves, at 5l. 10s. 27 horses, meares and colts, at 42l. 13s. 4d. 22 swine, at 4l. 6s. 9 score and 6 wedders, at 34l. 4s. 8d. 12 score and 12 yowes, at 42l. 35 tuppes, at 4l. 17s. 7d. 5 score and 12 hoggs, at 11l. 4s. Corne in the staggarth and in the barne, 58l. Upon the earth, at 20l. Hai, at 29l. Pleughe-gcre and wane-gere, at 5l. Houshold-stuf, apparell, playt and all such things as doyth belonge to the house, at 41l. 11s. The leace of Swaynston, at 10l. Malt in the gardner at Hardwicke, 20s. Colles and behives, at 40s. In mony, 15l. 13s. *Summa* of the goods praised is 520l. 6d.

Detts owing to the said Mysteres An Hebborne *vidua* as following :—

Rychard Cottesworthe, 5l. 6s. 8d. William Skaythlocke, 3l. 10s. Jhone Ferrey, 46s. 8d. Jhone Thomson, 6s. 8d. Croisbei, 3l. 2 men of Morden, 15s. Tod of Sedgefeld, 23s. 4d. Rychard Gregson, 10s. Rouland Hicson, 14s. Thomas Dinsdall, 40s. Thomas Stellin, 9s. George Medcalf, 40s. Ingram Tayler, 6s. 8d. William Pine, 6l. Umphrey Blaxton, 6l. 13s. 4d. Umphrey Blaxton [*sic*], 30s. Uswolde Mydforthe, ... Edmond Parkinson, 18l. 6s. 8d. Mayster Anthony Hebborne, 20s. Summ of the detts awing is 56l. 8s. *Summa totall.* is 579l. 19s. 6d. Whereof detts awing to the testator as followithe :—

Imprimis: To hir doughter, Ellinor Hebborne, 40l. To William Heghington, 40s. To Johne Cay, 12l. To Johne Dent, 20s. The farme of Swaneston, 5l. 13s. 4d. To Mr. Gray, 5l. To Robert Hebborne for a horse, 5l. 6s. 8d. To Rychard Eland, 56l. 6s. 4d. To Ellenor Hebborne for a stott, 40s. To Anne Allan, 6s. To the webster, 3s. To Umphrey Blaxton, 5l. 8s. To William Hebborne, 4s. For

---

[1] The lady, the inventory of whose goods is now printed, was Anne, sister of Sir Christopher Metcalf, knight, and widow of Richard Hebburn of Hardwick, by whom she had issue four sons and five daughters.

the sesment of Shotton, 22*d*. Jhone Bellerbe, clerke, 4*l*. 14*s*. To William Hebborne for his child's portion of his father's goods, 20*l*. To Robert Hebborne for his child's portion of his father's goods, 20*l*. To William Hebborne, 3*l*. 13*s*. 4*d*. For servant wage, 4*l*. 6*s*. 3*d*. To the smythe, 2*s*. 2*d*. For funerall chargs, 5*l*. 18*s*. 8*d*. Summ of the detts owing is 140*l*. 14*s*. 5*d*.

WILL OF JOHN HALTON.

May 27, 1569. John Hawton of Newcastle, master maryner, etc. To be buried in the church yarde of All Saincts. To my eldest son, John Hawton, my seatte house that I nowe dwell in and to his heires, then to Roger Hawton, my son, then to my daughters, Agnes and Elizabeth Hawton. I will that John, my son, shall pay yerely to each of my daughters 105*s*. during the tearme of 20 years. To John, my son, my best silver whissell and chayne and one quarter of my shippe called the "Mary Galland," and my thre houses and a certan waist in Gatished nowe in the teanor of Robert Anderson, yeoman, John Hollis, mariner, and Agnes Bell, wedowe. To Roger, my son, my house in Sandgatt now in the tenor of John Hall, blacksmith, and my four tenements therunto adjoininge with a key nowe in the tenor of John Story, maryner, Andrewe Loggan, yeoman, Thomas Blaikden, maryner, and Elizabeth Lighton, wedowe, and one quarter of the abovesaid ship and my second silver whissell and cheyne, and he to paye yerly for 5 yeres to my sonne-in-lawe, William Moore, shipwright, 40*s*. To my said son Roger the rent of 7*s*. by yere from a shoppe on the bridg now in the tenor of Rauphe Craggs, merchaunte, and the yerely rent of eight shillings from a tenement now in the teanor of John Jackson of Newcastle, merchant. To Agnes, my daughter, one tenement in Sandgate, now in the tenor of Reynold Soppet, cordiner, and a tenement in Sandgate now in the tenor of Thomas Anderson, maryner, and one haulfe quarter of my said shippe, and one haulf of my close in Gatished now in the tenore of John Pressick and Nicholas Hedley, merchant, and one halfe of my tenement in the Syd now in the tenor of George Farnaby, marchant. To Elizabeth, my daughter, my 3 tenements, waist and gardinge on the Burne-bancke and the other half of my tenement in the Syd in the tenor of George Farnaby, marchaunt, and one half quarter of my ship, and the other half of my close in Gatished now in the tenor of John Pressick and Nicholas Hedley of Newcastle, marchaunte. To each of my said daughters, sex silver sponnes. To John Redheade, shipwright, a new russet gowne. To William More, my sonne-in-law, one hole sea rayment. To everyone of my lait sister's, Jennet Readhead, children, one bowle of wheat. To my servant, Jenet Swaine, 10*s*. To my servant, Margaret Dixon, 10*s*. To George Cooke, clarke of the Trinitye-housse, 5*s*. To my wife, Agnes Hawton, my seathouse for life. Overseers, Maister Richard Hodshon, merchant, and George Pearson, to each 10s. Witnesses, Angues Fife, Roger Raw, baker, George Pearson, tailor, both of Newcastle. Jennet Wilkinson, Elizabeth and George Cooke of the Trinite-house with others.

WILL OF ELEANOR COOK.

June 26, 1569. Elloner Cook of Newcastle, widowe, lait wife of Christofer Cooke of Newcastle, marchant, etc. To be buried in the churche of Alhollowes as nighe unto my husband as may be. I give to my trustie frend, William Selbey, of Newcastle, marchaunt, for the use of my daughter, Elizabeth Bewick, 20l.; and if she overlive her husband or dye before him, the said sum to be divided amongst her five childring, Christofer, Robert, Elleonr, Agnes and Gillian Bewicke, also I geve to each of them more towards ther prefarment in mariag, 40s. I geve and bequiethe to my very trustie frends, Richard Hodshon of Newcastle, alderman and marchaunt, and to Isabell, his wyfe, 20l. for the use of my daughter, Margerie Dickinson, wife to William Dickinson, if she outlive her husband, and if she die before him to be divided among her children. And I gyve them more for ther prefarment in mariag, 40s. a pece. I gyve to my trusty frends, Richard Hodshon and William Selby of Newcastle, marchant, for the use of my daughter, Agnes Brigham, wyfe to Humfrey Brigham, 20l. if she overlive her husband, and if she dye before him to be devided among her children ; to each of them 40s. a pece. I give unto my said two friends for the use of my daughter, Jellyan Girdler, wyfe unto William Girdler, 10l. if she overlive her husband, and if she dye before him the said sum to be divided among her children ; 40s. a pece to each of them. To Christopher Cooke, my son, 30l. out of my keyles, and a lyghtner. To my son, John Cooke, 10l. in money. To Christopher Elmer, merchant, 60l. and my best keyle and my best lightner. To Elizabeth Langton, five marks. To my kelemen, 30s. To Oswald Jackson, five marks. To his daughter, Marion Jackson, 20s. To Isabell, wife of Richard Hodshon, fouer old ryalls. To Mistris Scryvener, one olde ryall. To Mistris Selby, wife to William Selbe, one old riall. To Clement Ogle and his wife, an old angell each. To Mrs. Roxbey, now wife to Lawrance Rokesbye, one old angell. To Elizabeth Goundrie, one old angell. To Mawde Wilkinson of Winlinton, 5s. To my sister, Hilton, 10s. To my sonne in lawe, Humfraye Brigham, a goblet of sylver. To William Girdler, a playne pece of silver. To William Dixinson, halfe a dossen silver spownes. To Androw Bewick, halfe a dossen of sylver spownes. To my daughters, Elizabeth Bewick, Margere Dixinson, Anne [sic] Brigham and Gillian Gyrdler, one chist of lynning napperie, to be devided amongst them. To my daughter, Elizabeth Bewick, one brasen morter and one pestell, one gown lyned with unwattered chamlet and a kyrttell of the same, belonginge to the same gowne, and my next best beltt and a paire of silver crooks belonging to the same, for life, then to Ellon, her daughter. To my daughter, Anne Brigham, my best gowne and kyrttell and my best beltt. To Margere Dykkinson, my worsted gowne and kyrtell. To William Cookson's wife, one old angell. To Mr. Richard Hodshon, fower old ryalls, and to Mr. Selbe, one old riall. To the poore colyers of Winlington, 3*l*. among them. To John Hedley, 5*s*. To the poore howsholders within the towne of Newcastle, 40*s*. To Mr. John Killinghall, an old angell, and the same to his wife. To William Cocks of Newcastle, an old angell. To Christofer Elmer, one payre of fyne lynen sheets, etc. To my brother's sonne, Thomas Elmer, 10*l*. I will that my foresaid 2 friends shall sell the house in which I dwell within one year after my death for the use of my daughters and I make them my executors. Supervisors, William Selbe and Climent Ogle. Witnesses, William Selbe, William Brown, clarke, John Horne.

CODICIL. Whereas it haithe pleased Almightie God to call unto his mercie before my death my sonne, John Cook, therfore I will that suche legacye as is gyven unto my said sonne, John Cooke, shall be gyven to John Cooke, his basterd sonne, which he had by Isabell Robson, and I also gyve to him all suche proffetts as he shall receyve by the administracon of the goods and cattals of my said son John, save onelye the lease of the Sowthefeld which I give to my sonne, Christofor Cooke. And whereas it haith pleased Almightie God to call my dowghter, Jellyan Gyrdler, to his mercie, I will that all suche legacie as is gyven to her in my said will, be distributed equallye among her 3 daughters. I gyve to Sir William Browne, clerke, one old angell. I gyve to John Horne, servant to Mr. Richard Hodshon, one olde angell besydes the reward of my trustie frends for writting of my said will. I gyve to my two madens nowe being my servants, 20*s*. a pece. I gyve unto Richard Brakenby, 10*s*. I gyve to my daughter, Elizabeth Bewick, one mylke kowe. I gyve to Elioner Dixkynson, daughter to William Dixkinson, one demey bellt that I bowght last which cost 16*s*. Witnesses, William Browne, William Selbe, John Horne.

WILL OF MICHAEL FETHERSTONHAUGH.

Aug. 14, 1569. Michell Fetherstonhaugh of Stanop, esquyer, etc. To be buried within the quyere of the parishe church of Stanhop. To my wyfe, Isabell Fetherstonhaughe, the thirde part of all my goods. To my dowghter, Johan Fetherstonhaugh, on hundredth pounds to mary her withall and she to be ordered by my son, John Fetherstonhaugh. To my son, Lancelot Fetherstonhaugh, one annuitye of 4*l*., and in defalt of such payment he to enter on the tenement called the Hole. I gyve to him 20*l*. for his portion. To my sonne, John Fetherstonehaugh, eightene oxen going at Stanhope and twelve kye with ther calves and foure score youes, one hundreth wethers, and one sylver salt double gylt, one sylver pece and a doson sylver spoynes, left unto me as heyrelumes perteyning unto the house. And I give him my hole lease of Stanhope mylle for the better mayntenanc of his house. I owe unto Henry Welden, 20*l*., and to Christofer Welden, 6*l*. 13*s*. 4*d*., to be paid unto them in full contentacion and satissfaction of ther child's porcions and of the arreragies of these.

INVENTORY OF THOMAS TEMPEST.

Aug. 22, 1569. INVENTORY. Thomas Tempest of Stanley, gent. 26 draught oxen, 55*l*. 599 wethers, 132*l*. The halffe of one shipe, with hir furnyture, in comen with Mr. Robert Tempest, 60*l*. *The hall, etc. The butterye, etc. The kitchyng, etc. The chamber over the buttrie, etc.* Courtings of read and greane say with a valence and frenge of the same bed, 12*s*. *The chamber over the larder, etc. The wright's chamber over the milke-house, etc. The chamber over the stable, etc. The chamber over the parler, etc. The chamber over the maids chamber, etc.* One flanders chist, 3*s*. 4*d*. *Mr. Marlees chamber, etc. The loft over the kitching, etc. Plate. Imprimis:* One standing pece, weing 14 ounce, dobel-gilt, 3*l*. 10*s*. One other standing pece with a cover doble-gilt, weing 16 ounce, 4*l*. A nest of goblitts and a cover doble-gilt, weing 30 ounces, 7*l*. 10*s*. 2 saltes with one cover doble-gilt, weing 15 ounces, 3*l*. 15*s*. One drinkin pott with a cover doble-gilt, weing 14 ounces, 3*l*. 10*s*. 2 dosen spoones white, weing 26 ounces, 5*l*. 12*s*. 8*d*. One salt with a cover white, 4 ounces, 17*s*. 8*d*. His apparrell in all, 13*l*. 6*s*. 8*d*. The leace of Kealaws, 26*l*. 13*s*. 4*d*. In Lanchester, 6*l*. 13*s*. 4*d*. The leace of the Lady-landes, etc. Clement Ogle of Newcastell owes him 38*l*. Mr. Jhone Billingham, for arrerages of rent, 7*l*. 10*s*. The leace of Kiolaws geven to Mrs. Agnes Hodshon, his mother. Plate geven to Nicholas Tempest, etc. *Declaro* 593*l*. 3*s*. 4*d*.

WILL OF ROBERT BEST.

Dec. 8, 1569. Robert Best of Gaynforth. To be buried in Gaynford churche yerde.[1] To the poure men's boxe, 12*d*. To Martyn Best, my youngest sonne, one hawked whye, one youe and a lambe, and to everyone of my childreing a yowe and a lambe. The residewe to Margaret my wife and my five children, whom I make my executors. Witnesses, Thomas Hode, Anthony Blaxton, George Carter, Christofor Robynson, curatt, William Kyng, Nicholas Car.

Debts owing by this testator: To my brother Thomas Best of his child's portion, 4*l*. 4*s*. To my brother Peter Best, 8*l*. 3*s*. 4*d*. To my sister Margaret Best, 8*l*. 10*s*., and to my sister Allison Best, 16*s*.

The inventory of testator's goods, exhibited Jan. 24, 1569/70, amounted to 48*l*. 19*s*. 4*d*.

---

[1] According to the *Gainford Register*, the testator was buried Dec. 7 (*sic*), 1569.

INVENTORY OF ROGER BLAKISTON.

INVENTORY of Roger Blaixton of Gybsyde,[1] gent., proved by
Nicholas Porter of Bekley, gent., etc., Feb. 4, 1569/70.
The hall. Half a dosen silver spoines, 18s. *The parler, etc.*
One flanders chiste, 2s. One dosen sylver spones, 48s. Fyve broken
spones, 10s. *The chamber above the hall, etc.* One flanders chist,
2s. 8d. *The mayden chamber, etc. The chamber next the mayden
chamber, etc. The chamber above the parler, etc. The servants'
chamber above the old buttrie, etc. The chamber above the kytchen,
etc. The old buttrie, etc. The kytching, etc. The brewing house, etc.
The lairder howse, etc. The utter milke-howse, etc. The ynner milke-
howse, etc. The. stable, etc. The kill, etc. The barne, etc. The
stake yeard, etc.* Cattell, etc., at Gybside, Marley Hill, and Thorpe.
To Anthony Barras for my teithe, 40s.

WILL OF MARGARET HARTBURN.

March 8, 1569/70. Margaret Harteborne, wedowe, lait wyff to
Richard Harteborn of Newcastle, yeoman, deceased. To be buried
in the churche of All Saincts, Newcastle, nye to my husband. To
my husbonde's daughter, Margerye Morland, one sylver salt, withe
a cover. To hir two sonnes, halfe a dosen sylver sponnes betwixt
them. To Richard Harrigaite, one olde riall and the goblet of
sylver that my husbonde boughte, and to his wyffe one angell. To
John Lyme one angell and a goblet of sylver which lyeth in pawnde
to me of 3l. 12s. To John Gibson, merchaunt, one angell, and to his
wyffe, one doble duckat. To Thomas Johnson, my husbonde gold
ringe and one old riall. To Roger Morley, one coppe of masor edged
with silver and one olde ryall and 3l. To Janet Horssley, one angell,
and to her daughter, one halfe crowne. To Thomas Stewart, halfe a
duckatt. And for the two sylver sponnes which James Garnett's wyff
layed in paunde to me, I will that she have the one spone delyvered
and she shall gyve to hir daughter that I christened two shillings.
To Margaret Hutcheson, 3 bushells of malte. To Henrye Brewester,
5s., and my sister Cicilie husband one Fransh crowne and to hir my
best silver croks and my brode reade kyrtle, provided that at her
deathe she give them to one of my sister's children. To Anne
Haswell, 5s. And wheras Mastris Brigham owes me 20s., I will that
upon payment of the money she have hir pawnd delivered. To my
sister, Isbell Marwoode, all the malt, wheat and rye within my house
and all the beaffe (except one load of malt which I give to Margerye
Morlaye). I also give to my sister Isabell Marwoode, in money,
10l. To Elisabeth Marwodd, 3l. 6s. 8d. and as much brodde
clothe as will make her a gown and worsett to lyn it with. To

[1] Roger Blakiston, son of William Blakiston of Coxhoe, married one of the
daughters and coheirs of . . . Marley of Gibside.

Jayne Marwodd, 3*l.* 6*s.* 8*d.* and my better brod reade kyrtle. To Margerye Marwodd, 3*l.* 6*s.* 8*d.* To Edmunde Marwodd, 3*l.* 6*s.* 8*d.* To Thomas Marwodd . . . . My husband's 2 brothers. To Robert Bettlestonne's wife, halfe a crowne. The iron chymney in the hall to remayne allways in the house, provided Roger Morley give to my sister, Isbell Marwoode, one of his chymneys for it. To Anne and Margaret Harrigaite, halfe a crowne each in money. To Margaret Marwodd, the iron chymney in the lofte. To Rauff Collinge wyffe, half a crowne. To Richard Tompson, 5*s.* To Margerye Morley and Elisabeth Marwodd, all my brewinge vessell. To my sister, Isabell Marwod, my best gowne. To Beil Marwodd, wife to Archbould Marwodd, my worsted kirtle. To Richard Marwoodd, the chiste which I bought upon Hobkirk. To my maid, Elisabeth Atkinson, 10*s.* beside her wages. The rest of my houshold stuffe to Isabell Marwodd, my sister, for her daughters, except the cubbord in the hall, which I gyve to Margaret Marwood, and I give her to Richard Marwood till she be 21. I will my sister Isbell shall pay to my sister Cecilie, 20*s.* Supervisors, Richard Harrogait,[1] master and maryner, Thomas Johnson, yoman, John Gibson, merchaunt.

WILL OF HENRY KIRKBY.

March 18, 1569/70. Henry Kirkbye of Northe Awkland. To the poore people, to be distributed at the discretion of my executors and supervisors, 20*l.*, of whiche to the poore folkes of Kendall, 10*l.*, to the poore folkes of the parish of Sancte Andro Awkland, fyve marks, and to the poore people of Kirkbye Irelaith neir the crosses, 6*l.* 13*s.* 4*d.* To Elisabethe Tompson my suster daughter, 10*l.*, one gowne clothe of Flanders dye, sex dishes, 4 platters and 4 causors, beinge London vessell, etc. To my suster, Elisabethe Craycall and her children, 10*l.* To my sister Margaret, wife of John Tompson, and her children, 10*l.* To Jennat Todd of Kendall, wedo, 4*l.* To every one of my godchildrin, 12*d.* a peace. To the churche where yt shall please Almightie God that I shall be buryed in, 3*s.* 4*d.* To one Ranold Dawson and his childrin, 6*l.* 13*s.* 4*d.* To Thomas Tomlynson and his wyffe, aither of them, 10*s.* To Roger Nicolson, Gawan Watson, Lyonell Kaylame and Thomas Herryson of Weste Slikborne, 40*s.*, that is to every one of them, 10*s.* To William Mudye, 12*s.* To the poore people of Bedlington, 40*s.* To every one of my uncle's childrin that is not named herein, 6*s.* 8*d.* To my uncle, Rauff Herryson and his childrin, 40*s.* To my brother, Thomas Kirkbye wiffe and her children, 3*l.* 6*s.* 8*d.* To William Kirkbye, my cosing and uncle sone, 20*s.* and to John Kirkby, his brother, 6*s.* 8*d.*, and

---

[1] Richard Harrigaite was the owner of premises on the Quayside, Newcastle, now represented by the Three Indian Kings. *Cf.* Welford, *Newcastle and Gateshead*, vol. ii. pp. 367, 452.

I forgyve hym what he owithe me. To Allen Kirkbye, one sylver spone and I forgyve hym 13s. 4d. he owithe me. To Mr. Lancelote Pickeringe, one of the best sylver spones and one tyn pott. To Edward Hubberstee, 2s. in Spanyshe money, and to everye child that was Robert Hubberstee, one olde grote. To John Kirkbye of Durham, 6s. 8d. To Henry Brasse, 10s. To Henry Baills, 10s. To William Johnson the yonger, 6s. 8d. and I forgyve hym all he owes me in my debt booke. To Symond Johnson, 6s. 8d., and I forgyve hym all he owith me in my debt booke. To William Johnson the elder and his wyffe, 40s. To Anthony Dawson and his children, 5l., and I forgyve him what he oweth me. I gyve ten old angells of gold, that is in a brasselett, to be bestowed of Stramagatt bridge in Kendall at the oversight of Anthony Duckett and Nicholas Hodgson. To the wyffe of Rychard Barrell, a paire of hoose with yalloo tashes for a token. To Nicholas Maddison, 10s. and I forgive him what he owith me. To Thomas Tunstall, 20s., and to his sister Twissilton the rest of the money he oweth me. To Percivall Tesll, 6s. 8d. To my brother, Peter Kirkbye, 6l. 13s. 4d. To my brother Edmund, fyve marks. To Agnes Tompson and Richard Tompson, her brother, 4l. each, and to the said Agnes one cupbord that stands in my house at Awckland and sex platters, sex dishes, and sex sawcers beinge all London vessell. To Edmund Ridall, 10s. in gold. To Christopher Kirkbye, the one halfe of my lease of the water mylls in Beddlington, and the other half I bequieth to my executors for the performance of this my last will. I forgyve Henry Lockye 26s. 8d. of the some he owes me. To Roger Kirkbye of the crosses, a sylver spone. To Henrye Dobinson, son of William Dobinson, 5s. Whereas my brother, Robert Dawson, owes me for two packs of wool I forgive him the price of one of them. The residew to my brother, Edmund Kirkbye, and Robert Dawson, and my two sisters, Elisabeth Crawkall and Margaret Tompson, whome I make my executors. Supervisors, Anthony Dixon, John Brasse, William Johnson th' elder, Rychard Barrell, Anthony Duckett son of Roger Duckett, and Nicholes Hodgson, and I give to each of them 10s. Witnesses, Rauffe Baills, Symon Johnson, John Payckock and others.

Inventory exhibited Sept. 30, 1570.

INVENTORY OF WILLIAM WREN.

March 20, 1569/70. The inventaire of the goods perteyning to William Wren, laitelie departed to the mercie of Allmightie God, praised by Thomas Robinson, Anthony Cassope, Leonard Rypley, Thomas Compton and Ralf Cowton.

Fyrst, one cowe, price 20s. One almerie, one cawell with brasse geare, the price 8s. One acre and a half of herd corne, the price 20s. Hay, strawe and baltings, 4s., etc. *Summa total.* 3l.

Debts. Fyrst ; owing to Robert Mayson 4*l.* 14*s.* Owing to Lancelett Chapman, 30*s.* Owing to Henrie Kirkbye, 22*s.* Owing to John Sigeswike, 48*s.* Owing to Edward Crawe, 33*s.* 4*d.* Owing the wyff of Thomas Nichell, 2*s.* 8*d.* Owing to John Craw, 30*s.* Owing to Ralf Genison, 30*s.* Owing to Ralf Wren, 11*s.* Owing to Thomas Robinson, 5*s.* Owing to Robert Yong, 4*s.* Owing to John Robinson, 12*s.* Owing to Robert Pawson, 13*s.* Owing to Agnes Kay, 10*s.*

WILL OF ANDREW SURTEES.

April 15, 1570. Andrewe Surtys[1] of Newcastle, merchaunt, To be berryed in the church of Sant Nicollas at the laue westerne doore. To Geayne, my wyff, thys howsse I dwell in at the Calle Crosse for her life and my two howsses in the Brood Chayre, and after her deathe to my tenne chyldren, Tomas, Ouswoll, John, Jhams, Robart, Rauffe, Ellyn, Ayealls, Annas and Margerie Surtees. To Ayealls Surtys, the housse whare Nane Fostar dwells on the Castell moot, for her life. To Ellyn Surtys, the housse on the Moot that Dame Browne is in nowe tenand for hyr lyffe naturrall. To An Surtys, my daughter, the housse on the Moot that Genat Surtys dwells in, for her life. To Margere Surtys, my daughter, the housse on the Moot that John Golle dwells in, for hyr lyffe. To Rauffe Surtys, my yongast soone, the house on the Mootte that Beelle Wylleson dwelling in, to him and his ayears maylls. After the dysseasse of my daughters, I wyll that their housses shall come to Edward Surtys and his ayears maylls and his ayears, then to Tomas Surtys, then to Ouswolld Surtys, then to John Surtys, then to Jhams Surtys, then to Robert Surtys, then to Rauff Surtys. To Edward Surtys, my sonne, and his ayres maylls my hoouse that he dwell in nowe, in the Cloose, then to Tomas Surtys, etc. I wyll my wyff shallff a thryd, my ten chyldryn a thryd, and the othar thryd partt for my fyunerrrals and leggesses. To Rauff Surtys and Jhayne, hys wyffe, two angells nobels. To Maryan Surttys, my dowghter-in-lawe, one angell. The rest to my wife. Suprayvyssors, Master Herre Branlleng and John Hudsson.

INVENTORY OF CHRISTOPHER DALE.

An inventorie taken the 19 daye of Aprill in the yere of our Lord God 1570 of the goods and cattalls off Cristopher Dayll, lait disseasied, of the parisshe off Darlington in the countie of Durham,

[1] Andrew Surtees was apprenticed Oct. 18, 1529, to Robert Hely of Newcastle, merchant adventurer, and his name appears in the admission books belonging to the Company of Merchant Adventurers until Nov. 11, 1564. His will is signed with the wavering hand of an old and sick man.

inholder, prased by Cuthbert Storie, John Appelbie, Cristofor Dobson and Anthonie Ogell, with others.

In the Hall. Two silver peces weing 16 unces, at 4s. 4d. the ounce, 3l. 9s. 4d. 8 silver spoinnes, 32s. 12 pair of lyn sheits, 4 paire off harden sheits, 12 codwares, 40s. 2 cubbords, a long table, a counter, 2 formes, a longe-settell, 3 old chares, 16s. 6 puter platters, 3 latten bassons, a little puter basyng, 6 latton candellsticks and 10 old puter potts, 13s. 4d. An iron chymnaye, a pair of tongs, a por [sic] and a fyre shovell, 10s. *Summa, 9l. 8d.*

The Parlor above the Hall. One long table, one forme, one chare, one litle round table, a litle open cubard, 6s. 8d. Two stand-yng beddes, a trindell bed, furnished with bed and bolster, 40s. A litle iron chymnay, a bason and ane ewer, 2 putter candelsticks, 3 quysshons, 7s.

The Chamber over the Hall. Two standyng beddes, furnisshed with fether-bedd and bolster and other furniture therto belonging, two litle counters, one forme, 40s.

The Newe Chamber. 3 standing bedes furnished, one trindell bed furnished, a litle table, a carpet, 26s. 8d.

The Littell Chamber. 2 beddes, furnished for men servants, ane old chaire, a litle table, 10s.

The Loft benethe the doores. Two beddes furnyshed for women servants, 10s.

The Buttrie. One presse, 2 chists, one bord, a bread grate, 10s. 20 peces of puter, 10 sawcers, 12 puter plates, a litle brasen morter, 26s. 8d.

The Kychen. A capon cawell, 2 bords, 20d. Pott hookes, a pair of cob yrons, two dripping pannes, 3 speets, 6s. 8d. 2 cawdrons, 6 brasse potts, 4 pannes, 40s. 4 tobes, a brewing lead, a masfat, a troughe stone, a latin laver, 26s. 8d.

The Stable. Haie, one lode, 6s. 8d. 6 oxen, 2 kie, one horsse, 7l. Corne in the feild, 10l. One iron bound wayn, on long wayne, 4 yokes, 2 teames, one plowe and the plowe gere belongynge, 40s.

Summa bonorum, 40l. 19s. 4d.

Debts owyng to the said Cristopher Daill :—Cuthbert for a horsse, 26s. 8d. One Eland of Rippon, 46l. Cuthbert Nycholson, 14s.

Summa bonorum et debitorum quae debentur defuncto, 89l.

WILL OF RICHARD FARROW.

April 20, 1570. Richard Farroo, parson of Winston.[1] First and principallie I comytt my sowll unto Almightie God my Maker, Redemer and Saviour, my bodie to be buried wythin the chaunsell of Winstone aforesaid. I will and command that James Farroo. my brother's son, shall have in goods 24l. 8s., which I resaved for his

---

[1] Richard Farrowe was rector of Winston from 1559 to 1570.

barne partt by the deathe of his father. I will that the foresaid sum of 24*l.* 8*s.* shalbe taken furthe off my goods presentlye after my deathe ; and that Embrie Farroo, my brother, have the foresaid somme of 24*l.* 8*s.* till that James Farroo, my brother's son, shall com unto his lawfull ayge. I gyve and bequithe unto Jane Frend, my kynsswoman, a litle coffer. I gyve and bequiethe unto Jane Hyghley, my servaunt, a litle pott. I gyve and bequiethe unto William Atkanson, clerk, my best gowne. The resydew of my goods, quick and dead, not bequested, my debts and legaces paid and funerall expenses discharged, I gyve unto Embrie Farrow, my brother, and Jannett Farroo, my doughter, whom I maike my wholle executors to be jointlie togyther. I mayke and ordaine the supervisors of this my last will and testament, Mr. Ralffe Sighwicke and John Dowghtwhett : desyryng them, as my trust is in them, to se it performed in all points and things, and towards ther paines for a memorie I gyve unto Mr. Ralff Sighwicke the lesser of the Flanders chists and to John Doughtwhett the great Flanders chist. Witnesse hereoff, Mr. Ralff Sighwick, Jhon Doughtwhet, Peter Alwand, William Allandson, Henrie Robinson, Hewghe Rampshawe.

The Inventarie of all the goods moveable and unmoveable of Rychard Farroo, layt parson of Winston, praised May 25, 1570 : —

8 oxen, 11*l.* 6*s.* 8*d.* 6 kyne, 7*l.* One stirke, 6*s.* 8*d.* 10 clipt wethers, 32*s.* 45 wethers and a tupe, 8*l.* 13*s.* 4*d.* 11 yowes with ther lambes and 2 yowes without lambes, 44*s.* One horsse and a mare, 3*l.* 6*s.* 8*d.* 2 swyne and a bore, 24*s.* Geesse and hennes, 5*s.* *Summa,* 35*l.* 18*s.* 4*d.* Corne in the barne, 3*l.* 6*s.* 8*d.* Haye, 13*s.* 4*d.* Corne in the housse, that is, malt, wheat and rie, 40*s.* *Summa,* 5*l.* 13*s.* 4*d.* One long wain, with plow and plow gear, 20*s.* A cart, 10*s.* A systren, 13*s.* 4*d.* Lyme, 26*s.* 8*d.* *Summa,* 3*l.* 10*s.* The implements in the house. 2 caldrons, 14*s.* 10 pece of puder, 4*s.* 4*d.* 4 pots, 8*s.* A brasell morter and a pestell, 2*s.* 3 pannes, 1 drissing kniffe, 2*s.* 2 candelsticks, 6*d.* 2 reckyngcrooks, 16*d.* Tubbes, skeels and bowells, 4*s.* *Summa,* 36*s.* 2*d.* Implements in the hall. A counter, 2 tables, with two formes, 6*s.* 8*d.* All the bedding belonging to the housse with be[d]stocks, 47*s.* 4*d.* A cubbord with all in the buttrie, 33*s.* 4*d.* Flesshe, 6*s.* *Summa,* 4*l.* 13*s.* 4*d.*

Debts owing unto Rychard Farroo, parson off Winston, Anno Domini, 1570. Of Thomas Wilson of Barnard-castell, 11*s.* Rychard Edward, 11*s.* Robert Couler of Gainfurthe, 3*s.* John Bell of Conescliffe, 8*s.* Thomas Allanson, 8*s.* 8*d.* John Glynton of Barnard-castell, 12*s.* Mr. Thomas Menvell, 20*s.* John Frend, 4*s.* Robert Brumell, 2*s.* 9*d.* Thomas Horne, 19*d.* Edwarde Willie, 4*s.* Wedow Clayton, 3*s.* 6*d.* Thomas Dixson, 4*s.* 6*d.* Thomas Turner, 4*s.* A graie maire to Robert Doughwet, 20*s.* A bay maire to John Menvell, 26*s.* 8*d.* *Summa,* 7*l.* 17*s.* 11*d.* *Summa totalis,* 59*l.* 13*s.* All the corne of the earthe, wheat, rie and haver, 6*l.* 6*s.* 8*d.* All the dough, 6*s.* 8*d.* Two chists, 10*s.* *Summa,* 7*l.* 3*s.* 4*d.* *Summa totalis,* 66*l.* 4*s.* 5*d.*

INVENTORY OF RICHARD GREGGE.[1]

July 10, 1570. Rycherd Gregge, clark. 12 oxen and 4 stotts, 19*l.* 6 kie, 7*l.* 2 maires and two fooles, 3*l.* 13*s.* 4*d.* 2 staggs, 22*s.* The hole cropp in the feild belonging to Richard Gregg, the glebe as well as others, 23*l.* [Sum. 70*l.* 4*s.* 2*d.*]

Debts. To William Hardyng, vicare of Hart, 31*l.* 19*s.* 7*d.* For his lambe, wooll with other tends and reparacons, 40*s.* Paid to Mistres Lawson in borowed money of hyr, 20*s.* To Mr. Lawson for a closse farme, 20*s.* For drinke at certain tymes, 2*s.* To Richard Gregg, his son, 3*l.* 6*s.* 8*d.* To Sir Thomas Dawson, 26*s.* 8*d.* To Sir Thomas Bowes, 2*s.*

To him. William Atkinson of Barwick, 10*l.* Markendaill wiffe, Richard Porrett and Peter Gregge 4*l.* 10*s.*

INVENTORY OF ALEXANDER FEATHERSTON.

INVENTORY of Alexander Fetherston, lait of Wardell forest, deceased the 24th of Aug., 1570, praised by John Fetherston of the Hedrycloughe, Lionell Fetherston of Horsley, etc. : —

5 kien and 3 calves, 5*l.* One old cruked horsse, 13*s.* 4*d.* 5 whies, 3*l.* 6*s.* 8*d.* In housshold stuffe, 10*s.* 3 oxen, at 18*s.* a pece, 54*s.* 2 styrks, 10*s.* 3 yowes, 7*s.* George Leighe of Alstone-more owes him 6*s.* 8*d.*

He owes. To Hughe Whitfeld of Durham, 19*s.* To Rowland Nattresse of Wearshead, 13*s.* To Edward Sheill of Allandell, 4*s.* 3*d.* To Thomas Lighlye, 3*s.* 4*d.* To George Cotesforthe, 20*d.* To Peter Robinson of Allandell, 4*s.* To Nycholas Bowman, 8*d.* To George Hawdon, 8*d.* To Sir Mychael Horne, 12*d.* To George Hurde, 2*s.* To Margrett Yonger, 2*s.* To Jane Coltard, 20*d.* To Lionell Fetherstone, 20*s.* To Arthure Emerson, 3*s.* 4*d.*

WILL OF RICHARD JACKSON.

Sept. 27, 1570. Richard Jackson, husbandman in Denton, being off wholle mynd and perfect remebranc, praise be unto Almighti God, makethe and ordainethe this my present testament, conteining herein my last will, in maner and forme following, that is, first I commend my soull unto Almighti God, my Maker and Redemer, and my bodie to be buried in the churcheyard of Denton. I gyve and bequiethe unto my wiffe, Annesse Jackson, Robert Jackson, William Jackson and Thomas Jackson, my three sonnes, the lease of the Thornie closse whiche I bought of Mr. Girlington, but yf the foresaid Agnes doo marie, then wholie gyve it to my thre sonnes. I gyve unto Robert Jackson, my eldest son, the best ox at his judgment.

---

[1] Curate of Hart.

I gyve unto William Jackson, my son, one black stott, and also I gyve unto the said William, yff he will applie his books, fower yowes and fouer lambes. I gyve unto Thomas Jackson, my son, one colt fole. I gyve unto Janett Jackson, my doughter, one black calff. I gyve unto Eilinor Jackson, my yongest doughter, fyve nobles of money. The rest of all my goods and cattells I gyve and bequiethe wholie unto my wiffe, Annas Jackson, and to my sonnes and my doughters, which jointlie I maik myne executors, except onelie that I gyve unto my doughter, Annes Jackson, one branded cowe and 5s. in money. I gyve unto my doughter, Margarett Jackson, 5s. of money, and I gyve unto my doughter Janett 5s. of money which my mother dyd gyve and bequiethe unto them. In witnesse wherof Rychard Glover of Darneton, William Carter, Anthonye Garthe, Alexander Tued (?), Jeaking Thompson.

INVENTORY. Sum. 39l. 4s. 4d.

WILL OF JANET DALE.

Dec. 29, 1570. Jenet Daill of Archdeacon Newton, parish of Darlington, wedowe. To be buried in the parish church-yard of Darlington. I geve unto Anthony Dale, my sonne, the hole lease of my fermhold wherein I nowe dwell, and to have, occupy and enjoy the same during the terme of the yeres yet to come. I geve unto the said Anthony Dale 8 oxen and 2 stottes, with waines and waine-gear and ploughes and plough-gear and thinges belonging unto them. I geve unto the said Anthony Dale two of my best horses. Also I geve him a ledeall, my bruing vessell, a brasen mortar, a stone trough, a drawen table, the best chist that I have, a fether bedd and all thinges belonging unto it. I geve unto James Dale, his sonne, a fole, and to either of his daughters an ewe. I geve unto Margaret Dale a cawell, an ambry, the one half of all my houshold stuffe, a cowe, 3 shepe, a little cawdron and in mony 20d. I geve unto Alleson Stainsby the other half of all my houshold stuff, the best bed that I have but one, a pair of lynnen sheats, and a pair of harden, 2 blankets, 2 coverletts and my best gowne; also I give her a cowe and five shepe, and in mony 5 markes. I geve unto Christofor Stainsby five nobles that he doth owe me for a horse that I sold him. I geve unto his wife a cowe, and to every of his children an ewe. I geve unto Thomas Simpson's wife a cowe, a presser, the best chist that I have but one, and to Sissely, her daughter, a gret broad panne, and to every of her children besid, an ewe. I geve unto Margaret Dale a chist. I geve unto Agnes Dobson, my sister, a paire of sheats, a kerchif, a raill, one of my cotes and in mony 20d. I geve unto John Dobson 5s. in mony and to his wife two busshels of whete and to his yongest sonne an ewe. I geve unto Michaell Helcot one ox stirke of a yere old, to his brother and to every of his sisters an ewe. I geve unto Elizabeth Hackforth a kerchif, a raill, a smock,

an apron and all my workday rayment and in mony 3s. 4d. I geve
unto Jenet Dobson a kerchif of my best lyne. I geve to Edmund
Blackman's wife two busshels of malt. I geve to Richard Dobson
2 busshels of wheat, and to Robert Robson of Blackwell one busshell
of wheat. I geve to every of my godchildren, 4d. I geve to the
poure people of Darlington 20d., and to my curate for his paines, 2s.,
and to the clarke, 12d. All the residue of my goods, my debts
being payed and my funerall expenses discharged, I will that they
remaine unto the use of Anthony Dale my sonne, Agnes Stainsby,
Isabell Helcot and Margaret Simpson, whom I do make jointly and
severally executors of this my last will and testament, and also Mr.
Frankling overseer of the same, if plese him. These being wittness,
James Thornton, clerk, John Dobson, Marmaduke Farbarne, with
others.

WILL OF NICHOLAS BLYTHMAN.

Jan. 24, 1570/1. Will of Nycholas Blithman of the parish of All
Saints, Newcastle, bucher. Visited with the hand of Almightie God.
To be buried in my parish church nigh my father. To the poor of
the parish, 12d. My house I live in to John, my son. To Elizabeth
Blithman, my daughter, 10l. To Annes, my wife, 20 marks. To my
mother, for a token, an old angell. Supervisors, my cosing, William
Blithman, and my brother, John Blithman.[1]

WILL OF ROBERT BIRKENHEAD.

Feb. 11, 1570/1. Robert Birkehead of West-brandon.[2] I gyve to my
doughter Dorytye 20 marks for her child's porcon, and to my daughter

[1] 1566/7, Feb. 17. Edward Blythman, buried. *Gateshead Register. Cf.*
Welford, *Newcastle and Gateshead,* vol. ii. pp. 412, 444.
 Will of Edward Blythman. Feb. 14, 1566/7. Edward Blythman of
Gatisshed, butcher. To be buried in Gateshead churche. To the poore men's
box, 6s. 8d. For the repayringe of the churche, 6s. 8d. To Joane, my wife,
26l. To William, my son, my goods and 8 silver spones. To Edward Blythman, my son William's son, the third part of a division of a close called lower
Cole-close which I and my partners have . . . . of Thomas Gasqwen,
gent., and two of the foresaid spoones. To my sonne William, his two
daughters, Elizabeth and Jane, each two of the said spoones. George Blythman, my son William's bastard boy, the other two spoones. To my son in
law, George Martyne, and Jane, his wife, 4l. To each of Rauf Wealand's
six children, 8s.
 Inventory exhibited 26 Feb., 1566/7.

[2] Robert Birkehead of West Brandon married Isabella, daughter of Gerard
Salvin of Croxdale, and, as is recited in the will, enjoyed a beneficial lease of
Sherburn house from his wife's brother, Anthony Salvin, master of University
College, Oxon., who held the mastership of Sherburn Hospital with other
ecclesiastical preferments in the diocese of Durham.

Margarett, other 20 marks, in the custody of their mother and ther uncle, Jarrard Salving, and ther brother Lampton till they be readye to be maryed. To my wife, the leases of my farmehold at West Brandon to bring upp my children, and if she die before they come of age, I will that my son Jerrard shall have them. To my wife, my lease of Sherborne-house which my brother-in-lawe, Sir Anthonye Salvine, dyd gyve unto my wyfe and me. To my wife and yongest sonnes, George, William, Anthonye and John, together with Jarrard, my sonne, my lease of Thrislington for my yeares. To my doughter, Katheron Lampton,[1] a nute gilt with 11 peaces of golde of fyve shilling a peace, and to every one of hir children, 3s. 4d. To James Barbone and Thomas Wilfoot, 3s. 4d. each. To Anne Claxton, 6s. 8d. To Isabell Farrowe and Margerye Bracke, either of them, a gymer hogg. To Dorytie Corker and Janett Bracke, ayther of them, 12d. To Thomas Wilfoote wyfe and hir doughter, 12d. a peace. To Edward Patterson, 12d. To my sonne Jerrard, a yong graye colt. To George, my son, a yonge dune meare. To my brother-in-lawe, Jerred Salvinge of Croxdyall, esquire, 5l., for the which he haithe in paune 8 old ryalls of 15s. a peace which my mynd ys to have againe, paing unto him the said 5l.

Debts owing to me: 10l. lent to Mr. Anthonye Salvaine, clarke, which was payd to Mr. Readman of London for a part of payment of his annuitye out of Sherborne-house. Uswyne Ogle of Branspethe, gent., for a gray horse, 4l. Uswyne Ogle of Branspethe, gent., for otts which ys ordered by the curte, 32s. 6d. Anne Claxton, 56s., and a angell. Thomas Blacket, 20s. George Simson for a cowe, 23s. 4d. Supervisors, my brother, Jarrard Salvaine of Croxdayle, esquier, and my sonne-in-lawe, Thomas Lampton of Malton, gent., gyving to ayther of them a ryell for a token. Wittnesses hereof, William Claxton, Robert Conyers and Rawfe Emerson.

WILL OF BERTRAM ANDERSON.[2]

March 8, 1570/1. Bertram Anderson of Newcastell upon Tyne, alderman and merchaunte. To be buried within the churche of St. Nicholas in Newcastell aforesaide as nighe unto my wyffe as convenyentlye maye be. I bequithe to my dowghter, Barbary Anderson, for her full child's porcion of my goods, 400 markes, and hallfe hir mother's rayment, with the one halfe of hir beltes and bedes, and theis to be geven hir at the day of hir maryage or elles

---

[1] Thomas Lambton of 'Malton in Rydal,' third son of John Lambton of Lambton, married Catherine, daughter of the testator. Flower's *Visitation of Durham*, 1575.

[2] A biography of Bertram Anderson, some time mayor of Newcastle, may be found in Mr. Richard Welford's *Men of Mark 'twixt Tyne and Tweed*, vol. i. p. 47. The inventory of his goods is printed in *Wills and Inventories*, vol. i. p. 335.

when she, the same Barbarye Anderson, shall come unto the full age of eightene yeares, at suche reasonable tymes and dayes as shall be thought mete by the supervisers of this my testament and laste will.   And I will by theis presents that she, the same Barbarye, be in the custodie of my aunt, Maistres Barbray Thomlingson.   I gyve to my dowghter, Alyson Anderson, for hir full childe's porcyon of my goodes, 400 markes [*ut supra in omnibus*].   And I will that she, the said Allyson Anderson, be in the custody, care and government of my father-in-lawe, Mr. John Franckleyne, and my mother, his wife   I gyve to my sone, Bertram Anderson, for his full childe's porcion of my goodes, 400 markes.   I gyve unto my sone, Bartram Anderson aforesaid, his heirs, etc., my great howse and messuage, with the appurtenances in the strete called the Close in the said towne of Newcastell upon Tyne, sometyme in the tenure and occupacon of George Davell, alderman of Newcastle aforesaid, deceased, which howse with the appurtanances I bowght and purchased of Anthonye Bird.   I bequithe to my said sone, Bertram Anderson, all my howses with the appurtenances whatsoever in the towne and feildes of Morpethe in the countye of Northumberland.   I give unto my said sone, Bartrame Anderson, all my howses with the appurtenances, as well in the borowgh of Gateshed, as in the citye of Durham, and also my close lyeinge in the tarritorye feilds of Gateshed.   I will that all the mesne profetts arysinge yerelye of the said landes and tenements before bequithed to my said sonne, Bartram Anderson, shal be, remayne and come unto the use of my eldest' sone, Harye Anderson, unto such tyme the same my sonne, Bartram Anderson, shall fullye have accomplished the age of one and twentye years, for the intent and purpose that he, the saide Henrye Anderson, durynge all the saide tyme shall sufficientlye fynde unto the said Bartrame Anderson, my sonne, meat, drinke, clothynge and convenyent lernynge at scoolles. And further I will, by theis presents, that if it forton any of my said thre children, Barbraye Anderson, Allyson Anderson and Bertram Anderson, to depart from this lyfe before the accomplyshment of the yeres before lymyted, that the childe's porcion of my goodes, before to that child (so called to the mercye of God) bequested, shal be equallye divided to the other two then lyvinge and even so from one of them thre to the longest lyver of them.   And I will that if it shall happen my said sone, Bartram Anderson, to be called to the marcye of God before the accomplyshment of the aige of one and twenty yeares, that then the landes and tenementes with the appurtenances, before to hym bequested, shall remayne and come unto my right heires. I give to my dowghter, Eesabell Calverlaye, for a token, and also in full satisfaction of hir childe's porcion of my goodes, 100 markes ; over and besides that I do owe unto hir husband for lent monye and for my tythes of Haswell and Haswell Grandge, amountynge together to the some of 25*l.* 6*s.* 8*d.*   I gyve by theis presentes unto Barbraye Calverlaye, dowghter unto my said dowghter, Eesabell Calverlaye, to be paid when she, the said Barbraye, shall accomplyshe

th' aidge of fourteene yeares, for a token, the some of 20*l.* ; and to
John Calverlaye, sonne of my foresaid dowghter, Eesabell Calverlaye,
the some of 10*l.* to by him bookes when the said John shall
accomplysh th age of fivetene yeres. I gyve to my said mother-in-
lawe, Mrs. Isabell Francklyne, for a token of my assured good-will
toward hir, one goulde ringe and my best tablett of goulde. I gyve
my lovinge aunt, Mrs. Barbraye Thomlingson, for a token,
one gould ringe and wilst she, the same Mrs. Barbraye Thomlingson levethe, I will that she have so many coles to be taken
from my staythes in Darwen and Stubble Wood as she shall burne
for hir own fyer or fyers within hir owne house. I gyve to my
brother, Clement Anderson, all those numbers (?) of colles whatsoever
which Anthonye Thomlingson, presentlye baliffe of Gatished aforesaid, father-in-lawe of the said Clement, doth owe unto me. To my
brother, Harye Anderson, for a token, one angell-noble. To my sister,
Jane Metford, for a token, a dubble duckitt in goulde. I gyve unto
my sister Maryon Chapman, widowe, for a token, thre tennes of
colles to be taken of my stayth of Silverwood in Northumberland to
be taken within thre yeres, that is to saye, everye yere a tenne of
colles. To Humfrey Taylor, for a token, 13*s.* 4*d.* ; and to everye
brother of my layte wife, Allis Anderson, for a token, 10*s.* ; and to
Christopher Morpethe, for a token, 10*s.* ; and to my sister-in-lawe,
Elizabethe Anderson, layte wife to my brother, Frauncis Anderson,
deceased, 10*s.* ; and to Agnes Orde, my maydene, the some of 3*l.* ;
and to Jennet Heryson, late wife to Androwe Heryson, 20*s.* ; and to
Allis Heryson, hir doughter, 10*s.* I gyve unto Maryon Fenwick,
my sister's dowghter, over and beside suche portion as is given unto
hir, as well by hir owne father as allso by my father, so that she
wilbe ruled by my said sone, Harye Anderson, with whome I will
she, the same Maryon Fenwick, shall remayne, 5*l.*, and he, the same
my sonne Harye, to finde hir, the sayde Maryon Fenwick, con-
venyente meate, drinke, and clothes and other necessaryes, without
rebateinge any thinge of hir porcion therfore duringe all such tyme
as she and her porcyon doth remayne with him, the said Harye.
I give to my said father-in-lawe, Mr. John Francklyn, for a token,
my best gowne and 3*l.* 6*s.* 8*d.*, and to my brother-in-law, William
Jenyson, for a token, my gowne nexte the beste and the some of
6*l.* 13*s.* 4*d.* To my servaunt, Sir (*sic*) Thomas Keye, for a token, 10*s.* ;
and to my servante, Harrye Ayton, for a token, 10*s.* ; and to John
Robinson, my servante, for a token, 10*s.* ; and to Marke Birde, my
servante, for a token, 10*s.* ; and to Sanders Stote, my servante, for
a token, 10*s.* ; and to my servante, Thomas Richardson, 10*s.* And
also I forgive unto my servante, Cristofer Baxter, the remaynder of
the Frenche reckonynge for the which my ship, called the 'John,' was
stayed for at the towne of Newhaven in Fraunce ; and to my cossynge,
Harye Wyckylffe, for a token, 10*s.* I wyll that there be geven to
the poore people of the towne of Hambrowgh eighte tennes of my
colles, to be taken on my stathes on the northe side of the river of

Tyne, and they to paye bothe for the fitchinge of them from the staythes and custome with all other charges. I gyve unto my servaunte, Thomas Cleborne, (over and above a lease I will to be maid by my heire, unto hym, the said Thomas Clebborne, for the terme of 21 yeares of my farmhold in Seaton in the county of Durham,) for a token, 6*l.* 13*s.* 4*d.* And all the residewe of my goodes and chattells, moveable and immoveable whatsoever, I gyve to my said sonne, Harye Anderson, whom I ordeyne and make my soole and full executor, and he to be advised and to followe the good advise and councell of the supervisours of this my will, and especiallye, of my blessynge, by the advice of said father-in-lawe, Mr. John Francklyn, and of my said brother, Mr. William Jenyson, who do knowe most of my doynge and trades. I make my sonne-in-lawe, Mr. Thomas Calverlaye, and my brother-in-law, Mr. Christofer Metfordd, one of the aldermen of Newcastell, and my father-in-law, Mr. John Francklyn, and Mr. Christofer Morland of Pettington in the countye of Durham, gent., and my brother-in-lawe, Mr. William Jenyson, supervisours, and I gyve unto my said sonne, Mr. Calverlaye, for a token, one angell-noble; to my said brother, Mr. Christofer Mitford, one angell-noble; and to the said Mr. Christofer Morland, for a token, one angell-noble. Witnesses, Mr. Christofer Metford, Mr. John Francklyn, Mr. William Carr, Mr. William Jenyson, Harye Metford, Benet Chertesye, Robert Metforde, James Care, William Browne, John Stowte. [Pr. 12 June, 1571.]

WILL OF SIMON ELRINGTON.

Aug. 29., 1571. Symonde Elrington [1] of Hespershealls, parish of Bywell Peter. To Robert Boothe,[2] two olde angells. To my cossing, Thomas Boothe, two olde angells. To my cossing, Richard Booth, the same. To John Swyneborne of Wylome, and to his wyfe, two olde angells. To William Bayley, an olde angell. To Anthonye Hall of Durham, and to his wyffe, two olde angells. To Edwarde Hall, an olde angell. To Thomas Hall, an old angell. To John Wattson's wife, an olde angell. To Maistres Boothe, sex old angells, which she haithe in hir custodie, with the reste of all the angells the which I have gyven here before. To Mr. Davie Carnabie two old angells. To Mr. Anthonye Carnabie, one Franche crowne. To John Wattson within Newcastle, two old angells. To his wife, one old angell. To the said John Wattson, one golde ringe. To John Wattson, the foresaid John's father, one golde ringe. To the foresaid old John Wattson, all the reste of the olde angells that is

[1] Some account of the family of Elrington of Espershields may be found in the new *History of Northumberland*, vol. vi. pp. 209-211.

[2] Robert Booth of Old Durham entered his pedigree at Flower's *Visitation of Durham* in 1575.

in my chiste at Olde Durham. To all my servants and hyndes, one quarters wages, over ther wages due, and two yowes each. To my servant, Thomas Robinson, one yonge whye. To his wife, two yowes. To my servant, Symond Browne, a yonge whye. To Richard Teasdalill of Colpotts, all the debts, etc., he oweth me. To Henry Teasdalill, his son, my beste horse or meare and all the riding geare and all the rament that I did ride withall, that is to saye, dublett, hoose, jackett, and jerkine, one hatt, with one brooche sworde and dagger. To Symond Teisdaill, my yonge maire. To Jennet Teisdaill, thre kyne and 3 calves. . . . . To Alise Teasdaill, two yowes. To my syster Elizabeth, thre kine . . . . and 20 yowes. To Alice Browne, wedow, two yowes. To Dorithy, her doughter, 2 yowes. To John Smyth, my mylner, 2 yowes. To John Maughan's wife, 2 yowes. To Richard Whitfeilde, 6s. 8d. To William Carre of Colpotts, 2 yowes. I will that Lancelott Carre, my servant, shall have 21 yeres of his father's fermehold which is my land in Unthanke, after my deathe. To my syster, John Smyth's wife, a kowe. To my sister, Thomas Redeshawe's wife, one kowe. I will that Edward Hall of Durham shall pay to Richard Teasdaill of Colpotts 26s. 8d. he oweth me for one horse. To Thomas Benson, clarke, parson of Edmondbiers, 6s. 8d. for his panes. To Anthony, Edward and Thomas Hall, my woole. To Richard Coltman of Consyde, 20 sheep. To Christofor Hall, 20s. To Christofor Fenny, two Franche crownes. To Edward Hall's wife, 5s. To Richard White, 5s. The rest to my uncle, Roger Boothe, and my cossing, John Wattson of Durham, whom I make my executors. Supervisors, Mr. Anthony Ratlyffe and Mr. Cuthbert Ratliffe, his sonne, to aither of them, one angell. Witnesses, Maister Anthonye Ratliffe, Mr. Cuthbert Ratliffe, Mr. Anthonye Carnabie, Richard Whitfeild and Thomas Benson, clarke, parson of Edmondbiers.

WILL OF ROLAND BLENKINSOPP.

Sept. 30, 1571. Roland Blenkynshop, preiste, one of the petti-canons of the cathedrall churche off Durham. I bequithe my sowlle to Almightie God, Father, Sonne and the Hollie Gooste, and Jesus Christe, by whoise meritts I trust to be the childe of Salvacion. My bodie to be buried at the Nyne Alters besyde Sir John Byndley. I gyve and bequithe unto the poore people the daye of my buriall, 6s. 8d. I gyve untó every one of my fellowes the petticanons, 12d. I gyve unto every one of the singing men, 8d. I gyve unto every one of the queresters, 4d. I gyve and bequithe unto the two virgers, to aither of theym, 8d. I gyve and bequithe to the two bell ringers, to aither of them, 8d. I gyve and bequithe unto my brother, Sir William Blenkinsop, two olde ryalls. I gyve unto my singuler good frynde, Mr. Christofer Chayter, one olde angell. I gyve unto my hoostes Baker one old angle. I gyve and bequithe unto my syster Katheryn, and Esabell, hir doughter, 4*l.*, that is, to aither of theyme, 40*s.* I gyve unto my syster Kateryn my syde gowne furred with whyte lambe and faced blacke lambe. I gyve unto Essabell, hir doughter, one shorte gowne furred with blacke lambe. I gyve and bequithe unto Anthon Tayler, my nephew, 40*s.* I gyve unto my saide nephew,' Anthon Tayler, one sleveles jackett. I gyve unto Agnes Neile, 5*s.* The resydew of all my goodes moveable and unmoveable, nott bequithed, my debts paid, legacies fulfilled, and my funerall expenses deduct, I gyve and bequithe unto my brother, Christofor Millit, and to my syster, Alice Millit, his wyffe, whome I maike, name and ordaine myne executors of this my present will and testament, desyreing my welbeloved brother, Sir William Blynkinshopp, to be supervisor of this my laste will and testament. And I will that this my present testament, with all things herein written, shall stande and abide for my very laste will and testament, ande none other nor other wise. In witness whereof, I, Rolande Blenkinshop, to this my testament haithe subscribed. Wittnessis, William Blenkinshop, William Wattson. [Pr. Oct. 13, 1571.]

WILL OF CHRISTOPHER MOISER.

Nov. 23, 1571. Christopher Moiser[1] of Newcastle on Tyne, glover. To be buried in St. Nicholas church besyde my wyfe Elizabeth. To my neighbours, poore honest householders, 20*s.* I gyve to my syster, or servaunte, Florance Moyser, 20*l.*, with all my househowld stuffe—playte, and jewells onely excepted—and my lease of the halfe teythes of Killingworth which I have of Mr. John Wilkinson and Cuthbert Carr, esquier ; remainder to my sone, Cuthberte. To my brother George 5*l.*, my best russite gowne, a chamlete jackete ; and 6*s.* 8*d.* To my brother, Lawrence Moyser, 6*s.* 8*d.*, my beste gowne and broide clothe jacket. To my brothers Lawrance and George's wyffs 5*s.* 8*d.* To Elisabeth Moyser, doughter to my said brother Lawrence, 3*l.* 5*s.* 8*d.* To Thomas Sawer, 5*s.* 8*d.* To Thomas Hall, 5*s.* 8*d.* and to Anthonye Hall, 12*d.* To Thomas Morpeth all the moneye he owes me for two bucks skynnes for furre to his weddinge gloves. To Mrs. Hallyman, 10*s.* To Christopher Morpeth, 10*l.* To Margaret Grene, one Frenche crowne. To Richard Reid, 10*s.* To Martyn Hallyman, one Frenche crowne. To Robert, son to George Carr, sadler, 3*l.* 5*s.* 8*d.* To Christopher Morpeth, my lease which I have of Cuthbert Carr. To Rebecca Carr, my wyffe's wedding gowne lyned with chamlete, cramseye coler. I give the residue to my sone,

---

[1] The testator, Christopher Moiser of Newcastle, glover, was fifty years of age when, Oct. 26, 1568, he was witness in a cause at Durham respecting the will of Thomas Wilkinson, with whom he had served his apprenticeship. *Cf.* Welford, *Newcastle and Gateshead*, vol. ii. p. 423.

Cuthbert Moyser, and appoint him sole executor. I will that Christopher Morpeth and my sister Flowrance shall have the tuition of my sonne Cuthbert duringe his nonage ; and in case of the death of my said sone the whole of my estate to come to my sister Flowrance and my bretherne Lawrance and George. Supervisors: Robert Hallyman and Humphreye Tayllor. Mr. Cuthbert Musgrave oweth me 5s. Witnesses : Humphray Tayllor, Valentyne Baker, John Ladecastell, Henry Tayllor and William Tayllor. [Pr. 1572.]

WILL OF CUTHBERT GALLOWAY.

Jan. 13, 1571/2. Cuthbert Galloway, clerke, of Northe Warmothe. To be buried within the churche of Northe Warmeothe aforesaid. I bequithe to Issabell Hadrike 4 yeards of whyte wollen clothe. I bequithe to Allice Whetley 4 yeards of white wollen clothe. To Jennet Hebburne, 4 yeards of meld russett. I bequithe to Annes Thomson and to Annes Tayler and to aither of them, 3s. in money. I bequithe to William Hutchenson and to his wiffe the occupacion of all my goods for there liffe naturall to the use of there children. I bequithe to Janet Hutchenson, the yonger, 2 yowes and 2 lambes. To Agnes Pyg, one yowe and one lambe. I bequithe to the said William Hutchenson 32 shepe to his owne use. The reste of all my goods not bequethied nor geven, my debts and legasies faithfullie content and paid, I bequithe to Richerd Hutchenson, John Hutchenson, William Hutchenson and Janet Hutchenson, whome I maike my full executors, they to dispoise to the pleasure of God and the healthe of my sowle. Witnesses, Edmonde Stapleton, curet, Thomas Atkinson, Robert Newton, Rauffe Pyg, with others moo. [Pr. May 19, 1572.]

WILL OF ROLAND CLARK.

Feb. 14, 1571/2. Roland Clarke, parsone of Dinsdaile.[1] Being of perfect remembrance, thanks be unto God, yett fearinge the houer of deathe and trusting to be saved by the merits of Christe, I maike and ordayne my will ande testament as folowithe. Firste, I freelye committ and gyve my sowle unto Almightie God ande to his onlye sonne Jesus Christe my Saviour and Redeamer and my bodie to be buried wher yt shall please Almightie God to call me unto his mercye. I gyve unto the poore man's box of Dinsdaill, 2s. I gyve unto my syster, Jannett Robinson of Byers-greyne, one crowne of golde for a token. I gyve unto my syster, Jane Prierman of Heighington, one crowne of goulde for a token. I gyve unto my syster, Margerye Welfoott of Redworthe, one crowne of golde for a token. I gyve unto Roger Clarke, my brother sonne, 20s. I gyve unto Edward

---

[1] Roland Clark was rector of Dinsdale from 1561 to 1571.

Robinson, my suster sonne, 10s. I gyve unto Edward Welfoot, 10s. I gyve to Nycholas Welfoott, 10s. I gyve unto Rauffe Welfoott, 10s. I gyve unto Percyvell Welfoot, 10s., and all my rament belonging unto me, so that he learne and applye his books, or ells to have nothing, but to retourne unto myne executors. I gyve unto Richerd Johnson of Mydleton one crowne of goulde, and to his wyffe, a crowne of goulde in remembrance. I gyve unto Jeane Prierman, my suster doughter, 20s. I gyve to Essabell Prierman, 20s. I gyve to Sisseley Prierman, 20s. I gyve unto Margery Robinson, 20s. I gyve unto Essabell Welfoott, 20s. The resydewe of all my goodes, moveable ande unmoveable, my debts, legacies and funeralls paid and discharged, I gyve and bequithe unto Thomas Robinson, my suster sonne of Byers-greyne, and Jeanne Prierman, my suster, of Heighington, whome I maike bothe joyntlie togyther executors, ande thus to committ my sowlle to Almightie God, both nowe and ever more. Amen. The daye and yere above written. I gyve to my suster doughter, Sisselly Prierman, two coverletts, thre puther dishes, twoo harden sheytts, two blancketts, with an amerye, and I requeste my speciall frinde, Mr. Robert Place, to be supervisor of this my last will and testament. [Pr. Oct. 20, 1571.]

WILL OF JOHN SIMPSON.

April 7, 1572. John Simpson of Houghton in the parishe of Denton. I gyve my sowle to Almightie God my Saviour and Redeamer, by whose meritts and passion I triste to be saved, and to all the celestiall companye of heaven, my bodye to be buried in churche, or churche-yearde of Denton, what tyme yt shall please God to call me unto his mercye. I gyve to Roger Sympson my sonne one browne kowe. I gyve to John Sympson one cowe. I gyve to Roland Sympson one spangit whye. Also I gyve to Annes Sympson, my doughter, sex gymmer hoggs and two ewes, and two lambes. I gyve to Elsabith Sympson two why calfes, that is, yere-olds, and eight gymmer hoggs. I gyve to Roger Sympson, my sonne, plewghe-geare and wayne-geare after my wiffes deathe. I gyve to John Sympson, my sonne, one baye foole. I gyve to Rolande, my sonne, thre ewes ande thre lambes. I gyve to my brother, George Sympson, 2 gymmer hoggs and to his wiffe one gymmer and to every one of his children, one gymmer lambe. I gyve to Roger Sympson that maried my sister, one gymmer hogg. I gyve to Margaret Sympson one gymmer. I gyve to Henrie Sympson and his brother John two gymmer lambes. I gyve to Thomas Wylle, 4 ewes with there wooll. I gyve to Christofher Cockfeilde and John, his brother, two lambes. I gyve to Thomas Wyllies sex children, sex lambes. I gyve to my two doughters, Annes and Elizabeth marages, twentie marks a peice I gyve to the churche warks 16d. I gyve to William Thomson, clerke, 12d. I gyve to Roger Sympson my closes at Redworth.

I gyve to John Sympson my houses in Awckland. I gyve to Roland Sympson my house in Yearme. The resydew of my goods, my debts and funeralls discharged, I gyve to my wiffe, Janet Sympson, Roger Sympson and John Sympson, whome I maike my full executors joyntlie togyther, they to dispoise yt to the honor of Almightie God and the healthe of my sowle. Wittnesses, William Preston, Roger Shawter, Roger Sympson, William Megger, William Thomson, curat, with others. [Pr. July 19, 1572.]

WILL OF GAWEN HOPPEN.

April 11, 1572. Gawayne Hoppen of Hoppen in the parish of Bambrough.[1] To be buryed in my parych church of Bambrough, I give to my syster, Elynor Hoppen, all my manor of Hoppen and also the tower of Hoppine for hir life, and after her decease I geve and devise the same to Henrye Hoppen, son of Thomas Hoppen of Newcastle, merchant, and his heirs. I give the residue of my estate to my syster, Elynor Hoppen, and appoint her sole executrix. Mr. Thomas Forster of Edderstone the elder, Thomas Forster the younger, and Henry Swinno of Mossen, supervisors. [Pr. 1572.]

[1] An account of the township of Hoppen may be found in the new *History of Northumberland*, vol. i. pp. 243-248. The history of the old owners, who took their name from the place, is supplemented by Sir David Smith, purporting to quote the *Feodary's Book*, who states that Cuthbert Hoppen of Hoppen, vicar of Warkworth (1538-1571), had a bastard son, Thomas Hoppen of Newcastle, merchant, who was the father of Henry Hoppen, to whom his grandfather (Cuthbert) and Robert, his grand uncle, conveyed the estate of Hoppen. That Henry Hoppen committed a murder upon Henry Ord and fled, whereupon Gawen Hoppen, his grand uncle (the testator), entered, but died without issue, whereupon Eleanor Hoppen, the great aunt, entered, and at her death was succeeded by the two daughters and coheiresses of her aunt, wife of . . . Bradford of Bradford. These two sisters sold Hoppen to Thomas Bradford, baron of Bradford, who *circa* . . . conveyed it to (Edward) Conyers, who had married his daughter. (The nuncupative will of Edward Conyers is printed in *Arch. Ael.* 2nd series, vol. ii. p. 197.) There was a fine levied at Michaelmas term, 15 Eliz. (1573), by George Clerkson, gent., and Robert Lamb, plaintiffs, and Elienora Hoppen, *alias* Hoppon, deforciant. Warrant against the said Elianor and her heirs for ever, to hold to the said Elianor for her life, and after her decease to remain wholly to Thomas Hoppen, *alias* Hoppon, and his heirs for ever. *Feet of Fines* (Northumberland). In spite of this attempt to settle the estate, it is known that it did ultimately pass into the hands of Edward Conyers.

The following is the will of a member of the family who had settled at Newcastle :—

March 21, 1557. Roger Hoppine (of Newcastle). To be buried within Alhallowes church. I give my house to my wyfe for hir lyfe, and after hir decease to come to my son Robert Hoppyne; and furder I geve my said sonne Robert Hoppine to Robert Hoppine and my daughter Annes to his wyfe ; and my daughter Margaret Hoppine I do geve to Margaret Pereth ; and furder I geve my daughter Isabell Hoppine to Ellinor Hoppine, sister unto the said Robert Hoppine of Hoppine ; and furder I geve my wyfe my son Richard Hoppine. I am owinge to George Swineborne 20s. ; to Missress Selbye 53s. 4d., whereof hir promyse was to me to geve me 40s. for my goynge to Bladen for helpinge to make hir a shipe, whereupon remainethe to hir 13s. 4d. I appoint my wife executrix. [Pr. 1559.]

WILL OF JOHN MARSHALL.

Feb. 21, 1572/3. John Marshell of the parishing of Chester. To be buried in the churche at Chester with oblacions there due and accustomed. In legasies, I bequithe to Frances Marshall, my doughter, all cattells which came of a kowe geven hir of Richerd Scott. I gyve to Marie Watter 3*l.* 6*s.* 8*d.*, to be paid when the said Marie comes to full yeares or to hir mariadge. I gyve to Raufe Swalwell one scott [*sic*] of thre yeares olde. I gyve to George Franche one oxe stirke of a yere old. I gyve to Francis Franche one whye stirke of a yere old. I gyve to the churche of Chester, to remayne, one Bible conteyning the Old Testament, in parchement texed. I gyve to Martyne Halliman one Bible prented in paper. I gyve to Richerd Vacye one New Testament in Englishe, and one arball.[1] I gyve to the poore people one boll of harde corne. I gyve to Robert Halliman one booke named the Golden Flese in Englishe. Also I gyve to the said Robert Halliman my knage stafe. I gyve to Agnes Marshall, my wife, my lease during hir wedoheid in the demaynes, and after to Frances Marshall my doughter, during my yeres. The residewe of my goodes, moveable and unmoveable, my debts paid, with the funerall expenses, I gyve to Agnes Marshall, my wife, whome I maike my executrix. Wittnes hereof, Leonard Sanders, Thomas Whelpden, with others. [Pr. June 6, 1573.]

WILL OF EDMUND PARKINSON.

April 6, 1573. Edmunde Parkingson.[2] I will 12 freis gownes to 12 pore men to attende me to my grave. Also whearas I receaved of Symond Welberye for agremente for the deathe of James Hyrdson, 150*l.*, wherof I paid to my syster Dorathe, lait wyffe of James Hyrdson, 50*l.*, I will that other 60*l.* be devided among his children, and as for the other 40*l.* I dyd spend in costs and chardgs abowt the sewet against the parties that mordered the said Hirdson. To my brother, John Parkinson, one meare and two kye, and two kye and two stotts or 4*l.*, and 40*l.* towards the purchissinge of his fermehold which he now dwellith upon. To my nevy, Edmund Parkingson, son to John Parkingson, my brother, one horse, with a cote, a cloke, one hat, one paire of hoese, one sword and one buckler. To my brother, James Parkingson, my best horse and one ring of gould called a signed and two ould angells. To my systers, Dorathe and

---

[1] *i.e.*, a herbal.

[2] Edmund Parkinson of Newcastle, in 1565, purchased the manor of Hulam, co. Durham, of George Claxton. His widow Alice remarried James Carr, and of the two daughters who were their father's coheiresses, Barbara became wife of Henry Mitford of Newcastle and Jane the wife of Ralph Lawson of Nesham, co. Durham. *Cf.* Welford, *Newcastle and Gateshead,* vol. ii. p. 458.

Anne, eather of them, a mylke cowe and 12 yowes and one murninge gowne. To my nevye, Edmunde Ellener, sonne to my syster Dorthe, one cowe and 4 shipe. To everye child of my bretheringe and systers, 10*d*. To my daughter, Jane Parkynson, beside her porcon, 80*l*., to the custodye of Mr. William Lawson of Thrope Boulmer for her use. To Barberye, my daughter, 80*l*. Provyded alwaies that such moneye as is paide, or shalbe paide, by the said Edmunde Parkingson or any for hym, to Raufe Lawson for his exebicion at the Innes of the Curte, shalbe allowed of the said 80*l*. To Alys, my wyffe, one dosen sylver sponnes of the best. To my brother, Oswold Mydfurthe, in lawe, and hys wyffe, 20*s*. To my brother-in-lawe Robert Wilson, and his wyfe, my syster, 20*s*. To my brother Byddycke and my syster Annes, hys wyfe, 20*s*. To my brother-in-lawe Thomas Greine, and his wyffe, 20*s*. and one mylke-cowe. To every poure househoulder dwelling in a streat called the Close, 12*d*. and to every poure house-houlder dwellinge in the parishe of Hessledone, 12*d*. To Anthonye Mydfourthe, my servant, hys hoille yeare's waidges, being 20*s*. 8*d*. To Richard Collingson, my servant, 26*s*. 8*d*. To Margerye, my servant, 3*s*. 4*d*. To Thomas Turner, 6*s*. 8*d*. Executors, my daughters Barbarye and Jane. Supervisors, Mr. Christofor Mydfurthe of Newcastell, alderman, and Mr. William Lawson of Thropp Bolmer. To each of them an old angell. Witnesses, John Parkinson, Robert Ellyner, Rychard Collyson.

WILL OF NICHOLAS CLARK.

In ye name of God, Amen. I, Nicholas Clarke, servant to the right worshipfull Sir John Foster, knt., and warden of Middle Marches, etc., doithe make this my last will and testament the 26th of June in the 15th yeare of the reigne of our soverigne laydye Elizabeth, quene, etc., [1573], in manner and forme following, that is to saye, I bequeath and fraielye geve my title and claime of the one halfe of the tythe woull and lambe of Emelton parish, as it is expressed in my lease, unto Gerard Wetherington and Thomas Sakeilde. Before these witnesses, Edmunde Thewe, Edwarde Woodson and Jane Dawson, with others.

WILL OF WILLIAM CARTER.

Aug. 17, 1573. William Cartar of Denton, within the countie pallentyne of Durham, husbandman. To be buried in the churche or churche-yearde of Denton, withe my mortuarye dewe and by the lawe accustomed, what tyme yt shall please God to caull me to his marcye. I geve to Elizabeth Howington, the yonger, 40*s*. I geve to my sonne, Peter Carter two sonnes, two gimmer lambes. I geve to William Whitfeilde fowre childer 4 gymmer lambes. I geve to Elisabeth Howington the elder, one bowle of wheate. I geve to my godsonne, William Thompsone, one gymmer lambe. I geve to the poore-menes boxe, 12*d*. I will that John Carter and Marmaducke Carter, my two sonnes, perfourme all covenants and orders agreed upon my parte to John Bucke and William Wormeley as touchinge the mariadge of my doughter Margerye. And they also to do the licke on there partie to Myles Bucke, as my trist is in them. The rest and resydew of all my goodes, moveable and unmoveable, my debts and legacies paid, and my funeralls dischardged, I geve to my two sonnes, John Carter and Marmaduke Carter, whome I maike my full executors joyntlie together of this my present last will and testament, they to dispoise yt to the honor of Almightie God and the healthe of my sowle. And I desyer theis gentlemen, Mr. John Witham and Mr. George Tounge, and my brothere, Sir Peter Carter, as my speciall trustie freindes, whome I maike the supervisors of this my will, to se yt fullie perfourmed, as my truste is in them. And thus I committ me freelye into the handes of Almightie God, my Maiker and Redeamer, trustinge to be saved by the merites of Jesu Christ, my onelye Savyor and Redeamer. Theis wittnesses, Alexander Tuerde, Anthonye Garthe, William Pigge, William Thompson, curat, with others. [Pr. May 22, 1574.]

WILL OF MARTIN BRACKENBURY.

Feb. 20, 1573/4. Martyne Brakenberie of Killerbie, in the parishe of Heighinton, within the countie of Durham, gent. First and principallie, I geve and moste frelie bequeathe my soull to the Holie Trinitie, and to all the blessed companye of heaven, and my bodie to be buried in the churche or churche-yearde of Gainfourthe,[1] with my mortuarie dewe and by the lawe accustomed, what tyme it shall please Almightie God to call me unto his mercie. I geve to the poore-man's boxe at Heighington, 20*d*., and to the poore-man's boxe at Gainfourthe, 20*d*. And my funeralls and fourthe bringinge to be at the discretion of my wyfe, Margret Brakenberie. Also I will that my wyfe Margret shall have the occupacion and governemente of my farmehould to the upbringinge of my children duringe hir lyfe, and after hir deathe I will that the lande that I purchaised shall my sonnes Oliver and Thomas Brakenburie have, and after my wyff's deathe the said Oliver and Thomas shall geve to ther brother, Richarde Brakenburie, for a tokinge of remembraunce, 6*s*. 8*d*. yearle and not before. The residewe of all my goods, moveable and unmoveable, my detts dischardged, and my funeralls, I geve to my wyfe, Margeret Brackenberie, Oliver Brakenberie and Thomas Brakenberie, whome I doe make jointlie together my full executors, they to dispose all things to the pleasure of Almightie God and the healthe of my soulle. And I charge my executors to se my detts trulie paid.

[1] The testator was buried Aug. 2, 1576. *Gainford Register*.

And I desire theise gentlemen, Mr. Raufe Tailbois, Mr. Anthonye
Tailbois, Mr. George Tonge, Mr. John Witham, as my speciall truste
is in them, for the love of Almightie God, to be good to my wife and
small children, with youre helpes in all ther busines. Theise witnesses, Richarde Wetherelde, Robert Smythe, Raphe Barton, Thomas
Tompson, Peter Hutcheson, Raphe Wright, William Tompson, clarke,
with others. [Pr. Oct. 26, 1576.]

WILL OF CUTHBERT THURSBY.

Sept. 21, 1574. I, Cuthbert Thursebye, beinge hole of mynde
and of perfyte memorye, do ordaine and make this my last will and
testament, and my bodye to be buryed in the church or chappell of
Barnard-castle under my father stone before queare, with my
mortuary dew and by lawe accustomed. I geve and bequeathe to
Robart Thursebye, my sonne Thomas sonne, one cupbord standinge
in the hall howse. I geve and bequeathe to my sonne, Thomas
Thurseby, one arke, one trowe, one presser. I geve and bequeathe
to Margerye, my doughter, all the rest of my howsehowlde stuffe
not bequeathed. I geve and bequeathe to everye one of my childers
childringe one lambe. I geve to my doughter Margerre all my
sheipe. I geve and bequeathe to my doughter Margerye, 6l. 13s. 4d.
for hir chyld's porcion. I geve and bequeathe to James Loidman one
whye stircke. I geve and bequeathe to Lancelote Alurgill a cote
and a paire of hose. I geve and bequeathe to my sonnes, Thomas
Thursebye, and Gabriell Thursebye, my lease of the demaynes duringe
my yeares yet to come. The resedew of all my goods, my detts paid
and funerall expences discharged, I geve unto my sonnes, Thomas
Thursebye and Gabriell Thursebye, whome I ordeane and make my
full executours of this my last will and testament. [Pr. March 11,
1574/5.]

WILL OF THOMAS OGLE.

Dec. 14, 1574. Thomas Ogle of Tritlington, gent. I give all my
lands in Tritlington to James Ogle, my son, and his heirs, and if it
can be proved that he cannot taike naturall witt and reason to
govern hymselfe then to go to Martyn, my son,[1] and James to have
sufficient yearly to keep him out of the said lands at the sight of
my brother, James Ogle, Martyn Fenwicke, Mathewe and John Ogle,
my brethren. I will that my wyfe shall have my purchased lands

[1] June 21, 1575. 'James Ogle of Cawsie Parke, esquire, Mathew Ogle of
the same place, gent., and Martin Fenwick of Este Hedwayne, gent., were
appointed guardians of Martin Ogle, son of Thomas Ogle, late of Trittillington,
deceased.'

in Tritlington according to the condicion of one obligation wherein my brother, James Ogle, and I stande bound to Mr. Hedworthe of Haraton for the performance of the same. I desire the Right Honourable, my Lord Ogle, to be good to my wyfe and children. To my daughters, Agnes and Juliane Ogle, 60*l*. to be paid out of my goods and the maynes of Trittlington. To Margaret Ogle, my wife, and my two daughters, my lease, tytell, terme of years, graunt or graunts of the tythe corne of Prestewike. To my daughters, all my goods and the corn and oitts on the ground, etc., of the maynes in Tritlington, excepting my wife's thirds. To my two sons, my lease and terme of years of the tythe corne of Benrighe, paying such somes of monye as I stand bounde to paye to Agnes and Elizabeth Symson by an order maid by the counsell of York. I give to Margarett Midforth, to hir marriage, 10*l*. My sons executors. Supervisors, my brethren abovesaid and John Hedworth of Harradon, esquier. Witnesses, James Ogle, Lewes Ogle, John Ogle, Mathew Ogle, George Turner, Robert Wederington, John Heron, Andro Rutlodge, Thomas Donne and Edward Townes.

WILL OF RICHARD BAYLES.

Dec. 16, 1574. Richerd Baylls, parson of Cockefeild. I geve to Nicholas Ludge and Christofer Ludge, 3*l*. 6*s*. 8*d*. to bye two sommer nages. To Jenkyne Myddleton one whye, or ells 13*s*. 4*d*. To John Bell of Rumbey parishe, 3*l*. 6*s*. 8*d*., if my goods will serve to dischardge all suche. To Isabell Bell, 40*s*. To Anthony Harrison, 40*s*. To James Temple . . . . To Richerd Johnson, his wife and children, 20*s*. To the wife of John Tompson, one whye, or ells 16*s*. To Henrie Johnson, 20*s*. To Thomas Hodgson, 40*s*. To Anne Johnson, 40*s*. ; William Baills, 40*s*., and to Anne Baills, 40*s*. John Kiplinge, 20*s*. To the wife of Christofer Ludge, 40*s*.—if there remayne to dischardge all things 4*l*.—also one brass pott which was her father's. To Richerd Baills, one counter. To Elisabeth Baills, one cupborde. To Margaret Harrison, two ewes. The rest of my goods, unbequithed, I geve to John Baills of Shotton and Richerd Baills, whome I maike my hole executors of this my last will and testament. I will that Richerd Arrasmythe and James Arrasmythe, when all my legaces and other things is dischardged by John Baills and Richerd his sonne, then they to be partaykers of that which remayneth with John and Richerd Baills. I will that Nicholas Ludge and Christofer Ludge be supervisors of this my will and testament and they to have all there costs and charges borne when as they go to any place to the perfourmance of the same. Witnesses, Raphe Waitt, Symon Wait, Raphe Ludge, Nicholas Ludge, Michaell Arrowsmethe, Robert Browne, with others. [Pr. Jan. 14, 1574/5.]

WILL OF THOMAS PENTLAND.

Jan. 4, 1574/5. Thomas Pentlande of the parishe of Sainct Gyles, in the suburbes of the citie of Durham. I most hartelie geve and bequithe my sowle to Almightie God, my onlie creator, and to his sonne, Jesus Christ, my onlie Savior and Redeamer ; my bodye to be buried within my said parishe churche of St. Gyles, whereas my freindes shall thinke most convenient. And for my goodes as here-after followeth :—I geve and bequithe to Christabell Darlinge, wedo, one sylver spoone. I geve and bequithe to the poore folkes in Sainct Oswoldes parish, 4s. I geve and bequithe to the poore folkes in St. Gyles parish aforesaid, 5s. I geve and bequithe to Elinor Hawell my servaunte, 5s. I geve and bequithe to Christofer Grcine, minister, my best gowne. I geve and bequithe to Thomas Snawball, my goodsone, 5s. I geve and bequithe to Richerd Bell a sylver spone. I geve and bequithe to the said Richerd Bell wife, 5s. I geve and bequithe to Roger Bell, his sonne, to be paid in two yeares next after the dait hereof at two payments, 20s. I geve and bequithe unto John Cooke, 2s. 6d. I geve and bequithe to Thomas Fawell, 5s. I frelie remitt and forgeve John Mawer, th' elder, 6s. 8d. which he oweth me. I geve, will and bequithe unto Edward Wilkinson and Mergerye, nowe his wife, all my hole righte, title, interest, use, possession and tearme of yeres which I have, might, should, or ought to have, of, in and to all my burgage and acre of medow in Giligate aforesaid : to have and to holde the said burgage, and acre of medow, with all and singular th' appurtenances thereto belonginge, to the said Edward Wilkinson and Mergerye his wife, and there sequels *in jure* according to the custome of the courte there holden. I will that the said Edwarde and Mergerye, and there assignes, in consideracion therof shall paye, or cause to be paid, unto John Thomson, my sister sonne, yerelie every yere during his life naturall, 10s. of lawfull Englishe money, and he to have an honest bedd-roome frelie at all tyme and tymes when and as often as shall convenientlie resorte and come thither. The resydew of all my goodes not legated nor bequested, my debts paid, legacie deducted, and funerall charges perfourmed, I geve and bequithe to the said Edward Wilkinson and Mergerye his wife, whome I ordaine, constitute and maike my full and sole executors of this my said testament and last will. Witt-nesses hereof, Thomas Cornefourthe, th' elder, George Tayler, Richerd Bell, John Cooke, Thomas Fawell, etc. [Pr. Jan. 15, 1574/5.]

WILL OF ROBERT ELRINGTON.

Jan. 25, 1574/5. Robert Elringtone of Espersheles. I commende and bequeth my soull unto Almightie God, my Creator and Redemor, trusting in his grace and mercy to be one of his elect children. I bequeth unto Johne Elringtone, my sonne, all my whole intereast, right and title in all my lands, tenements, houses, pastours, comon of pastours, of the towne of Elringtone ; and all my interest and title in all my lands, etc., at Hadenbridge, specified in one dead of gifte made by me to the said Johne, my sonne, to continue unto him and to his heyres for ever. I bequeth unto the foresaid Johne Elringtone tenne oxen, etc. I bequeth unto Martin Elringtone, my sonne, all my whole intereast of one fermeholde in Unthanke of the rent of 20s., with all things thereto belonging; and also 6s. 8d. of one fermeholde in the said towne of Unthanke, now being in the tenor and custodye of Edward . . . . —if the lawe will permitte the same—and if it ﹅will not, I will that my heyre shall paye out of the foresaid two fermeholds unto the sayd Martyne Elringtone, my sonne, 26s. 8d. yearly induring his naturall lyfe. I bequeth unto George Elringtone, my sonne, one fermeholde of the rent of 13s. 4d., being now in the tenor and custodye of Janet Elringtone, my step-mother, lying in the towne of Cronckly, after the death of the said Janet; and one other fermeholde of the rent of 13s. 4d. yearly, being now in the tenor and custodye of Robert Parker in the foresaid towne of Cronckley—if the law will permitt the same—and if it will not, I will that my heyre shall paye out of the foresaid two fermeholds unto the said George Elringtone, my sonne, 24s. 8d. yearly induring the said George naturall lyfe. I bequeth unto William Elringtone, my sonne, one close of the rent of 36s. yearly, being now in the tenor and custodye of Thomas Robisonne and John . . . . and one close called the mill . . . . of the rent of 6s. 8d. yearly, and one corn mill, the rent of the same when it shall fall—if the lawe will permitte the same— and if it will not, I will that my heyre shall paye out of the foresaid closes and mill the foresaid some of yearly rent unto my foresaid sonne, William Elringtone, yearly induring his naturall life. I bequeth unto Marrion Elringtone and Agnes Elringtone, my doughters, the yearly rent of 10s. out of one fermeholde in the towne of Unthanke, being now in the tenour and custodye of John Robisone; and also 5s. rent yearly of one fermeholde in the foresaid towne of Unthanke being now in the tenour and custodye of Thomas Swinhowe yearly during their naturall lyves, or ells I will that my heyre shall paye unto my foresaide two doughters 20 marks, that is to saye, 13l. 6s. 8d.—to either of them 6l. 13s. 4d.—and then my heyre is to have the foresaid two fermeholds. I bequeth unto Johne Elringtone, my sonne, being base born, or bastard, 4 shepe to helpe him to ane occupatione or science. I bequeth unto the children of Johne Carre, my sonne in lawe, eavry one of them a shepe. I bequeth unto Richard Carre, sonne to the said Johne Carre, one quye stirke. I ordeyne and make Custance Elringtone, my wyfe, Johnne Elringtone, Martyne Elringtone, George Elringtone, William Elringtone, my sonnes, Marrion Elringtone and Agnes Elringtone, my daughters, my true and lawfull executores. Supervisors, Johne Carre, my brother in lawe, and Hary Wallace of Knarsdale. Witnesses, Robert Andro, Robert Nesome, Edward Warde, Thomas Bensone, clark, parsone of Edmondbyer.

WILL OF CHRISTOPER FAWDON.

Oct. 5, 1575. Christopher Fawdon, servaunte to Mr. Christopher Conyers of Horden. To be buried in Esington churche-yearde as my executors will. I geve to Mr. Christopher Conyers, my master, 4*l.* I geve hyme my horse and geare. I geve hym two stotts. I geve to Philip Fowdon, my brother, 4*l.* I geve hym a cowe and (his) sonne a calfe. I geve to Robert Fowdon, my brother, 10*l.* I geve to my two systers 20*s.* to be devyde equallie betwixt them. I geve to my felowe servauntes in house 15*s.* I forgeve Jhon Frinde of Durham 3*l.* he owethe me. I geve Jhon Frinde's wyffe 26*s.* 8*d.* I geve to his sonne 26*s.* 8*d.* when it comes to the hands of my executors. I do geve to Jhon Scott's childeringe, of Hathorne, all my shepe. I geve to Jhon Scotte himselfe one stotte. I geve Mr. Conyers, elder, 10*s.* in golde. I geve Mrs. Elizabeth Conyers 10*s.* in goulde. I geve to Mr. Ashe 15*s.* I make Mr. Christopher Conyers and John Hathorne my executors, to whome I geve the rest of my goods and debts owinge me, viz., Jhon Symson and William Beere, 8*l.*, of which 6*l.* is to be payd at St. Jhon day in Christenmes, and the said William to paye 43*s.* 4*d.* at Easter next coming. Mathewe Currye dothe owe me that ys to be paid at St. Andrewe day, 3*l.* 15*s.* and William Richardson of Thorpe, 53*s.* 4*d.* Witnesses heareof, Jhon Joley and Christopher Jackson, with others.

WILL OF THOMAS CHAYTER.

Dec. 15, 1575. Thomas Chatter of the parish of Saint Jones, Newcastle, wever. To be buried in St. John's near my wife. The lease of my house to my son, Cuthbert Chatter, and he to pay to my son, Oswould Chatter,[1] during the years of the lease, 20*s.* a year. My lome to Cuthbert, my sonn ; and to Oswold, my son, the lome he works on. To my son, Nicholas Chatter, 20*s.* Remainder to my two sons, Cuthbert and Oswyne [*sic*] Chatter. To George Graye, curate, 2*s.* 6*d.* To the poor, 12*d.* [Pr. July 31, 1577.]

WILL OF HUGH WHITFIELD.

Jan. 26, 1575/6. Hughe Whitfeild of Durham, draper.[2] To be buried in St. Nicholas. I give to the maintener or officer of the

---

[1] For some notices of Oswald Chaytor, for thirty-eight years clerk of St. John's, see Mr. Richard Welford in 'Local Muniments,' *Arch. Ael.* vol. xxiv. p. 153.

[2] 1575/6, Feb. 28. Emma, wife of Hughe Whitfield, buried. *Reg. St. Nicholas'*, Durham.

[3] The following is the will of a member of the same family :—

Oct. 21, 1578, eight in the eavninge. Thomas Whytfelde of Durham, draper, in the house of my cosyng, George Whitfeilde, in Newcastle. To be buried in the cathedrall churche of Durham, in the east end of the sayd churche, without the queare, if it can be obtayned, otherwise in Saint Marye's church in the

towne for the maynteininge of the pannte and for that use 20s.
My daughters, Jane and Agnes Halliday. To my son, William
Whitfeild, a silver peace, a signet of gold, 6 silver spoones, with a
mazer cup tipte with silver and gilte. To my son, Thomas Whitfeild, 100l. My brother, John Whitfeild; my sister, Magaret
Stokoe; her (?) daughter, Agnes Anderson. The wife of my brother,
Henry Whitfeild, deceased, 20s. To my sonne William Whitfield, my
dwelling house in Silver Street, also my two burgages or tenements
in Flesh-gate in the said city. To Hugh Anderson, the residue of all
my goodes. Witnesses Sir William Headlam, curate, William Watson,
clerke, Edward Hendspeth and Richard Walton. [Pr. Jan. 18, 1577.]

WILL OF JANET GIBSON.

Feb. 18, 1575/6. Janett Gibson of Wosinghame, widow. To be
buried in Gateshead church-yard.[1] To Matthew White of the Read-
hughe, co. Durham, gent., my house in Gatishead which was my
father's, John Unthanke's, deceased, lyinge upon the east parte of the
Quene's streate, betwene a tenement somtymes William Langeshow,
and after dyde belonge to the chaplen of the chantry of the blessed
Trinitie, in the churche of Gatished, upon the northe parte of the
over Kirke Chaire. To my daughters Mary and Elizabeth Stobbes,
30s. apiece. To my daughter Alice Gybson a cowe in the keepinge of
Edward Stobbes. Residue to my four doughters Jane, Maryon, Alice,
and Elizabeth Gybson, whom I make executors.

WILL OF HUMPHREY MAIRE.

Mar. 9, 1575/6. Umfraie Maire of Hedlehoppe. To be buried
at Lanchester. I give to my son, John Maire, 26s. 8d. To my son,
Lanselot Maire, 26s. 8d. To my brother, Richard Mayre, 13s. 4d.

Northe Baylye, as nighe my wyfe as may be convenientlye. To the poor of
the parish I dwell in, 6s. 8d. by year till 20s. be spent. To the poor of Newcastle, 20s. To my son, Robert Whytfelde, 10l. To my daughter Elizabethe,
wife of Thomas Wilson, 11l. 13s. 4d. To my son, Anthony Whytfelde,
6l. 13s. 4d. To my daughter, Katherine Whytfelde, 20l. and as much cloth
as will make her weddinge apparell, to the value of 5l. To my son, Robert
Whytfelde, a belt with a head and a pendyse of sylver and gylt moreover;
my best gowne and my best sworde. Jennet Hutchinson, my wife's sister.
To my daughter Jennet, the lowse sylver geare in my chyst. My son Roger
Whytfelde's son Raynold, 6l. 13s. 4d. To my son-in-law, Thomas Hopper, a
dublett with damask sleves. My cosyng, George Whytfeilde, his wife, his
mother, and his son Henry. John Whitfelde of Durham, tayler, Edward
Whitfelde, son of Anthony Whitfelde, and his other children. Thomas
Stokar's wife, my cosin. Roger and Anthony Whitfelde, my sons, and
Thomas Hopper, my son-in-law, executors. Mr. Hedworth of Harraton,
Maister Lampton of Lampton, Mr. Bellasye of Jarray, Nicholas Cokson of
Pittington, supervisors. [Pr. Nov. 15, 1578.]

[1] 1575/6, Mar. 13. Jane Gibsonne, buried. *Gateshead Register.*

To my master, Mr. William Hodgshon, 10s. My son, Robert Maire. My curat, Sir Richard. My wyfe and three sons executors.[1] [Pr. 1576.]

WILL OF CUTHBERT SMYTHE.

Mar. 26, 1576. Cuthbert Smythe of Ketton, gent. To the poor house-holders in Acliffe parish on the day of my burial, 4l. To the reparations of Acliffe church, 20s. To my sister, Margaret Grymstone, after the death of her husband, Martyn Grymstone, 20l. To my sister, Custannce Stellinge, after the death of her husband, William Stellinge, 20l. To my sister, Frances Layton, after the death of her husband, Robert Layton, 20l. To my sister, Isabell Sotheren, after the death of her husband, Christopher Sotheran, 20l. To each of my sister's children living when I die, 20l. To my cosyng, William Smythe of Eshe, and his son, George Smythe, all my leases, etc., on the grange, manor and farm of Ketton, and of the tythe corn, sheves and haye of Ketton. To my said cosyng, George Smythe, 20l. for a token. To my cosyng, Margaret Smythe, my cosyng William Smythe's wife, 20l., to by hir a nage. To my cosyng and landlord, Sir William Bellasses, knight, 6l. 13s. 4d. for a token, to buy him a geldinge, and to my ladye Bellasses, his wife, 3l. 6s. 8d. Remainder to my cosyng, William Smythe of Esh and George Smythe, his son, a third part to my nephew, William Sotheren. Witnesses, John Lambton, John Swinborne, Richard Lumley, etc. [Pr. May 10, 1578.]

WILL OF CUTHBERT HILTON.

April, 1576. Cuthberte Hilton of Greate Useworthe, parishe of Washington. To be buried within my parishe churche of Washington with my mortuarie dewe by lawe. I geve to Elizabethe Hilton, my wyfe, my lease and farmehoulde in Great Osworthe duringe the tyme of hir wedowe-heade, excepte the moitie or one halfe of 2 mylnes conteyned in the same lease, and yf yt shall fortune the said Elizabethe to marie or die before the said lease be expired, then I will that William Hilton, my sonne, have my said farmehoulde in Great Oswourthe, except the mylnes before excepted; and in defaulte of the said William Hilton and his lawfull yssue, to Thomas Hilton, my sonne; and in defaulte of the said Thomas and yssue of

[1] Thomas Mayre of Plawsworth, another member of the old Durham family of Maire, made his will, Jan. 26, 1583/4. To be buried in the churchyard of Chester. My eldest son, John Mayre; my goddaughter, Alison Silvertop; my son-in-law, John Lidell; William and Thomas Silvertop. Residue to my wife Katherine and unmarried children, viz., Christopher Mayre, John Mayre the younger, and my daughter, Isabel Mayre the younger. Pr. 1584.

The very close connection of the families of Maire and Silvertop has continued to the present day.

hym lawfullie begotten, to come to George Hilton, my sonne, and his children, in maner as before said. I geve to Anne Hilton, my doughter, myne intereste and righte of my twoo mylnes belonginge to my farmhoulde in Great Oswourthe, for and duringe hir naturall lyfe; and yf she die before the years of the same be expired, I will then that the years and righte of the same remayninge and unnrune cum to William Hilton, my sonne, provided allwayes that the said [Anne] and hir successors paye the rente yearlie, and sufficientlie repare the same, duringe ther tymes. I will that Elizabeth, my wyfe, have the custodie of my children and ther goods dureinge ther noneaidge to suche tyme as honeste mariges or other prefermente maye be provided for them by the advice of there said mother with there freinds, yf she kepe hir wedow, but yf she marie or dye before my childrene be fourthe with ther portons, I will that then William Hilton, my sonne, have the custodie of my [children] and ther goods, provided alwaye that whensoever William Hilton, my sonne, shall enter to . . . . hould . . . . Great Osworthe in maner aforesaide, my will is that within 2 yeres nexte . . . . the said William Hilton, my sonne, or his executors, administrators or assignes . . . . cause to be paid forthe of my farmehoulde aforesaid, beinge lawfullie demanded . . . . of the said farme in Osworthe aforesaid to five of my children to ther . . . . administrators or assignes the some of 20l. in maner and fourme folowing, that is to . . . . to Thomas Hilton, 3l. 6s. 8d. To George, 3l. 6s. 8d. To Margaret Hilton, 6l. 13s. . . . . Elizabeth Hilton, 3l. 6s. 8d. And to Elynor Hilton, my doughter, 3l. 6s. 8d. . . . . geve to my sister, Margret Scurfeild, one bowll of wheat . . . . [g]eve to Robert . . . . one boull of rye. I geve to Margaret Godsricke one pecke of wheat and to Cuthbert Godsricke one pecke of wheat. I geve to my god-doughter Katheren . . . . one gymmer and to my god-doughter, Margaret Harle, one gymmer lambe . . . . To Thomas Hilton, my sonne, one dune nage of 4 years oulde. Also I will . . . . right worshipfull Sir William Hilton of Hilton, knight, to be supervisor, and I geve unto his worshippe one oulde angell. The reste . . . . I geve to Elizabethe, my wyfe, whome I make full and whole executrix of this my last will, whome I also charge to paie all my proveable detts . . . . Witnesses, William Bainbrigge, Richarde Harle, Thomas Cat . . . . Phillip, William Sparrow, Robert Sparrowe and George Morden, curat, with others. [Pr. Feb. 1, 1576/7.]

WILL OF ROBERT COOK.

Aug. 14, 1576. Robarte Cooke of the citie of Durham, in-habitante and teacher of the grammer scoole there,[1] whole of minde

---

[1] The testator was master of the Grammar School at Durham, at which ancient institution John Baliol, king of Scotland, received part of his education. *Cf.* new *History of Northumberland*, vol. vi. p. 53.

and of perfite health and remembrance, make this, my last will and
testament. First, I commende my sowle unto Almighty God, through
Christ only trustinge to be sayved, and my bodye to be buryed
where my frinds shall thinke most meyte and convenient. Also
I demise, will and bequith unto Margerie Lynge, *alias* Procter,
daughter of Thomas Proctor of Loughborowe, in the countie of
Layster, yeoman, otherwise called Margerie Cooke, wiffe of me, the
said Robart Cooke, all that my messuage, tenement and farme with
th' appurtinances in Skeythbye in the countie of Yorke, and all my
interest, title, tearme and yeares therein, for and to the goode education and preferment of my children, upon condicion that the said
Margerie shall not goe about to sell, demise, surrender or alien the
same or any part thereof, whereby the same maye not lawfullye, after
the decease of the same Margerie dyinge within and duringe the
tearme and yeares aforesaid, come to suche children as she now
haith or heareafter shall have by me, the said Robart. The residew
of all my goods and chattels, my debts payed, I doe give to the said
Margerie, and to Thomas Cooke, Elizabeth and John Cooke, the
children hade betwixte me and hire, the said Margerie, whom I make
the executors of this my last will and testament. In witnes wherof
I have written this my will with mine owne hande and thirunto
sett my hande 14th Aug., anno domini 1576. By me, Robert Cooke ;
George Lightfote, Cuthbart Claxton, Jerrard Salven. [Pr. Dec. 5,
1579.]

WILL OF EDMUND SHADFORTH.

Dec. 4, 1576. Edmund Shaldforthe, parish of All Sayntes, Newcastle, master and maryner. To be buryed within my parishe church
or churche-yearde according to the lawdable custome of Christian
men. To Allysone, my wife, the house in the Broad Chaire in which
I nowe do dwell in, duringe her lyfe, and then to John Leiche, sonne
to my syster, Elsabethe Leiche, and his heirs ; then to Belye Leiche,
his syster, etc. ; then to my nevye, Robert Hynmers, sonne to
Mathewe Hynmers, etc., and then to my rightus heires. To the
foresaid John Leiche, two tenements in Pandon (when of age). To
my syster, Elsabethe Leiche, the house she nowe dwelleth in and the
tenement adjoyninge. To the said John Leiche, a whysell with a
chyne of sylver with my sea gowne and all the rest of my sea close,
and a bagge with a lock of sylver. To the foresaid Robert Hymmer,
a whysle of sylver, and to his sonne one ould angell. To my brother,
William Huntley, my sworde and one horine garished with sylver.
To my father in lawe and my mother in lawe, a French crowne each.
To my aunt Coke, 5s. The rest to my wife, she executrix. [Pr.
June 10, 1583.]

WILL OF THOMAS WRAY.

Oct. 13, 1577. I, Thomas Wraye, the sonne of Richerd Wraye, laite of Barwick upon Twede, weaver, and nowe of the aige of 32 yeares, being of hole mynde and purfyt memorie, and having occacion to travile into Flannders to serve as a soldior, maikes and ordaynes this my last will and testament in maner and forme foloweng. First, I geve my soule to th'ands of Almightie God and my bodie to the earth where it shall please God to call me. To my brother, Nycholas Wraye, my house upon the Grenes nowe in the tenor of Raphe Wraye, my brother, without any letts or trobles. [Pr. 1584.]

WILL OF ROBERT CLAXTON.

May 10, 1578. Robert Claxtone, clerke, master of the Hospital of St. Edmonde the King in Gateside.[1] To my sister Jane Wardell, 40s. To my cosin, Nicholas Denman, and my cosin Agnes, his wife, 6s. 8d. each. My cusin Hall and his wife . . . . To Robert Hall that I dyde christen, 10s. and the rest of the money that Mr. Deane dothe owe 'unto me; I wyll that William Hall sewe for it. To Michael and William Hall, my syster's children, and Agnes Woormell, 40s. that Thomas Mallett shulde have payd for the executorshipe of his uncle, the Deane of Lincolne, the which he dide borowe of me when I was at Lincolne. I forgyve James Lasenbie 4l. that I dyd paye for him to Rynyane Shaftooe for wyne. To my sister, Agnes Lasenbie, 3l. 6s. 8d. To Agnes Surtes, 10s. To Ammonde Claxtone, 13s. 4d. To my aunte Selbye, 5s., and to Christopher Selbie and each of his sisters, 5s. To Elynor Selbye, daughter of William Selbye, merchant, whom I christenyd, 20s. and a fyllett. To Robert Marche, 3s. To the pore folkes in Elvett parishinge in Duresme, in their booke of the collectors of the pore, 20s. And I gyve in lyke maner unto the pore folkes in Gatesyde, 20s. To Margerye Claxstone, 40s. that my brother, Roger Claxstone, did give her for my part of the executorship, and 40s. of my owne, and one gowne that is in Duresme, and 2 yeards and a half of brode reade, that she dooe use hir-self well and honestlye and dooe please my brother, Richard Claxstone; and I wyll the velvett be taiken of the gowne to another use as shall please my brother; and she doo the contrarye, then my executor to use hir at his discretione. To my brother, John Claxstone, 13l. To Alexander Fetherstonehaughe, 33s. 4d. of my parte of executorshippe. Remainder to my brother, Richard Claxstone: he executor. Witnesses, Thomas Thomlingesone, gent, etc. [Pr. Jan 19, 1578/9.]

---

[1] Robert Claxton was collated to the mastership of St. Edmund's Hospital, Gateshead, Aug. 15, 1552, and held the same until his death. He was buried Dec. 3, 1578 (*Gateshead Registers*). *Cf.* Welford, *Newcastle and Gateshead*, vol. ii. pp. 286, 512.

WILL OF GEORGE BURLINSON.

Aug. 17, 1578. George Burlessone of Woodhorne, yeoman.[1] To be buried within the church or churchyard of Woodhorn. To my son, George Burliesone, a swanne oxe, a hauked oxe, and sinimounte oxe, a blacke stote in using, a brown and a branded in Chepingetone. I give to my son, George Burleisone, my dune horse and 20 ewes. To my wife a third part of my goods. To my sone, William Burlessone, 20 ewes. To my son's daughter Jennett Burlesone, 2 quies which are at New Close with John Cloughe. To my sonne's sonne, Thomas Burlessone, a brown mare and 4 hogges. To my son's daughter, Margaret Burlessone, 4 hogs. To Elizabeth Burlessone, 4 hogs. To James Burrlesonne, two roughe hogs. To my son's son, William Burlessone, a basant foole. Witnesses William Graye, John Shevyll, smythe in Woodehorne, and John Hedley.

WILL OF JOHN GLENTON.

Dec. 3, 1578. John Glentone. To be buried in the chappell of Bernerde-castell with all devine service nowe moste godelye sett forth. To my cosine, Ambrose Watsone, my house lyenge betwixt my nowe dwellinge house and the burgage of George Simpsone during my wife, Genet Glentone's wedoweheade, or till she marye. To Genet, my wife, all my lands and leases in Bernard-castell and Strateforthe, as by my evidences, escripts and writings may appeare, for life if she be my widow, and then to my cosine, Ambrose Watsone, and the heires of his bodie lawefullye begotten for ever. The said Ambrose Watsone, and his heirs, yeldinge and payenge yearlye for ever unto the hands of the four and twenty of the parishe, or chappellarie, of Barnarde-castell for ever, and to the use of the pore people inhabitinge within the toune of Bernarde-castell 26s. 8d. at 2 severell tymes in the yeare. That is to saye, 13s. 4d. at the feaste of Penthecoste, and 13s. 4d. at the feaste of Martyne the busshope in Wynter yearlye, within 14 dayes after eyther of the said feasts and if the said yearlye rent of 26s. 8d. of currante Englishe monye, or any parte or parcell therof, shalbe behinde and unpayed 14 dayes after eyther the saide feasts, that then it shalbe lawefull to and for the four and twenty of the parishe or chapelrie of Bernarde-castell, from tyme to tyme so beinge, to enter upon the said burgage in Bernarde-castell and lands on Stratforthe and distreyne, and the distresses so taken with them to leade, dryve or carrie and the same to impounde or withholde tyll that the rente then behind and unpayed be

---

[1] The family of Burlinson owned a small freehold estate in the township of Woodhorn, which, by the last of the family, Frances Byrletson, spinster, by will dated June 7, 1700, was given to her cousin, Byrletson Shell. *Cf.* Woodhorn MSS., Woodman Collection.

throwelye answeryd and payed. To my cosins, Ralphe and Francis
Saire after my wife's death, or marriage, my two other burgages in
Bernard-castle and they to pay to the 24, yearlye, for the same
13s. 4d., etc. My lands and edifices in Mickelton of the annual rent of
6s. 8d. to my two godesonnes, Edwarde Hutone, sonne to my brother
John Hutone, and Anthony Hutone, sonne to my brother in lawe
George Hutone, and their heirs. To my especyall frend and cosine,
William Applebie of the Gyll-feilde, a velvett nighte cappe for a
simple token. To my cosen, Nicholas Applebye, my beste tafeta
doublett if it wyll please him to weare it. To my cosen, Anthony
Applebie, 10s. To my cosine, Ambrose Watsone, 10l. To James
Midletone, his bill of 5l., one suite of my apparell and my swearde.
My cosen, Elizabeth Persevell. To my brother, George Hutone, an
olde ryall and my better cote of plaite. To my sister Elyner, his
wife, an angell. Her daughter, Cecill Hutone, and my brother, George
Hutone's other children. My brother, Ambrose Huttone. To Robert
Huttone, son of Alixander, a younge colte of twoo yeares olde, brede
under the soare meare that was George Taylor's. To Jane Hutone,
his sister, 26s. 8d., which her mother owes me. Ther brother,
Frances Hutone. My sister, Cycile Hutone. My brother in law,
John Hutone ; my sister, his wife ; his son John and his two daughters.
My olde frend John Watson of the Sheils. To the right worshipfull
Mr. Christofer Chaytor, an angell for a simple token. To Mr. Henrye
Middletone, 10s. which he owes me, and to his daughter, Elizabeth
Middeltone, my gode-doughter, a whie. To my cosine, Ambrose Masone,
my best cloithe gown and a grogrome jackett and my dagger ; and to
his son, Frauncis Masone, my gode sonne, a stole and all the bookes that
were my brother's. To my cosinge, Thomas Hutone, 30s. towards
the buyinge of a nage. To my cosine, John Tweddell of Londone,
haberdasher, 40s., and to his brother, Jeffraye Tweddall, 20s. To my
cosine, Ralphe Saire, my soare meare and hir fole, and my bowe and
quyver. To my cosine, Frances Saire, 3l. 6s. 8d. and the sweard,
etc., that was my brother's. To my cosyne, Issabell Saire, their
mother, 20s. she owes me and 46s. 8d. besides, and a gowne of
huswiefe's clothe lyned with lambe and faced with conye. To my
cosyne, Marmaduke Simpsone, 40s., and I forgive him what he owes
me. To my cosyne, Henry Simpsone, his brother, 40s., and to
Anthony Simpsone, his brother, 3l. 6s. 8d. To their sister which is
married, 53s. 4d. ; and to ther sister married to George Applebie,
one angell. To Edward Simpsone, sone to John, 40s. To his sister,
Grace Simpsone, 40s. To John Hiltone, 10s., and his sister, towards
hir maryaidge, 40s. To my cosin, John Parkine's wife of Larting-
ton, 30s. To my cosin, William Wharton's wife of Eglestone, those
of the feather-beddes which came from Darneton. My cosin, John
Jackeson's wife of Baudersdale, 10s. To Mr. Oswyne Mettfourthe of
Newcastell, 3l., which his father-in-law, Mr. Hunter, owes me, and
46s. 8d. more. To Matthew Coperwhate, clarke, curate of Whorlton,
2 olde angells. To Thomas Reade, 3l. 6s. 8d. And I wyll that an

angell which my brother, Sir Gefferaye Glentone,[1] dyde gyve and bequeathe unto Sir Arthore Shaftowe, be gyven unto him (with) th'one of my blacke clokes that were my brother's. To Ralphe Barnes, 10s. To my cosin, John Hill, his wife, 10s. To Dorothy Whitfelde's son, 10s. To Grace Mill, wife of Robert Miller of the Horse Markett, in Richmond, 10s. To Thomas Thursbie's son, which is my godesonne, 20s. To Christopher Anderscne of Richmond, butcher, 3s. 4d. To Ambrose Glentone, 10s. To the mendinge of the heywayes about Stratfoorthe, 40s. To the pore of Bernard-castell, 12l. To the mending of the heywayes and streates within the precincts of Bernard-castell, 6l. I gyve, as my brother appointed me, 20s. to mend the heywayes on and aboute Heddone and Eatche-wicke, and 20s. to twentie of the porest householders in Heddone. My wife executrix. Sir George Bowes, knt., and Mr. John Clopton supervisors. [Pr. Jan. 28, 1578.]

WILL OF ROBERT HARBOTTLE.

Jan. 12, 1578/9. Robert Harbotell, gent., parish of Tainefeld. To be buried in the church-yard of Tainefeld. To my brother's daughter, Mabell Bell, 40s. To Ralphe Harbotell, son of my cosin, Robert Harbottle of Beamishe. . . . . To my brother in lawe, William Shafto, an ould angell. To my son, Thomas Harbotell, my best graye horse, and he to be sold, and six silver spones, etc. To my daughter, Elinor Harbotell, six selver spoones. Remainder to my wife, Barbarie Harbotell, and my two children, Thomas and Elynor Harbotell. To my wife, my two farmholds in Tanfield for her life. Witnesses, Roland Shafto, Robert Harbotell. (The children minors). [Pr. Feb. 28, 1578/9.]

WILL OF BARTHOLOMEW CRASTER.

July 26, 1579. Batholmew Craster of Stobes-wood, parish of Morpeth. My bodye to be buried within the parish church of Vulgham paying my accustomed duties, etc. To my youngest brother, Lewes Crastor, one lin loome and one pott. To my doughter, Jane Craster, one cow with calfe, and I will that John Craster, William Craster and Christofer Craster shall have the ofspring and proufe of the sayd cow to the use of Jane, my doughter, until she come of lawfull age. I give to the sayd Jane, my doughter, one presser, a[l]mire and one cawell. I gyve the rest of all my goods, moveable and immoveable, to Margret Craster, my wyfe, and Jane Craster, my doughter. Witnesses, Thomas Tayler, Robert Coward, Wylliam Craster, Thomas Wray, curate, with others. [Pr. April 7, 1580.]

[1] Galf. Glenton was vicar of Heddon-on-the-Wall, 1547-1577. Arthur Shafto was vicar of Stamfordham at the same period.

WILL OF WILLIAM MADDISON.

Oct. 14, 1579. William Maddeson of Aldergill, parish of Stanhopp in Wardill, gent. To my wife, Dorothy, my gray horse, and my best gray meare and two goulden ringes. To Stephen Maddeson, my sonne, my yonge graye meare, or els 4*l.*, a yonge gray horse, a cubbourd, fower silver sponnes, a gilted dagger, my lute, my best hose and three coots, one of tuffed taffitye, two of blacke brode clothe, the one laced with lace, and a yocke of yonge oxen. My daughters Anne, Frances, Elianer and Ursuly. To my daughter Ursuly, a silver sponne being dubbel gilted. My son, Roland Maddeson, 40*s.* Supervisors, Mr. John Feddersonhaughe, esquier, Lyonell Maddeson, of the Newcastle, gentleman, and Lancelote Maddeson, my son. I give to Mr. John Featherston, a crose bowe. To Lionell Featherston and Alexander Featherston, a peacer called a curreare and 5*s.* of monye. [Pr. 12 March, 1579/80, administration being granted to Dorothy Maddeson the widow, tutrix of Stephen Maddeson and the daughters, minors.]

WILL OF WILLIAM SURTEES.

Dec. 27, 1579. William Surtes, of the parish of Ovingham. To my wife, Elizabeth Surtes and unto Thomas Surtes, my sonne, all my farmoulde and the lease of Hughes Close. John, Christopher, Roger, Ralph, and Agnes Newton, my daughter's children. Christopher Surtes, my brother's son. My daughters Dorothie, Grace and Katherine Surtes. John Surtes, son of William Surtes, my son. My wife, Elizabeth Surtes, and my son, Thomas Surtes. Thomas and Richard Surtes, my sons. Grace, Katherine and Dorothy Surtes, my daughters. Witnesses, Thomas Roderforth, gent., Rowland Surtes, etc.   [Pr. March 22, 1579/80 and administration granted to Elizabeth and Grace Surtes—Thomas, Richard, Katherine and Dorothy Surtes, being minors.]

WILL OF JOHN MORTON.

April 19, 1580. John Mowrton of Unthank, within the countie palentyne of Norham, gentelman.   To be buried in the parish church of Twedmouth. To my sonnes, Anthonie and George Morton, whom I do maik my full executors, my landes, etc. To Custance, my wyfe, my water corne myll in Spyttell and my houses and tenements there, for her lyfe. To my doughters, Jane and Phillis Morton, 6*l.* 13*s.* 4*d.* each. My loving frend, Thomas Graye of Wark, gentelman, and my cossyn, Robert Morton of Barwick, burges, supervisors.   Witnesses, Robert Morton, Humfray Duglas, Thomas Revely. [Pr. 1581.]

WILL OF ROBERT BOWES.

April 22, 1580. Robert Bowes of Barwicke, in the diocesse of Durham, gentleman. I bequeath my soule to Almightie God, my Maker and Redemer, and my bodye to the earth. My will is that my house-stead in Barwicke shalbe sould by myne executors toward the payment of my debts. I also will that 30*l*. which is dew unto me for my pencon at Barwicke goe also towards the payment of my debts. I give to my nephie, Raphe Bowes, my gold chine. I give to John Pecocke 10*l*. I will and give by these presentes my house in Giligate to my brother Anderson and his heires and they to pay the rent of the same unto the poore people in Pittington parishe in the countye of Durham. I will and give unto Thomas Appelbye, servant unto Mr. Treasuerer, a blacke meare goinge at Nunstanton. All the residewe of my goods and chattels, my debts, legaces and funerall expences discharged, I give to my said brother, Henrye Anderson, esquier, whom I make my sole executor. I give by this my will to Mr. Treasurer of Barwicke my beste horse. Witnesses, Raphe Bowes, Thomas Appelbye, George Shepperson, George Swinborne, James Gascoigne, John Pecocke and William Kellome. [Pr. Aug. 22, 1580.]

WILL OF JOHN COLLINGWOOD.

May 23, 1580. John Collingwood of Newcastle, weaver. To be buried in the church of St. Andrews, my parishe churche. To my daughter, Margerie Graye, wiffe to Umphrey Graye, taillore, 24*s*. per annum out of my houses and lands, and I charge my brother, Thomas Collingwoode, as he will aunsweare att the dreadful daye of Judgment, to pay this. Agnes, James and Roberte Graye, sonnes to the said Umphrey Graye, to either of them, a pottle potte. To my brother, Thomas Collingwoode, all my workhouse geare as yt standyth belonging to the science of weavers. My sister, Jennet Dodes. Margaret Collingwoode. My wyfe, Ellenor Collingwoode. Iszabell, daughter of Umphrey Graye. To my brother, Thomas Collingwoode, all my houses and lands for his life and then to his heirs; failing them, to my daughter, Margerie Gray and her heirs. Residue to Thomas Collingwoode and Umphrey Graye, they executors.

WILL OF JOHN WATSON.

June 24, 1580. Johne Watsonne of Durham. To be buried in the parishe churche of St. Oswoolds, in the place where my wyffe was buryed.[1] To Elizabethe, my wyffe, my leace of my two ferme-

---

[1] 1580, June 29. Mayster John Watson of th'age lxxx yeres, for wysdom, gravyte, honeste, sobryete, and other godly vertews, worthe to prased, was buried the xxix day of June, beinge the feast day of Peter th'apostle. *Registers of St. Oswald's*, Durham.

holds in Synclyffe duringe here lyfe, etc. To my sonne, William Watsonn, for his fyliall portione, 10*l.* To my sonne, Mr. Christofer Watsone, for his chyld's portione, 10*l.* To my sonne, Anthony Watsonne, for his chyld's portione, 10*l.* To my sonne, Roger Watsone, my lease of the tythe corn and shayves of Pyttingtone. To my sonne, Johne Watsone of Newcastell, my lands cauled the Ryddinge, with all the evydences therto belonginge. To my sonne Jhone's wyffe, my gretesse sylver spoune. To my sonne Johne doughter Margrett, 40*s.* To his yongest doughter, Agnes Watsone, 20*s.* To my sonne, Roger Watson, on yonge coult goinge at Newtone Hansworthe. To Elinor Mydford, wyffe to Robert Mydfourde, for a tokene, on ould angell. To my sonne John's sonne, Robert Watson, sexe wedder sheepe, and to his other thre sonnes, Roger, John and Cuthbert Watson, to everye of theme 6*s.* 8*d.* To my doughter, Elizabeth Thorpe, on sylver spone. To my doughter, Margrett Thorpe, on sylver spoune. To my doughter, Elinore Cartere, on sylver spoune. To my sonne Johne's sonne Robert, on syvler spoone. To Jane Watsonne of Richemont, 26*s.* 8*d.* To my cosinge, Myles Whyte, one dubbell duckett. My sonne Johne was executor to my brother, Doctor Watsone, dysseaced. Mr. Christofer Chaytor, esquier, supervisor, and he shall have one ould angell for a tokene. My sons John and Christofer executors. To my sonne Roger, for his full portione, 10*l.* To the poore of Elvet, 40*s.*

WILL OF WILLIAM COWLEY.

Aug. 12, 1580. William Cowley, one of the gunners belongeng to the Quene's Majestie's great ordinance in Barwick upon Twede. My daughter, Margaret Cowley. Mr. William Larkyn, the master gunner of Barwick, and my loving cosyn, William Preston, pencioner. To Alice Johnson, my brod mowthed pott, etc. To John Browne, the cowper, my yealowe britches. To Grace Jackeson, my maiden servant, hir whole wages till Martinmes. To Ann, George Pawlin's wife's daughter, 10*s.* To Thomas Raye, my table. To John Frost, my biggest brass pot. To Malle Frost, my biggest brass pan. To Jerrerd Martin, 5*s.* To Robert Potter, the jerken and britches, I do weare everie daye. My will and request is that ther be 10*s.* in money, or bread, bestowed upon the poore upon the daye of my burial. Also I will that there be bestowed in a banket upon my fellowes and frendes the daye of my buryall, 6*s.* 8*d.* [Pr. March 31, 1582.]

INVENTORY OF CHRISTOPHER FORSTER.

Feb. 15, 1580/1. Inventory. Christofer Foster of Darlingtone.[1] *The Hall:* 7 silver spoons, 25*s.*, 6*l.* 13*s.* 4*d.* *The Greate Chamber:* A led mal, a staffe and a jacke, 3*s.* *The Litle chamber, etc. The*

---

[1] Christopher Forster's will is dated Jan. 18, 1580/1.

Inner chamber: All his apparell, 30s. A broade stall of 3 bords for sellinge of fleshe, 20d. *The parlour .beneth the hall, etc. The Buttrye, etc. The Kitchin:* One bedstede, 2 linsey wolsey sheets, a brake, a tub, a swingling and a siff, 6s. A wrist stone, a tub, a maskfat, a chiese presse, a gimlet and a litle siffe, 5s. All the shopgere, 6s. 8d.

He owes : To his eldfather, Georg Fenny, 4l. To Georg Dodsworth of Jolby, 50s. To my sister Maw and her children, 4l. John Clesby of Clesby owes him 9s. 6d. Widow Burnet of Brekhouse, 26s. John Burnet, 6s. 8d. Marmaduke Batmansone, 10s. 10d. John Crathorn of Darlington, 2s. 8d. Francis Parkinsone of Whessey, 14s. 6d. Widow Vavisour of Denton, 6s.

Summa bonorum, 34l. 10s. 8d. *Debitorum,* 16l. 7s. 2d.

WILL OF RALPH CATTERICK.

April 23, 1581. Rauphe Catricke of Wolvestone, yeoman. To be buryed within the parishe churche of Billingham. To Rauphe Catricke,[1] my elldeste sone, and his heires my messuages, cotages, lands, etc., in Wolvestone (except the messuage and lands I boughte of Mr. Claxton and by me gevene to my sone William Catricke), two goledd stottes, etc. To my sone, William Catricke, two branded stotts, one brocked stotte, two kye called Goldelockes and Prymerose, and one graie meare which I boughte of John Alynne of Foxden. To my sone, Nicolas Catricke, one kowe I boughte of Thomas Laton and one goolded oxe. To my sone in lawe, George Davisone, one kowe called Shevells. My sone in lawe, William Laken. To John Manwel, curate of Billingham, 12d. To Thomas Watson, parishe clarke, 4d. I will the soile or donge aboute my house that my sone Rauphe have that in the fawde garthe and at my coate howses. To my son William, a paire of syles. The plowe heades, stillts and plowe beames aboute my house to be dividid. My son William sole executor. [Pr. March 6, 1581/2.]

[1] The testator's son, Ralph Catrick of Wolveston, made his will April 26, 1591. 'To be buried in Billingham church. I give to my wife, Alison Catrick, all my lands, etc., which came to me by inheritunce in Wolvestone. To my sonne and heire, John Catrick, all my lands and hereditaments (except before excepted) in Wolveston. My daughter, Margaret Catrick, etc. I give to the chappell in Wolveston on gimmer lambe. To the reparinge of Billingham brigg, 2s. I give to every child whome I helped to christen 12d., and to the poore of Wolveston, 2s. To Richard Catrick, my brother's sonne, etc. To John Watsonn, my brother-in-lawe, 10s. To Agnes Lackine, a whie calfe. To my sister, Jane Lackinge, a whie. To every of my sister's three sonnes, 12d. To my curate, John Mandell, 5s. Overseers, George Thorpe and Robert Watsonn.

WILL OF THOMAS SMITH.

July 9, 1581.   Thomas Smith of Old Angarton, yeoman.   I give
my farmhold in Angarton, and my office of baylywick there, unto
my eldest sonne, Cuthbert Smith, with the favourable consent and
good will of the right honorable the earle of Arundell and the Lorde
William Haward, my lande-lordes and good maisters.   I bequeathe
my sonne Cuthbert unto the said right honorable William, Lord
Haward, humbly beseching his honour to be good lord and maister
unto my said sonne ; and failing issue of the said Cuthbert, to my
son, John Smith, and, in default, to my third son, Roger Smith.
I give to my base begotten sonne, Ralph Smith, two younge quies.
I will that Richard Smith, my brother, shall have the tuicon of the
said Ralph and his portion.   My wife, Isabell, to have her hole third
part.   I give the residue to my five children, Cuthbert, John, Roger,
Margaret and Agnes Smith.   Cuthbert Pie of the Abbuy-milne,
Martin Fenwick, and my brother, James Smith, supervisors. [Pr.
March 13, 1581/2.]

[INVENTORY exhibited Sept. 29, 1581.]

WILL OF SIMON WELLBURY.

Aug. 13, 1581.   Symon Welberye of Castle-Eden, gentleman.
To be buried in my parish church of Castle-Eden.   To the poore
people of Castle-Eden, 10s.   To the poore people of Monke Hesselden,
6s. 8d.   To the poore of Shotton, 5s.   To Ralphe Hedworthe and
Christofer, his sonne ; my daughter, Margaret Bone, and hir sonne
John ; William Todd ; John Welberie, sonne of my sonne Philipp
Welberie ; Symond Welberie, sonne to my sonne John Welberie ;[1]
and my sister, Margaret Trolopp, to every of theym one oulde riall.
To Mrs. Conyares, wife to Mr. Richard Cònyars, and to Symond
Welberie, sonne to Phillip, to eyther of theyme one ould ryall.   To
my cosens [sic] Mergery, Isabell, Elizabeth, Barbara and Elliner
Welberie, daughters to my sonne, Anthony Welberie, everie one of
them twentie markes.   To my cosen, Robert Welebrie, sonne to my
sonne, Anthonie Welberie, my title, etc., to the tithe of garbe and
grayne in Harte and North Harte as I have the same of the demise

---

[1] June 8, 1585. Will of John Welbery of St. Ellin Aukland. To be
buryed in the porche of St. Ellin's, wher my wife sittethe. To my sister
Bone, one dowsan of silver spones. Whereas I mayde a lease to my neavye
Toode of certayne tenements in St. Ellin Aukland for the tryall of the title
therof, and a lease of two parts of the demayne, I will he shall resigne the
same to my wife. Also, I borrowed of a gentlewoman fyve marks, and I lent
hir husband as muche. I will, therfore, that th'one shall acquite th'other. I
will that my wife's children shall have ther portions payd whiche is dewe unto
them by ther owen father's will and everye of them 20l. I promysed them ; of
the which I have payd alredye 10l. to William Williamson, my wife's eldest
sonne, and he to have the rest when 21. The rest to Symonde and Tymothy
Welbery, my two children, and Dorothy, my wife, they executers. My
brothers Anthony and Phillippe Welbery and my neavye William Todde,
supervisors.

and graunt of Mr. Thomas Cotton, esquire. To my sonnes, Phillipp
and John Weiberie, 40*l*. apiece, *i.e.*, to eyther of theym 20 marks,
in the handes of Henrie Bulmer, gentleman, which he oweth me
for a geldinge. To my sonne, Phillipp Welberie, one annuitie of
3*l*. 6*s*. 8*d*. and a yearlie rent of 53*s*. 4*d*. which I have heretofore
gyven him out of Castle Eden. The residue to my cosens, Robert
and John Welberie, sons of my sonne Anthony: they executors.
And I make my said sonne Anthony their gardien. Witnesses,
Charles Vicars, clerke, Thomas Spark. [Pr. 1583.]

WILL OF MICHAEL REVELEY.

Aug. 14, 1581. Myckell Reivelye (of Chatton). To be buryed in
the quyer of Chatton. My wife Essabell and my son Thomas
Reivelye. My children, Thomas, Clemens, William, Forton, Essabell,
Elenar and Gennat Reivelye. Stevne Reivelye supervisor.

He owes to the lorde of Haggarston, 30*s*; to the lorde of Morton,
8*s*.; to Thomas Reivelye, 20*s*. [Pr. July 21, 1582.]

WILL OF GYLES ANDERSON.

September 26, 1581. Gyles Andersone (of Newcastle, taylor).
To be buried within the churchyarde of St. Nicholas at the easte end
of the sayd church. All to Jane Anderson, my wife, George, Gyles,
Margerye and Isbell Anderson.

INVENTORY. A glasse caige, 2*d*. On quiver for arrows, 4*d*. 4
hespes of harden yarne, 6*d*. 2 hallings, 16*d*. Two stults and a
trow stone, 6*d*.

In the shope: A shop-borde, 16*d*. On pressinge iron and two
payre of sheares with 3 pinkinge irons, 2*s*. On chiste, 16*d*. A
brydill with two cloge ropes, 4*d*. 2 tubbs and on sea, 12*d*.
Summa, 6*s*.

On quyver of straw withe carten shaftes, 6*d*. 3 chistes and a
stole and a braik, 4*s*. A brandon of iron, 6*d*. A lance, 4*d*.

The Companye of the Taylors is owinge unto me 8*s*. 1*d*.; Mr.
Thomas Swan, 3*s*. 1*d*.; Robert Mytfoord, 7*s*. 4*d*. [Pr. November
29, 1581.]

WILL OF MARTIN LAWSON.

Nov. 15, 1581. Martin Lawson of Bywell, gent.[1] To be buried
in my parishe church of Sanct Andrew, Bywell. To the poor, 30*s*.
To my basse begotten doughter, Margaret Lawson, 10*l*. The rest
to my basse begotten sonne, John Lawson: he executor. My sister,
Barbarye Lawson, and William Asheton, clerk, vicar of Bywell
Andrewe, supervisors. [Pr. 1584.]

---

[1] The will of testator's brother, Edward Lawson of Bywell, is printed in
Wills and Inventories, vol. i. p. 432, and a short pedigree of the family is given
in the new *History of Northumberland*, vol. vi. p. 239.

WILL OF HUGH CLARK.

Nov. 21, 1581. Heughe Clerke of Berwic, milner.[1] To Robert
Cowper, my brother in law, my whole staite and parte of my myll
in Twedmowthe, and my howse in Ratton Raw, *alias* Revensdon,
for tene yeares, paying for the rent unto my sonne, Thomas Clerke,
alias Sawer, and to his mother, Elizabeth Sawer, 30s. per annum :
he a miner.   Eme Johnson, my sister's daughter.   Bartilmew
Cowper, my brother's sonn.   My sister and her children.   Supervisors, my master, Mr. Robert Vernon, and Thomas Sallesbury.
Witnesses, Barnard Vincent, clerk, etc.

WILL OF HENRY AYTON.

Dec. 20, 1581. Henrie Ayton of Newbottle, yeoman.   To be
buryed within the parishe churche of Houghtonne.[2] To the
poore of the parish of Houghton, 20s.   To William Ayton,
my sonne, the leases of my farmholdes in Fyshburne, etc., and
my wife Agnesse Ayton, his mother, shall have the occupation
of it duringe his minoritye, paying 4l. per annum : to take new
leases at the discretion of my wife, my cosinge, Robert Furrowe of
Fyshburne and Christofer Wharton of Offerton : if he die, to come
to Isbell and Barbarye Ayton, my two dawghters.   My will is
that Robert, Agnesse and Jenett Chilton, my children in lawe, shall
have theyr hole portione dewe to theym by the administration of
their father, William Chilton.   To John, *alias* Raynolde, my
bastarde sonne, 6l. 13s. 4d.   My sonne in lawe, Roberte Chilton
. . . . To the amendinge of Newbridge lonninge, 12d.   To William
Ayton, my best coate.   To John Ayton, my seconde coate.   To
William Ayton, one yron chimney whiche was my mother Hobsons,
a porre, two rostinge crookes and a recken crooke.   To Barbarye
Ayton, a millaine brasse potte.   Remainder to my wife and two
daughters.   Supervisors, my cosinges, Christofer Wharton of
Offerton and Robert Farrowe of Fishburne.

WILL OF JOHN WARDLE.

Dec. 23, 1581. John Wardaill, of the parish of Shilbottle. To
be buried in the parish church of Shilbottle. To Marion Clerke,
my sister-in-lawe, a browne quie. To Richard Wardaill and John
Wardaill, either of them a yewe and a lamb at Whitsunday. All
things betwixt Hugh Pallaser and me is cleare and that he can

[1] 1581, Dec. 4. Hew Clarke buried. *Berwick Register.*

[2] 1581/2, Mar. 1. Henry Aiton of Newbottle buried. *Houghton-le-Spring
Register.*

claime or challence nothinge of my wiffe and children hereafterwards. I give the rest of my goods to John Wardaill,[1] Hugh Wardaill, Thomas Wardaill and Agnes Wardaill, my children, whom I make executors ; my wife, however, to have hir thirds to bring up children until lawful years. [Pr. Jan. 25, 1581/2.]

WILL OF ANTHONY PRESTON.

Jan. 5, 1581/2. Anthony Preston of East Murton, gent. To be buried in the parish church of Cundell.[2] I give to Dorothy, my wife, my farmes, etc., at Brontoft. To Marie, my daughter, 20 nobles out of my lease at Yowlethorpe and Melsinbie (?). My sister Curwen, one lode of wheat, one loode of rye and one loode of pease. My cosen, Elinor Curwen, 20 nobles. My cosen, Anne Blakeburne, 40s. My wife and my son Francis executors. Witnesses, Anthony Claxtone, William Chilton. [Pr. June 16, 1582.]

INVENTORY. Feb. 8, 1581/2. A stone stagge, a colt stagge and a graye fillie, 4l. 2 litle graye fillies, 1l. 13s. 4d. A litle bawsant stagge, 1l. 5 maires and 5 foales, 8l. 6s. 8d. 2 ridden horses and 2 maires, 4l. 10s. 2 tweeld boardcloathes, 2 tweelde towells, 5 lynnen board-cloathes and 2 harden boardcloathes, 2l. The apparell of the testator, 6l. 13s. 4d. 2 stilewats, 2 jacks and other furnytor for warr, 2l. Playte : 12 silver spoones, a silver salte with a cover parcell gilt, and a silver pott with a cover, 6l. 13s. 4d. 11 silver spoones, 2l. 4s. Goods at Brountofte, etc., etc.

He owes : To Mr. Thomas Preston, 6l. 13s. 4d. To Mr. William Gravin, 6l. 13s. 4d. To Mr. Mawlbie of Yorke, 1l. 16s. To Dame Clibburne, 11s. To Mr. Swifte, 6l. Funerall expences, 11l. 17s. 9d.

Summa, 329l. 15s. 8d. Debts, 62l. 15s. 8d.

WILL OF GEORGE ELLISON.

Jan. 10, 1581/2. George Elyson of the towne of Newcastell-uppon-Tyne, shippwrighte. To be buryed within the parryshe churche of Alhallowes. To my syster, Margrett Eleson, 50s. To my brother, Stephen Elyson, all my worke-towles and my silver whistle, he to pay unto my wyfe 26s. 8d. ; also 3 paire of breches and a motlleye slope, mye fustian doblett laide wythe lace. To my brother, Andrewe Elyson, all my shepe whyche I have in the

[1] John Wardale held in messuage and husbandland land in Shilbottle in 1585. New *History of Northumberland*, vol. v. p. 427.

The testator's brother, Thomas Wardell, also of the parish of Shilbottle, made his will Aug. 14, 1581. ' To be buried in Shilbottle church. I give all my goods, moveable and unmoveable, to my wife Alice and my two sonnes, Richard and John Wardell, they executors ; my brother, John Wardayle, supervisor.' Proved Oct. 11, 1581.

[2] Cundall, a parish in the West Riding of Yorkshire, six miles from Ripon.

countrye, which ys in nomber eighte or thereabouts. To my brother, Cuthberte Elyson, my blacke doblett laide wythe laice. To my sister, Ann Elyson, 10s. My brother, Jhone Elyson, owes me 20s. Jhone Readheade of Rothberrye do owe me for 2 Frenche cappes, 7s. George Strangwyche doth owe me for a sworde, 16s. I owe unto my Mr. Thomas Smythe 4s. Remainder to my wife, Isabell Elyson, she sole executor. Witnesses, William Liddell, Gerrard Errington, etc. [Pr. March 13, 1581/2.]

[INVENTORY exhibited Mar. 7, 1581/2.]

WILL OF MARTIN GARNETT.

Feb. 17, 1581/2. Martyn Garnett of Barwicke upon Tweed, alderman.[1] To my wife, Agnes Garnett, my farmehold in Buckton, the tower with all things belonging, and all the store upon it; my house wherein I dwell in Barwicke in Marye-gate; the next house to it, wherein nowe Captain Case dwelleth, for her life; and another tenement called the mill-house; another tenement in the Wester-layne wherein Christopher Ogle dwelleth; the lease of a tenement in Marye-gate; my lease of 8 sheete of salmon fishing in the Heugh sheile and 8 sheete salmon fishing in the South Yarrowe dureing my years; my farmhold in Orde, both water and land, which I have of Nicholas Manners. To my sonne, Rowland Garnett, 20l. To my sonne, William Garnett, 10l. To my sonne, Nicholas Garnett, 20l. To my daughter, Jaine Garnett, 100 marks. I will that my wife shall bring up Robert Garnett, the eldest sonne of my sonne Rowland Garnett, if his parents be soe contented, at her proper costs and chardges; and after my death, I will that she shall take in like manner the younger boy, Ralph Garnett. All my lands to the said Robert and his heirs, and failing issue, to my son, Ralph Garnet, and failing issue, to my two daughters, Margaret and Jane and their heirs. To the church in Barwicke, 20s. to buy a carpett to the Communion table. My wife executrix. Supervisors, Mr. Robert Carvill, and my sonne in lawe, Bartilmew Bradforth. To Mr. Robert Carvell, my best horse. To Bartilmew Bradford, the next horse unto my best. To my daughter at Beverley, 6l. 13s. 4d. Witnesses, Thomas Clerke, vicar of Barwicke, Bernard Vincent, clerk. By me Bartholomew Bradforth. [Pr. May 12, 1582.]

Dec. 4, 1653. The original will was delivered to Mr. Ralph Taylor, scrivener, for the use of one Mr. Lewen, merchant in Newcastle, who married one of the daughters of the deceased and had hir sole interest in the said will, as he alledged.

[1] A biography of Martin Garnett, who was a leading public man at Berwick, may be found, Scott, *Berwick-upon-Tweed*, p. 290.

WILL OF JOHN LASSELLS.

March 18, 1581/2. John Lassells, of the towne of Newcastell upon Tyne, marchannte.[1] My bodye to be buryed wethein my parishe churche of Sancte·Nicholas in Sancte George porche soo nyghe my wyffe, Anne Lassells, there buryed as convenyentlie maye be. To the poore men's boxe of my sayd parishe churche, to be distributed to the poore at the discretion of the churchewardens, 3s. 4d. To my sonne, George Lassells of Darlington, my beste gowne faced with blacke budge, my beste dublett of satten, my blacke chamlett jackett, garded with velvett, 16 silver spoynes with lyons on there ends, 1 white sylver peece, 1 standinge bedd of waynescott, 1 flanders chiste, 1 chiste of waynescott, and a dubblett of blacke worsett. To my doughter, Margarete Sheiles, 2 sylver spoynes, 2 payre of lynnen sheits, 1 flanders chiste and 10s. To my doughter, Elizabethe Tennand, 2 sylver spoynes and 10s. To my doughter, Anne Casson of Houghton, 2 silver spoynes, 1 paire of lynnen sheates and 10s. To my servannte, Elizabethe Donne, one fether bead, with one paire of blanckettes, one paire of sheates and 1 paire of coverlettes, and also 13s. 4d. To Anne Lassells, wedowe, 3s. 4d. All the reste of my goodes to my sonne, William Lassells, whome I doo make my executor; he to ordayne and dyspoyne the same to the pleasure of Almyghtie God as he shall thinke beste. And I doo ordayne and make my welbeloved in Christe, Mr. William Selbye, alderman, supervisor of this my laste will and testamente, desyringe hym for the love of God, and as my speciall truste ys in hym, to see this my said will probate and putt in execution accordinge to my trewe meaninge, and I doo gyve unto hym for a small token one olde angell. Wytnesses, Edward Collingwood, William Chamber. [Pr. Oct. 16, 1582.]

WILL OF MATHEW WILKINSON.

April 18, 1582. Mathewe Welkensonn of Newcastle, smethe. To be buryede within the churche of All Hallowes. To my wife, Elizabeth Welkenson, the house I dwell in. To my daughter, Elizabeth Welkinson, my two tennements at the Lyme-kelles. To my sonne, Roberte Welkensonne, my lands in Tendaill, in a place called the Fawleye within the barrendrye of Warke. Residue to my wyfe, Elizabeth Welkeson, Robert Welkenson, my sonne, and Elizabeth Welkenson, my doughter, whom I appoint executors; they thre to dispounde the same to the pleasure of God. [Pr. March 26, 1583.]

[1] John Lassels was apprenticed, Feb. 2, 1527, to Thomas Horsley of Newcastle, and was admitted free of the Merchant's Company circa 1536. Dendy, Newcastle Merchant Adventurers, vol. ii. p. 189. He was sword-bearer of the Corporation of Newcastle. Cf. Welford, Newcastle and Gateshead, index.

INVENTORY. 2 heedsheets, 2s. 4 cod pillyvers, 18d. A demye with head and tache and a paire of croukes, 17s. *The brewhouse:* A wortt-tub, a guylle fatt and a masken fatte, 4s. 5 standes, 20d., a seye, 2 washinge tubes, 20d. A brewinge cawdronne, 5s. 4d. A seive, 5s. A wheye, 10s. *The Shope:* 3 score 16 dossen showlles, 5l. 10s. 8 grett hammers, 4s. 4 up and downe hammers, 4s. 7 small hammers, 3s. 4d. 4 stand spike bores, 5s. A duble-take boie, a singel-take bore, 2 heckenall bors, 2 tengell bors, 2 takett bores and a small tangell bore, and a lednall bore, 3s. 4d. 8 payer fyer tonges, 4 hewers and 24 punches, 4s. 2 paire of penchers, 8d. 3 bowlsters, 5 small boulsters, 12d. 2 half quarter C. wyghts, on 10 *li.* wyghte, on 7 *li.*, on 5 *li.*, on 4 *li.*, on 3 *li.*, on 2 *li.*, on *li.* and half a *li.* 3s. 4d. 2 grendstones with trowes, 12d. Irron stedye with an irron byker, 6s. 8d. A casten sledye, 8s. 2 paire of bellyses, 14s. a paire of new bredes with a skene to cover thym, 6s. 8d. *Summa,* 8l. 19s. Mr. Robert Errington owes him 18s. 7d. He owes to John Shaftow, 3l. 6s. 9d. To Fraunces Anderson, 33s. 11d. For his buryall, 12s. 6d. His chiste and the makinge, 5s. His forthe bringinge, 14s. 2d. Etc.

WILL OF THOMAS HARRISON.

April 26, 1582. Thomas Harryson, parish of St. Marie's, in the North Balie [Durham], singingman, beinge longe before this tyme visited with extreme sicknes, the messenger of my mercifull God wherebie to put me in remembraunce what I am, yet beinge of mynde, manner and forme followinge. First, I gyve and bequeath my soule unto Almightie God, trustinge that by the blodie deathe of that sweete Saveyor Jesus Christe, I shalbe one of those that he, at the last day, shall say unto 'Come unto me ye blessed of my Father and inherite the Kingdome which is prepared for you,' and my bodie to be buryed in the Gallolie as nie my uncle, Mr. Bromley, as may be. My welbeloved wyfe, Barbarie. To my sonne, John Harrison, 100l. and my gould ringe for a token, which weigheth an ounce, and my blessing withal, and my will is that he and his porcion, when he commeth to the age of 12 yares, shalbe delyvered unto my worshipfulle frende, Mr. John Clopton, esquier. To my sonne, Christofer Harrison, 100l., and for a token I gyve hym a dozen and a halfe of silver buttons, with my blessing withal—my good cosyn and frend, Mr. Oswold Carr of Newcastle, merchaunt, to have him. To my daughters, Margaret and Barbarie Harrison, 80l. each. Also I gyve to amend our churche stock 5s., trustinge that the parishioners will fynde meanes that I may have my money paid to my wife I have laid out for the building of the newe house. To the poore of our parishe, 6s. 8d.; South Bailie, 3s. 6d.; St. Nicholas, 6s. 8d.; St. Oswoldes, 6s. 8d.; St. Margaretts, 6s. 8d.; St. Gyles, 6s. 8d. Also, I gyve unto the pant, 10s., to be bestowed

theron as the alderman for the tyme beinge shall thinke convenient.
To my aunte Barbarie, one old angell.   To my cosyne, William
Haryson of Rabie, one old angell.   To my brother Wardhaugh,
my blewe coote and my lether dublett—his wife, son Thomas and his
daughters Elynor,' Janet and Barbarie . . . .   To Thomas Humble,
my newe canvesse dublett, my blacke britches and a crowne of
goulde, trustinge that yf he chaunce to be a townes man he will
have care of my children to see theme do well, as I have had of
hym.   Supervisors, the right worshipfull Mr. Doctor Burton, Mr.
John Clopton, Mr. Christofer Chaitor and Oswolde Carr, and I gyve
unto every one of theme one old angell a pece.   To my gossopp,
Symon Comyne, one Frenche crowne.

WILL OF JOHN SOTHERAN.

May 16, 1582.   John Sotheran, of the towne of Newcastell upon
Tyne, marchant.   To be buried in the church of Sancte Nicholas.[1]
The howse I dwell in to Florence, my wife, for hir lyfe, and then
to my sonne, Thomas Sotheran, and his heirs; then to my sonne
Nicholas and his heirs : then to my sonne John and his heirs.
Whereas my brother, William Sotheran, upon ane olde reckening
dothe owe me 20*l.*, I give it to his fowre sonnes, Rowlande, Roger,
Robert and Cuthbert.   To my nevew, William Sotherane servant to
Mr. George Lawson, 6*l.* 13*s.* 4*d.*, if he do not troble my heres or
executors for his executorship unto my father in law, Robert
Robenson.   To my sonne, Thomas Sotheran, and his heres my tene-
ment and close in Gateshed.   To my pore neghbores, being hows-
holders, 40*s.*   To my brother, William Sotheran, for a token, 10*s.*
To his wife, 6*s.*   To my brother in lawe, Rafe Harle, 10*s.*, and to
my lovinge sister, his wife, 6*s.*   To my nevew, James Harle, my
apprentice, 3*l.* 6*s.* 8*d.*   To my neece, Margarete Harle, 3*l.* 6*s.* 8*d.*
George Armarer owes me 10*l.*   To Leonard Harle, an olde angell.
To Mr. Nicholas Hedley, one old angell.   To Mrs. Hedley, his loving
wife, one Frenche crowne.   To my cosen, Thomas Horsley, 20*s.*
To my frend, John Watson, 10*s.*   The remainder to my wife and
five children.   [Pr. June 13, 1583.]
[INVENTORY exhibited July 3, 1582.]

WILL OF JOHN GALLON.

Aug. 25, 1582.   John Gallon of Alnewicke, gentleman.   To be
buried within the church of Saint Michaell in Alnewicke as nighe
my father, Pervicall Gallon, where he lyeth, and my other brethren

---

[1] The testator was buried at St. Nicholas's, May 19, 1582 ; his two daughters,
Agnes and Florence, were under age at the time of their father's death. *Cf.*
Welford, *Newcastle and Gateshead*, vol. iii. p. 12. The inventory of his goods
is printed in *Wills and Inventories*, vol. ii. p. 68.

and sisters. To William Gallon, my sonn (a minor), and his heires male, my lands, burgage and earable, etc., in myne owne occupation and free purchase of Mr. George Middleton of Silkesworth, co. Durham, gent., within the towne and feilds of Alnewick; failing him, to my son Cuthbert Gallon (a minor) and his heirs male; remainder to Edward Gallon (a minor), sonne of William Gallon,[1] my elder brother son ; remainder to the daughters of my son, William Gallon ; remainder to the daughters of my son, Cuthbert Gallon ; remainder to Alice Gallon, my daughter. My wife, Jane Gallon, to pay 20*l*. to Cuthbert, my son, when he comes of age. To my wife, my terme of yeares of the quarter of the tieth corne and sheaves of corne of Emelden. My daughter Alice (a minor): Jane Gallon, my brother William's wife. Isabell Gallon, my brother William's daughter. John Ellicar. George Forster of Newham and his wife. I give to Edward, son of John Gallon of Alnwick, two young nouts, my wife to bring him up. Edward Gallon, my brother's son, his land at Trewick. Residue to my wife. Mr. Cuthbert Collingwood and Mr. Cuthbert Forster, supervisors.

WILL OF GAWEN ROTHERFORTHE.

Sept. 16, 1582. Gawen Rotherforth of Rochester, parish of Ovingham, esquier. To be buried in my parishe churche or chancell. All my goods, etc., to Margarett, my wiff, and she sole executrix, to order and dispound my goods to the health of my soule by the counsell and consent of my brother in lawe, David Carnaby, and my sonne in law, Thomas Ereington of Beukeley whom I make my supervisors. My children to have there porcions fryndley without suite of lawe. Also I will that my daughter Grace's porcion be maid 40*l*. Witnesses, Thomas and John Routherforth and Thomas Herington.

[INVENTORY exhibited Oct. 5, 1582.]

WILL OF THOMAS BARROW.

Sept. 29, 1582. Thomas Barrowe, quartermaster serveinge in Berwicke upon Twede. To be buried in the church-yarde. My cosen, Thomas Hogben, lait souldier in Berwick and nowe dwellinge

---

[1] A pedigree of the family of Gallon of Alnwick is given in the new *History of Northumberland*, vol. ii. p. 486.

The testator's brother, William Gallon of Alnwick, made his will Nov. 4, 1574. 'To be buried in the parish church of St. Michael. I give my land in Trewick (Trewitt) and my son Edward to my brother, John Gallon, till my said son be of age. I give my daughter, Beyll Gallon, to my sister, Margaret Forster, the old good wife of Newham. My brother, John Gallon, and my uncle, John Gallon, executors. Rauf Collingwood of Sheiply, supervisor.' Pr. Dec. 16, 1574.

Two early deeds relating to the Middleton property at Alnwick are printed in *Arch. Ael.* vol. xxv. pp. 74, 77.

in Kent, my executor, and I give him all, and he to kepe my daughter, Ursulea Russell, with sufficient meat, drinke and apperrell as an honest man's child ought to be found; and if her husband, John Russell, be deade, or that she can gett a devorsement from her husband, the said Thomas do see her honestlie bestowed in mariage upon some honest man. To Mrs. Larkin, 10s. To Thomas Savage, my best cloke. To John Selbie, horseman, 5s. To my cosin, George Hamon, dwellinge in Kent in the parish of Hearonhill, 5l. My cosen, George Hamon's thre sonnes, Adam, John and Christopher, 20l. each.

WILL OF JANE AYNSLEY.

Oct. 6, 1582. Jane Aineslye, late wyffe to William Ainesley of Bradforth, parish of Bolam, beinge in this time of God his visitacion in good and perfect remembrance. To be buried within the church earth of Bolam. To Robert Rochester of West Whelpington, 10s. To his sister, Janet Rochester, 10s. To his sister, Isabell Rochester, 10s. To my brother, Martyn Atcheson, 10s. The rest of my goods to my good maister, Marmaduke Fenwick, whom I make my executor and supervisor, desyreing him to dispone thes goods amongst my brethren and poore friends. Witnesses, Marmaduke and Roger Fenwick, John Cutter and William Heaton. [Pr. Feb. 15, 1582/3.]

WILL OF WILLIAM BURRELL.

Oct. 10, 1582. Wylliam Borralle (of Chatton). To be burryd in the churche yearde of Chatton. Robert Atcheson, John Brown, Jennat Borrale, my wyff, and Essabelle Elder my executors. Witnesses, Edward Cowston, vicar, etc.

He owes to Mr. Thomas Forster 14s. and to John Revelye 3l. 4s. 4d.

WILL OF THOMAS CRANE.

Oct. 18, 1582. Thomas Crane of Crawhaull. I give to Agnes, my wyfe, the thyrd of my lands and goods. I give to Elizabeth Crane, my daughter, the yerlie somme of 10s. out of Caughton [sic] in Hexhamshire. To each of the children of Margarett Ledall, my sister, 3s. 4d. To each of the children of Katherin Awgood, my sister, 3s. 4d. To Nycholas Rydley of Wyllimonstswyke, esq., 3l. 6s. 8d. To John Crane, sonn unto Jhon Crane of Barwyck, my black humbled cowe. To Thomas Rydley, the wrighter hereof, 6s. 8d. To Nicholas Rydley, sonn unto William Rydley of Leehouse (?), 6s. 8d. To eyther of the two daughters of Luce Heron, my daughter, 6s. 8d. To Alexander Rydley, my grene venecon hosse.

To my sonn, Nycholas Crane, my black nagg, sadell, brydle, jack, sword, etc. The marriadge of my sonn, Nycholas Crane,[1] to be att the discrecion of Nycholas Rydley, esquier, and Mr. William Vauxe most earnestlie desyringe at ther hands that they wylle a staye unto hym, remayninge with his mother, and with ther good councell, agde and assistance, to be a meane thatt he be keptt and mayntayned att scoole and in the travell of good learninge. The remainder to my children, viz., Mare, Barbare, Elsabeth, Margret and Jayne Crayne, my daughters.

NUNCUPATIVE WILL OF RICHARD CLIFF.

Memorandum that Rychard Clyffe, layt of the South salt pannes, neire to the South Sheiles of the parish of Jarro, of the diocess of Durisme, now deceased, whylst he lyved beinge of good and perfytte remembrannce, the 5th day of December last, 1582, mayd and declared his testament and last wyll nuncupative, before certeine honest witnesses herunder named in maner followinge, in effect *videlicet*, I gyve my sonne, John Clyffe, and my boote to the sayd John his use, unto you, Thomas Bridggs, here present. And he then declared that he had payed unto Mr. Edward Taylor 20*l*. and declared that he had had the occupation also of a close for certeine yeares for redeminge of a salt panne that was morgashed to hym by one John Carre ; and sayd that the sayd Edward owed to him xiii[en] foure chaulders of cooles. He also sayd : Executors of my last wyll and testament I constitute and make Elynor Clyffe, my wyffe, and my sonne John Clyffe, and doe praye my sayd wyffe to be good to my sayd sonne, John Clyffe. Whyche woordes or the lyke in effecte he sayd, spoke, declared and wylled to be done, and constituted executors as above, the daye and year abovesayd in the presence of Stephane Kaye, Thomas Bridggs and Alyce Wallas.

WILL OF RICHARD CRAWFORD.

Dec. 2, 1582. Rychard Crawforthe of Headlame. To be buried within the parishe church of Gainforthe.[2] To the church, 3*s*. 4*d*. To my sonne, Christofer Crawforthe, all my right, etc., of all my leases and tenements. To Sythe Garthe, one of my brother Thomas his doughters, 6*l*. 13*s*. 4*d*. To Jennett, wyffe of Anthone Garthe, Agnes, wyffe of Thomas Hoodde, and Margaret, wyffe of George Wetherald, 10*s*. each. To my brother Thomas Garth's daughters, Margaret, Jenett and Anne, a bushell of hardcorn each. To the poore, 20*s*.

---

[1] Nicholas Crane of Crawhall, in the parish of Haltwhistle, in 1615, on the marriage of his daughter Margaret with Ralph Clavering of Bowsden, settled upon them and their issue his lands at Crawhall, Bradley-hall, Housesteads, Thorngrafton, etc. Hodgson, *Northumberland*, pt. ii. vol. iii. p. 329.

[2] 1582/3, Feb. 19. Richard Crawforth buried. *Gainford Register.*

I will that my brother, Sir Robert Crawforthe,[1] shall have one chamber and meatt and drynke duringe his lyffe of the proper costes of my sonne Christofer, yf it please him to be so contended, and to use him as his lovinge and naturall unckle, as my trust is that he wyll do. Robert Shipsyde, one of my sister Jaine's sonnes, 13s. 4d. Remainder to Christofer my sonne and George Crawforthe, his son. Anthonie Garthe and Thomas Hoodd, my sonnes in law, supervisors. Witnesses, Ambrose Lancaster, Wylliam Elwyne, Rychard Garthe, Cuthbert Garthe, Richard Crawforthe. [Pr. April 20, 1583.]

WILL OF THOMAS CORBY.

Dec. 7, 1582. Thomas Corbye, of hir Majestie's towne of Barwicke counstable. I give to my servante, Elynor Kitchyne, a flecked calfe, my freesse cloocke of Newcastle frease, etc. I give to my daughter, Margaret Reade, my best cloocke that my lord of Bedfoord gave me. To my son, Thomas Corbye, my dune horse with a read sadle and bridle. Residue to my son in law, John Read and Margaret, his wife. [Pr. Feb. 18, 1582/3.]

WILL OF RICHARD HUTTON.

Dec. 31, 1582. Richard Hutone, maior of the towne of Hartillpole. To be buryed in the churche of Sainct Hilde in Hartillpole in the mydd halleye before the quiere dore. To Richard Hutone, the eldeste son of William Hutone, my sone, my burgage in Hartillpole in Southe Streite to him and his heirs; then to John Hutone, second son of William Hutone. To everye one of my children, William, George, Margaret and Agnes Hutone, 10s. Remainder to Isabel Hutone, my wife—she executrix.[2] My brother, John Hutone, supervisor. Witnesses, John Browne, allderman, John Stappltone, clarke, etc. [Pr. Feb. 6, 1582/3.]

[1] June 26, 1583. Will of Robert Crawforthe of Whitworth, clerke. If God call me to his mercie here at Whitworth, I will that my bodye be buried in the quere of the parisshe churche ther. To the reparinge of the seyd churche, 6s. 8d. To the poore of Billingham parishe, 10s. To the poore of Gaynforth parisshe, wher I was borne, 10s. To Thomas Garthe, his foure daughters yet lyvinge, everye of theom, 5s. To Christofer Crawforthe, my brother's sonne, his thre systers, everye of theim, 5s. To Elizabeth Lynne, widow, my cosinge . . . . My (late) brother, Richard Crawforth. Christofer, my seyd brother's son.

The following is the will of a kinsman: Sept. 8, 1583. Edward Lynne of Whitworth. To be buried within the queire very neare wheare my mother laie. To Robert Crawforth, a angell of golde to praie for me. To the aiged poore people, penie daile; also, I gyve my godchildren 12d. a peice, and to those children whiche I held under the busshope, every on 12d. a pece.

[2] The will of the testator's widow, Isabell Huton of Hartillpole, is dated Mar. 8, 1583/4. 'To be buryed within the churche of Sanncte Hilde in Hartillpole, nigh unto the grave of my late husbande, Richarde Huton. My sons, George and William Huton. My son-in-lawe, Rauffe Thompson, and Ann his wife, my daughter. My son-in-lawe, Gilbert Nicollsone.' Pr. 1584.

WILL OF ROBERT FORSTER.

Jan. 19, 1582/3. Robert Foster, clarke, vicare of Dalton.[1] **My**
bodie to be buried in the quere of Dalton hard at the outsyde of the
wall of my clossett. Also I bequithe to my servante, Beale Dunne,
one brandid quye that wente at Shotton, a cawell, 2 puther dysshes,
a bedd of clothes, my best brasse pott sayf one, hir whole yeare
waiges, a kyrcher and two bourds to maike hir a chist upon. Allso
I geve to Jenett Ranoldsonne, my old servant, two kyne, one called
Throssell and the other Chyrry, a wyndowe clothe, the beste hewed
coverlett I have, a tempes, two longe bourds, a puther platter and a
great tre dubler. Allso I geve to John Ranoldsonne a browne
upheaded stot goinge in the northe feild, a dune horse, thre paire of
house syles and other wood that ys att Hesselden, a dossinge doore
bourds, a newe cowpe wayne, a paire of longe wayne blayds, and thre
axell trees, and two of the best mowlde bowrds, halffe my plewghe
heads and halfe my plewghe styltes, a newe plewghe, half of my
clethinge bowrds, and two yoicks whiche was bowghte of Thomas
Yonge of Morton. Also I geve to Allesonne Ranoldsonne, wife of
John Ranoldsonne of Hawthorne, a brandid quie with calfe. Also
I geve to Dorathye Dune, *alias* Allay of Sehame, fowre gymbers
or yews. Also I geve to Agnesse Dunne, to Elizabethe Dunne and
to Brydgitt Donne, everye one of theyme a gymbre. Also I gyve to
Robert Robinsone two oxen, one called Brownebeird and th'other
Prowdlocke, and my cropp growynge upon the grownde att Dalton,
and a paire of longe wayne blaydes. Also I gyve to Agnesse Robynson, wife of Robert Robynsonne of Dalton, a almerie, a peuther
charger, a great pott, a basynge and a bedde. Also I geve to William
Thomson of Hawthorne my warday gowne. Also I geve to Jenett
Ranoldsone 10 shepe. Also I geve to John Ranoldsonne of Hawthorne 10 shepe. I geve to Robarte Robinsone of Dalton 10 shepe.
I give to my goodsone, Robarte Fall of Dalton, my beste bowe of
ewe. Also I give to John Foster of Hesselden, my brother, one
yocke of my beste oxen unbequithed. I give to John Ranoldsone one
quarter of wheate, one quarter of otes and one lode of pees, to be
delivered presentlye after my deathe. I will that my executor shall
give yearlye durynge the tearme of five yeares, to beginge att
Chrystenmasse next after my deathe, to the poore of Dalton parishe
4s., which in the whole ys 20s. to be distributed as aforesaid. I gyve
to George Fell of Ryop 3l., in recompence of certen tougher which
he clameth of my brother, John of Hesselden, and to his wyfe and
children, 20s., which some of 5l. 2s. in the said George Fell hand.
The reste of my goods, moveable and unmoveable, unbequythed, my
debts paide, my legaces and al things in my will and testament discharged, I gyve yt to John Foster of Hessleden, my brother, to

---

[1] Called *Richard* Forster in the list of vicars of Dalton printed by Mr.
Surtees in his *History of Durham*, vol. i. pt. ii. p. 3.

Richard Foster, to Thomas Foster and Robert Foster, his sonnes, whome I mayke whole and joynte executors of this my laste will and testament. Witnesses, Thomas Yonge and Anthonie Downne of Morton, Robart Sharpe and John Shaldfoorthe of Hesselden, William Toodd and George Dayle of Dalton, Peter Thorpe of Dalton, and Thomas Easterbye, clarke, vicarre of Sehame, wythe others. [Pr. Feb. 9, 1582.]

NUNCUPATIVE WILL OF JOHN SMITH.

John Smith of Shercborne, within the parrish of Pittington, deceased, in the yere of our Lord God 1582/3, the 24th daye of Januarii, did utter his mind at divers tymes concerninge his last will and testament, both before he was sicke, and also lyinge upon his deathe-bedd, as followeth: First he did say to William Shauld-forth of Sherborn, long before he was sicke, that Allyson Smith, his wyfe, should have all his goods that he had, duringe hir lyfe, and that after hir death all the saide goods should come to George Smyth and Isabell Thropp, whome they had brought upp and which did helpe them in theire nede, and did make them two sole executors of the same to theire owne proper use and commoditye. And at an outher tyme he did speake the same words to Herry Cooke and Thomas Cooke of Shereborne, and upon his death-bedd, a little before he dyed, he spake the same to Thomas Dobson of Shereborne. All which said persons will testyfye the truth hereof upon there othes when nede shall require.

INVENTORY. 27 April, 1585. One ould ambre and one chawwell, 2s. Two chists, 2s. One ould and one borde, 7d. Fower stoles to syt on, 4d. Two bras pots, 6s. One kettell and two lytle pans, 2s. 10d. Eyght peace of puder and two lytle sawcers and one salte puder, 5s. One candelstycke, 8d. Two coverleds, 5s. One lynnynge shete and two lynnynge towels, 3s. 8d. Two lynnynge kyrthchers (?) and two lynnyng rayles, 22d. Eyght other ould lynnyng clothes, 23d. Two ould cod pillowes of lynnynge, 9d. Fyve ould harne shete, 3s. 8d. To harne aprans and one ould borde clothe, 8d. Seven ould cods, 8d. Thre woman's coots and one ould clokke and ould waystcoote and one payre of sleves, 5s. 8d. Thre ould skrede happins, 8d. Certayne wood vessell, 3s. One spinnyng whele and thre payre of ould cayrds and thre baskets, 10d. Fyve ould pockes, 7d. One hallinge clothe and fower ould bords, 8d. One rackkin croke, one hatchet, one payre of iron tongs and iron bars, 12d. Two hens and lytle chikkens, 8d.

WILL OF GEORGE TOPIAS.

Jan. 30, 1582/3. George Topias of Busshopweremouthe, yeoman. To be interred in the churche of the said Wermouthe under my owne stall where commonlie I used to sitte. To the poore of the parishe of Tinmouth, to be distributed to them in bread, 3s. 4d. To the poore of Washington parishe, in like manner, 3s. 4d. To the poore of Munckewermouth and Busshopweremouth, likewise, 3s. 4d. each. To the repayringe of the churche of Busshopweremouth, 2s. 6d., forgevynge the said church 4s. which it was indetted unto me at the makinge herof. To the poore of Standwrope parishe, 3s. 4d. To the poore of Barnard-castell parishe, where my father is interred, 20s. To the poore of Gainforthe parishe, where my mother [1] is interred, 20s. To John Bell, my sworde and dagger. To Richard Thomsone, my wives sonne, 19s. My brother, Thomas Topias. To Francis Topias, son of William Topias, my bowe of two peaces. Jane Topias, his daughter. My brother William's children. To the three children of John Craddocke, 2s. 3d. a peice. To my brother Craddocke, 2s. 8d. [Pr. March 9, 1582/3.]

WILL OF JOHN HORSLEY.

Jesus. March 17, 1582/3. John Horsleye of Milburne Grainge, gentleman.[2] To be buried within the parisshe churche of Pontyland. All my goods, etc., I give to Lancelotte Horsleye, the sonne of Lamerocke Horslye, my sonne, of Newhame, and my said sonne Lamrocke to have the tuition of him. I make the said Lancelote my executor. Oswould Ogle of Shilvingetonne, gentleman, supervisor. Also I will that myne executour deliver unto Robart Horsley, the sone of Edmund Horseleye, my sonne, departed, seaven heade of nawte. Witnesses, Oswould Ogle and Lamrocke Horseleye.

WILL OF JOHN BROWN.

May 3, 1583. John Browne of Newcastell, armorer. To be buryed in the church-yard of St. John. To my doughter, Anne Browne, my howse that I nowe dwell in. To my sonnes, John and Henrye Browne, the shop that is in my howse to worke in. To my sonne John, the greate vise, the study and the belles, and my sonnes John and Henrie to have all the shope geare, viz., iron stufe, plates, harmes, crosbowes and gonnes. To my sonne John, a chiste with the fyer locks therein, a payr of hose of buffe leather, a jerken to the same and a bufe skyne of lether. To my sonne Henrie and his heires, my howse which standethe nere the Whit Crose in the Neate Market, the leser vise in my shop and a bufe jerkin. My brother William Browne, my work-day apparell. My mylne in New Heton to

---

[1] 1577, July 23. Widow Topias buried. *Gainford Register.*

[2] The testator purchased Milburn Grange, Aug. 23, 1566, from Bertram Anderson of Newcastle. His name heads the pedigree of Horsley of Bolam given in Hodgson, *Northumberland*, pt. ii. vol. i. p. 335.

my children. My welbeloved frends, William Errington, gent., and Thomas Browne, tayler, supervisors. Names of those which are indepted unto me : Sir George Radclyef, knight, 38s. ; Martyn Trotter, 53s. 4d. ; Humfreye Graye, 6s. 8d. ; Mr. Francis Ralclief, 6s. ; Thomas Atkinson, 21s. 6d. ; Mr. Thomas Gascoyne, 12s. [Pr. June 10, 1583, by Anne Brown the widow.]

WILL OF WILLIAM BLENKINSOPP.

June 14, 1583. William Blenkinsop, clerk, one of the peti canons within the cathedrall churche of Durham.[1] My bodye to be buried within the cathedrall churche as nighe where as my brother, Rowland Blenkinsop, was buried as may be. To the poore people, within the citie of Durham there as most needing, 40s. To my sister, Alleson Myllott, widow, 10l. To Davie Taylior, my syster's sonne, 10l. To Anthony Taylior, my systers sonne, 10l. To Agnes Neyle, 3l. 6s. 8d. To John Bucles, 5s. To William Foster, 6s. 8d. To William Smythe, clerke, one old ryall of 15s. To Richard Johnson, one old yaungell of 10s. To Beale and Francis Wright, children to William Wright, marcer, 5s. betwen them. To Richard Buckels, sonne to John Buckels, 5s. To Elizabeth Buckles, syster to the said Richard, 3s. 4d. To everye peti canon within the cathedrall churche, 12d. a peace. To everie of the lay singinge men ther, 8d. a peace. To the master of the choristers, 12d., and to everie chorister, 4d. a peace. To Robert Skepper, 5s. To Myles White, 3s. 4d. To John Haykins, 12d. To everie of the poore men, 6d. To the bell ringers of the said church, for makinge my grave and such thinges as they have to do for me, 6s. 8d. To Roger Malham, 5s. I will that my bookes shalbe geven and distributed as the said William Smyth, clerke, Davie Taylior and Richard Johnson shall thinke good, so that some of them be bestowed of Christofer Mallam. Also, whereas George Jobson oweth me 5l., I gyve that debte to Edward Jobsone, his sonne. To William Walton, my godson, 6s. 8d. To John Robinson, his wife, 10s., and to Suzane Robinsonne, my goddoghter, 3s. 4d. To the said Davie Taylior my soulden sylver spone, and to Alis Taylior, his wife, one old ryall of 15s. To Margaret, wife to the said Anthony Taylior, one other sylver spone. The residue of my goodes, etc., to the said Alleson Myllot, my sister, Davie and Anthony Taylior, my sister's sonnes, whom I make executors.

[1] A minor canon of the cathedral of Durham, whose bequests betoken more good feeling towards the 'inferior members' than towards the 'dignified clergy' of that body. He may possibly have been one of the family of Blenkinsop settled at Birtley. His sister had been married to a Millot, another Chester-le-Street name ; her husband was perhaps a humble member of the house of Whitehill Millots.

WILL OF WILLIAM BELL.

July 15, 1583. William Bell of B̓enwell, yeoman, of good and perfect memorie, I prayse God for yt, and yeat visited with syknasse, God comforte me. To be buried in St. John's church-yarde, where my ellders lyethe buried. To Thomas Bell, my sonne, one baye mare that usethe to goe in the wayne, beynge about syx years of age. I give my farmes to Agnes, my wyff, durynge hir lyff. Thomas Bell, my younger sonne. Margaret Bell, daughter of Robert Bell, my sonne, deceased.

WILL OF WILLIAM SHELL.

July 24, 1583. William Shell of Alnewicke, merchant.[1] I bequeath my sowle to Almightie God, my Creator, and to Jesus Chryst, my Redemer, whose death and passion I acknowledge to be only sufficient for my salvation : assured herof by the earnest of God's Spirit who hathe regenerate me into a most certeine and lively hoape of the blessed immortalitie. And I will that my bodie be buried in the churche of Alnewicke with such reverence and rites as are now used in the Church of England. My wyfe Agnes executrix. [Pr. 1584.]

INVENTORY OF JOHN SHAFTO.

Oct. 4, 1583. INVENTORIE. John Shafto of Newcastell, marchante. Praised by Wylliam Greenwell, Mathewe Chepman, Rauffe Coxe and Frances Andersonn, marchants. 1 small cowbartt with a fleare and on presse for napkins, 10s. On bassinge and on ewer and 8 dansk potes, 26s. 8d. 2 panted hallinges and a . . . . , 3s. 8d. On . . . . croke, on lydginge yrone, 2s. 6 cushings, nott stoped, 16s. 4 danske chestes, 20s. *The shoppe :* 69 shepe skenes, 3l. 3 laste of flaxe, 75l. 38 ends yron wes, 110 stone, 6l. 2d. Owtome towe and 37 dossen and a haufe hempe 8l. 3s. 4d. 7 hauffe pots off James F . . . . , 3s. 10d. One danske cheste, etc.

WILL OF JOHN HIND.

Oct. 8, 1583. John Hind of the Houshell Fourd, within the forast of Stanhope and in the county of Durham, yeaman. My body to be reverently inhumated or buried in the church garth of Stanhop, in

[1] Feb. 22, 1573/4. Will of Wylliam Shell of Allnwicke, blackesmythe. I give my howse to George Gray, my uncle Ralphe Graye, his sonne. I give my worke house to Henry Shell. I give my study (*i.e.*, anvil) in Barwick to John Shell. The remainder to my sonne, Nicholas Shell, and I give him with his portion to my uncle, Ralphe Gray, whom I make executor. Pr. 1584.

sertayn sure hopp of resurreuion and eternall lyffe through Jesus
Christ our Lord. I geve to my sonne, Robert Hind, a quie styrke.
The ryst of all my goods, both moveable and unmoveable, wyth my
detts and legesses and fenerall descharged and payd, I geve to Alener
Hind, my wyffe, whome I make my full executor. In wettnes
whereof this my last wyll and testament, Wylliam Stobes of the West-
yeat, Robert Stobes, Rychard Younger and John Stobes. [Pr. Nov.
9, 1583.]

WILL OF MARTIN SHELL.

Nov. 7, 158[3]. Martine Shell of Barwicke, one of her Majesties
canenores of the great ordinance.[1] To be buried at the discretion of
my sonne, Henrie Shell. I give the howse I dwell in to my son,
Henrie Shell, and then to his sons John, Martin and Henrie Shell
and their heirs male respectively, and then to their unckell, Rowland
Shell. I give to my sonne, Rowland Shell, all my tooles the which
I wroughte withall in my smythe's shopp. I give to my sonne John
Shell's daughter, Christien Shell, a howse, and to her sister, Esabell
Shell . . . . My daughter in lawe Alles Shell, wedowe. To my
dowghter Custannce Ryveley and her seven children, 40s. To my
daughter Jennat Lambert's son, Thomas Lambert.[2]

WILL OF ANTHONY FENWICK.

Dec. 1, 1583. Anthony Fenwik of Treuwick, within the countie
of Northumberland, gentleman. My bodie to be buried in my
parishe churche of Bollam. To my brother, Robert Fenwik's thre
sonnes, 2 whies sterkes and 2 yowes. To my brother Robert, 4
bowilles of ottes, to helpe hym to sawe his ottes sed, and one browne
maire. To my brother Nycolas Fenwik, 3 bushell of ottes. To
Jane Fenwik, my wyffe, sex of my best oxen, and the therdes of all
my goodes. To my thre dowghters, that is, Mabell, Agnes and
Kathern Fenwik all the rest of my goodes. To my sonne, William
Fenwik, my yrone chemley, a golding broche and all suche old
airelowmes as was leifte me by ansitors. To my wyffe, all my fermhold of Trewik, so long as she is my wiffe, to bring up my childring,
and after her marage to have her thirdes of my farmhold. My wiffe
and my childring executors. I put my brother in lawe, Mr. Rauffe
Fenwik and Robert Fenwik, my brother, in full trust to my wiffe
and childering; and especially my brother in law, Rauffe Fenwik,
with my sonne William, if in caisse my wiffe do marie, to se hym

[1] 1583, Dec. 8. Martin Shell, gonner, buried. *Berwick Registers.*

[2] The testator was evidently a kinsman of Robert Shell of Berwick, whose
will is printed in *Wills and Inventories*, vol. i. p. 132. In that document
Thomas Shell of Alnwick is mentioned.

well browghte upe in learninge, and to se the rest of my farmhold well occupied. Wetnes, George Carre, gentilman, Thomas Fenwik, Robert Fenwik, my brother, William Thompson, etc. [Pr. 1584.]

INVENTORY. Feb. 27. 7 oxen, 8*l.* 10*s.* 9 kye, 3 stottes, 2 blak stirkes, a bull and 2 stottes, 18*l.* 13*s.* 4*d.* One gray mare, 20*s.* Household stuffe, 5*l.* Corne sawen and unsawen, 16*l.* Wanes, plewes, yokes and yrons, yron sownes and haros, 46*s.* 8*d.* *Summa,* 45*l.* 10*s.*

WILL OF ALICE ANDERSON.

Dec. 25, 1583. Allice Anderson of Walbottle. To be buried in my parrishe churche of Newborne. My daughter Margret and her two sonns, Roger and Thomas Shafto ; her towe other sonnes, Gawyn and Alexander Swinborne. My daughter Mabell and her young sonne, Jhon Cammont, and her daughter Mary. Gawyn Anderson, my husband's bastard sonn, and Mabell, Dorothy and Margaret Anderson, his daughters. Isabell and Thomas Anderson, my son Jhon's children. To my sonne Cutberd, one halfe net of fishinge upon the lorde's water. My sons Roger and Cuthbert executors. [Pr. 1584.]

WILL OF GAWEN CHARLTON.

Jan. 14, 1583/4. Gawen Charlton, the parish of Bellyngham, yeoman. To be buryed within the churche of Bellyngham. I gyve my son, John Charlton, into the hands of Mr. Edward Charlton, lord of Hesslesyd, gentleman. My base begotten daughter. Remainder to my wife, Elsapeth Charlton, the child she is with, and John Charlton, my son, they executors.

WILL OF THOMAS BELL.

Feb. 3, 1583/4. Thomas Bell of Bellisis,[1] in the parishe of Stannington in the countye of Northumberland, gentlemen. I will that my bodye shalbe honestlie buryed within the southe porche of Stannington churche. My wife Elizabeth to have a thirde part of all my goodes, and one other full thirde I gyve to my children, Christofer, George, John, Janet and Elizabeth Bell, equallie to be devided amongst them. To William Robynson of Seaton Delavall, 3 yeawes. To Thomas, sonne of Arthur Newton, one yeaw and one lambe. To the children of Thomas Alanby, 3 shepe hogges. To Thomas Rey of Horten Graunge, one you and one lambe. All the

[1] Apparently the father of Christopher Bell of Bellasis, whose name heads the pedigree of that family entered at St. George's *Visitation of Northumberland* in 1615.

rest of my goodes, etc., to my two younger sonnes George and John
Bell and to my two daughters Janet and Elizabeth, equally to be
parted among them, provided that this residue of my goodes remayne,
in the handes of my wife Elizabeth duringe her wedowhead. I
gyve all those my landes, etc., in Bellisis which I lately purchased
of Sir George Ratclif, knight, unto my eldest sonne Christofer and
his heires male for ever, then to my second sonne George, then to
my third and youngest sonne John, to be helde of the cheif lorde of
the fee thereof by the services thearefore dew. And in default of
such issue male of my sonne John, the said landes, etc., shall come to
the next right heire of me, the said Thomas Bell. My wife Elizabeth
sole executrix. Witnesses, Richard Hancocke, clerk, and James
Rey of Horton Graunge.

INVENTORY. Eighte oxen, 9*l.* 7 kye, 7*l.* 4 stottes, 40*s.* 3
whyes, 30*s.* A horsse, 40*s.* 4 schore and tenn yowes, 15*l.* 6*s.* 8*d.*
30 hogges, 3*l.* 28 boules of hard corne, 5*l.* 12*s.* 20 boules of otes,
53*s.* 4*d.* Waynes, plowgere and plowes, 26*s.* 8*d.* The insighte
geare, 3*l.* 6*s.* 8*d.* 4 shottes, 2 geese and a gander, 6*s.* 8*d.* 3 bee
hyves, 10*s.* *Suma totalis,* 53*l.* 13*s.*

WILL OF WILLIAM RIPPON.

Feb. 22, 1583/4. William Rippon of . . . . parish of Lanchester. To be buried in the church of All Hallowes at Lanchester.
I give to my son, Robert Rippon, a silver spoone, and to William
Rippon, my son, two silver spones. To Nicholas Forster, my son,
a silver spoon, one pair of silver crookes that was my wyfe's, one
graye mayr and all my intereste of one close that I have at Wollye
of Mr. Conyers ; falinge he cannot have the close, I will that the said
Nicholas shall have all the money that whiche Mr. Conyears did
receve for the same close, which is 51*s.* 8*d.* My daughter's children.
William Brigg's two sons. William Rippon, my sone's son. My
daughter's son, William Forster. To the mendinge of the ways
aboute Lanchester, two ewes. To my curat, a kowe. To my son
William, a pair of beades that was my wife's. The rest to William,
my son, whom I give to the charge of Thomas Tempest and William
Hodshon till he be 21. Witnesses, John Rippon, George Foster and
Richard Milner, curat.

WILL OF EDWARD JENISON.

March 22, 1583/4. Edwarde Jenison [1] of the towne of Newcastell. To be buryed wythin the churche yearde of Alhallowes. I
give to the poore, 6*s.* 8*d.* To Christofer Bewyke, a stott. To

---

[1] The name of Edward is unknown in the pedigrees of Jenison of Newcastle
and of Walworth given in Surtees, *Durham,* vol. iii. pp. 263, 320, 322.

Barbarye Bewycke, a read hawked kowe. To the children of William
Jenison, 2 whie stirkes. To Elizabethe Bewycke, a quye. To Peter
Bewyck, 2 stottes in Horton Gragnes. To Henry Jenison, a stott.
William Jenison do owe to me for a sieive, which I did sell him
for his wife's churchynge, 2s. 8d. I owe to Dame Bowmer, 12d.
To Malley Jenison, a kowe. To Henry Swan, a kowe. To Robert
Bullocke, two stottes. To Richard Hartbowrne, a kowe. To William
Thompson, a fylley.   To George Bullocke, a quye stirke.   To
Elizabeth Bewicke, 5s. To Arche Noble, 6s. To Steaven Raisley,
12d. The rest to Peter Bewyck and Robert Bullock, they executors.
Witnesses, Cuthbert Ewbank, curate, Rauff Wilkinson and Robert
Wylde.

WILL OF CHRISTOPHER WOLDHAVE.

April 8, 1584. Christophore Woldhave, of the parish of St.
John's, Newcastle, surgeant. To be buried in the churche-yearde of
St. John's besyde my two wyves. To Oswold Delahaie, my first
wyve's sonne, 3l. 6s. 8d. and all such instruments of surgery as was
his father's. I bequeath to my wyffe Anne and my sonne Henry all
my goods and I appoint them my lawful executors. To my sister,
Alice Craggs, 6s. 8d. To my sister Janet, 3s. 4d. To my brother
in lawe, Robert Craggs, 3s. 4d. To my brother, Bartrame Waddhave,
my best dubblet. I forgyve my brother two bylls of debt of the sume
of 5 marks. To my two brethren, William and John, 3s. 4d. a piece.
To Alexander Craggs, my russet gowne. My friends, Humphraye
Graye and George Nicollson, supervisors.

WILL OF THOMAS KAYE, CLERK.

April 8, 1584.   Thomas Kaye of Newcastle, clerke.[1]   To be
buried under the thorne tree in St. Nicholas's churche-yarde.   To
the church of St. Nicholas, 40s. To the poore of the towne, 40s.,
by the distribution of my right worshippfull maister, Mr. Henry
Anderson. To everye my said maister his children, 10s. To my
said maister his brother, Mr. Bartrame, 6s. 8d.   To my lovinge
maistres, Mrs. Anderson, 10s. To the two daughters of Sir . . . .
Brandlinge, knight, deceased, as yet unmarried, 10s. each. To Thomas
Pearson, parish clerke, in St. Nicholas, 3s. 4d. To Janet Moore,
widow, my best gowne. To John Wallace, singinge man, and to the
under clerk of St. Nicholas, eache of them 20d. My right worshippfull maister, Mr. Henrie Anderson, my sole executor.   Witnesses,
John Magbraye, clerke, and Bartrame Andersone.

[1] The testator was senior curate of St. Nicholas's, Newcastle. Cf. Welford,
Newcastle and Gateshead, vol. iii. p. 36.

WILL OF ANTHONY BRADFORD.

April 8, 1584. Anthony Bradford of Barwicke, foyman. To Dorrity, my wyffe, my house in Briggat wherin now she dwellethe. To my son, Thomas Bradford, my other house in Briggat. To my daughter Ellenor, 40*l*. To my sons Rowland and Thomas, 60*l*. each when of age. My wife executrix. Witnesses, Thomas Clerk, vicar of Barwicke. Lyonell, Nicholas and Bartholomew Bradforthe, John Morton, etc.[1]

WILL OF WILLIAM LIDDELL.

April 27, 1584. William Liddell of the towne of Newcastell upon Tyne; sicke in bodye. To be buried with[in] the church of Alhallowes on the north syde, in the place which I have therunto already appoynted. To my sonne Steaphen Liddell, 10*l*., to be delivered unto him when as he shall come to lawfull years. To my sonne Humphray Liddell, 10*l*. To my sonne Andrewe Liddell, 12*l*. To my sonne Francis Liddell, 15*l*. (when of age). To my son Christopher Liddell, two angels of 10*s*. a pece. To everye one of my bretheren and their wyves, and to everye one of my wyves bretheren and their wyves, an owld Edward 12*d*. To my sister, Agnes Robson, 12*d*. To my sister, Janet Henderson, 20*s*. The rest to my wyf, Margrete Liddell, she executrix. My cosin, Francis Comin, and George Liddell, merchaunt adveanturer, to be coadjutors and supervisors. [Pr. Sept. 12, 1586.]

WILL OF CUTHBERT RIDLEY.

April 25, 1584. Cuthbert Redlye of Newcastell, gent. To be buriede within the easte ende of the pariche churche of St. Nichollas. I give to Johne, sonne of Alexander Redlye of London, yeoman, all my lands, etc., to him and his heires mayle. Remainder to Francys Redlye, his brother, and failing him to Johne Redlye, son of Wylliam Redlye of Sclattesfelde, co. Northumberland, my eldest brother's sonne, and his heirs male. Remainder to the nyxte of my name and bloude. To Johne Redlye, my eldest brother's sonne, 5 marks. To Nychollas Redlye, his brother, 5 marks. To William and Gilbert Redlye, their brothers, 40*s*. each. To their sister, Dorryte Redlye, 40*s*. To John Redlye, son of my brother Clement Redlye, 5 marks. To my syster, Jane Redlye, 5 marks. To my sester, Roger Storey wyffe, 40*s*., and to her three sonnes 40*s*. each. To Alexander Redlye, my base begotten son, 10*l*. To Edward Redlye, my eldest brother's sonne's sonne, 40*s*. To Jhone Parker wyffe, nowe dwellinge without the Neweyett in Newcastell, 6*s*. 8*d*. To Elizabeth, lat wyffe of

---

[1] 1584, April 17. Antho. Bradeforth, marchant, buried. *Berwick Registers.*

Frances Andersone of Newcastle, 6s. 8d.   I will that my wyffe,
Cristibell Redlye, shalbe honnestlye and substancially foune with
a woman sarwant to attende and wait upone her by my truste
frends Mr. Wyllme Selby of Newcastell, alderman and his wyffe,
Elizabeth Selby (whom I make supervisors).   The remainder, my
fenerall expences, etc., discharged, I gyve to Johne Redlye, sonne of
Alexander Redlye—he executor.

[INVENTORY exhibited Nov. 1, 1595.]

WILL OF WILLIAM GIBSON.

June 25, 1584.   William Gibson of Straunton, in the countie of
Durham, yeoman.   My bodie to Christen buriall within the churche
of Straunton, nere unto the place where William Kyrton was buryed.
To the reparacions of the churche aforesaid, 3s. 4d.   To the poor
people of the same parishe, 3s. 4d.   To my sone Robert, a lytle
cubborde at the chamber dore, two sylver spones, the counter, a
paire of iron bound wheales, and the yonge black geldinge, together
with my coote of plate, and all my furniture of warre, as bowe, arrowes,
sword and dagger.   To my sonne Nicholas, my whyte fillie or mare,
and 2 yowes with a black brocked stotte.   To my sonne William,
my mare and a fole, with two yowes.   To Elizabeth, my daughter,
the newe cubbord and the yonge brynded cowe, with 3 gymmer
shepe.   To Agnes, my doughter, one browne cowe.   To Margaret,
my doughter, one browne whie and 5 shepe.   My will is
that Alyson, my wif, shall have 2 angells of gold, and that she
shall enjoy all my ferme and landes which I holde of my Ladye
Gresham, and allso my other ferme which I have of the Quene's
Majestie by leas, during her wedowheade, to educate and bringe
upp my children, but yf she fortune to marye againe, my will is
that Robert, my sonne, shall have my said fermes, etc.   And my
will is that Cuthbert Raynton and Richard, the sonne of Robert
Johnson, shall have the bringinge upp of my said sonne Robert
and his childe's parte, after the mariage of my wife againe.   I gyve
to my sister, the wife of Robert Johnson, one swarm of bees.   To
Jannet Hall, *alias* Swallwell, and Jannet Sklater, my systers, everie
of them a bowle of wheat.   My father, Henrye Gibson, to have paid
yearlie unto him out of my fermes, 20s.   To Richard Johnson, the
blewe clothe which I have to make him a coote, with sylke and
buttons and all thinges necesarie thereunto.   To William and Robert
Swallwell, my syster's sonnes, to either of them a gymmer lambe.
To my syster Hal's children, everie of them 12d.   To Robert
Johnson, the yonger, my best gymmer lambe, and my booke of
the Newe Testament in Latyne and Englishe.   To Cuthbert Raynton's wif, one swarm of bees.   To Mr. Vicar, one loode of wheat.
Alyson my wif and Nicholas my sonne, executors.   My trustie frendes,
Robert Johnson the elder and John Kirton the elder, supervisors.

WILL OF RALPH COLE.

Sept. 7, 1584. Ralphe Coale [1] of Newcastle, merchant and merchant adventurer of Englond. To be buried in decent and comelie order where it shall please God to call me. To Robert Coale, my base begotten sonne, 40*l*. To Elizabeth, daughter of Thomas Hopton of Newcastle, merchant, 20*l*. To James, Ralphe and Jane Coale, children of my brother, Nicholas Coale, 3*l*. 6*s*. 8*d*. each when 21 or marriage. Whereas the good shipp called the 'Robert Bonaventure' of Newcastle, whereof I am parte owner, is now departed upon her voyage pretended to be made with her into the realme of Fraunces, where she is by Godde's grace to receyve and take in her ladinge : I gyve my moytie of the foresaid shipp and of the instruments, tackle and apparell of the same, as also all such ladinge of salte and other merchandyes as she may be laden with, to my brother, Richarde Coale. To my brother, Richard Coale, my greate house, in the occupacion of Clement Anderson, merchant, at the Keyside, which I late bought of John Ruksbie of Newcastle, merchant, and the houses in Newcastle I latelie bought of Henrie Anderson the younger, now mayor of Newcastle. I give to my brother, Nicholas Coale, my house in Pilgryme Streate, in the occupacion of one Marcus Antonio, Italian, which I purchased of the forenamed John Ruksbie. I give my house in Gateshead, in the occupation of my mother, Jane Coale, widow, to my brother, Thomas Coale, and 40*l*. To my welbeloved mother, Jane Coale, wydow, one doble rose noble of golde for a gentle remembrans. To my welbeloved friendes, William and Jennett Lame, children of my late Mr. Robert Lame of Newcastell, one rose noble of golde a pece, and to Thomas Hall, now servant and apprentice of the foresaid Robert, an angell of golde for a gentle and freendlie remembrans. To Mr. George Stiles of Newcastle, now depewtie of the worshipful companie of Merchantes Adventurers, resident in Middleburghe, one rose noble of golde for a gentle remembrans and token of my good will. To Mrs. Margaret Lame, myne olde mistress and wif of the foresaid Robert Lame, an angell of golde for a token of remembrance. To the poore of Gateside— where I was borne—3*l*. 6*s*. 8*d*. To the poore of St. Nicholas's parish, 20*s*. To the Almosiners of this towne of Middleburghe, to the use of the poore—if it please God here to call me to his mercie— twentie shillings Flemishe. Whereas there is a certeyn variance and controvarsie upon an accompte of long time dependinge betwene me and John Butler of Newcastle, merchant, I forgyve him of all suche mony yet due. I give the rest to Richard Coale, my brother—he executor. My trustie and welbeloved freendes, Robert

---

[1] The inventory of testator's goods is printed in *Wills and Inventories*, vol. ii. p. 134. He was the son of James Cole of Gateshead (whose will is printed on p. 66 of that volume), and he was apprenticed, May 12, 1564, to Robert Lamb of Newcastle, merchant. *Cf*. Dendy, *Newcastle Merchant Adventurers*, vol. ii. p. 210.

Lame and Henry Tennat of Newcastle, merchants, and my brother Nicholas, supervisors, and I gyve to every of them for theire paynes for a gentle remembrans and token of my good will, thre angells of golde a pece. I give my messuage in Hornesbies chayre to my executor. To my mother, Jane Coale, one pece of golde of foure ducketts. Witnesses, Cuthbert Anderson, Christopher Eland, George Stile, Ralphe Coise, scriptor.

WILL OF GEORGE STROTHER.

Oct. 14, 1584. George Strother of Abberycke, gent. To be buried in the parishe churche of Allnwycke, as nyghe unto my father's bodye and othere my ancestors as convenientlye maye be. To my mother, Jenat Strother, two yowes. To my cosyn, Robert Clarke, sone of John Clarke of Alnwyck, my howse in Fenkel strett, in consyderacion of the great travell and charges that he hayth bestowed in the lawe abowte the obteining of the same; and the goodwyl and ryght of a farmold in Sowthe Charltone, nowe in the tenore of Odnell Selbey. The remainder to Jenate, my wife, and John Clerke, my cosyne, whom for the frendshype and love he beares I praye to be a husband and faythful frend to my wyff. Witnesses, Thomas Armerer, Henrye and Jenat Strother. [Pr. 1585.]

WILL OF THOMAS ELSTOB.

Jan. 11, 1584/5. Thomas Elstoppe of the parishe of Darlington. To the pore in Darlington, 3s. 4d. To John Woodfall, minister there, 3s. 4d. To Lewis Ambros, 3s. 4d. Towards the mendinge of Skerne Brigg, which is at the east end of the churche, to be payde when it is amendinge, 3s. 4d. To Anne, my wyffe, the howse which I nowe dwell in, with all barnes, stables, selleres and soulars, looftes, kittchen, buttrie and outhowsses, curtelas, orchardes, gardens, back garthes and ther appurtenances, for her lyffe, and after her decease to Thomas and Richarde Elstoppe my sonnes, and there heres for ever, conditionally that yf ether of them doe or will sell his righte or title therein, he that so dothe shall not sell his righte to none other but one other, but one of them shall sell his righte to th'other, and yf they bothe doe and will sell the same house to eny but one of them to the other then the saide house shalbe reverte and come to Henry Elstoppe, my yongar sonne, and his heres for ever, and yf Henry will sell the same, then to come to James Elstoppe, one of my sonnes, and his heres, and yf James will sell, then to John Elstoppe, my youngest sonne. To Anne, my wyffe, a rawke cowe. To my sonne Henry, 6 yewes over and beside his owne 4. To my sonne Richarde, 4l. 6s. 8d. To my sonne John, 2 ogge lambes, and to James, my sonne, other towe. To Elynour, my dawghter, a fatte yewe and 40 markes, to be paid at her mariedge, or when she come to 21 yeres. The rest of my goods, etc., to my wyffe and to Henry, James and John, my sonnes. My wyffe Anne my executor. Witnesses, John Woodfall, minister, Francis Lowson, Robert Nicholson, Thomas Colin, Christofer Dent, William Teasdale.

WILL OF ELIZABETH DONKIN.

Jan. 19, 1584/5. Elizabeth Donkin, wedowe, fyrste wyffe of Rycherde Rand,[1] tanner, of Gateshead, and lastlye wyffe of William Donckin of the same towne, marchant.[2] Fyrste I comend and yealde up my sowle into the handes of Allmyghtye God, my Creator, Redemer and Sanctyfyer, trusting by faythe in Chryste Jesu my onelye Savior to be receyved into Abraham's bosome after my departur, and my bodye to be buryed in the parishe churche of Gateshed so neare the bodye of my fyrste husband as convenyentlye may be. To the poore, 10s. To my eldest sonne, James Rand, pastur at Norton, one sylver salte with a cover pershell gilt. To his sonn, Rychard Rand, all my sheep at Norton except one which I bequeathe to my brother's dowghter. To my seconde son William Rand and his heirs, two tenements in Hillgate which did belong to my yongest son, Raphe Rand, by vertewe of his father's will, but he haythe conveyed them unto me in respect of certain somes of monye bestowed upon hym at the Universytie of Cambrydg; also one sylver goblet. To my thyrd son, John Rand, one tenement in Hillgate and fyve sylver spoones. To his son, Richard Rand, the rent of a tenement. To Forton Rand, his daughter, a yonge cowe. To my yongest sonn, Raphe Rand, fowre sylver sponnes. My son in lawe Raphe Potts, and my daughter Margaret his wiffe. To my daughter, Margerye Rand, 30l. My second husband's sonn, John Donckin. My sister, Margerye Harle. Residue to my daughter, Margerye Rand. Witnesses, James, William and John Rand.

WILL OF ELIZABETH FENWICK, WIDOW.

Jan. 24, 1584/5. Elizabethe Fenwick of Easte Matfen, wedowe. To be buried within my parrishe churche of Stamfordham. To the powre, 6s. To my sonne, Gerote Fenwick, my lease of the tythe corne of Easte Matfen, etc. The rest of all my insighte geare to my doughters, Agnes and Margrett Fenwick. The reste of my goods to my children, William, Arthur, Agnes and Margaret Fenwick. To

---

[1] The will of Richard Rand of Gateshead, dated July 3, 1569, has been printed by Mr. Welford, *Newcastle and Gateshead*, vol. ii. p. 427.

[2] 1570, July 2. William Donkinge and Elisabeth Rande married. *Gateshead Register.*

1584/5, March 11. Elisabeth Doncken buried. *Ibid.*

Roger Fenwick, George Fenwick's sonne, a boull of wheat. **My doughter** Agnes and her portion to my father, George Fenwick, gent. My son William to my brother, Roger Fenwick. My sonne Arthur and my daughter Margaret to my son Gearrit Fenwick, dessiringe him to kepe my sonne Arthur at scowlle untell he can perfectly writ and reade. My son, Gerote Fenwick, sole executor. Witnesses, Clement Cocsone, clarke, Roger Fenwick, etc.

[INVENTORY exhibited May 6, 1585.]

WILL OF RICHARD STROTHER.

March 17, 1584/5. Richard Strother of Caldmartin, parish of Chatton. My wife executrix. Sir Thomas Graie of Chillingham, knight, and Mr. Rauff Graie of Hortone, supervisors. To my sone, Thomas Strother, 10*l.*, and I give hyme frelie to my master, Sir Thomas Graie. To William Strother, my son, 10*l.*, and I leve hym to Mr. Rauff Graie of Hortone. To my sone, Lyonell Strother, 10*l.*, and leves hym to Mr. Edward Graie, constable of Morpeth. My sone, Richerd Strother to Mr. Robert Carr (?) and 10*l.* My son Arthur Strother and 10*l.* to Mr. Arthur Graie. To my daughter Barbara, 10*l.*, and I leve her to my ladie Wotherington, and 30*l.* more at her mariage. Witnesses, Thomas Watsone, Rauffe Selbie, Thomas Lilborne, etc.

WILL OF GERARD FENWICK.

March 17, 1584/5. Jerarde Feninck of the parish of Hedden de Wall. To be buryed in Hedden church. To John Fenwick of Barwick, my brother, my twoo tenements in Ovington unto such tyme as Marmaduke Fennicke, sonne unto my brother Martyne Fennicke, come of lawfull age, and then he to deliver them to him, provided that in the meane tyme my said brother John shall fyne them in his owne name, and he to bring uppe the sayd Marmaduke with meat, drink and cloth, and to keppe him at the scoole all the sayd tyme—and if he dye then—to the heirs male of my sayd brother John, then to the heirs male of my brother, Ambrose Fenwik, then to the heirs male of my brother Martyne Fennicke. To my brother Martyne, ten bowlls of rye, in Long-witton, this yeare and ten bowlls next yeare. To Georg Shaftoo, 12 shepp with John Carnaby of Langlye, etc. To the pore of Heddon parishe, 4 bowlls of rye. To Eden Fennick, 20*s.* To Anne Read, 10*s.* To George Raymes, one bushell of rye. The rest to my brethren, Ambrose and John Fennicke. To my brother Martyne, all the cattle of myne he haithe aboute his house except the 16 which is now gone a jestinge.[1]

---

[1] *Agisting :* the taking in to pasture. *New English Dictionary.*

To Sir James Hobson, one bowll of rye.   Witnesses, Mr. Martyne Fenick, George Fenick, Edward Criswell, George Raimes, James Hobsone, vicar, etc.

[INVENTORY exhibited April 30, 1585. *Summa*, 205*l*. 19*s*]

NUNCUPATIVE WILL OF ELIZABETH WARRENER.

Memorandum that about St. Ba . . . . day last, 1585, Elizaoethe Warrener, late of the towne of Newcastell upon Tine, beinge crased in hir bodie yet whole in mind and of perfecte memorie, did in the presence of Jane Readhead and Marian Watson, in the sicke man's house nighe Newcastell, say and declare that she did give all hir goods and hir filiall porcion to hir welbeloved mother, Agnes Warrener, and so died upon extraimitie of hir sicknes the same day.

WILL OF MATTHEW DAGLISH.

April 21, 1585.   Mathew Dagleis, of the parishe of Southe Sheilds in the countie of Durham. My body to be buried within the chapell of St. Hiles [*sic*]. I give and bequiethe the right of myne house and salt panne unto my wife and children, and yf my wiffe should marye againe I appoint hir to paye unto ech one of my children fyve marks a peace.   And my will is that Anne Chamber be broughte uppe and have like porcon as myne owne children. I give and bequiethe unto my sonne Thomas my whistle. I appoint that Jannet, my daughter, shall have fyve marks, yf she sue for it. I doe owe unto Mr. Henrye Midforthe, for two tennes of coales, 3*l*. 10*s*. I do owe unto William Swinburne, for one tenne of coales, 33*s*. 4*d*. I owe unto Thomas Scott 58*s*. I do owe unto one John Fisher 20*s*. I doe owe unto Stephen Prestwigg, beare brewer, 5*s*. 4*d*. I do owe unto one Kaye in Hull, a roper, 10*s*.   Things that are betwene Humfraye Elleson and me he hathe them in writing, saving 20*s*. of lent money which I owe him. I doe owe unto Richard Hevisyd, for one weighe and an halfe of salt, 37*s*. 6*d*. I do owe unto Mr. Barker, 12*s*. William Sare owethe me 6*l*. whereof I have his bill.   Richard Hevisydes owethe me for brinning home harth-stones. John Carr owethe me 7 bowles of salt. Richard Hevisyd owethe me for 12 pound of twyne, 7*d*. a pound. One William Gipson of Ruisewigge owethe me for salt, 5*s*. Mr. Whithead owethe me for a cable of 21 stone weight, 2*s*. 6*d*. a stone, and for 9 bowels of salt, 3*s*. a boule. I have an house at the steithes to me and myne of one Mr. Ratclif. The rest of my goods both moveable and unmoveable I give and bequithe unto my wife and 5 children whome I ordeyne, constitute and appoint executours of this my last will and testament, to se my debts paid and funerall costs discharged.   Witnesses hereof, William Bramall, our curat ; John Carr, clarke ; John Wilkinson, Robert Burton, George Henderson and others.

WILL OF THOMAS WOUMPHREY.

April 24, 1585.   Thomas Wympraye of Dreridge.   To be
buryed in the chappell of Widdrington.   To my brother, Wylliam
Wympray, my jacke, steale capp and my speare.   To my brother,
John Wympray, my bowe and bagge with th'arrowes.   Residue to my
wife Margaret and my children.   Witnesses John Wympray, Robert
Wympray, Roger Almorye, etc.

WILL OF NICHOLAS COXON.

Sept. 14, 1585.   Nycholas Cocksonn, of the parrishe of Pittington.   To be buryed att my stall end in my parrishe churche of
Pittington.   My farmhold of South Pittington to Syssill, my wyfe,
so longe as she keepith hir selfe unmaryed, and then to Robart
Cockson, my sonne; then sons Mychaell, Nycholas and Henry
respectiveley.   To my daughter, Elizabeth Cockson, 40*l.*   To my
daughter, Ann Ironside, fower yowes.   To the poore of Pittington
parrishe, 6*s.* 8*d.*   To my brother, Robert Cockson, 40*s.*   To Robart
Murraye, vicar of Pittington, 10*s.*   To my mother, Allysonn Cocksonn, one olde angell, desiringe hir to be good graundmother to
my children in consideracon of certaine charges which she knoweth
I have bene att.   To my brother, Charles Cockson, two anngels.   To
my brother Mychaell, one anngell.   To my cosinge, George Johnson,
one angell.   To Mr. William Appleby of Gildfelde, 6*s.* 8*d.*   To my
brother, Anthony Applebye, 5*s.*   To my sister, Anne Trotter, and
hir husband, three boolls of corne.   To my sonn, Robart Cockson,
one trotting gray horse and my hauke.   The rest to Syssill, my
wyfe, and my fower sons, Robart, Mychaell, Nycholas and Henry
Cocksonn, whom I make executors and I committ them unto the
tuytion of my wife.   The right worshipfull Mr. Henrye Anderson of
Newcastle and my cosinge, Nycholas Hedley of the same, supervisors, and I give to the said Mr. Henry Anderson my black geldinge
and to Nycholas Hedley one black rackinge colt which is att
Cowpighell.
[INVENTORY.   Oct. 6, 1585.]

WILL OF JOHN PATTERSON.

Sept. 14, 1585.   John Patteson [1] of Aklington, in the parish of
Warkworth, yeoman.   To be buried in the church of Warkworth.

---

[1] The following is the will of another person of the same surname :—
Nov. 1, 1606.   Robert Paterson of Amble, in the parish of Warkworth,
husbandman.   To be buried in the church of Warkworth.   I give to my
nephew, Nycholas Scrogges, 2 oxen.   To my niece, Elizabeth Scrogges, one
boule of oates.   My wife, Elizabeth Paterson, and my children, executors.
[Pr. 1606.]
Inventory, 49*l.* 5*s.* 6*d.*

I give to Robert James, my cousin's son, 2 oxen, 1 oxe stirke and 2 kyne. To my sister, Isabelle Fintche, 2 ewes and 2 lambs. My wife, Alice Patteson, sole executrix. [Pr. 1585.] INVENTORY, 18*l*. 3*s*. 8*d*.

WILL OF THOMAS TOBIE.

Nov. 7, 1585. Thomas Tobie of Newcastell, barber surgen. To be buryed nye unto my wiff. I geve my son George Tobie to my frend Rauffe Tate, with the booke of Marters,[1] the Erball,[2] the Bible, Johannis de Vigo,[3] Bullins booke,[4] with a mettall pott and a bason. To Thomas Tobie, the lease of the shopp with the seller, with the lavor and plat, a paire of the best syssars and the syne att the dore, and I will that my said son Thomas shall remaine with George Fuscter with my case of implements moreover. Executors, Robert Tobie and Annas Toplyffe. Witnesses, Cuthbert Ewbank, curate, William Burrell, etc.

WILL OF JOHN ALLISON.

Jan. 16, 1585/6. I, John Allenson of the parishe of Denton, being sicke of bodye, but of a perfect memorye doe make my last will and testament. First, I bequiethe my soule into the hands of Allmightie God who first gave it me, when he first created my bodye in my mothers wombe, nothinge doubting but this my Lord God will receave my soule and place it in his glory. As touching this my bodye even with a good will and free harte I geve it over, comitting it to the earthe wheare of it was first maid, nothing doubting but at the last daie I shall receave it in feaire better state then it is nowe. Now as touchinge my temperall goods, first I bequiethe unto Anthoni, my sonne, one hawked cowe and 8 sheepe. Also I bequiethe unto the said Anthonye one baye meare, with my saddle and bridle, my sword, 2 temes, one shekle, 2 louse crokes. Also I bequiethe

[1] The first edition of John Fox's *Acts and Monuments of these latter and perillous Dayes touching Matters of the Church wherein are comprehended and described the great Persecutions, and horrible Troubles that have been wrought and practiced by the Romishe Prelates especially in the Realme of England and Scotlande*. etc., was published in London in 1562.

[2] William Turner, a native of Morpeth, published several books upon herbs. That mentioned in the will was probably his *Herbal*, printed at Cologne in 1568, folio.

[3] John Vigo, *Workes of Chirurgerye*; translated by Bartholomew Traheron. London, 1543, folio.

[4] Probably either William Bullein's *Gouvernement of Healthe*, London, 1558, or his *Bulwarke of Defe[n]ce against all Sicknes, Sornes and Woundes that dooe daily assaulte Mankinde*. London, 1562.

unto Agnes, my doughter, 2 kyene, 8 sheepe. Also I doe geve unto my brother's children 2*d*. a peace. All the rest of my goods, my funerall discharged, I doe give unto my wif Elinor, whome I doe make my whole executrixe. Witnesses, Mr. Gilbert Marshall, Henry Mane, Thomas Crowe, per me Thomam Horton, *Curatum de Denton.*

WILL OF WILLIAM PRESTON.

Feb. 11, 1585/6. William Preston of Houghton in the Syd in the parishe of Denton, being sicke of bodye but whole and perfect of memorye, doe make my last will and testament. First I bequiethe my soule into the hands of Allmightie God, who of his fatherly goodness gave it me when he first created this my bodye in my mother's whombe, nothing dowghting but my Lord God will receave this my soule and place it in his glory for his mercie sake. As concerning this my body, even with a good will and free hart I give it over, committing it to the earth wheareof it came, nothing doughting but at the last daye I shall receave it in feare better state then it is now. As touching my temperall goods, first I bequiethe unto Raphe, my sonne, the lease of my farme. Also I do give unto Raphe, my sonne, and Dorithe, my doughter, my 4 oxen to be equally devided betwene them. Also I do give unto Raphe, my sonne, all my ploughe and wayne geare. Also I give unto Agnes Simson one blacke mear and to Dorithe, my doughter, one acre and a half of wheat and one acre and a half of otts. Also I give unto Agnis, my doughter, all my corne that is in William Burdon's feild. Also I give unto Agnes, my doughter, one graye mear and one graye fillye. Also I give unto Agnes, my doughter, 3 key, one branded why and one blacke stot. Also I give unto my wife, 2 key and thre lode of haye to find them upon the ferme, the said hey to be mowen and brought whome, of my sonnes charges, at the sight of 2 honest men. Also I give unto my wife 6 ewes, to be found upon the farme, and one graye mear, to be found upon the farme. Also I give unto Agnes, my doughter, my begest cawldron. All my houshold stuf I give unto my wife. Also I give unto Janet Burden, my servant, 2 ews and yf they do not prosper, 2 gimmer hogs. Also the rest of corne I doe give unto my wife and Agnes, my doughter. Also I give unto my wyf one acre of land in a feild to be plowed and sowne at my sonnes charges. I give unto everye one of my god-children 6*d*. and unto the churche 12*d*. ; all the rest of my goods, my debts and funeralle discharged, I doe give unto my wife.

WILL OF WILLIAM STORY.

Feb. 12, 1585/6. Jesus. William Storye of Corbridge. To be buried in the parish church of Corbridge. I give the best of my weathers to the poore, to be sodden and dealt for me yf I chance to die upon a fleshe day. I give to my daughter Elizabeth two kye which are in the hands of Thomas Frissell of Haydon Bridge. To my brother Roger's son George, the lease of my house, etc. To James, another son of my said brother Roger, a kowe which is in Jerrerd Marshall's hands. To Bartie, one other of my said brother Roger's sons, one of the two kye in his father's hands and the other kye to William Storey, son of James Story. I give to my brother Edward one rigged ox which is with my brother Roger; and I give to Ellen and Christobell Hudspeth, daughters of Roger Hudspeth, one sheepe apiece. Residue to my daughter Elizabeth Storey and George Story my brother Roger's son when I make executors. Supervisors Hector Carnabbe and George Milbourne.

INVENTORY OF STEPHEN AYRE.

Inventarium bonorum Stephani Ayre de Barwick, departed the 10th of August, 1586. One rapier and a dagger, 10*s.* A clocke bag, being an old one, 12*d.* One beadstead with canapie and curtains of carrell, etc., 5*l.* 10*s.* One pece, flaske and touch box, 20*s.* Six silver spons, 48*s.* One old holbart, 2*s.* 8*d.* One graven murrain, 16*s.* Two old murrains, 7*s.* 6*d.* One pece, flask and touch box, 13*s.* 4*d.* One horse, 4*l.* In readye money and ticket that was in the house, 3*l.* 16*s.* 4*d.* One black mourning clock, 20*s.* One black hat, 20*d.* One littell black armour, 6*s.* 8*d.* One black clock linned with tafetye, one red skarfe, one brush and a seing glase, one old saddell, nineteen yards of linnen cloth, one jerkin and a paire of hose of murraye. All these things were geven away as he laye on his death bed.
Summa, 38*l.* 7*s.* 8*d.*

WILL OF GAWEN MITFORD.

Aug. 10, 1586.—Gawen Mytforth of West Slikborne, parish of Bedlyngton. Sicke in bodie. To be buried wythin the church porch of Bedlyngton. My five children to be my true and lawfull exequitoures, and my wife to remayne wyth my children so longe as she and they can agre and as long as she is unmaried, and when she marieth to take her owne and to depart. I give to Janet Stamp one kowe and to Gawen Stamp, sone to George Stamp, one quie.

INVENTORY OF WILLIAM READ.

INVENTORY. 1586. William Reade of Newcastle upon Tyne, marchante. *The shopp:* Thirtie thre cannes, 3*s.* 6*d.* 33 wanded bottelles, 5*s.* 5 pair of querenes, 20*d.* 20 lbs. annetsedes, 4*s.* 4*d.* 12 brushes, 12*d.* A yeard and a half of yelow satton, 6*s.* *The chamber:* Fyve ribbin shetes, 13s. 4d. 1 twilte bourd clothe, 3s. His beste gowne, 30s. His worse gowne, 20s. 2 dublets, 6s., etc., etc. Some of his goodes, 87l. 13s. 11d. He owes to John Ponchon of Chester, priest, 11s. 8d. To Mr. William Hardinge of Newham, 16s. For his ferme at Burradon, 3l. 6s. 8d. For the tythe at Burradon, 6s. 8d. For the hyndes' boule corne, which is 22 bowlles, 5l. 10s. To the smythe, for ploughe geare, 20s. For the hyndes' wages, 26s. 8d. For the maides' wages, 12s. For the sheringe of the corne, with the charges of the same, 3l. For his buriall, 40s. The charges of the household, since his deathe, 5l. For suertishipp to John Hall of Marley Hill, for Henrie Orde and Bartram Orde, 7l. Some of his debtes, 79l. 8s. 11d.

Debtes owinge unto him, moste parte supposed desperate debtes: Olde Mrs. Lawson, deceassed, 16s. George Heron of Riplington, 4s. 6d. William Heron, Jerard Heron, suertie, 2s. 6d. A reckenninge of John Blenkinsope, supposed to be nothinge. John Riddele, a Scottisman, 9s. 2d. Mrs. Ogle of Adon Sheales, 10s. Gowan Reid of Riddesdaill, 11s. 5d. John Foster, tynkler, 2s. 9d. David Dawhethe, Scottishman, 8s. John Montelande of Lyntes Ford, 14d. Edmond Strother of Alnwicke, 4s. 2d. Robert Peapedye, wever, 6s. 8d. Mrs. Swarmaye of Bromehaughe, 11s. Bertram Parkin, for Mrs. Millett, 37s. John Collingwode of Weteslade, 20d. Nicholas Lawson of Sighill, 20d. Robert Marley of Kio, 8s. 9d. Alexander Marley of Urpeth, 20d. The lorde of Meldon, 13s. 4d. Sir Christofer Houghell, preist, 23d. Richerd Hall, in the countie of Carlesle, 14s. 6d. Oswolde Wuddrington of Beddell, 6s. 8d. William Warter of Broughin Stanmore, 6l. 3s. 10d. James Elwood of Warwickbrigg, 5s. William Selbie of Cocklawe, 4s. The old good wyfe of Shafto, 18d. Gawen Swynbourne of Braiklay, 15d. Thomas Middleton of Belsaye, 7s. 10d. Thomas Grenwell of Bromeseild, 13s. 2d. Mr. Richerd Baker of Belsaye, 13s. 10d. Robert Stott, merchante, 8l. 19s. 1d. The some, 127l. 13s.

WILL OF WILLIAM BATES.

Jan. 20, 1586/7. William Baits of the towne of Bromeley, parish of Bywell Peter. To be buried in the church of Bywell Peter. Thomas Usher and my wyffe, Barbarie Baites, executors. I give to my said wyffe my tytell of a tenement or farmehold in Bromeley and my goods. In case anything doth come to the said Barbarie Baits but good, then George Baits, my brother, to have my tenement in Bromeley. To George Wilkeson and John Wilkeson, one lamb betwixt them. Witnesses, Blease Baits, Thomas Usher, George Lawson, George Baits. [Pr. 1586.]

WILL OF JAMES DUNN.

Feb. 8, 1586/7. James Don of Clappotte, within the parrishe of St. Nycholas in Durham. To be buryed in St. Nycholas churchyarde, neare where my wife was buryed.[1] To my maister, Mr. John Hethe of Keapyere, th'elder, one olde anngell, and to Maistres Thomazin Heth, his wife, one olde angell. To Mr. John Heth the younger, one olde anngell, and to Maistres Elyzabeth, his wyfe, a goulde ringe with a deaths heade. To Thomas Hethe, one correll stalke tipt with sylver, and to Thomazin Heth, my younge maister's daughter, one plaine gould ringe. To Maistres Agnes Heth, my olde maister's syster, one correll stalke tipt with sylver. To Mr. Edward Heth one Frenche crowne, and to Maistres An, his wyfe, one of my least sylver spones without a knopp. To Mr. Robarte Throckmorten, vicar of Ayckley, one Elisabeth anngell. To John Franckleyne of Kepyere, 20s. To everye of my fellowe servannts in my maister's house, bothe men and women servants, 12d. a pece. To William Marche, sadler, 5s. and to his wife a litle sylver key. To John Watson, clercke, curat of St. Nycholas churche in Durham, 5s., and to William Murray, clercke, curat of St. Giles, 10s. To John Cooke, bailyfe of Gilligate, 2s. To the poore folke in St. Nycholas parrishe, 20s. To the poore folke in St. Giles parrishe, 20s. To Christofer Don, my sonne, the lease of my house wherin I now dwell, and a tablet of sylver gilt sett aboute with white pearle. To Elizabeth Don, my daughter, a sylver harte gilte. Executor, Mr. Robert Throckmorton, vicar of Aickley. Supervisors, Mr. John Heth of Kepeyre, the elder, esquire, and Mr. John Heth, the younger. Witnesses, Rychard Conyers, etc., William Murraye, clerck.

WILL OF RICHARD HARRISON.

March 22, 1586/7. Richard Harison of the parish of Whickham, yeoman. To be buried in the church yard of Whickham, at the queer end.[2] To my son, Nicholas Harison, my title of mine inheritance of the halfe of . . . . closes commonly called the Brigg-medowes in Whickham, and I give the tuition and guerdnership [sic] of my said sonne to my welbeloved uncle, Mr. John Hedworth, and to my father n lawe, Antonie Barras, till he be 21. The rest, together with 5l. legasies due to me by the last will of Nicholas Harison, my father, disseased, to Gennet Harison, my wife. She executrix.

INVENTORY OF THOMAS SMITH.

INVENTORY. March 24, 1586/7. Thomas Smythe of Sandgate, Newcastell, shipwright. Twelve silver spounes, 48s. One silver whissell with a chaine, 40s. Two silver gobletts and a silver salte,

[1] 1586/7, Feb. 12. James Dunn buried. *Registers of St. Nicholas'*, Durham.
[2] 1587, Mar. 25. Richard Harrison buried. *Whickham Registers.*

6*l*. 13*s*. 4*d*. Baye salte, 4*l*. *In the backe chamber:* Fowertie one ores (?), 3*s*. 4*d*. 40 fur dailles, 20*s*. 120 linge fishe and 100 cod fishe, 4*l*. 6*s*. 8*d*. 4 bowles of rye, 20*s*. 18 shoules, 2*s*. 6*d*. *In the sellor of the backside:* Thre bases, with other implements, 13*s*. 4*d*. 2 pipes and 3 barrells of beife, containing 160 stone, 9*l*. 6*s*. 8*d*. *In the sellor above John Dobsons:* Eighte duble barrells of tar, 4*l*. 4 barrells of pitche, 24*s*. Five hundrethe prones at 14*s*. per 100, 3*l*. 10*s*. 8 Norwaye bords, 10*s*. One houndreth and a halfe of clapbordes, 24*s*. One skipp, 6*s*. Thre thousande trenailles, 20*s*. *On the key and other places:* Sixe peices of tymber, 36*s*.   8 peices of tymber, 21*s*. 4*d*. 100 planks and swalls, 10*l*. 17 bords of one ynche and a half thicke, 34*s*. 60 of little croked peices, 20*s*. One olde shipp boote, 26*s*. 8*d*. 15 small peices of tymber, 20*s*. 2 swalls for rother peices, 8*s*. 24 anker stocks, 8*s*. 4*d*. *The shippes and lighter:* The shipp, callid the 'Mary Grace,' with hir furniture, 200*l*. Thre quarters of the shipp, callid the 'Jesus,' with hir furiture, 195*l*. One lighter, 27*l*. *Owen unto him:* Mr. Edwarde Lewen, 20*l*. 7*s*. 11*d*. James Middleton, 5*l*. 11*s*. 8*d*. Anthony Pottes, 8*l*. George Hurde, 51*s*. He owes to Mr. Marke Shafto, 5*l*. 8*d*. The funerale expenses, 10*l*. Some totall, 546*l*. 13*s*. 5*d*.

WILL OF MARGARET MIDDLETON.

April 25, 1587.   Margaret Myddelton of Connyscliff, in the bishopricke of Duryrm, wydowe. I gyve to my lord William Haward 20*l*. and to my ladye, his wyfe, 10*l*., desyring theyr speciall goodnes to my kynsman Lancelot Salkeld and Nycholas Salkeld his sonne, that the said Lancelot and Nycholas, may injoye my hole yeares which I have in the leases of Conyscliff and Osmotherlaye. To my brother, Mr. Lawrance Bannister, 5*l*., and to his eldest sonne, Richard, my best silver salte and a dossen silver spones, and to his sonne Robert 10*l*. To the poore in Kendall parishinge, 5 markes ; to the poore within the parishe of Lancaster, 40*s*. ; to everie poore howseholder within this parishe of Conyscliff, 12*d*.   For the mendynge of the highe waye from Conyscliff mylne to Gallowe hill, 5 markes, to be delivered to Nycholas Cowpland and Thomas Gibson to see it properlie bestowed. To my cosin, Margarete Travys, 40*s*. ; to my goddaughter, Margaret Kyrbye, 20*s*. ; and to my goddaughter, Margaret Bateman, 10*s*. To Margarete Robinson, 20*s*. To Thomas Chambers, my godsonn, 20*s*., and to Margarett Wadeson, my god-daughter 20*s*. To George, Anne and Bessie Robynson, 20*s*. a pece. To John Lowghanbye, 5 markes. To Margarett Hobson, 40*s*. To Ellyn Tuner, 20*s*. To Den Tompson, 20*s*., and I will she be kept at this house duringe my lease. To everie one of my servantes, half a yeare's wages above that he hath served for ; and I will that everie two betwixt them have the beddes they lie in. To my neace, Anne Brian, 4 angeles, and to my kynsman, Nycholas Curwen, 5*l*. ;

to his daughter, Ellyn Burrell, 40s., and to Dorathe, his daughter, 20s. To James Anderton, my neace's sonne, 5 markes, and to myne olde servant, Nycholas Cowpland, 5l. To Francis Salkeld, my neace's sonne, my second silver salte and 6 silver spoones. To my neace Salkeld, seaven payr of sheates which ar twoo heads and a half. To Anne Salkeld, thre payr of eln brode sheates, and to Jane and Anne Salkeld, to eyther of them 4 payr of my next sheytes, and a garnyshe of puther vessell. To Nycholas Salkeld, my neace's sonne, the inherytance and all my estate in twoo tenementes, the one in Conyscliff, the other at Hawlatrasse, in the countye of Lancaster. To Anne Vycars, 20s. The residew of my goodes, etc., to my lovinge neace, Elizabeth Salkeld, and hir daughters Jane and Anne Salkeld, and I mayke my welbeloved kynsman Lancelot Salkeld, and Nycholas his sonne, executors. Witnesses, Thomas Orpwood, Rychard Curwen, Nycholas Cowpelande, John Haisteye and John Lackenbye. [Pr. May 5, 1587.]

INVENTORY. May 2, 1587. Two syde sadles and one hackney sadle, with furnyture, 3l. One swearde and a dager, 2s. 6d. All the implementes in the bread chamber and aple chamber, 3l. The implementes in the lime house and haves house, 50s. Plaite and ringes, 20l. Her apperell, 13l. 6s. 8d. Summa totalis, 167l. 11s. 6d. For lyinge hir corpse in the churche, 6s. 8d. In expences at the buriall, 25l.

INVENTORY OF ROBERT BROWN.

INVENTORY. May 3, 1587. Robert Browne of the Northe Shyldes. Two salt pannes, newly buylded, standinge at the west end of the seyd Sheiles, with all kynde of implementes, thereunto belonging, 140l. One quarter of a shippe, called the 'New Elisabethe,' with her furniture, and victuales, 38l. One quarter and halff a quarter of a shippe, called the 'Olde Elisabethe,' with her furniture, 37l. One new coble, for the sea, with th'appurtnancis, 46s. One coble and a halff coble more, to the sea, with theyr furniture, 26s. One boat, for the towne, called a towne boat, 16s. Certeyne weys of salte and coles, remayninge in the gardner, 50l. One new dublet of rashe, one payer of breches, etc., one prevy coat, one sword and one daggar, 3l. 6s. 8d. One mariner's sylver whystle, with a crowfoot, and 4 silver spones, 40s. All the old nettes, 20s. All the Spaynishe yron, in barrs, 3l. 10s. All the stringes and fyshinge lynes, 40s. Debtes to him, 325l. 9s. 6d.

WILL OF PETER MADDISON.

May 11, 1587. Peter Maddeson of Gainforth, sicke of bodye, etc. ; my bodye to be buryed amongst the Cristians whereas my freands shall thinke good.[1] I geve to the poore man's boxe, 12d.

[1] 1587, May 15. Peter Maddison buried. *Gainford Registers.*

I geve to Thomas Maddesone, my sonne, one baie fillye and a whye stirke of a yeares old, and a rude of wheat at the Spure briggs and a rude of Langcrosse landes, and a rude of otts at the townes end. I geve to Jane, my daughter, the eldest branded cowe, a whie stirke of one yeares old, a rude of wheate at the Spurre briggs and a rude of the Langecrosse lands and a rude of otts at the towne end. I geve to my sonne Anthonye my lease accordinge to the custome of the maner. I geve the said Anthonye my waine, plewgh, yocke and teme and all other implements of husbandre that is aboute the house, and a branded stotte of 4 yeares old. I geve to Kathirine, my daughter, one redde cowe called 'Cherrie,' a rude of wheate at the est end of Hethorne, beinge the westermer rude, and the westermoste rude at the garth end being otts. I geve to Agnes, my daughter, one belled cowe, the estermore rude at the est ende of Hethorne, and a rude of otts at the garth end. I geve to Dorithe, my daughter, a read whie and a whie stirke of 2 yeares old, a rude of wheate at Grascame carre and a rude of otts at the garthe end. I geve to Richard Stele, my brother in lawe, 3s. 4d., and to Nicholas Maddeson, my brother sonne, 3s. 4d., whome I make the supervisors of this my last will and testament. The residue of all my goods, my debts paied, my funeralls discharged, I geve and bequeth to Anthonye my sonne, to Thomas my sonne, Kathirine my daughter, Agnes, Dorithe and Jane my daughters, whome I make the executors of this my last will and testament.

Debts that I doe owe: To Richard Stele, 11s.

Debts that is owinge to me: First, George Seton's wiffe, 2s. 5d. William Watson, 8d. John Bode the elder, 6d. Robert Clifton, 16d. Georg Shalwell, 20d. William Johnson, 4d. John Bode the younger, 4d. William Taller, 6d. John Marginge, 7d.

I geve to Anthonye, my sonne, a great trowe to salt his fleshe in. All the implements of houshold, as pewder, brasse, wollinge and lining, and wood as amenerye, cawell, bordes and chist, I geve to my daughters. Witnesses at the makinge hearof, William Thompson, Thomas Bode, William Kinge and John Swainston, with other more, Richard Stele and Nicholas Allen.

INVENTORY. Four oxen, 6l. 13s. 4d. 3 kyne and 2 horses, 7l. 2 twinters, [*sic*] 16s. One stotte, 26s. 8d. 3 horses, 4l. One fillye, 20s. 11 sheep, 36s. One sowe and three piggs, 6s. 8d. One plewe, one waine and the course furniture belonging there too, 13s. 4d. In corne uppon the earth now growinge, 13l. All in the fowre house, 20s. The chamber, 13s. 4d. His apperell for his bodye, 6s. 8d. *Summa*, 38l.

WILL OF ROGER BRASS.

July 1, 1587. Roger Brasse of Preston uppon Skirne. To be buryed within the parishe churche of Aycklife, as neire to my freindes as possiblie cann be. My fermhold to Jennet, my wife, for hir life and then to my youngest sonne Edward. To my eldest sonne, Richard Brasse, the title of his ferme. To my second sonne, Robert Brasse, my ferme laitlie in the tenoure of Anthony Arrossmythe. My sonne Richard's sonne and daughter, Robert and Barbary Brasse, begotten by his first wyfe. My daughter's daughter, Esabell Heslerton, 10s. The rest not bequested to my wife, Jennet, she executrix.

WILL OF WILLIAM RAW.

July 9, 1587. William Raw of the citye of Durham, yeoman. My bodye to be buryed in the chappel of St. Margretts of Durham.[1] To my wiffe the house I dwell in during her wedowehoode. Also I doe geve and bequeth to my said wiffe the some of 26l. 13s. 4d. for her and the bringing of my thre children begotten by her. I geve to Robert, my sonne, the house and shopp next adjoining to the house I now dwell in. I geve to Margrett Alison a hawkt whye of two yeare old, to be kept in my grounds till she bring her a calfe and then she to have both cowe and calfe. I geve to my doughter Elisabeth my house with th'appurtenances in Fleshergate. I geve to my good freand, Roger Rawe of Newcastle, one old ryall in hope that he will take so much paines as to be an overseer of this my last will and testament. I geve to his wiffe an old ryall for a token of good will and to her doughter the like peece of gold. I geve to Edward Hall, my good neighbour, for a token of kindness, the some of 6s. 8d., praying him to joyne with Mr. Rawe in overseing of this my last will and testament. The rast, etc., to the discretion and distribution of my sonns William and Christofer, my executors, to be devided amongst them and the rest of my children of my first wiffe. Witnesse, Germayne Gardyner, Edward Hall, Hugh Tallentyre, Robert Rawe.

INVENTORY, 1587. *Inter alia:* The lease of Chilton poole, 20l. The lease of the myll, 20l. 2 flanders chists, 5s. 8d. 19 stone of wool, 3l. 16s. A payre of clariots, 6s. 8d. 10 brasse potts, a morter and a pestall, 40s. 12 spoones, 5l. One goblett and certen old monye, 4l. A salte, 37s. His apperell, 4l.

Memorandum that Christofer Rawe and William Rawe, executors of the said deceased, did pay to there mother in law, wiffe to the said deceased, in consideration of hir thirds and wedowe right, and legacies, or whatsoever she should have of the said deceased his goods, the some of 36l. 13s. 4d. and are to pay to her 2 fothers of haye yearlye during the tyme of 16 yeares next.

[1] 1587, July 12. William Rawe buried. *Registers of St. Margaret's,* Durham.

WILL OF WILLIAM BURDON.

July 17, 1587. William Burden of Stockden upon Tease, parish of Norton. To be buried in the chappell of Stockden. To the power man's boxe, 5s. To my son, William Burden, my house held by Roger Huchinson; an akre of arable land in every cornfield about Stockden, for his life; in the west field at Marle Potts two riggs, in the Castle-feild two riggs of short akers, and a rigge of longe lands in the Northe feild. To my son, Henry Burden, my house in which I dwell. My wife Anne Burden and my daughter Jane Burden, etc. To my son, Roger Burden, 4 marks. To my son, Thomas Burden, his children, 3l. 6s. 8d., the eldest 26s. 8d. and the other two 20s. Witnesses, Rowland Burden, Thomas Fewler of Stockton, Thomas Edgar, clarke, curat at Stockton, etc.

WILL OF EDWARD BEWICK.

Aug. 6, 1587. Edward Bewicke of Newcastle, baker. To be buriéd in the churche of All Sainctes. To my wife, Annes Bewicke, the howse wherin I nowe dwell, with all my other landes, for her life natural, savinge one howse in Pillgrim Streete, nowe in the tenore of Jhon Armestronge, locksmith, which said howse I geve unto Elizabeth Errington, daughter unto Robert Errington, master mariner, and she to enter into the same at the daie of her mariage, and failinge that she marie, the said howse to come unto my next of kinne. I will that my said landes, after the death of my wife, shall come to my two halfe-brothers, Thomas and Jhon Read, and to their heires, and failing such, then to come unto Cristofer Hall, sonne to Edward Hall, and his heires, and failinge suche, to William Hall, sonne to George Hall, and then to my nexte of kinne. To the said Christofer Hall one seller, now in the tenore of Edward Bartram, and one lofte over the same, in the tenore of Roberte Errington, with nyne balkes, or rigges, belonginge to the same, whiche I bought of Mathewe Mattfen, and nowe in the tenore of George Barker, cordener. To the said Christofer Hall, 20l., which said Christofer, and all his portion, I commit, duringe his noneage, to Robert Jhonson, master mariner. To my unkle, George Hall, 4l., and part of my clothes, as my wife shall thinke meete. To my uncle, Edward Hall of Barwicke, 6l. To my brother, Robert Errington, 3l. To my brother, Christofer Errington, 3l. To my cossen, Edward Hall, 3l. and my best gowne. To William Eden, one tonne of beare, and my best cloake. To William Hall, sonne to George Hall, 3l. To Barbara Harbottle, my halfe-sister, 3l., and I do acquite all thinges betwene her and me. To Robert Jhonson, one duble duckett, and two old angels, to make him a ringe and at his deathe, he to give it unto his sonne Edward. To my servant, Raphe Collingwoodd, 20s. To my servantes, Jhon Saire and William Rawe, 10s. a pece. To

Lionell Mair, 10s.   To Isabell and Elizabeth Hall, daughters to
William Hall, my uncle, to eche of them 6s.   To my cossen, Anthonie
Errington, 30s.   To Sissilie, wife to Michell Hall, 20s.   To Andrew
Bewicke, merchante, 10s.   To Jhon Carr, merchante, 10s.   To Ales,
wife to Robert Errington, one old angell.   To Margaret, wife to
Christofer Errington, 10s.   To Leonard Diggles, 20s.   To Anthonie,
sonne to Robert Errington, 10s.   I will that my mother, Isabell
Read, shalbe my sole executrixe, and Christofer Errington of New-
castle, merchante, supervisor.   To Edward, sonne to Edward Hall,
brewer, 20s.   To Ralph Boutflower, Alis Boutflower and Jane
Boutflower five shillings apiece.

   INVENTORY.   A silver salt and 5 silver spons, 3l. 8s.   In the
kytchynge: A byll stafe, 3s.   A polke, 5s.   In the chamber: Fyve
Spanyshe cuchyns, 10s.   The ships perteynynge to him: A quarter
and halfe a quarter of the 'Spedwell,' 53l. 6s. 8d.   The 'May Flour,'
a thred, 16l. 10s.   The 'Danyell,' a quarter, 70l.   A thred of the
'Chanswell,' 65l.   80 linges, 40s.   64 carvell plankes, 10l.   In
Annes Bewicke lofte, 96 lynges, 48s.   100 codes, 33s. 4d.   A
half hundrethe of lynges, 30s.   For two laste of rye, whiche came
from the este contrey, of his adventor, 26l.   The frights due
from the este contrey for Edward Bewicke's part: For his parte of
the 'Chanswell,' 22l.   For his quarter of the 'Danyell,' 17l.   For
a thred part of a quarter, that was sold to Richard Hodgshon, of
the 'Danyell,' 30l.   The some total of his goodes and debtes is
467l. 6d.

WILL OF RALPH SINGLETON.

   Aug. 12, 1587.   Rauffe Singleton of Langton, within the parish
of Gainforth.[1] My bodye to be buryed within the parish churche
yeard of Gainforth, paying the dewties there accustomed to be payd.
I geve and bequethe unto my sonne, Henrye Singleton, all my
furniture of husbandrye, with the intereste of all my tenements and
leases in Langton, according to the custome of the lordshipp of
Barnard-castle.   Also I will that Margaret Singleton, my wiffe, shall
have the moytye and halfe of the sayd tenements during her wedow
head, and that Anne, my doughter, shall kepe and abyde with hir
mother or brother and be found of the said tenements untyll such
tyme as hir said mother and brother doe provyde a maryage for hir
at there discretion.   Also I geve and bequethe unto Anne Singleton,
my doughter, thre score pounde, and that Henrye, my sonne, and
Margaret, my wiffe, shall have the usaige and custodye thereof
untyll such tyme as these with the advyse of Robert Spencer, my
brother in lawe, doe at there discretions provyde a sufficient maryage
for my said doughter, when they shall se tyme convenyent for the

[1] 1587, Aug. 17.   Rafe Singleton buried.   *Gainford Registers.*

same. All the rest of my goods, moveable and unmoveable, I geve and bequeth unto Margarethe, my wiffe, and Henrye Singletone, my sonne, whome I make my onlye executors joyntlye together. Also I make supervisors of this my last will and testament Ambrose Lancaster of Headlome, gentleman, and my brother in lawe, Robert Spencer of Langton, to se this my will executed according to the trew meaninge hereof. In consideracon whereof I geve unto the sayd Ambrose Lancaster, 20s. And also I geve unto the said Robert Spencer, 2s. I give to Rauffe Singleton, my brother sonne, on whye stirke, and to Margarethe Hewetson, my mayde servant, one yewe and a lambe, and John Browne, my servant, one yewe and a lambe. Witnesse, Ambrose Lancaster, Robert Spencer.

Aug. 19, 1587. INVENTORY. 6 oxen, 14*l.* 7 kye and whyes, 10*l.* 10*s.* 4 younge calves, 23*s.* 4*d.* 2 horses, 53*s.* 4*d.* 35 old sheepe, 4*l.* 10*s.* 40 lambes, 53*s.* 4*d.* 3 swyne, 9*s.* 6 gease, 3*s.* 4*d.* 12 pullaines, 4*s.* Unmoveable goods. *Suma,* 36*l.* 6*s.* 8*d.* Pewder vessells, 20*s.* Brasse vessells, 4*l.* One cupbord, ambree and cawell, 43*s.* 4*d.* A mashine tubb with other wood vessells, 8*s.* A table, a counter, 4 formes, 12*s.* A cote of plate, a capp, bowe and arrowes, 13*s.* 4*d.* One waine, 2 coupes, 2 paire of wheles with all other furniture, 46*s.* 8*d.* 4 teames, 4 yocks, one iron oxe harrowe, 13*s.* 4*d.* 3 horse harrowes, 12*d.* 14 double acres of corne, 16*l.* 13*s.* 4*d.* 8 lode of haye, 40*s.* 2 stand beds with all there furniture, 33*s.* 4*d.* 4 other bedds with there furniture, 20*s.* 2 chestes, 3*s.* 4*d.* 6 quishens, 2*s.* One spete, 8*d.* A paire of iron rackes, 2*s.* 6*d.* One racking crooke, 16*d.* 2 spades, 10*d.* One riding saddell, 20*d.* 2 lode saddels, 20*d.* Seaves and riddells, 12*d.* One wyndow clothe, 6*s.* 4 seckes, 4*s.* 2 pokes, 18*d.* One be, 16*d.* 4 hookes, 12*d.* Apperelle, 13*s.* 4*d.* *Summa,* 35*l.* 16*s.* 8*d.*

Debts owinge to him: Robert Parkin, 7*s.* Anthonye Elstobbe, 20*s.* Anthonye Thompson, 11*s.* 8*d.* William Cardwell, 8*s.* *Summa,* 46*s.* 8*d.*

Summa totalis, 74*l.* 8*s.* 6*d.*

WILL OF JOHN READ.

Aug. 27, 1587. John Read of the parish of Sainte Margaretts, of the citye of Durham, turner, being of whole mynd, etc. My bodye to be buryed in the church or churchyeard of Saint Margretts, in Durham, at the discretion of myne executors.[1] I geve and bequeth unto the poore people of St. Margretts parish, 13*s.* 4*d.*, to be distributed by the hands and at the discretion of the churche-wardens of the said parish. I will that all such debts and dewtyes as I owe of right or consince to anye person or persons be well and trulye contented and paid by myne executors hereafter naymed without delaye or contradition, etc. I geve and bequeth unto Anne, my

---

[1] 1587, Sept. 3. John Read buried. *Registers of St. Margaret's,* Durham.

wiffe, all that my tenement in Cross-gate, with all and singular th'appurtenances thereunto belonging, together with all such right as I have or might have by anye maner of meanes, to her and hir heires for ever. Also I geve and bequeth unto my said wiffe the best of my kye, at her choyce, and also a lode of haye. I geve unto my sonne, Rowland Read, my house at Mylbourne whereine I nowe dwell, and also that peace of ground called Prests Parcke, latelye bought of Mr. Christofer Mayer, in full satissfaction of his childe's portion, and I doe comitt him unto the good bringing upp of my good neighbour and freand, Cuthbert Hutcheson, the younger. And for my other three children I doe comitt them unto the keeping of my wiffe, William Yley and Frauncis Browne, with there porcons of my goods proportionallye as shall fall out unto them, that is 'to saye, my doughter Anne to my wiffe, with her portion, my doughter Elizabeth, to William Yley with her portion, and my sonne John to Frauncis Browne with his portion ; and that my said children, Anne, Elizabeth and John, as also Rowland, to have there severall porcons delivered to them as followeth, viz., the ladds at the age of 21 yeares and the lasses att those yeares, or there several dayes of maryage. And if it shall happen that anye of my said children departe this worlde before theye accomplisshe the said age of 21 yeares, or there dayes of maryage, that then I will there porcions so dying shall be equallye devided amongst the rest of my children then being living. I geve and bequeth unto my sister, the wiffe of William Yley, the some of 10s. I geve unto my godsonn, John Yley, 14s. 4d. I geve unto William Yley, Cuthbert Hutchesonn the younger, Thomas Hoorde and Frauncis Browne, whome I ordeyne and make executors of this my last will and testament, to each one of them for there paines 5s. The residue, etc., I wholie geve and bequeth to my three children, John, Anne and Elizabeth Reade, to be delivered to them in maner and forme abovesaid. Witnesses heareof, Germayne Gardiner, John Preston, John Robyson and others.

WILL OF JOHN FERRY.

Sept. 3, 1587. John Ferrye of Ferrye one the Hill, being seike, etc. I will that Agnes, my wife, and Thomas Ferrye, my sonne, shall have and peaceablie posses my farmehold for the space of 21 yeares for the bringinge upp of my children, and after the expiratione of 21 yeres I will that my sonne, John Ferrye, shall enter unto the said farmehold, and he, the said John, to enter uppon the corne sowen one the ground, and at the said John Ferrye entrance to paye to everrye one of his brethren and sisters 5l. a peece. If anything happen him, then to my sonne Thomas Ferrye ; then to my sonn Robert Ferrye and so on. If my wife Agnes marrye, then my son Thomas to have the said farmeholde for the said yeares to bring upp

my children. To my sonne, Thomas Ferrye, the house that Christofer
Heighington dwelleth in, to enter after certayne yeares. Also,
whereas there ys certaine covenants and promisses maid betwixt
Henrye Jacksone and me, and the same to have been passed over
before a justis of Assise, which upon the said Henrie's parte ys
not performed, accordinge unto the evedence and his former woords,
notwithstandinge my request and desire ys, as my service, truste
and confydence ys in the said Henrye Jackson, accordinge to the
speciall trust that I have reposse in him, that he will consider and
performe all things contened in the evidence betwixt him and me,
as my sure trust is in him. I geve and bequethe to Henrye Jacsone
and his heires for ever the moitie or one half of my baren, that is
to saye frome the particione of the said barene north ward, unto
the tonne-gaite; and also I will he shall have the quantitie of my
fould garthe, so much as reaichethe betwixt the said barene and my
seate house, towards the tonne-gaite, accordinge unto a former
bargaine and sayle, maide betwixte the said Henry Jackson and me,
as doithe apeare in writinge before sufficient witnesse, that he hath
paid me for the same, allwaies provided that I, the said John Ferrye,
my heires and assignes for ever, shall have a passage through the
saide fould to passe and repasse as neid shall require. To my
brother, William Ferrye, a bushell of wheat. To my daughter,
Agnes Ferrye, a quie calfe. I will that my sonne, Anthonye Ferrye,
shalbe kipte att skoole for the spaice of tenn yeares at the charges
of the executors. My mynd and will is, that all suche covenants
and bargaines maide betwixte Henrye Jacksone and me I doe before
[sic] all suche bargaines unto my brother, Robert Ferrye, and he to
discharge all things betwixt Henrye Jacksone and me and quietlye to
enter of the same for the space of twentye and one yeares, and my
wife to have the comoditie of the same for this yeare. To Robert
Ferrye, Thomas, Anthony, Margrate, Marye, Elizabeth and Agnes
Ferrye, childringe, everye one of them, an ewe and a lambe. The
rest, etc., to Agnes, my wife, and Thomas, my son, whom I make
executors. My brother, Robert Ferrye, supervisor. Witnesses,
Richarde Kaye, Raulf Donne, John Geilson, Cuthbert Smith and
Robert Kirkehouse.

INVENTORY praysed by John Geilson, Robert Laxe, Christofer
Heighingtone and Robert Ferrye. Nov. 28, 1587.

Debts he oweth: To Henrye Jacksone, 9*l*. To Wedow Ruter for
6 bushells of bygge and 5 bushells of otts . . . . To John Graye of
Ferrye, 10*s*. To Thomas Peirsone of Durham, 8*s*. To Robert
Kirkehouse, 12*s*. To George Borrowe of Durham, 5*s*. To Anthonye
Hall's sonne the draper, 2*s*. 4*d*. To John Woorneer, 12*s*. To John
Helcott, 6*s*. 8*d*. To Thomas Graye, 3*s*. To John Rychardesone, 12*d*.
To John Leddell the smithe of Ferrye for worke, 6*s*. To Persevell
Todd, 2*s*. 8*d*.

Debts owing to him: Christofer Heighington of Ferrye Hill, 50*s*.

WILL OF EDWARD COLLINGWOOD.

Sept. 27, 1587. Edward Collingwood of the parish of All Saints,. Newcastle, yeoman.[1] To the power man's boxe where I shall be buried, 20*d*. To my Mr. James Middleton one gould ringe, and to my dame, his wife, one Englishe crowne of gould for tokens. My brother William Collingwood, 5*s*. and to his wife and son, John Collingwood, 2*s*. as tokens. My brother Raphe Rand and his wife and Robert his son. I forgive to Thomas Rand all demands, etc., provided that he doe pay to one William Grenewell of Newcastle, marchante, 9*s*. for one bowle of rye which he had of him, for the which I became the suretie. I give to my three godsons, Robert Rande, Edward Barker and Ralph Booker, whom I helped to christen,. 12*d*. apiece. My sister, Allinson Wilkinson. Elizabeth, my wife.

WILL OF STEPHEN CHAMBER.

Oct. 15, 1587. Stephen Chamber of Blackwell, within the parishe of Darlington, in the countie of Duresm, yemon. My bodye to be buried on the north side of the font within the church of Darlington aforesayed. I give to Katherine, my wife, all my land lying in Darlington field, with the crop on the same. I give unto Alyson [2] and Elizabeth Chamber, my two daughters, eache of them 20*l*. I give to Leonard Chamber, my sonne, 4*l*. I give to John Chamber, my sonne, plough and plough geare, waine and waine geare, and a blacke stagge with a whyte bridle starre in the forehead ; and I give all my sheepe, except ten, which I give to Katherine,. my wyfe, to be devyded equally betwene my sayed sons John and Leonard Chamber. I give to Alice Hobson, the daughter of John Hobson, 40*s*. I give to my brother Lawes, his six children, each of them 5*s*. I give to John Pape, 3*s*. 4*d*. and to his thre children 10*s*. amonge them. I give toward the repairinge of Blackwell brige, when the work goeth forward, 3*s*. 4*d*. I give to Hellenor Tod, my wives daughter, 20*s*., conditionlly that she shall not be hurtfull to my sayed children, and if she be, she shall have no part of the same. I forgive John Middleton the five nobles wich he oweth to me. I geve to Lewis Ambrose, scholmaster of Darlington, 4*s*. I geve to the poore 20*s*. All the rest of my goodes not bequethed, my debts payed and funerall expens discharged, I geve to be equally devided betwene my sonne Leanard and my two daughters, Alison and Elizabeth Chamber, and I make my sayed towo sons, John and Leonard Chamber, executors of this my last will and testament. Witnesses, Lewis Ambrose, William Lawes, John Pape, William Pape.

---

[1] *Cf.* Welford, *Newcastle and Gateshead*, vol. iii. p. 45.

[2] Allison Chambers died July 5, 1588, having made a nuncupative will,. concerning which there were proceedings in the court at Durham. *Cf.* *Depositions and Ecclesiastical Proceedings*, p. 328.

INVENTORY praysed by Robert Emerson, John Sober, Laurence Ward and Robert Jefferson. Oct. 19, 1587.

Inter alia : A cupbord, 26*s.* 8*d.* 8 bras pots, 3 kettles, 2 candlestiks, and a brasen morter, 50*s.* 2 par of copyrons. 4 reckencrooks, a broiling yron, etc., 15*s.* 47 peces of puder, 3 salts, 4 candlesticks and 4 salters, 50*s.* 10 quishings, wol and yarne, 7*s.* His apperrell, 25*s.* 3 coops, 4 par of stangs, a longe waine, 7 ploughs, 8 beames, an oxharrow, 5 horsharrowes, 11 asseltrees, 4 floks and wod in the helme, 5*l.* 10 teems, 4 shakles, 6 axel nails, 4 reñers, 6 lin pins, 4 par of cutwides, 2 horse temes, 4 yron taldwides, 5 sacks, 3 coulters, 7 yoks, spades, showels, mucforks, pickforcks, moldraks, waine ropes, traces and halters, 42*s.* 6 sadles and a spining whele, 13*s.* 4*d.* 20 heds, sheths, hedtrees, handles and mold bords, 8*s.* Corne on the ground; in Darlington feeld, 16*l.* 13*s.* 4*d.* In Blackwell fielde, 26*l.* 13*s.* 4*d.* In hay and corne beried and unberied in the lath and staks, 66*l.* 13*s.* 4*d.* *Summa,* 104*l.* Quick goods, 62*l.* 7*s.* Debts ought to the sayed Stephan. *Imprimis :* James Morland of Maltbie, 40*s.* John Pape, 26*s.* 8*d.* Nicholas Copland, 40*s.* Robert Emerson, 21*s.* 4*d.* Georg Wordye of Cunsley, 3*l.* William Helcot, 21*s.* Debts which he ought. *Imprimis :* To John Robinson, 4*s.* To John Pape . . . . [blank]. To William Laws, 3*l.* 6*s.* 8*d.* To Georg Wheatley . . . . [blank].

INVENTORY OF JAMES BRIMLEY.

Oct. 20, 1587. INVENTORY of James Brimley of Hart, deceased, valued by Gilbert Nicholson, John Dune, John Pasinor, William Tood.

Imprimis : The said James his filiall portion, vizt., 3*l.* 4*s.* 2*d.* The younge fyllye which was by legacye geven unto him, 20*s.* Two ewes and two lambes so geven unto him, 10*s.* One lambe which remained synse, 12*d.* One ewe more, 2*s.*

The debts whiche were and be now owen unto the said James Brimley.

Imprimis : The executors of William Brimley are oweinge unto the said partye, deceased, 48*s.* 4*d.* John Toode of Hetton-in-the-Whole, is indebted unto him, the said James, the some of 13*s.* 4*d.* Christofer Robinson of Houghton-in-the-Springe, 7*s.* Mathew Ferbecke, 2*s.*

The totall some of all the aforesaid goodes and credets is 8*l.* 7*s.* 10*d.*, out of which some is to be deducted the debts whiche the said partye did and dothe owe, vizt., to George Harrison of Hartlepool, 4*s.* ; to Jarrye Meburne, 20*d.* ; and to Peter Watson, 6*d.* ; and his funeralls, 20*s.*

Some of the which deductions is 26*s.* 2*d.*, and so the some cleare is 7*l.* 20*d.*

WILL OF PETER BEWICK.

Nov. 7, 1587. Will of Peter Bewicke of Newcastle, yeoman.
To be buried at St. Andrew's. I give my dwelling house to Annes,
my wife, for her life, and then to my daughter Barbarie and her
heirs; then to my daughter Elizabeth; then to my daughter Margaret.
To my brother Andro, 10s. To my sister Bullock, 10s. To my
master Mytford, thre daills of medow in Brunton. Residue to my
wife and my daughters, Elizabeth and Margaret Bewick. I desire
my master, Mr. Mytford, to bringe up my daughter Barbarie.

WILL OF JOHN DOBSON.

Nov. 15, 1587. John Dobson of Barnardcastell. My bodye to be
buriede in the churche of Barnardcastle, the dewtyes therto
accustomed, consentede and paied. I geve to my brother, Reignold
Dobson, 60l. of that money which he oweth me. I geve to the
children of my brother, William Dobson, 20l. equally to be parted
amonge them. I geve to John Teasdaile, Anthonie Teasdell and
Brigidde Teasdaile, the children of Robert Teasdaile and my sister,
every of them, 20s. I geve to Reignolde Dobson and William
Dobson, sonnes of my brother John Dobson, ether of them 20s.
I geve to the sonne of my brother Bartholomew, 20s. I will that
Reignold Dobson, my said brother, do consider the paines of Henry
Allanson that he takethe with me, and lykwise Thomas Whorton
and his houshould for there goodnes towards me, at his discretion.
I will that my said brother Reignolde do bestow 40s. at my funerall
of the moste substantiall neighbours that take paines with me, and
to rewarde the poore at his discretion. Finallye, the residue of all
my goods whatsoever not before bequeathed, my debts and legacies
discharged, and my funerall expences deducte, I geve to my said
brother, Reignold Dobson, and him I ordayne my whole and full
executore of this my will and testament trusting that he will se the
same performed accordinge to that confidence which I have alwayes
reposed in him. Wittnesses, John Ullocke and Mychaell Walker,
with others.

Nov. 29, 1587. INVENTORY praysed by William Cotes, Thomas
Whorton, John Priston and Mychaell Walker.

Imprimis: His apperell, price 22s. 2 chestes, 4s. A yeard
of whyte and other implements in the chestes, 6s. In ould money in
a purse, 11s. In another purse, 18s. 4d. A sadle, a sword and a
dagger, 12s. Some, 3l. 13s. 4d.

Debts owinge to him. Imprimis: His brother, Reignold Dobson,
of his childe's portion, oweth him 66l. 13s. 4d. The said Reignold
oweth him, appearinge by the thre bills, 20l. The said Reignold
oweth him in lentt money, 3l. John Sympson of the Abbey, 10s.
John Lawes of Stainton, 12s. Richard Pattinson, 10s. John

Huganson, 40s.   Thomas Langstaffe, 2s. 3d.   Robert Benison,
10s. 4d. Thomas Morgan, 2s. 6d.   Some, 94l. 5d.
   Debts that he owghte. Imprimis: To Helayne Symson, 21s.
The tyme of his visitation and his funerall expences, 6l. 5s. Sume,
7l. 6s.

INVENTORY OF HENRY JACKSON.[1]

Nov. 17, 1587.   Goods at Bitchborne and Ferrye-on-the-hill.
Imprimis: 13 kyne and 7 calves, 26l.   A bull and a steere,
40s. A fatt oxe and a cowe, 4l.   8 draught oxen, 18l.   5 waines,
3 paire of wheles and whele timber, plugh, harrowes, yocks, with
all other things apperteyninge to the wayne and plugh, 5l. 3
horse and mairs, 6l.   42 score wethers, 7l. 13s. 4d.   68 ewes
and tuppes, 11l. 6s. 8d.   46 sheepe hoggs, 4l. 12s. 20 fatt sheep,
3l. 6s. 8d. Waynes and plughe at Ferrye-on-the-hill, with other
implements, 20s. Swyne, 26s. 8d. Geese and pullen, 13s. 4d. Corne
in the barne at Bitchborne and at Ferrye-on-the-hill, 15l.   Corne
in the earth, 3l. 6s. 8d. Hay, 12l. Wodden vessell and implements
in the hall and butterye, 6l. Wodden implements in both parlers,
3l. 6s. 8d. Of implements in the upper weste chamber and newe
loifte, 4l. In the 2 chambers at starehead, 26s. 8d. Implements
of wood in the kytchine and milke house, 20s. All iron implements
for the house, 15s. Of brasse and batrye in the kitchine, 53s. 4d.
Puther in the hall, 4l. Puther in the buttrye, 25s. 6d. Puther in
the parler, 11s. 6d. Milkan (?) implements in the hall, 26s. 8d.
His furnyture and apparell, 12l. 6 mattresses, 30s. 3 fether bedds
and bowlsters, 5l. 10 paire blanketts, 4l. 12 codds, 24s. 17
happings, 51s. 12 coverletts, 48s. 2 oversea coverings, 26s. 8d.
Hangings, courtinge and quishons, 46s. 8d. 11 paire of sheets, 6l.
13 pellivers, 20s.   Table clothes, towells and napkins, 26s. 8d.
Lynninge clothe, 33s. 8d.   Wollen clothe, 56s. 2 carpetts, 10s.
10 paire of harden sheets, 40s. In lint, 4l. 13s. 4d. In wolle, butter
and cheese, 46s. 8d. In joyned golde, 14l. 6s. 8d. In dollors and
milne silver, 3l. 5s.   Annewity of 8l. by yeare for 16 years to
come as is sett downe by will, 128l. In leasses, 27l. 6s. 8d.
   Goods at Sonnyside. Imprimis: 5 kyne, 20l. 12 calves, 6l.
3 stotts, 8l. 3 stotts and a bull, 6l. 5 steers, 6l. 13s. 4d. Five
score and 18 ewes and tuppes, 20l. Five score and 3 wethers and
deamnonds, 44l. Five score and 3 sheepe hoggs, 8l. 8 fatt ewes,
32s. A gray maire, 53s. 4d. Hay, 10l. A cupbord, 13s. 4d. A
table with other implements, 13s. 4d.   Some, 147l. 5s. 4d.

[1] The will of Henry Jackson of Smelt-house, near Witton-le-Wear, dated
Oct. 9, 1587, is printed in *Wills and Inventories*, vol. ii. p. 292. He was
father of Thomas Jackson, vicar of Newcastle, 1623-1630, afterwards the
distinguished president of Corpus Christi College, Oxford, and a voluminous
writer, who died Sept. 11, 1640.

Debts owinge to Henrye Jackson. Imprimis: Robert Wilfoote
th'elder, 45*s.*, dewe at Martimas next and 4*l.* 5*s.* the last of
February, 6*l.* 10*s.* Matthew Younger of Durham, 28*s.*, dew at
Mårtinmas next wherof recovered 21*s.* John Ferrye, 9*l.* 10*s.*, dew
May-day or the last of May, 9*l.* 10*s.* Henrye Swinborne, 16*s.* 8*d.*
Parcivale Vasey, 4*l.*, dewe at St. Andrew day next, 4*l.* Rowland
Penmore of lent money, 40*s.* Thomas . . . . erson, 20*s.* The price
of an oxe, 39*s.* 8*d.* The price of a steere, 17*s.* The price of a bull,
20*s.* The price of 15 ewes, 46*s.* 8*d.* Rent of Read Myers, 16*s.* 8*d.*
John Jackson for a filla, 13*s.* 4*d.* Sume, 32*l.* 10*s.*

Summa totalis, 554*l.* 18*s.*

Debts owinge by Henrye Jackson as followeth. Imprimis: To
Thomas Wilson of Wolsingham, 18*l.* 5*s.* 8*d.* To Thomas Hyghe,
7*l.* 12*s.* To Robert Danyell 20*s.* For the rent of Bitchborne, 7*s.* 6*d.*
For the rent of Sonnyside, 10*s.* For the rent of Wolsingham, 6*s.* 3*d.*
For the rent of Ferryehill, 2*s.* 2*d.* For 20 fother of coles, 6*s.* 8*d.*
For lint, 46*s.* 8*d.* Geven to the supervisors, 12*s.* For servants
wages, 22*s.* 2*d.* For geast, 41*s.* Geven to his three daughters by
lagacye, 128*l.* To Richard Jackson, 4*l.* For workinge coverletts,
7*s.* Geven to the church of Witton, 6*s.* 8*d.* Geven to Robert
Wilkinson, curatt of Witton, 20*s.* The price of yewes geven by
legacye, 16*s.* 8*d.* In funerall expencs, 6*l.* 3*s.* 4*d.* Some, 173*l.* 8*s.* 1*d.*
beside and the colle of silver which, taken out of the above said
554*l.* 8*s.*, there remayneth 380*l.* 2*s.* 3*d.* or thus 380*l.* 11*s.* 3*d.*
Heugh Hochssone, William Lawe, Thomas Todd, John Waddley.

WILL OF ANTHONY COOK.

Nov. 18, [1587]. Anthonye Cooke of the parish of St. Gyles in
Durham. My bodye to be buryed in the churchyard of St. Gyles.[1]
I geve unto my wife, Margaret Cooke, my house during her lyfe and,
after her, unto myne eldest daughter, Margaret Cooke, if it please
God she lyve and that she pay out of the said house 10*l.* unto my
younger daughter, Jane Cooke. Also I geve unto the poure of this
parish of St. Gyles, 10*s.* Also I geve to my sister, Elinor Cook, 3*s.* 4*d.*
To my brother, Cuthbert Storye, 3*s.* 4*d.* To George Cook, 2*s.* To
George Cook his wife, 2*s.* To my brother, Richard Anderson, 2*s.*
Unto George Thompson, 12*d.* To my cossinge, Symon Cooke, 12*d.*
To my manservant, Raphe Hall, 12*d.* Unto my maidservant,
Elizabeth Ridlye, 12*d.* and a payre of shoes. Also I geve unto my
sister daughter, Elizabeth Anderson, when she cometh to lawfull
yeares, yf my wyfe be at that tyme of habillitie to geve yt her, 20*s.*
The residewe of all my goods, my debts, legasses and funerall
expences discharged, I geve unto my wyffe, Margaret Cooke, and
to my children, whom I make executors. [Pr. Dec., 1587.]

[1] 1587, Nov. 23. Anthony Cooke, tanner, buried. *Registers of St. Giles',*
Durham.

INVENTORY of Anthony Cooke, late of Gilligate, tanner, praysed by Symonde Smith, Anthonye Reynardson, Roger Foster and Georg Cooke.

Inter alia. Imprimis: The cupborde in the hall, 36s. One litle olde cupborde and one olde table, 3s. 5 chists, 8s. 3 candlesticks on laver, 6s. All his apparrall, 30s. 7 oke bords, 20d. 3 stone of salte butter, 7s. 6d. 6 shifts of leather and 8 hyds in the backe house at 4l. the shifte, 27l. 3d. 3 sole hyds, 48s. 10 hydes readye dryed and tanned, 4l. 4 shifts of roughe leather in the lymes, 14l. 11 barke fatts, 4l. 2 dozen girthes, 2s. 6d. 7 loade of barke and a halfe, 5l. 3 shaveings, 10d. 2 workinge trees and 2 workinge knyves and 2 lyme crooks, 18d. One brydle and 2 saddles, a rydinge sadle and a loade sadle, 3s. 4d. 24 fatt staves, 6s. 8d. 8 thralles and one horse heeke, 12d. One leather bagge and 2 male bands and the lether therin, 12s. Halfe an acre of corne grounde, 6s. Halfe a loade of coales, 12d.

Debts owen unto the testator. Imprimis: Owene by Jerrard Carr of Durham, cordiner, 18l. Richard Trewhett of Lumley, 7s. John Newton of Brandley, 10s. Richarde Richardson of Shotton, 18d. George Smith of Wingate, 20d. Henrye Floode of Warmouth, 10s. Richarde Wilson of Wingate, 2s. 9d. Margarett Patteson, 4s. 10d. Thomas Pope of Trimdon, 7s. More of the saide Thomas Pope, 7s. 4d. Isabell Dawson, 6d. Mathew Shorte of Houghton, 5s. 8d. Robert Cornefurth, 34s. John Lawson of Lumley, 41s. George Jobson, 14s.

Debts owen by the testator: To Cuthbert Billingham, 8l. Christofer Hall, my apprentice for his halfe yeare's waigs, 4s. To my maidservant, Elizabeth Ridley, for her halfe yeare's waiges, 5s. To be paide to Thomas Lawson yearelie at the feaste Michaell duringe the space of 5 yeares, 20s.

WILL OF ELIZABETH NEWTON.

Nov. 20, 1587. Elizabeth Newton of Huton Bonvele, in the countye of York, wedow. My bodye to be buryed in the parish church of Hooton aforesaid. If it please God to call me to his mercye at this present then my will is that Lancelott Conyers and Christofer Burdone shall enter unto as much of my goods as shall keepe and discharge theme harmeless of my two doughters' porcons, that is to saye Allison Newton and Margaret Newton. Also I will that Henrye Newton in like maner shall have as much of my goods to be praysed unto him as shall discharge Georg Hacforth, James Hacforth and Anne Hacforth of there portions that is behynde and undischarged. I bequeth to Georg Hacforth, my sonne, one graye meare. I will that Jane Hacforth, my daughter, shall have one cowe goinge of this fermeholde during my lease. Also I bequeth to Jane Hacforth, Anne Hacforthe, Allison Newton and Margaret Newton, my daughters, all my holle houshold excepting the best bed with the furniture of bedd clothes there unto belonging, the which I will that John Hacforth, my sonne, shall have of my gyfte. Also I will that my said sonne John shall have temes, yocks and all other things apperteyning unto husbandrie, with a long table in the fyer house. All the rest of my goods not bequethed I geve unto Georg Hacforth, Robert Hacforth, James Hacforth, Jayne Hacforth, Anne Hacforth, Allison Newton and Margaret Newton, wome I make my holle executors of this my last will and testament. Witnesses, Lancelott Conyers, Henrye Newton, Christofer Burdone, and Peter Watson, with others.

The debts of the said Elizabeth Newton heare under written. *Imprimis:* William Bell, 10s. To my doughter, Jayne Hacforth, 32s. To Georg Hacforth, my sonne. 11s. 8d. To Robert Hacforth. my sonne, 2s. 6d. To my sonne, John Hacforth, 5s. In charges during her lyffe (and) att hir funerall expences, 12s.

Dec. 7, 1587. INVENTORY of Elizabeth Newton, laite wife of Marmaduke Newton of Hooton Bonvell, deceased, praysed by 4 indifferent men.

Imprimis: 6 kyne and a suckinge calfe, 13l. 3 spaning calves, 1l. 13s. An old whyte mayre, 1l. 6s. 8d. The hay of the ground, 5l. The corne one the ground, 5l. The corne in the barne, 5l. One graye meare, 2l. One sow and a pigg, 6s. 8d. 10 peces of pewther, 2 candlesticks and a salt, 16s. The best kettell, 15s. 2 old kettells and 2 ould panns, 4s. 3 brasse potts, 16s. 8d. A fryinge panne, 8d. A plew with plew-irons, 2 yocks, 2 temes and a waine shakell, 5s. One spet, one payre of iron racks and one broyling iron, 3s. 4d. One recking and one payre of tonges, 12d. Ane axe, a mattocke, and a spaid, 1s. 4d. One matters, 5s. 4 coverletts, 11s. 3 quisshings, 2s. 8d. 3 codes, 2s. A bed with a matteres, one payre of sheets and 3 happins, 5s. 4 lynning sheets, 2 codwares, a lynning towell and a harden bordclothe, 13s. 2 harden sheets and 2 happins, 5s. A sacke and 2 pocks, 1s. 8d. 4 paynted clothes, 1s. 4d. 2 chaires, 2s. 2 tables, 4s. One cupbord, 14s. One presser and one cawell, 13s. 4d. 2 shelfe bords, 1s. 4d. One chist, 2s. 6d. One tempse and a seve and a ryddell, 10s. 6 boards, 1s. 6d. 2 chopping bords, 6d. One old chyrne, 2 stands, one bottell and 2 skeles, 2s. 2 seyas, 1s. 8d. One trowe for kneding, 2s. 6d. Bowells, chesfatts, a sinker, 2 wood dublers and dishes, 2s. 8d. 4 drinking cuppes, 2 canes and a pycher, 8d. One tubb and a skepp with other implements, 12d. *Summa totalis,* 41l. 7s. 2d.

WILL OF ROGER SIMPSON.

Nov. 21, 1587. Roger Sympson of Houghtone, in the parish of Dentone. I geve unto Sieth Westweike 3l. 6s. 8d. I geve unto John Hewitson one redd whye. I geve unto William, my sonne, my iren bound waine with all things belonging to it. I geve to my sonne John my house and all my land at Redworth, and also I geve unto my said sonne John 4*l.* I geve unto my doughter Margarett 4*l.* I geve unto the curatt of the churche 2*s.* 4*d.* I geve to the churche, 16*d.* and to the poore 4*s.* I geve unto Henrye Marley childring 3 gimer lambes. I geve unto my brother Rowlande 3 childringe 6 lambes and to the youngest 3 lambes. I geve unto my sister's Pickering children 3 lambes. I doe maike Rolland Sympson the tutor of my childringe, and to have the occupacon of the ferme-holde to theire behove. I geve to my sonne John 4*l.*, and to Margarett 4*l.* The residue of all my goods, my debts and funeralls being discharged, I geve unto my thre children, viz., William, John, Margaret Sympson, whome I doe make my whole executors of this my last will and testament. Also I doe make Thomas Hycksone of Merrington and Henrye Marley of Hilton, the younger, supervisors of this my will and testament. Witnesses, William Sympson, Anthonye Rounseforth and Thomas Harton, curatt.

Debts which the said Roger Sympson is owinge as followeth. *Imprimis:* For his ferme, 5*l.* 2*s.* To Mr. Franckline for a horse, 3*l.* To Jane Browne, 12*d.* To Brood Annas, 12*d.* To Anthonye Rumforth, 20*d.* Unto my brother Rolland Sympson, 6*l.* His servant, William Sympson, for his wages, 7*s.* 4*d.*

Oweinge unto the said Roger: Martyn Nycholas of Denton, 10*s.* Thomas . . . . for one kenninge of wheate . . . .

Nov. 8, 1587. INVENTORY. *Imprimis:* 6 kyen and 2 oxen calves, 11*l.* 3 stotts and one whye, 11*l.* 3 maires, 2 horses, 7*l.* 4 oxen, 9*l.* 13*s.* 4*d.* 30 old sheepe, 4*l.* 6*s.* 8*d.* 15 hoggs, 30*s.* 2 swyne hoggs, 16*s.* 3 hyves of bees, 20*s.* 5 geese, 3*s.* 4*d.* Haye of the fermeholde, 4*l.* 5*s.* In harde corne unthrished, 7*l.* Bigg and otts besydes the seid praysed, 40*s.* The cropp uppon the earth with the sowing to it, 13*l.* 6*s.* 8*d.* 3 yocks, 3 teames, one cowlter, one seike, and one waine, 1 shekell, 8*s.* 3 pyche forkes, 8*s.* 3 sythes, 12*d.* 4 womell, one chessel, 12*d.* 2 axes, one iche and a mattocke, 18*d.* One spaid, one showell, 4*d.* 4 mucke forks, 4*d.* One gave-locke, 15*d.* 4 old raiks, 4*d.* One handsawe, a paire of cumpasses and a pussar, 8*d.* One mucke hacke, 4*d.* One sheete, 2 borde-clothes, 20*s.* One dawghe shete, 12*d.* One sylver spone, a ringe, 19*s.*, ... 2 frocks, one petticote and one russett frocke, 25*s.* 4 towells and one bedd hangings, 5*s.*, to the use of Margaret Sympsone. One old seike, 2*s.* 3 wheit blanketts, 3*s.* 4*d.* 2 coverletts, 10*s.* 3 happings, 6*s.* 5 beddcodds, 5*s.* One mattresse, 5*s.* His apperrelle, 20*s.* 4 chists, 2 bedstocks, 9*s.* 2 cupbords, one almerye, one presser and 2 chaires, 40*s.* One tabell, 2 formes, 3 chesebords praysed, 2*s.* 5 brasse potts, 2 ketteles and thre panns, 35*s.* One paire of iren bound wheills and a long waine, 46*s.* 8*d.* 12 pewder vessels, 13*s.* 4*d.* Coope the whell, 13*s.* 4*d.* 2 saltes, 5 candlesticks, 2*s.* 4*d.* 3 seiks and one poicke, 16*d.* 2 stands, a kyren and a gylfatt, 3s. Seves, ridles and 5 kuttells, 8d. Secks, pecks, a windowclothe, 2s. 2 reeles, a heckell and lyne, 12d. One racking crooke, one paire of tongs, 12d. One oxe harrowe, 5s. One new bedstocke, 12d. One old bedstocke, 8d. One old kneding tubb, 7d. One old chese presse, 4d. 2 lynnynge apprens, 2 linninge churchef, 3 napkins, one payre of lynne sleves, thre lyning vails, one fyne curchife, 4 patlitts, one payre of lynne sheets (a paire of codd pillibers [erased]) and a paire of blacke sleves, 16s. 6d. *Summa*, 82l. 5s. 3d. For his mortuarye, 10s.; for reparacons, 20s.; and funerall, 20s.

WILL OF JANET ANDERSON.

Dec. 4, 1587. Jennet Anderson of Barwik on the Hill, widow. To be buried in the church of Ponteland.[1] To my daughter Jane, wife of Thomas Anderson, one bowle of whet of Newcastle market measure, one chist that standeth now in my chamber window, one side saddle and a cradle. I give to Heugh Anderson, sonne of John Anderson, one sheepe hogge and one silver arrow. To John Anderson, brother of the said Heugh, another sylver arrow. To Thomas Anderson, one sylver ringe. To my sone, William Anderson, one bed of clothes, on ironspit and chair, and a caser with two bed-steads. The rest to my youngest son, Bartram Anderson; he executor.

WILL OF RICHARD GLOVER.

Dec. 7, 1587. Richard Glover of Darlington, in the countye of Durism, yeoman.[2] I geve to Annes, my wife, twentye marks. I geve to my sonne Peter my younge blacke horse and two horsgats in the parke duringe my lease. I geve to my daughter, Elisabeth Glover, one house with appurtenances, adjoyninge to the house wherin I now dwell, and a cupbord standinge in the same house, and a presser standinge in the deanry and twentye marks. I geve to Mychell

---

[1] The following is the will of another member of the same family:
May 4, 1565. James Anderson of Berwyke on the Hill, in the parish of Ponteland, yeoman. I give my farmhold to Elizabeth, my wife, so long as she keepeth herself soyll and unmarried, and yf she be now with child, then the sayd child shall have the farme as soon as it shall be able to occupy yt, and that Maister John Ogle, the godmane of Twyssyll, shall have the custody of the said child; and yf my wyfe be not with child, the farme to goe to Cuthbart Anderson, sone of Edward Anderson, laite of the towne of New-castell-upon-Tyne, marchand, deceased. Witnesses, John Ogle, John Masyl-john, Richard Anderson, Percivell Anderson, Sir Edward Allenson, curat. I will that Isabell and Agnes, my susters, be brought up and have ther lyvinge off my farmold in Barwick, according to my father's commandment.

[2] An account of the Glovers, one of the oldest families in Darlington, may be found in Longstaffe, *Darlington*, pp. 149-150.

Shipside, 20s. To Thomas Glover that now dwelleth with me, 10s. To Richard Glover, my brother's soone, 10s. To George Marchells, sonne of John Marchell, ane ewe and a lambe, and to Anes Marshall and Elizabeth Marchall, doughters of the said John Marshall, each of them an ew and a lamb. All the rest of my goods, not bequethed, I geve to be devided equallye betwene my wife Annes, my sonn Peter, and my daughter Elizabeth Glover, and I make my sonne Peter executor of this my last will and testament. Witnesses, Lewis Ambrose, John Marshall and others.

INVENTORY. Jan. 7, 1587/8. *Inter alia :* His aparell, 40s. A cubbord, 26s. 8d. 2 tables, a forme, a chare, and 4 buffett stules, 30s. 5 puder chargers, 20s. 48 other puder dishes, 3l. 28 salters and 8 pottingers, 13s. 4d. 9 salts, 5s. 11 candlesticks, 10s. A basen, a latten ladle and an old ewer, 2s. A quart pot and a pinte pot of puder, 2s. 3 chamber potts, 2s. 6d. 2 chaffing dishes. 2s. 6d. 2 reckon crokes, a fyre shoull, on pare of tongs and a brulinge yron, 5s. 2 carpetts and 8 quishings, 10s. A paire of tables, 20d. 18 chesses, 13s. 4d. Befe and bakon, 40s. 3 cubbords, 2 formes and a chaire, 30s. 5 litle brasse potts, 26s. 8d. 8 fetherbedds, 8 bolsters and 8 coods, 8l. 3 fetherbedds, 3 bolsters and 3 codds, 4l. Fower chistes, 20s. 15 paire of shets, 30s. 7 paire of blankets, 40s. 14 coverletts, 4l. A stand bedd, a treacle bed, a fether bedd, 2 coverings, 2 blanketts, a bolstr and a pillow, 3l. 6s. 8d. A table a forme and chest, 10s. A carpett and 6 quishings, 20s. 10 paire of lyn sheets, and 12 rodwaires, 4d. 6 towels, 12s. 18 napkins, 4s. 6 table clothes, 13s. 4d. 9 yardes of lyn, 9s. 3 pare of bedstocks, 30s. 6 blankets and 6 coverings, 20s. 4 bedstocks and a treacle bedd, 30s. 6 quishings, 20s. A bord and other implements, 5s. 20 salt fiches, 10s. Stands in the butterye, 20s. 5 brasse potts and thre dripping pans, 20s. Fower kettels, etc., in the kitchinge, 4l. 4 quarters of havere and 15 peckes of wheate, 3l. 2 kits of butter and 2 leaxes, 20s. 20 quarters of malt and bige, 20l. A cupbord, 40s. A presser, 20s. Coles, 3 formes, 20s. A blacke horse, 53s. 4d. Spare flekes and a paire of wheales, 40s. Corne and hay in the howse and stacks, 33l. 6s. 8d. 4 oxen, 12l. Corne on the ground, 20l. Wain, plugh, etc., 4l. 5 kye, 11l. 2 mares, a stagge and 18 sheep, 10l. 14 silver spoones, 4l. The lease of two horsgats in the parke, 4l. The lease of Haughton feild, 30l. 3 swine and certaine wod, 3l. A bedd at John Marshell's, 3l. 6s. 8d. *Summa totalis*, 219l. 7s. 4d.

WILL OF JANE NICHOLSON.

Dec. 7, 1587. Jane Nicholson of Darlington, in the countye of Durham, wedow, late wiffe of Cuthbert Nicholson of Darlington, aforesayd. My bodye to be buryed in good and Christian maner. I geve to my sonne Cuthbert twentye marks and to my sonne

Edward other twentye marks, to be paid them within five yeares after my decease. I geve to Thomas Dossye a boule of rye and land to sowe halfe a bushell of corne yearlye duringe 3 yeares. I give to John and Frauncis Dossy, sonnes of the said Thomas Dossy, each of them a gimmer hogg. I geve to Annes Stanton a bushell of wheate. I geve to Margerye Stanton a kercher and a vayle, and to Jane Stanton a kercher. I geve to my daughter, Annes Dossy, all my cotes, except my wedding cote, which I geve to Isabell Dossy, daughter of Thomas Dossy, and one red cote, which I geve to my sister, Margarett Wilkinson. I give to Jane Glover a kercher and a vaile, all the rest of my goods not bequethed, my debts payd and funerall expences discharged, I geve to my sonne, Christofer Nicholson, whome I make executor of this my last will and testament. Witnesses, Cuthbert Storye, Richard Stanton, Thomas Dossye, Lewis Ambrose and others.

INVENTORY. Feb. 15, 1587/8. *Imprimis:* Her apparell, 10s. An almerye, a table and 2 chairs, 5s. 7 peces of puder, 4 brasse potts, 2 kettells and 6 panns, 34s. A chaffinge dish, 2 candlesticks, 2 salts, a spite, cobyrons, reckencrooks and tonges, 5s. Skels, dishes, bouls, trenchers, a little tub with other woodgeare, 10s. 2 bedstocks, 2 shelves and befe, 11s. 8d. One fetherbedd, one mattres, 3 happinns, 3 coverletts, 4 paire of shets, a bordcloth, a towell, 2 codwares, 5 code hemp and yarn, 44s 4 oxen, 3 kye, 2 calves, a horse and a meare, 19l. Corne in the lath and one the ground with hay, 32l. 2 swine and 4 shepe, 26s. 8d. 6 henns, a cock and 2 gese, 5s. Waine and waingere, 40s. *Summa totalis,* 60l. 11s. 4d. Debts which he oweth, 5l.

WILL OF CUTHBERT RACKETT.

Dec. 10, 1587. Cuthbert Rackett, within the parishinge of St. Oswold in Durham, visited by hande of God, sicke in my boddye, and yet hole of mynde and of perfitt remembrance make this my last will and testament in maner and forme following. I bequethe my soule to Allmightye God and my bodye to be buryed within the parish church of St. Oswolds aforesaid.[1] I geve and bequeth my dwelling house to my wiffe and hir children, that is, John Rackett, George Rackett, Addelia Rackett, Margret Rackett, Elsabeth Rackett, Chatherine Rackett, duringe the tearme of 24 yeares after my decease. I bequeth to my sonne, John Rackett, the house that nowe dwells in John Kendre, to him and his heires, lawfullye begotten of his bodye. I bequeth to Georg Rackett my sonne, the house that nowe dwells wedowe Grayme, and the heires of his bodye lawffullye begotten, and for defawte of heires lawfullye of there bodyes begotten,

[1] 1587, Dec. 13. Cuthberd Racket buried. *Register of St. Oswald's,.* Durham.

to come to there fower sisters as is named afore. I geve to my wiffe the lease of the house that nowe dwells in John Thompson during the yeares. I geve to my doughter, Addelyn Racket, the awmerye that was hir mother's. The rest of all my goods, moveable and unmoveable, I geve and bequeth to my wiffe and hir children named before, whome I make my full executors, my debts and other my legacies discharged. In witnesse hereof, Anthonye Barton, John Shipson, Richard Scott, John Kendrey, John Ridley.

INVENTORY. 2 iron chimneys, one paire of racks, a paire of tonges, a parr, a spete, a droppinge pann, 13s. 4d. 4 almeryes with one litle almerye, 20s. One long table, a shorte table, 2 counters, 2 formes, 7s. 6d. 2 chaires, a payre of playing tables, a buffet stoole, a carpinge clothe, 2s. 4d. 14 peece of pewder, 2 baysings and 10 sawsers, 6 potting dishes, 13s. 4d. 7 candlesticks, a laver, a salt, a tynn pott, 2s. 6d. 5 brasse potts, 12s. 3 standbedds, a trinle bed, a bordid bed, 2 fether bedds, 2 mattresses, 2 bowlsters, 2 payre of blanketts, foure happings, 2 coverletts, a oversee covering, a payre of hingers, 3 paire of lyne sheets, 3 code mares, 3 payre of harden sheets, 36s. A Flander chist, 2 formes, 2s. 6d. A chaffing dish, a wod dubler, 2 formes, 2 skeylls, a stande, 20d. 5 chists, a presser, a forme, 2 hallings, 4s. 4d. 4 panns, a cawdron, 3 stone trowes, 3s. 10d. His apperell, 13s. 4d. A brede braike and 6 bords, 2 old arks, 22d. Serten haye, 3s. 4d. A brewe lede, a tapp stone, 4 tubbs, 13s. 4 pece of old harnesse, 4 jacks, 12d. A grene covering, a paire of hingers and 5 pece of pewder, 10s. An oversee covering, 6s. 8d. A brasse pott, 6s. 8d. The lease of the house that now dwelle John Thompson, 10s. The some, 9l. 5s. 2d.

Debts that the foresaid Cuthbert ought: To Dorritye Walle, 30s. To William Wall, 10s. 6d. To John Willson, 18s. To James Liddelle 12s. Andrew Hawkins, 12s. At his furth bringing, 12s. The some, 4l. 13s. 9d.

Debts owing to the foresaid Cuthbert Rackett: Thomas Fosser for a cowe, 13s. 4d. Thomas Fosser for a lode of malt, 10s. The some, 23s. 4d. The funerale expences and debts dischargede, the total some cleare, 2l. 5d.

WILL OF WILLIAM NEWBY.

Dec. 28, 1587. William Newbye of Cockefeild. My bodye to be buryed in the churchyeard of Cockefeild. I geve to John Newbye and Richard Newbye one graye meare and 4 wethers. I geve to Symon Newbye 10s. which my brother, Gregorye Newbye, is indebted unto me, and 3 wethers. To Jelia Newbye, one whye calfe and 4 ewes. To Raufe Newbye, 3 wethers. To Robert Newbye, 2 wethers. To Anne Newbye, 2 wethers. I give the lease of my ferminge to my wiffe duringe her lyffe naturall, provided allwaies that she continnue my wiffe. I will that when my wiffe dyeth, or marieth, that my said lease come to my sonne, Rowland Newbye. I will that my wiffe bringe upp my two youngest children uppon the ferminge, and if she dye I will that my sonne Rowland shall se them brought and that they have there portions paid when theye come to the lawfull yeares. The rest of my goodes unbequethed, my debts and funerall expencs discharged, I geve unto my wiffe, my sonne Symon and my doughter Jelia Newbye, whome I maike joint executors of this my last will and testament. Witnesses, John Jollye, Robert Dixon with others. Supervisors, John Wild, John Jollye, Thomas Wilde and Lancelott Wild.

INVENTORY. Jan. 8, 1587/8. *Summa*, 24*l*. 13*s*.

WILL OF JOHN SEDGSWICK.

[Dec. . . . . 1587]. John Sigswick [1] of Walworth moore, in the parishe of Heighington. My bodye to be buryed in the churchyard of Heighington with all dewtyes of right thereto belonginge. I geve and bequethe unto the poore people of my parishinge, 13*s*. 4*d*. I geve unto William Bilton 10*s*. I geve unto my brother in lawe, Raphe Preston, my best dublett, and my best hose. I geve unto my brother, James Sigswicke, my best frese cote and my lynninge dublett. I geve Oswolde Newton my olde frese cote. I geve unto everye one of the children whome I did help to geve Cristendome unto, 4*d*. I geve unto John Rowthe, the curate of Heighington, one lyninge sharte. I geve unto younge William Robinsone one harden sharte. I geve unto my sonne William and to my sonne Thomas, to either of them, four ewes. I geve to my doughter Jane and my sonne Richard tenn ewes and one lambe, equallye to be devided betwixt them. I geve unto my sonne George five ewes and one lambe. I geve to everye one of my youngest children two ewes. My debts, legacies and funeralls paid and discharged, the residewe of my goods I geve unto Agnes, my wiffe, and Thomas, William, George, Richard and Raphe, my sonns, and Jane, my daughter, whome I make my joynte and full executors of this my last will and testament. Witnesses, William Bilton, John Rowthe, clarke, and William Robinson.

INVENTORY. Dec. 31, 1587. *Imprimis:* 11 kyne and hay, 30*l*. Corne in stacke, 20*s*. 2 whyes, one maire and 2 folles, 4*l*. 6*s*. 8*d*. Threscore eleaven shepe, 15*l*. 6*s*. 8*d*. The geare in the workehowse, 20*s*. His apperrell, 20*s*. 4 paire of lynnen shets, 7 paire of harden shets, 3 coverletts, 10 happings, 6 pillowbers, 6 coddes, 2 mattresses, 2 paire of blanketts, 4 paire of bedd stocks and 4 yeardes of clothe, 4*l*. 4*s*. 20 pece of puder, 2 sawcers, 12 tin spoones, 3 candlesticks, 21*s*. 2*d*. 6 brasse potts, 4 kettells, 4 pannes, one litle ketle and

[1] A pedigree of Sedgwick of Thorpthewles is printed in Surtees, *Durham*, vol. iii. p. 82.

fryinge pann, 40s. 6d. 2 cupbords, one presser, and a cawell, 20s. 24 milke boules, 2 chirnes, 4 skeles, 4 stands and 3 tubbes, price 10s. One table, 2 formes, one laver, one leavinge trowghe, one chaire, one greater, one temps, 8 theft fatts and 2 quissions, 5s. 6d. 4 secks, 4 pockes, one load saddell, one ridinge sade [sic] and a bridell, 2s. 10d. 2 spets, 2 rackinge crooks, 2 axes, 2 p'sers and one wumble, price 3s. Butter, chese and flesh, 26s. 8d. One spade, 3 mold racks, one hay spaid, 6 raiks and a paire of tonges, 10½d. Bowe, one shafe of arrowes, one sword, one daggar, one stele capp and a lance staffe, 2s. 6½d. One carte with wheles, 5s. 2 swine-hogges, one goose, one gander, ducks, mallerts, hennes and cooks, 12s.

Debts owing to him: William Bilton, 20s. Thomas Deanhame, 20s. John Smythson, 16s. James Sigswicke, 20s. Simpson wiffe of Cockerton, 18d. John Richardson of Bolame, 16d. *Summa total.* 63l. 6s. 3d.

WILL OF JOHN PARKIN.

[1587.] John Parkinn of Barnardcastle. My corpse to be buryed in the churchyeard of Barn[ard]-castle. I geve unto my 2 doughters all my houshold stuffe, that is to say, puder and brasse vessell, bedds, bedclothes and all other wood vessell. I geve to my said doughters my 2 old meares and 4 kye and 5 whyes, and all the apperell that was there mother's and there sister's. I geve unto my sonne John my bay stagg. I geve unto my 2 sonns, Myles and John, all my land and leases in Barnardcastle and my fermehold in Lertinton, jointlye and equallye to be devided betwixt them. I geve unto my sonne Peter ten shillings in the yere to be payd to him by the foresayd Myles and John yearlye induringe his lyffe if he doe not sell it nor turne it over to som other. My debts payd and my funeralls discharged, I doe make my 2 said sonns, Myles and John, my hole and full executors. Witnesses, Thomas Cocke, curate, Lionell Jackson, Bartill Kiplin, Henrye Abram. [Pr. Feb. 3, 1587/8.]

INVENTORY praysed by Bryan Hutchinson, Christofer Bowswell, Henry Brunskell and Thomas Parkin. First: Potts, kettells and other brasse vessel, 3l. All his puder vessell, 22s. An ambrye, a cawell, bedstocks, tubbes, bourdes, chaires, with all other woode implements within the house, 40s. Tonges, spete, with other iron implements, 6s. 8d. Coverletts, sheets, blankets with all other furniture belonging the bed, 20s. All his apperell, 13s. 4d. Sacks and poakes, 3s. 4d. Lynnen clothe, yarne and towe, 33s. 4d. 4 kye, 7l. 10s. 5 younge newte, 5l. 10s. 2 meares and a stagg, 53s. 4d. A lease of a shopp and a fermhold, 36s. 8d.

Debts oweing to him: 37s. 1½d.
Debts which he owes: 5l. 10s. So remaineth: 23l. 6s. 9½d.

WILL OF THOMAS WILKINSON.[1]

Jan. 24, 1587/8. Thomas Wilkeson of Nether Buston, in the parish of Warkworth, yeoman. My body to be buried in the parish church of Warkworth. I give to my wife, Agnes Wilkeson, the third part of my goods. I give to my eldest son, William Wilkeson, one cow and a boule of malt. To my second son, Robert Wilkeson, and his heirs lawfully begotten, the interest and tenant right of my farmhold. My third son George and my fourth son Thomas. To my daughter, Dorothy Wilkeson, 5 shepe. Robert Hall of Ambell and George Gibson, supervisors.

INVENTORY 24*l.*

WILL OF HENRY DAWSON.

April 14, 1588. Henry Dawson, of the parishe of Sct. Oswoldes, next unto the city of Durham. My bodye to be buryed within the church or church yearde Seynt Oswolde beforesaid.[2] I geve unto my wyfe, Margaret Dawson, all my goodes, moveable, etc., duringe hyr naturall lyfe, and when it shall please God to viset hir she to have the distribusion of my said goods amongst my children at her pleasure and as she shall thinke good. I give unto my two sonnes Thomas and Hughe, to ether of theme, 2 silver spones with knoppes. I give to my daughter Margaret, toward hyr mariage, 10*l.* in housewold stofe. I geve unto 4 children of Thomas Bowes, that is, to Herrye, George, Marget and Beale, 2 silver spones. I geve unto my wyff the house in St. Nycholas parish where Isabell Willson now dwelleth duringe hir lyffe, and after hir deseace I give the same house unto my daughter Marget, duringe the lease of the same house. And of this my present testamentt, I make and ordaine the said Margret Dawson, Thomas Dawson, Hughe Dawson, and Marget Dawson, my children, myne executors, and I utterly revolt and annull all and other wills, etc. This witnesses, William Wright, Anthoney Barton, Charles Moberley, vicar of St. Oswolds. I give unto Margaret, my wyfe, the house wherein I doe dwell during hir lyffe, and after her decease shee to give and dispose the same accordinge to hir will and pleasure. Witnesses hereof, Anthoney Barton, Charles Moberley.

INVENTORY 36*l.* 12*s.* 2*d.*

---

[1] A pedigree of the family of Wilkinson of High and Low Buston is given in the new *History of Northumberland*, vol. v. p. 217.

[2] 1588, April 12 (*sic*). Herre Dawson buried. *Register of St. Oswald's,* Durham.

WILL OF THOMAS HONDLEY.

July 15, 1588. Thomas Hondley, clerk, vicar of Woodhorne.[1]
My bodie to be buried in Woodhorne churche, under the table, where
I have often celebrat the holie communion, to my great comfort; and
yf it shall please God, that I die not at Woodhorne, then I will that
my bodie shall be buried wher I die, at the discretion of my wife and
my supervisors, in such convenient place, as shall please them, being
assured through the ryghteousnes, deathe and passion of our Sauviour
Christ, and shedding of his most precious blood, that I shall have
full remission and forgiveness of all my sinnes and eternall life. To
Thomas, Jacob, Edward, Samuell and Moyses Hondley, my sonnes,
all my bookes, as well those which I have at Woodhorne, as also
those which I have in Hallifax vicaridge, in the custodie and keping
of Richard Midgeley. To my said sonnes all my whole apparrell,
with all my horse furniture, that is to saie, a jacke, plaite sleves,
gautlett, steele capp, foure dagges, one curriet and three swordes.
To Dyna, my wife, the third of all my goodes, etc., and my children
to be under hir tuicion until they come to age. To everie one of my
said sonnes, 20l. To my doughters, Katheren and Grace Hondley,
to either of them, 20l. To my other doughters, Susana and Rebecca
Hondley, to either of them, 10l. For my purchase that I made in
Newcastele, beinge goodes and chattels, I will it be praised among
the rest of my goodes, and my wife to have all the houses duringe
her life, and then to go to the next heire male of my bodie. The
rest of my goodes, etc., to my daughters Katheren and Grace, whom
I make executors. And I desior the worshippfull and my deare
frendes, Mr. Doctor Pilkington and Mr. Doctor Colmor,[2] to be
supervisors.

INVENTORY. Oct. 24, 1588. His apparele, 10l. Six chistes
and 2 coffers, 33s. 4d. 8 bedsteddes, 30s. 2 tables, 1 long board and
6 formes, 13s. 4d. In butter and honye, 3l. 6s. 8d. In oyle and
sope, 10s. Foure stone of hempe, 10s. One stone and a half of
wooll, 6s. 8d. 1 almebrie and 1 cupborde, 16s. 40 cheeses, 20s.
Tubbes, barrels, with other implements, 30s. 1 cawell, 2 lint brakes
and a payre of muster stones, 3s. 4d. Thre ranges and 2 spites
with other implementes of iron, 15s. 3 fether bedes with 3 boulsters,
50s. 5 payre of blanketes, 13s. 8d. 10 happinges, 16s. 8d. 6
fether coddes, 10s. 3 matrices, 10s. 1 greene coveringe for a bedd,
6s. 8d. 1 carpett clothe, 12d. Hanginges about the chamber, 6s. 8d.
4 cuishinges, 2s. 3 chamber pottes, 2s. 6d. 4 cheires, 2s. Pewder
vessell, 11s. 2 bult clothes and 2 heclles, 3s. 8d. 3 lance staves
with a bill staffe, 4s. 1 halbert and 1 speere, 3s. Pannes, pottes
and kettels, 24s. 1 twoe-handed sword, and 2 short swordes, 20s.

[1] Thomas Henley, Handley or Hondley was vicar of Woodhorn from 1569
until his death in 1588.
[2] Clement Colmore, D.C.L., rector of Brancepeth, 1584; rector of Gateshead, 1588; canon of Durham, 1590; died June 18, 1619.

1 gunne, 4 dagges and 2 steele cappes, 40s. 10 saches, and 1 window clothe, 13s. 6d. Bed hanginges, 2s. One plowe, 6 yokes, 3 iron teames, 2 culters and 2 sockes, 13s. 4d. Waynes and 1 oxe harrowe, 28s. 8d. Fyve turtle cockes and 2 henes, 10s. 7 swyne and 12 geese, 36s. 8d. 6 hyves of bees, 18s. 1 whyte geldinge, 8l. 1 horse and 1 mare, 4l. Corne in the stacke-yard, 40l. 38 shepe, 5l. 10 kyne, 15l. 7 stirkes, 3l. 10s. 4 oxen, 8l. 8 stone of lynt, 32s. 10 goates, 20s. 6 poundes of waxe, 10s. *Certayne goodes at New-castell:* Three oversee bedes, 6l. 1 mantill, 20s. I payre of blanketes, 8s. 18 yards of woollen clothe, 18s. 8 quishinges, 16s. 1 greene carpett clothe, 6s. 4 yards of vylett carsey, 16s. A dressen clothe, 16d. 37 peece of pewter vessels, 28s. 3 pewter candell-stickes and a lattin salt, 6s. 8d. One dosen of sylver spounes, 3l. Two sylver goblettes, percele gylt, 20 ounces in weight, 5l. In napperie, 40l. Houses in Newcastell, 60l. Debtes owing to the testator, 92l. 5s. 8d. *Summa totalis,* 341l. 13s. 6d.

WILL OF ROBERT ELRINGTON.

Sept. 9, 1588. Robert Elringeton of Elringeton, of the parishe of Hayden.[1] To be buried in the quere within my parishe churche of Hayden. To John Smithe of Anecke, my browne meare, with one branded stott going at Hayden with John Tadcastell, and also one oxe in the handes of Raynold Carnabye of Nobbock, one branded riged cowe, which is at my owne howse, with one white flecked cowe and calfe, in the handes of Rowland Nobell. To Janet Cowson, a branded whye, in the tenor of Alexander Cragges. To John Cowson of Elrington, a branded whie, in George Tadcastell handes, of the Deyns. To Thomas Cowson, a branded cowe, with hir calfe. To Jane, the wife of Robert Forest, a branded cowe and a calfe. To my syster, Elizabeth Elrington, a black cowe and a calf, in the handes of William Rydley of Baggery, and a riged stott. To Roger Armstrong, a cowe in his owne custodye. To my servant, Cristye Clerk, a branded cowe and calfe and a branded whie. To Ellen Clerk, a black cowe. To Cristye Clerk, a cubbord, in the handes of Thomas Jackson of Hexham. All the rest of my goodes, etc., I geve and legate to my syster's sonne, William Robsone, whom I make executor. I appoynt Allexander Cragge of Elrington to be tutor to the said William Robsone.

INVENTORY OF JAMES DODDS.

Oct. 25, 1588. INVENTORIE of James Dodds of Newcastell tanner. At Elswicke, a hirdle of baffines in the yard and on other in the burne, 10s. 4 olde quisions and on vallewer, 16d. On pair of curtings of yallowe and blew sarsenett with a paire of flyers, 10s.

[1] *Cf. supra,* pp. 61, 72.

2 dosen of silver spones, weainge 26 ounces and on half at 4s. per ounce, 5l. 6s. 2 saltes of silver, parcell gilte, the lesser hath a cover, they way 14 ounces and a quarter, at 4s. per ounce, 57s. On lyttell copp or pece of silver, weinge 3 ounces and a half, at 4s. the ounce, 14s. On masser sett with silver; which silver waithe 4 ounces, 16s. 3 silver spones, 10s. 13 bowles of hardcorne called massilinne corne sowen upon the grounde. . . . .

WILL OF ANTHONY ELLIS.

Jan. 7, 1588/9. Anthonie Eles of Whorleton. My body to be buryed in the chappell yeard of Barnard-castle with all maner of service and dueties to be done for me as is nowe dailie accustomed. I give to my sister, Allisone Bell, one sheepe hogge. I give to my sister's daughter, Esabell Menvell, one sheep hogge. All the rest of my goods and chattalls, moveable and unmoveable, my debts and funerall expences beinge deducted, I give and bequeth them to my wiffe, Margarett Eles, and to my two sonnes, Robert Eles and John Eles, whom I make joyntely together executors of this my presente last will and testament. In witnesse hereof, Anthonie Menvell and Thomas Heighlie, with others.

WILL OF MATTHEW FORSTER.

May 6, 1589. At Bamburgh. Mathew Forster.[1] To be bureed in the quear of Bamburgh, with my mortuary dew to the Quene's Majestie. My howse, which I do now dwell in to my sonne Mathew Forster and to his heares male lawfully begotten, and failling such, to my sonne Silvester Forster and to his heares, and failing such, to John Forster of Newham and his heares, and failling such, to Richard Forster's four men children of Tuggale Hall, to be equallie devyded amangst them. My burgage lying in th'east end of the towne, to my dowghter Annas Forster and to hir heares for ever.

Debtes which this testator dothe owe: To Oswold Younghusband, for 1 bole of wheat, and a bole of malt, 16s. To Robert Swan of Burton, for a bole of malt, 8s. To Mathew Stanton of Shoston, for a bole of malt, 8s. To James Cowdone of Edinburghe, for one hogshead of wyne, to be payed at Lambas, 4l. 10s.

Goodes belonging to this testator: Thre kyne and 1 calf, 3l. Four yowes and 4 lambes, pryse of everie yow, 4s. I geve by legasie to my doughter Elizabethe, 1 hog and 1 lamb. And these thre kyne, with the four yowes and four lambes, to be equallie devyded betwixt my wyfe and her children. And I doe make my wyfe, Mabell Forster, my sole executrix. Before these witnesses, Thomas Browne, John Watson, James Bowden and Patrick Broock, clark.

[1] The testator seems to have been a member of the family of Forster of Newham, whose pedigree is printed in the new *History of Northumberland*, vol. i. p. 276.

WILL OF JASPER BOWDON.

Aug. 30, 1589. Jaspar Bowdon, of the towne of Newcastle-upon-Tin, taller. My bodie to be buryed in St. Nicholas churche yarde, under the throughe stone wher my anncestors dothe lye. My howse whiche I doe nowe dwell in to Thomas Bowdon, my eldest son, when he doth come to lawful yeares. My son Thomas Bowdon, I give to my brother John Bowdon, and he to see him brought up in virtue and in the feare of God. In default of Thomas Bowdon and of his heires mailles, my house to Roger Bowdon, my son. In default of my son Roger Bowdon, then to come to my daughter Margaret Bowdon; and in default of Margaret, then to my daughter Elinore Bowdon; and in default of her, then to my brother John Bowdon; and in default of John my brother, then to my brother Steaphene Bowdon, then to Jasper Stoco, my sister's sonne, and then to the heires of my bodie. To my brother, John Bowdon, my russett taffaty dublat. To my brother, Steaphen Bowdon, my sword and dagger. To Nicholas Stoco, my workdaye gowen. To my sister, Margaret Stoco, a quye stirke going at Hebborne. To my brother, 20s. To Edward Edan, my phessan collered cloake, my hat lind withe velvett, and my dagger. To Oswold Chaittor, my head peace and other thinges belonging therto. To Cuthbert Chaittor, my Spanishe leather girkinge, my violate bretches, and a paire of violate stockings. To Margreat Forster, my wive's best hate. John Acheson, my apprentice, shall have all my shope geare, and a paire of broad clothe blacke bretches, laide with billamonte laise. To Barbarye Anderson, on gold ringe, in hope she will not se my doughter Elionor and the rest of my children lacke. To my father, James Nicholson, 5l. To my cosin, Robert Eden, 5l. To Ambrose Forster, one fraunche crowne. My brother Steaphen to have my house, if he continue in the towne, paienge yearelie for the said house 40s. My shoppe at the hile corner to be solde to the moste advantage, givinge Richarde Swan the offer befor any other. My son, Roger Bowden, I give to my father, James Nicholson, and his portion with him. My doughter, Margreat Bowden, I give to Grace Claverne and hir porcion with hir, whom my wife did give unto her befor hir death, requestinge hir to taike hir. My doughter Elionor I give to my welbeloved frend, Jean Barker, and if she will not take hir, I give her franklye unto hir godmother, Elioner Nicholson. All the rest of my goodes to Roger Bowdon, Margaret Bowdon and Elionor Bowdon, whom I make executors. My father James Nicholson, my cosin Robert Eden, my frend Ambrose Forster, supervisors.

WILL OF JOHN JACKSON.

Oct. 21, 1590. John Jackson, in the parishinge of Eshe. My bodie to be buried in the parishe church of Eshe.[1] I give unto William Younge my graie mare, with her saddle and bridle. I

---

[1] 1591, Oct. 18. John Jackson of the Flasse, bur. *Esh Registers.*

give unto Roger Younge and Catheren Younge, his sister, twelve sheepe whiche is att the Billey Raw. I give and bequeathe unto Marie Jackson and Margaret Jackson, my two daughters, either of them, a whie that is att the Billey Rawe, with either of them a cow, if that my goods will extend. I will that my brother Richard shall have my fermehold att the west side duringe his life, payeing unto my wife and my two daughters for thre yeares next ensueinge the daite hereof, 40s. And att three yeares end he to paie unto them dureinge his life 4l. yearelie, and that he shall paye all dues and doe all services thereunto belonging. I will that my wife and my two daughters shall be the executors of this my will and testament, my debts paied and funerall expencs discharged. I will that Mr. Anthonye Kendall, Robert Danyell and Peter Norman be the overseers of this my will and testament. Records hereof, Anthonye Kendall, William Brasse, Robert Daniell, Peter Norman, clerck, with others.

WILL OF RALPH COLLINGWOOD.

Jan. 4, 1590/1. Raiph Collingwood. My bodie to be buried in the chaple of Bolton.[1] To my sonne, Thomas Collingwood, all my leases in the balliwick of Bewicke, and to his heires maile of his bodie lawfullie begotten, and failing him to my sonne Alexander Collingwood, and failing him to Mr. Henrie Collingwood, or his brother, John Collingwood; and whosoever of the foresaid Thomas, Alexander, Henrie or John hath possession of the foresaid leases, shall pay unto my four daughters, Margaret, Janet, Kathrin and Thomasine Collingwood, 10l. a peece. To my sonne Thomas, four oxen and 4 stottes, and all the corne which the two plowes dothe in Bewick wynn during his mynoritie. To Phillis Hallowell, 2 ewes. To my sister, Elizabeth Bethoun, a cowe and a calfe which I boughte of George Greye. To my father in lawe, Mr. Robert Collingwood, the milne of Bewick, to bring upp my children. To my mother, Jane Forster, 40s. My doughters, Margaret, Janet, Katherin and Thomazine, my executrixes. Mr. Henrie Collingwood and his brother John, supervisors.

WILL OF RALPH BLAKISTON.

Jan. 8, 1590/1. Raiphe Blaikston[2] of Sehame. To my sonne, John Blaikston, 6 of my best kyne or quies whiche allredye I have appoynted, 10 ewe shepe, 1 maire, and 1 stagge, and 1 langsickle.

---

[1] Bolton was granted, April 9, 1553, to Robert Collingwood of Eslington, esq., and Alexander Collingwood, gent., and to the heirs of the said Robert. Cf. new *History of Northumberland*, vol. vii. p. 217.

[2] Second son of John Blakiston of Seaton, parish of Seaham, and his wife Margaret, daughter of Richard Buck of Tudbury. His father's will is printed in *Wills and Inventories*, vol. i. p. 251.

To Allesone Gunton, 1 cowe, and 1 bedd of close, with somme lynininge geare whiche was my wive's and dowghter's, deceased. To my sonne, John Blaikston, one bedd of close.   To Robert Perkynne of Sehame, 1 lyttle calffe.   The rest of my goodes to Adame Blaikston and John Blaikston, my sonnes, whom I make joynte executors.

INVENTORY, 25*l.* 13*s.* 9*d.*

WILL OF RALPH CATTERICK.

April 26, 1591.   Ralph Catrick of Wolveston, parish of Billingham.   To be buried in Billingham church.   I geve to my wife, Alison Catrick, all my lands, etc., which came to me by inheritance in Wolveston.   To my sonn and heire, John Catrick, all my lands and hereditaments (except before excepted) in Wolveston.   To the chappell in Wolveston, on gimmer lambe.   To the reparinge of Billingham brigg, 2*s.*   To every child whome I helped to christen, 12*d.*   To the poore in Wolveston, 2*s.*   To Richard Catrick, my brother's sonne . . . .   To John Watsonn, my brother in lawe, 10*s.* To Agnes Lackine, a whie calfe, and to my sister, Jane Lakinge, a whie.   To every of my sister's three sonnes, 12*d.*   To my curate, Johnn Manoell, 5*s.*   My daughter, Margaret Catrick.   Overseers, George Thorpe and Robert Watsonne.

WILL OF ROBERT ERRINGTON.

Oct. 31, 1591.   Robart Erington[1] of Denton, in the parishe of Newburne, in the countie of Northumberland, gentleman.   To be buryed wythin the queere doore of the churche of Newburne, and as I trust to have mercie and forgivenes at God's hande, so I freelie forgive all men without exception, requiringe all my brethren and frendes, and all my evilwillers to doe the same.   To the poore folkes of Newburne parishe, 10*s.*   To the churche of Newburne, 10*s.*, for the reparacion therof.   To my daughter, Alice Errington, one branded whie.   To my yongest daughter, Anne Erington, a redd lockt whie.   To my wife Barberie one redd whie and twentie sheep hogges.   To my eldest sonne Marke, two of the beste sheep hogges. To my yongest sonne George, one white cowe and her calfe.   To my servante, Elizabethe Patterson, one haacte whie stircke.   To my sonne Robart, six of my best yewes.   To Barbarie, Custons and

[1] The testator, Robert Errington, was son and heir of George Errington (second son of Roger Errington of Denton) by his wife Barbara, daughter of . . . Shafto of Bavington.   By his wife Barbara, daughter of . . . Blunt of Newcastle, he had, with other children, a son and heir, Mark Errington of West Denton, who married Catherine, daughter of Nicholas Tempest of Thornley.

Annes Erington, my brother Nicolas Errington, his daughters, to everye of them, one gimber hogge. To my mother, Barbarie Errington, one goldingt stott, whiche I bought of hir. To my brother Nicolas, two sommer best-gates of grasse in my pasture at Wharleton, during seven yeares next ensewinge. The rest to my wife Barbarie, my sonnes Marke and George, and my daughters Alice and Anne, whom I make executors, and I constitute and ordaine Mr. Marke Shafto of Newcastle, Mr. Marke Errington of Pontilande, and Mr. William Phenicke of Blackeden, supervisors. [Pr. Nov. 2, 1591.]

WILL OF GEORGE FUISTER.

April 20, 1592. George Fuister of the towne of Newcastle-upon-Tyne, barbar chysurgion.[1] My body to be buried in the churche yeard of the parishe of All Sainctes, before the weddinge church-doore. To my wife, Jane Fuister, all my goodes, whom I make executrix. To my daughter Margaret, 10l. To my daughter Elizabeth, 10l. To the childe wherewith my wife is, 10l. To my wife, two double ducates, and my golde ringes for a token. To Elizabeth Bell, an old angele. To Grace Flower, a french crowne. To my brother, William Herrison, for a token, 10s. To my uncle, Briane Stroother, 20s. To my servaunt, Edward Atchesone, my case of silver lanchers, more I give unto him my shopp windowe whiche I doe nowe keepe, withall the shelves and paynted cloathes about the same, provyded alwayes that he be good unto mye said wyfe. To my apprentice, Thomas Turner, a pott and a basen, with a case of scissors and combes, and all that belongs thereunto, and pleasing my wyfe well during her widowehood, I forgive him a yeare's service; more unto him, 3s. 4d. To my wife Jane, all the yeares I have in lease of the shopp next unto Edward Halles. To the poore of the parishe of All Saincts, 6s. 8d., to be distributed amongst them by the church-wardens. To my nurse, 2s. 6d. To my neigboures, Thomas Bowmer and James Spoore, to eyther of them for a token, an Edward shilling. To Johne Todderick, 12d. My daughters Margaret and Elizabeth, minors.

WILL OF GEORGE ROCHESTER.

Oct. 27, 1592. I, George Rochester, saidler,[2] howsoever sicke in body, yet perfect in memorye and well in minde, thankes be to my most mercifull Father, who hath graunted mee so gentle a summons, do, from my hart, with a lively faith in the name of my Saviour Christ Jesus, recomend my soull to them, that gave it, craveing

[1] *Cf.* Welford, *Newcastle and Gateshead*, vol. iii. p. 69.

[2] The testator was a saddler in Newcastle. *Cf.* Welford, *Newcastle and Gateshead*, vol. iii. p. 77.

mercy and forgiveness of my sinnes in the mediacion of myne only Saviour, being veraly perswaded that for the death and passion of the same, my soull shall be partaker of b[l]isse, presently after the departure of thereof out of my wretched body, and therefore I renounce my workes, seeme they never so good, and cleave onely to the mercy of my Heavenly Father, and Christ my Saviour. To Mr. Houldsworth, as our vicar and teacher, in regard of tithes, which, it may be, I have not so duely paid as I ought to have donne, 5s. To my three children by my first wife, that is to say, George, James and William, for their children's portion, 10l. to every one of them, also to each of them a cowe and twoe silver spoones. To George, my best gowne, a broadcloth cote, laid over with billement lace, and a black, round cappe. To James, my second gowne, and a black cloth coate, stitched with silke. To William, a russet taffaty doublet, and a pair of breeches of broad cloth, laid with velvet, and a clok of silke russet, laid with lace, and myne hatte. To the said William, the remaines of yeares of the house now in the tenor of William Kircus. I geve the said George and his portion to his uncle, George Carre, during his minoritie. I geve the said James, his portion and his other legacies, to his ant, Anne Dent, late wife of Robert Dent, tanner. I geve the said William to Thomas Swanne, cordener. To Henry and Jane, my children by my later wife, either of them, 10l. and one cowe. To Henry, two silver spoones, a black taffaty doublet, and a silke grograme coat, laid on with velvet lace. To Jane, the half of all myne houshold stuffe. To Mr. Henry Mitford, alderman, and to his wife, either of them, an angell. To Mr. Still, halfe an aungell. To Cuthbert Wimfrey, 5s. To my cosen, Thomas Swan his wife, halfe a crown in gold. To Anne Dent, 5s. To my sisters, Margaret Atkenson and Alice Fishe, either of them, 20s. To Thomas Rochester of Sandgate, my brother, 5s. The rest, etc., to my wife Agnes, whom I make executrix. Witnesses, Henry Mytford, alderman, James Bamford, minister, George Still, Thomas Swann.

INVENTORY. Feb. 12, 1592/3. *In the shoppe:* Thre duzen and a halfe of rydinge trees, 10s. 6d. 16 lode trees, 8s. 2 sid trees, 2s. 3 oxen hides and a bull hide, 36s. 8d. 4 horse skynnes and a half, 8s. 2 cushenates, 6s. 2 yellowe cotten saidles, 6s. A read carsey saidle, 4s. A blew and chek saidle, 6s. 8d. 2 dozen sturrupp ledders, 12s. 14 bridles, 7s. 6 housingirdes, 2s. 8 paire of stirrupp ledders, 4s. 6 sadle-trees redie for the coveringe, 12s. Another half dozen of sadle-trees, 3s. 9 gyrthes, 2s. 3d. A lod saidle, 2s. 3 presers, 6s. 8d. 9 yellowe bridles, 4s. 6d. 8 whit bridles, 4s. 2 shoppe bordes, 20d. 2 maill pynnions, 6d. Another syd of lether, 3s. 4d. 5 paire of brod stirrupp ledders, 3s. 4d. 27 of harnes buckles, 6s. 9d. 3 band of stirrupp ledder bouckles, 14d. Half a band of gyrthe bockles, 5d. Half a duzen stirrupp irons, 2s. 3 duzen and a half of beates, 7s. 22 small beates, 18d.

Some totall, 162l.

WILL OF CHRISTOPHER BARTON.

Nov. 6, 1592. Christopher Barton. I have gevin and granted all such debtes and goodes whatsoever unto my executors, Henry Rotheropp, leivetenant, and Quinten Stringer, aunscient, in as free manner as may be, to them and their assignes, in which they, the aforesayde, Henry Rotheropp and Quinton Stringer, standes charged to paye all suche debtes as the abovesaid Christopher Barton doth owe, beinge herunder written.

These are the debtes that are owinge to Christopher Barton, soldiare, of Barwick-upon-Tweed. William Glover owith me 5*l.* Auncient Stringer and James Smith, for the debt of Leivetenant Blisse, deceased, 5*l.* In Annas Hasslewoodes handes, in tickettes of my owne entestaynement of glovess makinge, 3*l.* 13*s.* In Captayn Careye's clarke's booke, 9*s.* Antony Colman, upon a tickett which I have in my owne handes, 18*s.* 8*d.* In the twoe yeare's paye, 4*l.* 5*s.* 6½*d.* In the yeare's paye, 5*l.*

Some totall is juste 24*l.* 7*s.* 2½*d.*

The note named, debtes and somes of money which I owe any maner of waye whatsoever : To William Faun, for halfe a yeare's rent, 6*s.* 8*d.* To my keeper, 12*d.* a weeke frome the 1st of October unto the [blank]. To Jane White, widdowe, 10*s.* To my hoste, Fries, 10*l.* Annes Hasslewoode, 14*s.* 6*d.* To my landlord, Thomas Grene, 5*s.* To George Gardner, 2*s.* To John Stones, 7*s.* More owinge for washinge, 1*s.* 6*d.* To John Harwoode, 2*l.* To the widdowe Harrisone, 4*s.*

I geve and bequethe 10*s.* for a clothe for the comunion borde. I geve also to the poer, 7*s.*, to be distributed att the discretion of my executors. Also iff the saide John Harwoode do sue the afore-named Christopher Barton, he muste have truly paiede hime 40*s.* more. Also I give to my brother, Bryan Bartone, the bedde which I lye upone, with a blankett to it.

WILL OF THOMAS FISHER.

Nov. 26, 1592. Thomas Fisher of South Hebborne, within the parish of Jarro. To Thomas Golightlie, sonne of George Golightlie, my obligatione of 5 markes of John Bangke, with all sommes of money therin conteyned. The rest of all my landes, goodes, etc., to my cosine, William Fisher of Durham, and Agnes Lytle, my servant, whom I make executores.

INVENTORIE. Fower silver sponnes and a mazer, 22*s.* 8*d.* 3 latten candlestickes, a morter and a pestle, and a latten stall with a cover, 8*s.* 4*d.* 4 peuder pottes and an ewer, 5*s.* 18 peece of puder, 13*s.* 4*d.* 3 latten basines, 8*s.* 2 tinne bottles and 2 glasse bottles, 3*s.* 4*d.* A gunne, a pistle, a bowe, a dagger, a basslert and a coot of plait, 27*s.* His woolling apparell, 4*l.* A bill staff, 12*d.* 2 pare of plate sleves, and one pare of male sleves, 2*s.*

WILL OF GEORGE BOURN.

Dec. 15, 1592. George Bourn of the towne of Newcastle upon Tyne, cowper, being in health of bodie, but of good and perfect memorie, thankes, be to God, do make and ordaine this my will and testament in wrytinge, as well concerning the disposicon of my small porcion of landes and tenementes, as allso of that lyttle quantitie of goodes and chattells whatsoever, which God haieth lent me at this time present to dispose. First, I commend my sowle unto the handes of Almightie God, who created me, nothing doubting but that for his infinite mercies sett forthe in the precious bloode of his dearlie beloved sonne Jesus Christe my onlie Sayour and Redeamer, he will accepte the same unto his glorie and place it in companie of his holie angels and blessed sanctes, and I will my bodye be buried in the parishe churche of All Hallowes. I give the house wherin I now do dwell in the Flessher Rawe of the said towne of Newcastle uppon Tyne, and all other my houses, landes, etc., in the said towne and the liberties thereof (except one house with th'appurtenance in the Mell Markett), unto Isabell, my well beloved wife, during her life, and after her decease to Marke Erington of Ponteland, in the countie of Northumberland, gentleman, and his heirs for ever. I give the aforsaid howse in the Meale Markett to my servante, George Clewghe, and the heirs of his bodie, and for lack of such to Marke Erington aforenamed. To the said Marke Erington, one presser of wainscotte standing in the chamber over the hall, and one fether bed, with a bolster and all the furniture thereto belonginge, with the coveringe of tapisterye worke, and one iron chimney, also one sylver pece, parcell guylte, which the said Marke boughte for me at London, one sylver pece with a cover, dowble guylte, in weight, 26 ounces. The rest of all my houshold stuffe to my wief Isabell. To my said wief, 20*l*., provided she shall not have, taike or claime or benefite of the moyetie of my goodes dew unto her in respect I have no children lyvinge. To Mistres Erington, wief to Marke Erington, one portingale peice in goulde. To Mr. George Brigges and his wief, and to either of them a double duccatt. To my good frend, Jane Surtis, wief to Thomas Surtis, one rose noble in gould. To my servante, George Clewghe, all my workinge geare, also all classbord and houpes which I shall have unwrought at the daie of my deathe. To the aforenamed Marke Errington, the moietie and half of all the residew of my goodes, and the other moitie to my wief, whom I make one of the executors, and Marke Erington the other. To Mr. Howlesworth, an angell. To my wife, all my tenure of yeares of Tenth Medowes, in the parish of Newborne, and also of the Dovecotte-close. To Henarie Fenkell and his wief, a dowble duccatt eche. To my servant, Alice Cleugh, 3*l*. 6*s*. 8*d*. To my servant, Cuthbert Gibson, att the appointment of George Clewghe, half a thousand howpes, that is to saie, barrell howpes and firkin howpes. To Thomas Dickson and his wief, an angell in gould a pece. To Christopher Clewes, a double duccatt. Witnesses, Robert Errington, Gawyn Ogle. [Pr. June 15, 1595.]

July 2, 1593. INVENTORIE of the goodes of George Bowrne. In readie moneye, 120*l*. A dossane banquittinge dishes and 4 sawcers, 4*s*. A gowne faced with bonge, 3*l*. 2 gownes, 30*s*. A cloke, 20*s*. A sattone dublette, 26*s*. 2 jerkins, 2 pare of bryches, and 3 par of stotkins, 20*s*. 2 hattes and 3 capes, 20*s*. A steal cappe and a sworde, 3*s*. A calever and a flaske, 20*s*. 4 chistes and a halbarte, 16*s*. 24 pare of line shettes, 4*l*. 13*s*. 4*d*. 6 head shettes, 13*s*. 4*d*. 8 dossan napkins, 40*s*. 24 cod pillow beirs, 30*s*. 7 borde clothes of line, and one of dyper, 40*s*. 5 table towells, 20*s*. 2 dresser clothes of dyper, 6 hande towells, 8*s*. All the above lynne in the cheiste in the butterie in the fire chamber. Fower hundrethe clabord, 4*l*. 20 dossane brode hupes, 5*s*. 8 hundrethe fyrkins howpes, 8*s*. 3 thousand fyrkyn howpes, 30*s*. 7 dossane of brode howpes, 28*s*. 35 irone howpes, 23*s*. 4*d*. 5 axes and 8 eaches, 8*s*. 20 pare cells and 8 compasses, 4*s*. 6*d*. 3 headinge knyves, 18*d*. 5 joynters and 4 irons, 5*s*. 6 wimbles and 4 sawes, 8*s*. Certaine trussing howpes, 2*s*. 2 cutting knyves, and 3 chessells, 20*d*. 4 crosses and 2 brandrethes, 2*s*. 3 hewe axes and 4 eaches, 2 headinge knyffes, 2 wembles, a theasle, 6 joyning irons and 6 shaving knyffes, 23*s*. 4*d*. 7 dossane fatte howpes, 16*s*. 10 dossane brode howpes, 3*s*. 4*d*. 4 thousand barelle howpes, 3*l*. 4*s*. A thowsand fyrkyn howpes, 20*s*. 3 dossene pypes howpes, 18*d*. A silver salte with a cover, parcell gilted, 22 ounces, 4*l*. 19*s*. A sillver salte with a cover, 49*s*. 6*d*. A dossane syllver sponnes, 22 ounces, 4*l*. 19*s*. A sponne of sillver, duble gilt, 2 ounces, 11*s*. 3*d*. 13 sillver spoones, 40 ounces, 4*l*. 10*s*. A sillver potte, parcell gylte, 16 ounces, 3*l*. 12*s*. A sillver peace, parcell and gylte, 15 ounces and a half, 3*l*. 8*s*. 2½*d*. A sillver peece, parcell and gylte, 25 ounces, 3*l*. 7*s*. 6*d*. A stone potte banded with sillver, 50*s*. A peece of sillver, double gylte, 18 ounces, 4*l*. 12*d*. A peece with a plate cover, double gylt 26 ounces, 5*l*. 17*s*. A taister of sillver, 3 ounces, 13*s*. 2 sillver whissells with a touth pyke and certaine oulde monye, 20*s*.

Debts due to the testator: Marke Erington, 60*l*. Robert Eden, apothecarie, 20*l*. Robert Fenton and Randale Fenton, 45*l*. Robert Brandlinge, merchant, 20*l*. Sampson Hudspethe, 20*l*. Thomas Tallantyre, 10*l*. Lancelot Carnaby, 7*l*. 4*s*. Christopher Denninge, 12*l*. *Summa totalis*, 476*l*. 14*s*. 4*d*.

WILL OF WILLIAM LORD EURE.

Dec. 22, 1592. I, William Ewrie, Lord Ewrie,[1] fullie perswaded of my mortall condycion, that in Godes good tyme, unknowne to

---

[1] The head of the family of Eure, which came of the ancient and noble Norman stock of the barons of Warkworth. The testator was the son of Sir Ralph Eure, knt. (who was killed in 1545, during his father's lifetime, at

men, ther must be a separacion of soule and body, give and bequeathe my soule to Almyghtie God, my most mercyfull creator, trustinge assuredly to be saved, by the merittes of Jesus Chryste, who, on the crosse, payd the full pryce of my redemption, and made satisfaction, for all my synnes. ·I gyve forty poundes to be disposed to the poore people of Inglebye, Wytton, Stokesley and other towns, parishes, and hamlettes, thereunto now adjoyninge.   To Fraunces Ewrie, William Ewrie[1] and Charles Ewrie, my yonger sonnes, my farme called Cowndon grange, and the west felde of Sawton, nowe in my occupacion.   To my sonne, Rawfe Ewrye, all my plate, housholde stuffe and armor.   To my daughter, Mary Ewrie,[2] wyffe to my sayd sonne Raufe Ewrie,[3] my best standinge cuppe of sylver, excepte that whiche Quene Mary dyd gyve mee, which I will shalbe and remayne an heyrloome.   To William Ewrie, sonne and heyre apparaunt to my sayd sonne Raufe Ewrie, my best basyn and ewer of sylver, parcell gylt.   To my daughter Ewrye,[4] nowe wyfe to my sonne Fraunces Ewrie, one of my beste sylver bowles.   To my thirde sonne, William Ewrie, one armor complete for his body.   To my fourth sonne, Charles Ewrie, one armer complete for his body.   To Anne Mallorye,[5] my eldest daughter, 10l.   To my seconde doughter, Meriall Gooderyche,[6] 10l.   To my youngest doughter, Martha Armyn,[7] 10l.   To William Mallory, sonne to John Mallorye, by my sayd daughter Anne, whome I chrystened, 5l.   To William Goodryche, sonne of Rycharde Gooderiche, by my daughter Meryall, whome I chrystened, 5l.   To Christofer Mallorie, sonne of the sayd John and Anne Mallory, nowe remaynynge with me, 10l.   To William Lampton,[8] sonne to Raufe Lampton, whom I chrystened, one sylver bowle.   To everie housholde servaunt I shall have, att the day of my deathe, one whole yeare's wages.

Panierhaugh, or Ancrum Moor, in Teviotdale), by Margery, daughter of Sir Ralph Bowes of Streatlam, co. Durham, knt.   He married Margaret, daughter of Sir Edward Dymoke of Scrivelsby, co. Lincoln, knt.   She was buried at Ingleby Greenhow, Sept. 15, 1591, and the testator was buried at the same place, Feb. 13, 1593/4.

[1] 1647, May 11.   Mr. William Ewry, esquir, bur.   *Bishop Middleham Register.*

[2] The first wife of his son Ralph, Lord Eure.   She was the daughter of Sir George Dawney, Sessay, co. York, knt.

[3] 1645/6, Jan. 29.   Mr. Raphe Ewry, esquir, bur.   *Bishop Middleham Register.*

[4] Elizabeth, daughter of John Leonard.

[5] Wife of Sir William Mallory of Studley, co. York, knt.

[6] 1578, Nov. 4.   Richard Goodrige and Merioll Eure, daughter of the Right Honorable Lord Eure, mar.   *Ingleby Greenhow Register.*

[7] 1590, April 26.   William Arminge, esq., and Martha Eure, daughter of the Right Honorable Lord Eure, mar.   *Ibid.*

[8] Afterwards Sir William Lambton, knt., son of Ralph Lambton of Lambton, co. Durham, esq., and grandson of Robert Lambton, esq., and his wife Frances, daughter of Sir Ralph Eure, knt., and sister of the testator.

To Cuthberte Pepper, my best amblinge geldinge. To my sonnes, Raufe and William Ewrie, my waynes, etc., at Ingleby, Broughton or Sawton. The resydue to my sonnes Fraunces, William and Charles Ewrie, and I will that they shalbe kepte, and convenyent intertayne-ment for suche of my servauntes, as will remayne ther, att the chardges of my sonne Raufe, duringe one quarter of a yeare, nexte after my deathe and towards the chardges wherof I gyve to my sayd sonne Raufe all my grayne and corn, and I make him my sole executor.

CODICIL. Feb. 4, 1593/4. To my sonne and heyre, Raufe Ewrie, 1,500*l*. towardes the buyldinge of a hous at Jerrowe. To Mr. Bynnion, 8*l*. which he owethe me, and a geldinge. To Mr. Brydges, a geldinge, of 8*l*. pryce. To my sonne and heyre, Raufe Ewrie, all my draughte oxen, att Litle Broughton and Ingleby, and all my yonge shepe. To my servant, John Pearson, 4 markes. To Adelein Thorppe, 40*s*. To everie one of my maydes, a cowe. [Pr. July 5, 1599.]

NUNCUPATIVE WILL OF GEORGE TONGE.

Memorandum : That about the 16th day of Marche in anno domini 1592/3, Mr. George Toinge of Denton,[1] esquier, crased in bodie but of perfect mind and memorie, in the presence of these wit-nesses followinge did declare his last will and testament nuncupa-tively in manner and forme followinge. First, he did give and committ his soule to Almightie God and his bodie to the earthe. Also he did give and bequiethe all his goods and chattells to his wif Helin Toinge, and to his sonn Cuthbert, and to his daughter Elizabethe, whom he did make and ordeyne the executors of his last will. Witnesses, Henry Tong, Georg Jehnison.

INVENTORY, 2 April, 1593.

WILL OF JOHN HARDING.

May 27, 1593. John Harding of Whickham, gentleman.[2] My bodye to be buried within the parish churche of Whickham, with that comlyness that appertaineth thereunto. To Elizabeth, my wife, and children, all my goodes, and I make thesse here nominated,

---

[1] George Tonge of Denton and West Thickley married Helen, daughter of John Lambton of Lambton, by whom he had a numerous issue. He was buried at Heighington March 25, 1593, and was succeeded by his son and heir, Henry Tong of Denton and Thickley, who was born *circa* 1550. *Cf.* Surtees, *Durham*, vol. iv. p. 4.

[2] The testator was probably a member of the family of Harding of Holling-side, in the parish of Whickham, whose pedigree is printed in Surtees, *Durham*, vol. ii. p. 252. He married, May 3, 1584, Elizabeth Robson, and was buried Aug. 13, 1593. *Whickham Registers.*

namely, Robart Hardinge, Rafe Harding, Jane Harding, my full
executors. To Annis Robson, my mother in lawe, 1*l.* To Margaret
Tesdale, my kinswoman, 3*s.* 4*d.* To Raphe Whittfilde, in lew of his
good service, 2*s.* 6*d.* To the porer sorte of the people of Whickham,
12*d.* Witnesses, Mr. Robart Fawden, Richard Barloe and Richard
Darham, minister of Whickham. [Pr. Nov. 9, 1593.]

WILL OF ROBERT HARBOTTLE.

Aug. 3, 1593. Robarte Harbotele of Bemishe,[1] in the parishe
of Tanfield and countye of Durham. To my doughter, Elizabethe
Harbotell, 100 markes, to be taken of a tenemente called the North
Calsy; and a close called the West-myll-close, and another cloffe
called Dobbes Gren, altogether of the yearlye value of 16*l.* 11*s.* 8*d.* ;
also I give unto her all my houshold stuffe, savinge my plate and
sartan percills to be herafter recited, and I appointt my sone Raphe
to have the tuicion of her duringe hir nonage. To my son Robartt,
100 markes, to be taken out of my mill, called Callsye mill, and he to
be under the tuicion of his brother Raphe during his nonage. To my
son Frauncis, all my title, etc., of a tenemente, called the Middell
the Calsye, with a paer of virginalls. To my sone Raphe, a
brasse pot, a great yron chimlaye, on great presser in my parler at
the Calsye, a paer of claricottes and two silk carpin-clothes of nedell
work. To my sister, Barbara Ruddesforth, on gould ringe. To Jane,
wife to Richard Hindmers (?), 20*s.* To Mr. Francis Anderson, on ould
angell, and I make him supervisor. The rest to my sone Raphe,
whom I make executor, and I charge him to paye unto my sone
Robartt, 10*l.*, within two yeares after he come out of his prentishipe.
Witnesses, Francis Anderson, Isaac Anderson.

WILL OF THOMAS LORENS.

Nov. 4, 1594. Thomas Lorens [2] of Walsend, gentleman. My
bodye to be buryed in the parishe churche of Walsend. I make my
wif, Isabell Lorens, sole executrix. For my children's portions,
I will they be set forthe at the sighte of Mr. Raphe Lawson, Mr.
William Fenwick, esquiers, my brother Robert Lawson, my brother

---

[1] Cadets of the family of Harbottle lingered in the neighbourhood for many
years after Eleanor, daughter and co-heiress of Sir Guischard Harbottle, had
carried Beamish in marriage to Sir Thomas Percy. Robert, son and heir of
Thomas Harbottle, was possessed of lands in Tanfield so late as 1615. *Cf.*
Surtees, *Durham*, vol. ii. pp. 223, 225.

[2] The testator, an extensive farmer and grazier, with live stock at Walls-
end, Blagdon, Horton, Benton, Brenkley, Kirkharle, Prestwick and Flatworth,
is stated to have been a younger son of Robert Lorraine of Kirkharle. *Cf.*
Hodgson, *Northumberland*, pt. ii. vol. i. p. 246.

William Fenwick, and my brother Randall Fenwick, gentlemen. I gyve my eldest sonne, Robert Lorens, to my younge master, Mr. Roger Lawson. I leave the rest of my children with all my brethren and frendes, with my wif. To my sister, one oxe whiche is at Kirkharle. To Symond Toore, thre yowe hoges. To everye of my house-holde servantes, both men and women, 2s. To the poore, 10s.

INVENTORY. Hard corne and otes at Matfen, 16l. Otes in Stickley, 25l. Wheat in Stickley, 9 boules, 4l. 10s At Blaigden: 7 yere-olde nolte, 3l. 10s.; 6 two-yere old nolt, 6l.; 3 elder nolte, 6l. At Walsend, 40 ewes, 9l. At Blaigden, 83 hoges, 13l. At Horton, 40 hogges, 6l. 13s. 4d. At Benton, 89 ewes, 20l. At Walsend, 3 nages, 6l. At Benton, 1 nage, 40s. At Walsend: nyne oxen, 20l.; 12 kie, 18l.; 5 gelde nolte, 3l. 15s. At Benton; two oxen, 4l. 13s. 4d.; 16 kie, 24l. At Brenkley, 1 oxe, 20s. At Kirkharle, 1 oxe, 20s. At Prestick, 1 oxe, 20s. At Benton old gate, 26 kedes, 3l. At Walsend: twentie bouls of wheat, 10l. 10s.; 40 bouls of otes, 10l.; 8 boules of peese, 53s. 4d.; waines and plewes, with th'appertences, 53s. 4d.; all the household stuffe, 10l. At Walsend, 10 bouls of corne sowen, 10l. At Matfen, 7 bouls sowen, valued to 21 bouls, 7l. At Stickley, 4 bouls sowen, 4l. At Flatworth, 20 bouls of big, 10l. At Kirkharle, corne sowen and in the yarde, 5l. At Flat-worth, 20 ewes, 6l. His apparell, 40s. Debts owinge to him, 3l. He owes for the rent of Flatworth, 50l. *Summa bonorum declaro,* 214l. 18s. 4d.

WILL OF THOMAS NICHOLSON.

[1595.] In the name of Jesus, so be it. I, Thomas Nicholson of Newcastle, maister of a good shippe, called the 'Nightingaile,' of Newcastell, now sick in bodie but sound in mynde, and of perfect memorye, do rest and staye myselfe only on Godes mercye, beleving verylie, throwghe the merites of Christes death, to have remission and pardon of all my sins, and everlasting salvation, and to the blessed Trynytie I commit my soule, who is best can conceive it, and my bodye to the earthe, from whence it came, being persuaded that at the last God shall compell my body and sowle togither agayne, and these my eyes shall see Him, in the land of life. Concerninge my temporall estate and business, being also in good and perfit memorie myndinge to leave my testament and last wyll in sech order, that neyther my wife nor freyndes shall fall at any disorder thereon my negligent forgetfulnes. I do therefore wyll that my beloved wife shall have and enjoye all my landes, howses and tenementes, the shipp and els all my arrables, the freight and my wages, and all that I have, for the tearme of her life; and after her discease, the head howse to come to the use of my cosin Cuthberte's sonne Thomas; and after his discease, to come to Gabryall, and to John; and after ther discease, to come to the narrowest of the name, and for the rest to doo with them as hir mynd serves. And for tokens of remembrance to my freyndes, I give to my uncle, Christofer Nicholson, an old angell, and to my brother, Thomas Dodes, the same, also to my sister, Margaret Nicholson, the same, and to my coosins, Cuthbert Nicholson, John Fórster, and Margaret Gibson, the same to eache of them.   To my old uncle, Robert Byttelston, a crowne of fyve shillinges.   To Richard Doune, my wife's brother, my whistell and my chyne of silver and to my boy, John Forster, half of my see clothes and shirtes, and my sea carde, with the other bookes ; and to my brother, Robert Mylburne, an old angell.   And at my being at Danske, I tooke upon the valewe of 10l., at Robert Sterrete's man, to pay at London to one Sheat, and 20s. to John Ampleforth, of London, which debts, I doubte not, but the shipp will see discharged, if God send hir in safelie.   In default thereof, my wife to paye the same, and she to be full executrix of my wyll.   Witnesses, Edward Cordmane, Thomas Kenneker, merchante.   [Pr. *circa*, 1595.]

WILL OF WILLIAM DAVEY.

Nov. 10, 1595.   William Davey.   To be buried in my parish churche of Rothburie.   I give to Robert Davey, my son, a farmhold in Thropton that Robert Richeson holds.   To Edward Davey, a cottage which I buylded, a stone house upon it, an aiker of land that perteyneth therof to the cottage, and another aker in Thropton feild, called Beanias aker.   To John Davey, my son, the farmehold that Marke Jefferson dwelleth in, with one cottage, save two foodder of hay yearely that my sonne William Davey shall have of the said farmhold of the New-towne for ever.   To William Davey, my sonn, two houses in Rothburie, one that lieth east of Rollie Grenes and one house that lieth west of Rollie Grenes, and east of Roger Dodshone, and one close called Lister-cloce.   To my son, Edward Davey, one free house in Rothburie that lieth south of John Davis and north of Thomas Watson.   To John Davey, my son, a blaicke cow and shott.   The residue to Robert Davey, my son.   Witnesses, Robert Davey, Mathew Storer, John Storer, William Sowerbie, minister, etc.

WILL OF LUKE OGLE.

July 5, 1596.   Luke Ogle of Eglengham, gentleman.[1]   To be buryed in the parysh church or chauncell of Eglengham.   To my thre reputed daughters, Isabell, Myrryell and Beile Ogle, every of them, 10l.   To my sonne's daughter, Myrryell Ogle, 20l., besydes hir porcyon.   To my late son, Christofer Ogle,[2] his sonnes, all my right

---

[1] The testator seems to have been the second of the four Luke Ogles who successively held Eglingham.   *Cf.* Sir Henry Ogle, *Ogle and Bothal*, p. 193.

[2] Administration of the goods of Christopher Ogle was granted, June 13, 1597, to Thomasine, his widow.   His children, Thomas, Tristram, Cuthbert, Elizabeth, Julian and Dorothy Ogle, all minors.

and tytle of the mill of Eglengham, and the tythe corne of Aylname. To my syster, Jullyan Ogle, 20 nobles, and to her sonne Lewes Ogle, 40s., and to Thomas Ilderton, 20s. To Lewes, Marke Ogle's sonne, one house in Anwik, lyinge in Bellygate, which I purchased of John Spence. To Jane Taylor, 40s. To my reputed sonnes, Lennard and Robert Ogle, 20 nobles. To my sonne Robert Ogle's sonne, Luke Ogle, one yoke of oxen, with the heyer-lomes of the house, that is to saye, the tables, boordes and formes, the great caldron, the great pott, with the brasen morter, the best bedd in the house, the raxe and spittes. To Trestrom, sonne of my late sonne Christofer Ogle, the fermeholde in Framlington, after Lainge's lease is expyred, with the freehold ther, and after the said Trestrom, to come to his brother Cuthbert, and the longer liver of them. I make Thomas and Trestrom, the sonnes of my said late sonne Christofer, executors, and Mr. Raffe Gray of Chillingham and Mr. William Lawson of Rock, supervisors. Witnesses, Roger Gray, Robert Gray, Thomas White, Thomas Snawdon, William Lawson, Martin Ogle, and Gregory Fenwick.

Debtes owinge to the testator : Sir John Forster, for wood, out of Thropp wood, 10l.; more he is owinge me for the rent of the Gambleston, the space of 10 yere and odd, the rent being 4s. the yere. The heires of his brother, Thomas Forster, is owinge me for the queene's rent of Wardane, Warneford, Newlandes, and Bassindon, the space of 9 yeres, at 20s. the yere. Sir Raffe Graye's executores and his wife, 23l. Thomas Collingwood of Litle Ryle, viz., rent, 3l., girsons, 7l. 10s. The hayres of Henry Collingwood of Ingrom is owinge for the tythe corne of Revely, 5l., and 40s. for rent, and for a gerson of the said tythe, 7l. 14s. The laird of Prendick, 9l. The laird of Barra, 4l. and odd money. The laird of Clennell, 43s. The laird of Trewhitt, 20s. John Rutless of Killom, 40s. Henry Swnhoe for a gerson, 5l. 6s. 8d. and 20 fir dales. Gawinge Forster, 47s. 6d. The tennants of Burton is owinge for ther rentes. . . . Nychollas Manners for a fyne for one ferme in Burton, 10l. The mylner of Lylburne-mill, for 3 bowells of corne, 40s.

Debtes owinge by the testator : Mr. Gray, for the Quene's rent, 23l. John Gray of . . . . , 20s. The lady of Craster, 53s. 4d.

WILL OF JAMES WIDDRINGTON.

Sept. 2, 1596. James Witheringtone [1] of Gateshead, in the county of Durham, gentleman. To be buryed in the parishe churche of the saide towne, within the qyer. To John Chapman, my man, the farmhould late in the occupacion of Mathew Stokey, payinge

---

[1] The testator was apparently a younger son of John Widdrington of Temple Healey, in the parish of Bywell St. Peter, whose will, dated Feb. 4, 1570, is printed in *Wills and Inventories*, vol. i. p. 320. *Cf.* new *History of Northumberland*, vol. iv. p. 240 n, and vol. vi. p. 170.

3*l*. 6*s*. and no more. To my man, Mark Maugham, 3*s*. To my mayde, Margerye Blackdene, 40*s*., besydes her wages. To my daughter, Annas Witheringtone, my howse, etc., in Gateshead, whiche I boughte, to her and her heires lawfully begotten, and for defaulte of suche, then to her sister Marye, and for defaulte of her and her heires, then to come to John, Robert and Henry Witheringtone, and theire heires, from the eldeste unto the yongeste. To my said two daughters, all my howseholde implementes and stuffe in the said howse, to part and devide yt equally between them. And further I give to my said daughters all my horses, noult, and sheepe and corne, to be praised equallie for the somme of 40*l*. to eche, and if yt will not reach unto so much, then I will that my sonnes, John, Robert and Henry, do make yt furthe, when they shall come to 21 yeares, or to be maryed. To my sonne John, my whole tythe, etc., of the townshipe of Halleden, savinge the neather milne, belonginge unto yt, and that I doe give unto Robert, for his life, and after to come to his brother John. To my yongest sone Henrye, my title of Whitsydelaw.[1] To my sone Robert, my tytle of the tithes and personage of Hartborne. I doe make my said three sones my executors, to see all my debts discharged, etc., by the sight of Mr. Henry Witheringtone, esquier, and Mr. Roger Witheringtone, his brother, and give unto each of them, for a token of remembrance, 20*s*. I doe owe my sister Anne, yet unpaide of her bonde, 20 markes. Witnesses, Nicholas White, Anthony Softly, John Chapman.

WILL OF THOMASIN HEATH.

Oct. 14, 1596. Thomazin Heathe [2] of Acklife, weadowe, I give unto my sonne, Mr. John Rippes, my nest of sylver tunes, and my silver salt, and a tappestre coverlet, for a rememberaunc of my good will. To Mr. Robert Throckmorton, my sonne, all my houshoold stufe whatsoever. To my doughter, Thomazin Rippes, 100*l*. to be given hir eyther at the age of 21 yeares or at the daye of hir marriage, wheather of them commethe furst, and if she be then livinge, desiring Mr. John Heath of Keper, th'elder, to be aidinge and helpinge of myne executors for and towardes the puttinge fourth of the 100*l*. for hir best commoditye and profit, payinge unto them yearly that shall have the tuycion of hir, unto the foresaid tyme of 21 yeares or marryage, after the rait of 10*l*. for the use of the said 100*l*. But if she shall depart this life before the age of 21 yeares or

---

[1] The small estate of Whiteside-law, in the parish of Chollerton, was conveyed by William Widdrington to William Milburn in 1654. *Cf*. new *History of Northumberland*, vol. iv. p. 301.

[2] Widow of John Heath of Kepyer, co. Durham. She was the daughter of Thomas Dearham of Cremplesham, co. Norfolk, and was thrice married; first to John Throckmorton of Werrington, co. Northampton, and then to John Rippes of West Walton, co. Norfolk. She had no issue by her third marriage. *Cf*. Surtees, *Durham*, vol. iv. p. 70.

marryage, then I will and bequeath the said 100*l.* to be equallye distributed betwixt my two sonnes, Mr. Robert Throckmorton and Mr. John Rippes, if they be then lyvinge, or to the longer lyver of them, provided that the 5 markes which my husband, Mr. John Heath, gave by legasie unto Thomazin Rippes at his death be accompted and reckned allwaise in the said some of 100*l.* To my sister, Jane Bayker, a gold ringe, with a deathes head, for a rememberanc of my good will. To my lord the bushop of Durham, 2 spure ryalls. To Mrs. Mathewe, one spure ryall. To my brother, Mr. Robert Dearham, an angell. To my brother, John Dearham, an angell. To my brother, Mr. Baldain Dearham, an angell. To my sonne in lawe, Mr. John Heath, th'elder, towe spure ryalls. To my doughter in lawe, Mrs. Elyzabeth Heath, his wife, a gold ringe with a dyomond. To my sone, John Heathe and his wife, to eyther of them, an angell. To my sone, Edward Heathe, a spure ryall. To my doughter Thomazin, a noble soveraigne. To my doughter, An Heath, wife of Edward Heath, my best gowne. To my sonne, Henry Smith, one spure ryall. To my 2 maid servants, which shalbe in servis with me at the tyme of my decease, to eyther of them, 5*s.*, besides all my workday wearing apparell, to be devided betwixt them at the discretion of my executors. To Dame Morland and to hir doughter, Thomazin Hindmas, to ether of them, 5*s.* To Ingram Tayllor and his wife, to eyther of them, 5*s.* To John Francklin and Harry Denton, to eyther of them, 5*s.* To my old servant, Richard Baytes, 6*l.* 13*s.* 4*d.*, to be paid him within six months after my decease. To Christofer Dune, 20*s.*, to be paid him at the age of 21 yeares if he be then lyvinge. To John Kaye, 10*s.* To Bryand Metcalfe, 5*s.* To the pour of Saint Gylles pareshe in Gilligait, 40*s.* To Marye Blaxton, wife of Robert Blaxton, my new clothe gowne. To Mrs. . . . . and my taffity apern. To Margret Kaye, my newe safe-gard. To Jane Volenbye, my forepart of taffity. To Thomas Morley and Thomas Thursby, my god-children, to eyther of them, 5*s.*, to by ether of them a yew and a lame. To my cuszen, Richard Dearham, an angell. To Robert Stevensone, scholmaster of Acklife, 6*s.* 8*d.* All the rest of my goodes, etc., to my 2 sones, Robert Throckmorton and John Rippes, whome I do maik my full executors. And allso I do maike my sonne, John Heath of Kepere, th'elder, supervisor.

WILL OF EDWARD HUDSPETH.

July 16, 1597. Edward Hudspethe, of the cittie of Durham, tanner. My bodie to be buried in the parishe churche of Sainct Nicholas in Durham.[1] I give to Allice, my wife, all my landes and

---

[1] 1597, July 17. Edward Hudspet, alderman, in templo. *Burial Register of St. Nicholas',* Durham.

tenements duringe her lyfe naturall, to bringe upp her children and myne withall. I give and bequeathe to Edward Hudspethe, my sonne, and to thee heirs of his bodie lawfullie begotten, my tanne-house, and after his decease, if he die without heires of his bodie lawfullie begotten. . . . . My will and meaninge is, and upon that mynde, meaninge and entent, after my wyve's decease, I give my landes called Ashes landes and Hedworthes landes to my eldest sonne, Thomas Hudspethe, and to Christofer Hudspethe and John Hudspethe, my sonnes. I give as muche as in me liethe and will that Tobie Hudspethe, my sonne, shall have and enjoye the lease which is taken in his owne name. I give and bequeathe to everie of my three daughters, Jane Hudspethe, Margaret Hudspethe and Isabell Hudspethe, a severall and equall portion of my goodes as all my goodes shall amount unto, my debtes being first paied. I give and bequeathe to my wife Alice, dureinge her naturall life, the Chapple close and the little close called Parradise, and after her decease I give and bequeathe the same groundes to my sonnes Thomas, Christofer and John, besides the dwellinge-house before bequeathed to them. I give and bequeathe to my two bretheren, Thomas Huds-pethe and Robert Hudspethe, and to my sister, Allice Hudspethe, to everie of them, an angell. I give and commend my sonne Tobie Hudspethe to my good freend and neighboure, Edward Wanlesse, to be fatherlie educated upon the sonnes duetifull behavioure. I bequeathe my sonn, John Hudspethe, to Mr. Lockwood, hys god-father, to be ordered and governed after his good and godlie discre-tion. I bequeathe my sonne, Christofer Hudspethe, to my good freend Mr. Henrie Smith, to be brought up and governed after his godlie discretion. And I make, ordeyne and appoint Alice Hudspethe my full and sole executrix whom I charge to paye my debtes and legacies.

NUNCUPATIVE WILL OF THOMAS HUTCHINSON.

Memorandum : That upon Sondaie next before Michaelmas last, in anno domini 1597, Thomas Hutchinson, of Saint Margarets, in the cittie of Durham, beinge of good and perfecte remembrance, though sicke in bodie, made his last will and testament by word of mouthe in manner and forme in effecte as followeth, viz. : --He said to Gregorie Hutcheson : Yowe see that I am sicke and not like to live, my will is that you have the keapinge and government of my wife and children, and I will that you see that everie of them have right and that my children and there goodes be well brought upp and husband there owne goods. And in conformacon that yow will performe in deid accordinge to my trust hearin reposed in yow, I take youre hand and promise, and the said Gregorie soe promised, and by his hand assured on his parte (as he willed) so to doe. And all my goods I give (he sayd)

to my wife Annas Hutcheson, Thomas Hutcheson, Cuthbert Hutchin-
son, Christofer Hutchinson, Isable Hutcheson, Elizabethe Hutchinson,
Jane Hutcheson, Margerete Hutcheson, Anne Hutcheson, and
Alesone Hutchesone, my children ; and I give to Roland Colingwood
and Heughe Ayre, to eyther of them, being servants, 8s. the peece.
Witnesses hereof, Roland Collingwood, Heugh Ayre.

WILL OF ALICE CRASTER.

Sept. 23, 1597. Alice Craister of Dunstanbrough[1] in the parish
of Emmelton. I give unto every one of my sonnes-in-lawe one
angell. I give unto Mr. Richard Grene, five marks. To James
Wilson, one angell. To my sonn, John Craister, my beddinge, with
pottes and pannes. To my doughter, Grace Armorer, all my lynninge.
To my man, John Brown, 20s. To Margarett Robeson, one bowle of
rye. To the poore, 10l. To my sons, Edmond Craister and Thomas
Craister, 20l. apiece. To my daughter Barbara Craister, 33l. 13s. 4d.
To my daughter, Ellen Craister, 33l. 13s. 4d. To my daughter, Jane
Anderson, 20l. To my daughter, Margaret Collingwood, 20l. To my
daughter, Isabel Ogle, 20l. To my mother, a ryall. Executor, my
son-in-law, Henry Collingwood. Supervisors, Richard Grene and
James Wilson. Witnesses, John Craister, Luke Ogle, William Armorer
and Richard Grene. [Pr. 1600.]

NUNCUPATIVE WILL OF GEORGE HORSLEY.

1597. A little before Michaelmas last, in this year, George
Horsley of Togston, in the parish of Warkworth, did give all his
goods, moveable and immoveable, to his brother Thomas Horsley,
his debts being first paid. Witnesses, Cuthbert Hunter, Isabella
Hall, and others.

Feb. 15, 1597/8. INVENTORY of George Horsley, late of Togston,
parish of Warkworth, praised by George Baird, Cuthbert Hunter
and Roger Taylor. 6 oxen, 1 kowe and 1 stirke, 5l. 6s. 8d. 1 maire,
3 ewes and 1 hogge, 1l. 10s. 1 sewe and 1 goose, 5s. Wanes and
ploughes, etc., 16s. 2 almryes, 1 cawell and 1 chist, 16s. 3 pots,
1 kettell, 10 doublers and 2 sawcers, 13s. 4d. 2 barrells and 1 malt
tub, 1s. 8d. 1 table, a firecrooke, a paire of tonges, an iron spit
and 1 chaire, 3s. 4d. His bedding and the rest of insight goods,
6s. 8d. 3 bowles of hard corne sown estimated to 9 bowells, 6l. 6s.
1 bowle of bigge sown estimated to 3 bowles, 1l. 10s. 5 bowles of
oats sowen estimated to 25 bowles, 4l. 10s. Total, 22l. 4s. 8d.

Debts owing by testator, 12l. 0s. 1d.

---

[1] The testatrix was Alice, widow of Edmund Craster of Craster and
daughter of Christopher Mitford of Newcastle. Her mother's will is printed
in *Wills and Inventories*, vol. ii. p. 30.

INVENTORY OF JOHN BURRELL.[1]

An INVENTORIE of all the goods and chattells, moveable and unmoveable, whereof John Burrell, lait of Langtonn, deceased, dyed possessed uppon, valewed and priced by Willam Garth, Henrie Cockfield, Anthonie Thompson and John Thompson, the last daie of September, *Anno Regina Elizabethae* 39, (1597).

Imprimis: Twelve oxen, 32*l.* Twelve kyne, 28*l.* Seaven stotts and whies, 11*l.* Seaven horse and mairs and one fole, 12*l.* 16*s.* 8*d.* Three calves, 24*s.* 43 olde sheep, 7*l.* 54 sheep hoggs, 7*l.* 10*s.* 14 swine, 46*s.* 26 geese, 6*s.* 8*d.* Pulleins, 2*s.* 6*d.* Corne and haie at Langton:—Six score and sixteen threaves of wheat and rye, 30*l.* Nyne score and ten threaves of oats, 20*l.* In beanes and bigg, 26*s.* 8*d.* In haie, 8*l.* Corne and haie at Headlam:—Fower score and ten threaves of wheat and rye, 21*l.* Fower score and ten threaves of oats, 18*l.* In haie, 24*s.* Houshold stuffe:—One cupbord, 20*s.* Two cawells, 6*s.* 8*d.* Three tables, 6*s.* Formes, chairs, long settle and stools, 3*s.* 6*d.* Sixtene brasse potts, 4*l.* 4*d.* One caldron, 20*s.* Fower kettles, 16*s.* Six panns, 6*s.* One chaffendish, 12*d.* Divers household stuffe, 20*s.* One morter, 12*d.* Six great chargers, 15*s.* Fower dozen and an half of smaller vessells, 48*s.* One dozen of sawcers, 8 candlesticks, one ewer, three tinn potts, six stiltts, 12*s.* Two penter basons, one chamber pott, 18*d.* Three spits, one pair of iron racks, recken crooks, tongs, potts, clipps, fryinge panns, dripping pan, boyling iron, fyer shovell, 12*s.* 8 pair of bedstocks, 20*s.* Fower feather bedds, 53*s.* 4*d.* A mattres, 3*s.* 4*d.* Ten covercloths, 30*s.* 20 happings, 13*s.* 4*d.* Nyne blancketts, 13*s.* 4*d.* One carpett, 2*s.* 6*d.* Tenn codds, 6*s.* 10*d.* Six bolsterrs, 9*s.* Twelve pair of linn sheets, 3*l.* 24 pair of harden sheets, 48*s.* 14 lynn pillobeers, 14*s.* A dozen towells, 8*s.* A dozen napkins, 16*d.* Three lyn table clothes, 6*s.* 8*d.* Half a stone of coulored woll, 3*s.* Three straken table clothes, 3*s.* Three harden table clothes, 3*s.* A lynn cupbord cloth, 8*d.* Half a dozen cuissions, 2*s.* Lynn, harden and woollen webbs, 46*s.* 8*d.* Wood vessell:—Fower bark-fatts, 13*s.* 4*d.* One lead, 26*s.* 8*d.* In bark, 8*s.* One mask-fatt, one gailefatt and eight other woodd tubbs, 10*s.* Barrells, bowells, skeeles, and othere wood vessell, 13*s.* 4*d.* Chirnes, cheesefats and flacketts, 8*s.* Waines and plough with other necessaries therunto belongeinge:— An olde iron bound waine, 20*s.* One unbounde [*sic*] two coops, a paire of new wheels and a paire of new blaids, 40*s.* Eight teames, 12 yoaks, three wainehead shackles, 24*s.* Three coulters, fouer stocks, axes and wombles, 10*s.* One iron harrowe, fower horse harrowes, 3*s.* 4*d.* One gavelock, dung forks, iron forks, waine-ropes, bridles, loade-saddles and traces, 8*s.* Axell trees, beames and other plough gear, 2*s.* 6*d.* Butter and cheese:—16 stone of butterr, 50*s.* 30 cheses, 30*s.* 9 secks, 16 yards of seckwebb and pokes, 20*s.* A winding cloth, a bushell, a peck, 2s. Staves, ruddles, scuttles and boll weights, 3s. 4d. Two spinninge wheels, three basketts, 20d. His apparell, 20s. 13 silver spoones, 50s. Money in his purse, 38s.

Debtts owinge by Johnn Burrell: Unto one Rashell, 20s. To Christofer Marley, 9s. 8d. To Henrie Cockfield, 13s. To Margaret Betsonn, 7s. To Ann Natteras, 5s. In rent for Headlam, 19s. 10d. In rent to the Chauntrie, 18d. In rent to Henrie Cockfeild 8l. 7s. 5d. In rent for Thompsonn house, 12s. In rent for Pearson house, 2s. In rent for Cardnall house, 2s.

Debtts owinge to Johnn Burrell: Anthonie Preston, 23s. 4d. Richard Morton of Morton, 3l. 6s. 8d. Richard Morton, 6s. John Pearsonn of Langtonn, 10s. 2d. *Leases:* The lease of the west close, 3l. 12s. The lease of Richard Mortonn, 13l. 6s. 8d. Rowland Pearsonn's lease, 30s. A lease of John Towler, 16s. A lease of Richard Cardnall, 3l.

Summa bonorum, 279l. 15s. 6d.

WILL OF HENRY RIDDELL.

Nov. 4, 1597. Jesus. In the name of God, Amen. I, Henrye Riddle[1] of the towne of Newcastle-upon-Tyne, merchaunt, beinge sicke of bodye, and yet of perfect remembraunce of mynde, dothe make this my last will and testament. First, I give and bequeathe my soule into the hands of th' Almightie, by whom I hope to be saved, and my bodye to be buried in the great churche att Elbinge. I doe give to my host and hostesse, Esender of Elbinge,[2] betwixt them, 20l. To Richard Peares, Gerrard Reede, Gregorie Blande, Thomas Selbie, William Selbie, Clement Reade, Isaack Sharpe, the younge frowe, the three maides, the nurse, and to the foreman, everie one of them, an angell. To Charles Horsleye, 100l. To Edward Waister, 16l. To James Harll, 10l., and my best cloake of blacke, and my velvet britches. To Richard Hodshon, 100l. To Richard Hodshon's wife, 20l. To everie one of my brethren, two angells, and to my sister, two angells. To my father and mother, everie one of them, an angell. To Elizabethe Liddle,[3] whom I did meane to make my wife, 50l. To Mr. Murton of Newcastle, preacher, three angells. To Mr. Smathwhaite of Newcastle, preacher, one Frenche crowne. To be devided amonge the poore, 6l. All the residue of my goods, my debts, legacies, funeralls, my doctor, barber,

---

[1] Henry Riddell was a younger son of William Riddell of Newcastle, merchant adventurer, by his wife Barbara, daughter of Bertram Anderson. *Cf.* pedigree of Riddell, new *History of Northumberland,* vol. iv. p. 284.

[2] Elbing is a town near Danzig in Prussia.

[3] *Dep. Lib.* : Eliz. *ux.* Wm. Sherwood *v.* Charles Horsley. Nov. 6, 1601. *Isaack* Sharpe of Newcastle, merchant, *æt.* 29, was present with Henry Reedle at Elbinge, where he did see and hear the said Henry make his will—he gave to Thomas Liddle's daughter (whom he said he intended to marry) about fiftie poundes, etc.

and other charges being paied, unto Charles Horsley of Newcastle,[1] who is my father's faithful prentice, whom I doe give it unto, and doe make him my whole executor. And so I comitt my soule into the hands of Almightie God, who I trust will receive me into his kingdome. Amen. In witnes of a true will, I have sette my hand, in Elbinge, this 4th of November, anno 1597. In witnes of theise, Richardum Peares, per me, Gregorium Bland, per me, Jaraerdum Reade, per me, Willelmum Selbye, per me, Jacobum Harll, per me, Isaacum Sharpe.

Sic subscript. Henry Riddell. [Pr. May 12, 1599.]

WILL OF RICHARD CLAXTON.

Jan. 22, 1597/8.   Richard Claxton of Croxdale.[2]   The house, which I have in the barony of Elvet, in the suburbes of the citie of Durham, with the garthes, etc., I give unto Christofer, sonne of Gerarde Claxton, who was brother of Robert Claxston, late of Burn-hall, and failinge the said Christofer and his heires maile, then I will that it come to Thomas, sonne of my brother, John Claxston of Strudder-house, and failinge him, etc., to Thomas, sonne of William Claxston, nowe of Water-house, and then to my right heires.   And to the said house I do assign one step-leade standing in the entrie, covered with slate, one brewe-leade, in the brewhouse, and the dry-fattes, made of timber, standinge in the low howse, nexte unto the garden, for perpetuall heir-lumes.   To the poore of St. Oswoldes and St. Margarets, in Durham, to eache parishe, 20s.   To Mrs. Anne Killinghall, a golde ringe.   To Thomas Wickliffe, now prisoner in Sadberg, one silver spoone, and to Phillippe Parkinson, now of St. Margarets parishe, in Durham, two olde angels, and to Anne his wife, one Englische crowne.   To Richard Wardel, and to Elynor Harbottle, to each 20s., and to George, sonne of the said Elynor, 20s. To my brother, John Claxston, 6l. 13s. 4d.   To my cosing, Henrie Hall of Yorke, a litle silver salte.   To Alexander Fetherstane-haughe, a mazer cuppe.   To Marie and Margaret Biggins, and to Margaret Huton, to everie of them, a French crowne.   To William Claxston of Waterhouse, 10s., and the same to his wife.   To Humfray Claxston, 10s.   The rest to my brother John and to my cosings, Alexander Fetherstanehaughe, whom I make executors.

Memorandum : That the 15th day of June, 1598, the said Richard Claxton did, by word of mouthe, give unto his cosen, Launcelott Claxton of Wyneyard, gent., and unto his heires male, one silver salte, gilt, having the Claxton's armes, and failing him and his heries, of the howse of Old Park, to come to his brother, John Claxton.

[1] Charles Horsley, son of Thomas Horsley, gent., was apprenticed, Feb. 7, 1590, to William Riddell, merchant adventurer.

[2] The testator was a younger son of Robert Claxton of Burnhall by Allison Selby, his wife.

WILL OF THOMAS HILTON.

Feb. 14, [1597/8.] In the name ,of God the Father, the Sonne [and] Holy Gost, Amen. I, Thomas Hilton,[1] weake in bodye by longe sicknes, but stronge in faith [tow]ards Jesus Christe my Saviour, assured in hope of eternall joy, and in memorie of orderinge my worldly affaires perfecte and sounde, doe make this my last will and testament in manner and forme followeinge, viz. : First, I commend my sinnes to the Lorde's everlastinge mercies, myself into the hands of Allmighty God my Creator, my soule into the hands of Jesus Christe our Saviour, throughe the blessed sanctifying of the Holy Gost.

Secondly, my earthly bodye I doe commend unto the earth from whence I received it. All other my worldly blessinges wherof the Lorde hitherto hath maide me steward I bestowe and bequeath as followeth, but first of all I make my loveinge wiffe, Anne Hilton, and my children, George Hilton, Robert Hilton, Fraunces Hilton, Matthew Hilton and John Hilton, the sole and . . . . ite executors of this my last will and testament. Farther, I doe give and bequeath to my sonnes, George [and Ro]bert Hilton, and to ye longer liver of them, my lease of Farneton H[a]ll which I lately . . . . by lease of the . . . . cene. I d[o] give and bequeath [to my] sonnes Fraunces Hilton, Matthew Hilton and John H[ilton], the whole rectorie or parsonage of Monkewer-[mo]uth with all the purtenances th[ere]unto belonginge equally to be disposed amonge . . . . my three sonnes for their three lives and to the longest [liv]er of them three accordingly, after whose decease my w[ill] is that the inheritance of it returne unto m[y] eldest sone and heire, Henrie Hilton, and unto his heires mal . . . . [l]awfully begotten . . . . ever, and faileinge thereof t . . . . to returne to my executors and their heires . . . . ever. I doe give and bestowe upon my wyf [A]nne Hilton, all my title and tearme of yeares of the Foorde . . . . lde which I tooke lately of my father. My quicke moveing goods I doe give and bequeath to my wyfe and my two daughters, Jane Hilton and Marie Hilton, tow[ards] their better preferment in honest mariage. I . . . . give unto my servant, Thomas Teesdall, for his f[ai]thfull service doon and to be doon to my wyfe and he . . . . the lease of his father's farme in Awsten-moore for twyntie and one yeares. To my olde servant, Richard Vasey, I give a newe lease of his farme, in reversion of his former, freely without anie fyne.. I do give to my servant, Nichall Todde, fortie shilling. To ye poore people of my owen

---

[1] Thomas Hilton, the testator, was son and heir of Sir William Hilton of Hilton, knight, and died *v.p.* By his wife Anne, daughter of Sir George Bowes of Streatlam, knight, he had issue eight sons and two daughters. His widow remarried Sir John Delaval of Dissington, knight.

The original will is much decayed.

Cf. p. 178 *post.*

parrish I doe give five [m]arkes in monie.   All my dettes dew
to me I give amongst my executors.   All other my goods and
ch[att]ls what forme soever not formerly bequeathed I doe give and
bestowe upon my executors, my detts, if anie ther be, my legacies
and honest and seemelye funeralls oute of all my goods first discharged.   I doe also order and charge all my children, sonnes and
daughters, to be obedient and duetifull to their mother, whome I
doe constitute and a[ppo]inte to have the government both of
them and their po[rti]ons untill my sonnes be of lawfull age by
lawe to [ha]ve the use of their estates in their owen hands, and untill
my doug[h]ters, with the consent of their m[o]ther, be coupled
in honest mariage answerable to t[heir] father's childr[en].   Lastly,
I doe make and constitute by my earnest intre[ty]e my father [Sir]
William Hilton, my brothers Talbot Bowes, Robert Bowes, George
Bowes and Raphe Bowes, supervisers . . . . iringe good orderes of
this my last will and testament, whose brotherlye . . . . faithfull
favour for the loveinge performance in true peace of . . . . premises
in all love I crave of them to see unto.   [I ch]arge my wyfe and
children, to [be] advised and directed . . . . by their goodly wis-
domes in all good counsels [t]o eache of them I doe for
remembrance . . . . a ringe of golde to be worne by them.   In
cons . . . . tion and testimonie of this my last will and testament
I have this 14 of F[ebr]uarie subscribed my owen name and putte
my seale of armes.   Witnesses, William Hilton, Mychaell Constable,
William Constable, Robert Smith, etc.   [Pr. 1598.]

WILL OF WILLIAM ERRINGTON.

May 30, 1599.   William Errington, laite of the towne of Newcastle upon Tine, gentleman.   I commend my soule unto Almightie
God, my heavenly Father, assuredly beleving to be on of his elect
children thrugh the mirittes of Jesus Christ, my only Saviour.   My
body to be buried in the parish church of Alhallowes, within the said
towne of Newcastle upon Tyn.   To the poore of the parishe of
Alhallowes, 8s., and to the poore of the parishe of Gaytsyd, 5s.   To
my brother, Edward Erington, 3l. 6s. 8d. yearly, to be payed unto
him during the lease of my farmould in Benwell ; if he die before the
said lease be expired, then the said 3l. 6s. 8d. to John Erington,
the sonne of Robart Erington of Linalls.   To my brother, Edward
Erington, my gowne and my gould signet.   To William Stevenson
and his children, 3l. 6s. 8d. yearly during the foresaid lease.   To
William Errington of Linalls, my best cloke.   To my sister, Ellener
Josephe, 40s., and to hir sonne, Peter Herison, 6l.   To William
Stevenson, his children, every on of them, 20s.   To Doritie Jackson,
20s. ; and to hir sonne, William Jackson, 10s., and to hir doughter,
Doritie Jackson, 5s.   To Doritie Taylor, the wyfe of Thomas Taylor
of Benton, 10s.   To Agnes Atkinson, the wyfe of Christopher

Atkinson, 10s. To Elizabeth Stevenson, the wyfe of William Stevenson, a gould ring, which was my weding ring. The rest of my goodes
unto Anthony Stevenson, the sonne of William Stevenson, whom I
made my soll executor. My well beloved frendes, Robart Erington
of Linalls,¹ William Stevenson and my brother, Edward Erington,
the supervisors of my will.
    INVENTORY. Sept. 1, 1599. *Somma*, 6l. 5s.   Debtes owing to
him, 38l. 7s. 4d. His funeral charges, 6l. 6s. Other debtes, 37s.

WILL OF CUTHBERT COLLINGWOOD.

[1599.]   Cuthbert Collingwood of Angram.²   My body to be
buryed in the parysh churche of Angram. I will that after my
sepulture my sonne, Henry Collingwood, have given unto him two
oxen and one cowe, and that my sonne, Robert Collingwood, have
lykewise two oxen and one cowe and a calf. To my two dowghters,
Jane and Dorythye, eyther of them one ox and two kyne.   To my
sonne, Henry Collingwood, two brasse potts, the speyts, racks and
yron crooks, boards, tables and two almaryes, the stand beddes, and
one of the bedclothes with all the best furnyture thereunto belonging.
All the rest of myne insyght goods to my said two dowghters, Jane
and Dorythye.   To Cuthbert Butymond, one rygged whye, one
rygged calfe and thre styrks, and I comytt him to my executors,
wylling them to use him as one of my children.   To my eldest son,
Henry Collingwood, my best clooke, and to my eldest dowghter, Jane,
all hir mother's clothes.   To Robert Collyngwood, sonne of Anne
Glashoope, my jerken, bryches, hatt, stokyngs, shirts, bands, dagger
and my work-day apparell, and also my meare, with hir furnyture,
paying to Elizabeth Collingwood, dowghter of Elizabeth Carr, 24s.
John Thompson of Newcastle is owying me 40s., I give it to Elizabeth
Collyngwood aforesayd. My two sonnes, Henry Collyngwood and
Robert Collinwood, executors, comytting them duryng the tyme of
their minoritye to the tuition of my brother, Mathewe Collingwood
and Edward Carr, gent., whom I do make tutors and guardians of
all my children, to see then brought up in the fear of God.   The rest
of my goods to the benyfitt of my children and the discharge of a
good conscience. Witnesses, Cuthbert Collingwood the elder, John
Stephenson, Robert Burne, John Clarkson, Henry Clarkson, etc.
    The will, which is without date, was proved Sept. 4, 1599, by
Matthew Collingwood of the parish of Ingram and Edward Carr of
the parish of Alnwick, the tutors of Henry and Robert Collingwood,
children of the testator.

    ¹ The Linnels, on the Devils-water, was held of the earls of Northumber-
land by the family of Errington for several generations.
    ² An unidentified scion of the wide spread family of Collingwood who
resided in the parish of Ingram.

WILL OF JAMES GREY.

Aug. 16, 1599. James Gray[1] of the towne of Newcastle-upon-Tyne, draper. To be buried in the parishe churche of All Saints, wherin I am a parishoner, at the north syde of my late wief, her grave being in the south syde of the east ende of the said churche. To my eldest sonne, Raphe Gray, my dwelling-house, with th' appertenences, seytuat in the Sandhill, to him and his heires, and for lack of such, to my sonne James, then to my sonne John, and then to my daughters Margaret and Elinor Gray and their heires for ever. To my said sonne Raphe, 100*l.*, one goblet of silver, and a cover. To my sonne James, 100*l.*, with my whole estate, right, etc., of my lease of certayn cole mynes in the lordshippes of Whickham [and Gateshead], out of the leasse, called the grande leasse, provyded that he paye unto his sister 5*l.* out of the said cole mynes. Also I give unto him one goblet of silver. To the said Margaret, my daughter, 110*l.*, one whyte silver peece and a cofer with lynen, which I have appointed out for her. To my daughter Elinor, 110*l.*, one dozen of silver spones, and one coffer with lynnen. To Robert Gray, my apprentice, 20*l.* To his brother Raphe, 6*l.* 13*s.* 4*d.*, and the like sume to John Wilkinson. To my aunt, Elinor Mitford, 10*s.*, for a token. To my cozen, Isabell Lyons, 10*s.* To my cozen, Laurenc Mitforth, 10*s.* To my sister Gray, 10*s.* To Isabell Mitforth, 10*s.*, and to her sonne, which I christened, 10*s.* To my cozen, Cuthbert Gray, 10*s.*, and to eche of my servantes, 10*s.* To my sonne John, 110*l.*, and one goblet of silver. To my brother William Jenyson, Isabell Jenyson, and Robert Jenyson, for a token, a Frenche crowne a peece. To my cozen, William Gray, 10*s.* And whereas my said children, Raphe, James, John, Margaret and Elynor, be very yonge, I give them to my frendes followinge, that is to saye, to my brother Cuthbert Bewick, I give the tuycion of Raphe; to my brother, Robert Bewicke, I give my sonne James, and my daughter Elinor I also give to him and to my sister, his wife; I give my daughter Margaret to my sister, Margaret Bewicke, at the charge of my said brother Cuthbert Bewick; and as touchinge my youngest childe, John, I appoint him to the tuicion and good education of my loving frend, Thomas Pateson of Lodworth [*sic*] intending when convenyent tyme shall serve, and then to be put fourth apprentice to a merchante adventurer of the towne of Newcastle. I appoint my said children executors, and I make my loving frendes, John Lyons and William Gray, overseers, and I give to eche for his travail, 13*s.* 4*d.* Witnesses, Henricus Anthony, notarius publicus, John Smaythwait, Cuthbert Bewick, Robert Bewick, Thomas Pattison, William Graye.

[1] James Grey, a wealthy Newcastle draper, married Elizabeth, sister of Cuthbert Bewick of Newcastle, by whom he had, with other children, an eldest son, Ralph Grey, ancestor of the family of Grey of Backworth. *Cf.* new *History of Northumberland*, vol. viii.

INVENTORY OF HENRY MITFORD THE YOUNGER.

Oct. 8, 1599. An INVENTARYE of the goodes of Henrye Mitford of the towne of Newcastle, merchaunt, deceased, praised by Bertram Anderson, merchaunt, George Briggham, merchaunt, Matthew Milburn, weaver, the eight daie of October, 1599.
Imprimis: Three sackes of hoopes, 3*l.* Foure bunches of latts, 2*s.* .... 11 mugges, 8*s.* 2 paire 2 pound skales, 2*s.* One basterd muskett, 4*s.* One sea chist, 2*s.* 6*d.* One deske with ½ a pound tobaccho, 3*s.* 4*d.* One muskett, with furniture, 6*s.* 8*d.* 13 dailes and twelve sparres, 9*s.* 4 bowles of beanes, 16*s.* 15 hundredweight of tow, 7*l.* 40 stone of lint, 7*l.* In good debts, 3*l.* In desperat debts, 3*l.* Some is 25*l.* 13*s.* 6*d.*

WILL OF JOHN CLEOBURNE.

Dec. 27, 1599. John Cleoburne of Hyendon, parish of Cockfeild, etc. My bodye to be buried within the church of Cockfeild. I give to my sonne, Richard Cleoburne, the lease of my farminge of Colby. I give unto my said sonne one grisselled mayre. To my sonne, William Cleoburne, one grisselled mayre, beinge about fyve yeares old. I give to my sonne, Henry Cleoburne, one graie fillye of two yeares old. I give to my sonne-in-lawe, William Sidgeswicke, one read belled cowe. I give to three of the youngest children of Christofer Ducket, everye of them, one lamb. To Moyses Newbye, one lambe. To Margarett Lee, one lambe. To John Willis, one lambe. To Jan Perkinson, two ewes and one cloacke. To the poore, 20*s.* To John Bincks, one jirkin. To the parson of Cockfeild, 3*s.* 4*d.* I give to my sonnes Richard and William Cleoburne, and to my daughter Jane Sigswicke, all my houshould stuffe, to be equallye devided amongst them. The rest of my goods unbequeathed, my debts and funerall expenses discharged, I give unto my sonnes Richard, William and Henry Cleoburne and to my daughter, Jane Sigswicke, whom I do make joynt executors of this my last will and testament. Witnesses, John Metcalfe, John Bincks, with others.

WILL OF HENRY SINGLETON.

Dec. 31, 1599. In the name of God, amen. Henrie Singleton of Langton, within the parish of Gainforthe, sicke in bodie but well in remembrance, etc. My bodie to be buried in Gainforth churchyeard.[1] I give unto Raph Singleton, my sonne, all my waines, ploughe and plough-geare and all other furniture to them belongeinge. I give unto Margaret Singleton, my daughter, 16*l.* of lawfull English money, in full payment and satissfaction of all her

[1] 1599/1600, Feb. 10. Henry Singleton buried. *Gainford Register.*

childes porcon, or filiall porcon, to be payed to her when she cometh
to the aige of 16 years. I give unto John Thompson, my servant,
one lambe. Alsoe my will is that my wife, Anne Singleton, shall have
all my farmehold in Langton to bring upp my children withall
untill my sonne come to the aige of 21 years. But yf my brothere
in lawe, Lawrence Katherick of Darlington, shall not think my
children well brought upp, then I will my said brother in lawe,
Lawrence Katherick, shall have my sonne in his keepinge and half
of my farmehold duringe the tearme abovesaid; and which of eythere
of them that have my sonne and his porcon of my farme whether
soever that be shall paie for all the charges of renewinge of the lease
of my farme att her Majesties Exchequer at London att their proper
costs and charges. My debtts and legacies payed, and my funerall
expences discharged, all the rest of my goods, moveable and unmoveable, I give unto Anne Singleton, my wife, whome I maik my whole
executrix of this my last will and testament. In witness whereof I
have sett my hand and seall before the witnesses followinge. Given
at Langton the last daie of December, 1599. Anthonye Thompson,
Lawrence Kathericke, John Tompson, John Spencer.

WILL OF ROBERT SWIFT.

The last will and testament of me, Robart Swift[1] of Lincolne's
Inne, written with myne owne hande, January 14, 1599/1600, at
London.

Blessed be the holy name of God, Amen. I, Robert Swift of
Lincolne's Inne, in the county of Middlesex, attornaie, considering
that I am a sojourner upon earthe, and knowe not howe soone it
will please the Lorde, my God, to take me out of this perplexed
simple state of life, unto the Mount Sion and to the citye of the
livinge God, the celestiall Jerusalem, to the glorious companye of
innumerable angells, to the assembly and congregation of the firste
borne, which are written in heaven, to the spirites of just and perfect
men, and to the presence of the mighty God, where there is
satietye of joyes for ever more. Therefore, for the ordering of
my goodes and chattells, after my decease, doe make this my last
will, etc. First, I recommend my poore sowle into the handes of
Almighty God, the Father, the Sonne, and the Holye Spirite, thus
trustinge to be saved only by the sufferinges and death of Christe,
my Lorde and Saivioure, and I bequeath my body to the earth,
whence it. came, there to repose, till the resurrection of the deade,

---

[1] The only son of Robert Swift, LL. B., spiritual chancellor of the diocese of
Durham until 1577, prebendary of Durham and rector of Sedgefield, by Anne,
daughter of Thomas Lever, master of Sherburn Hospital and sometime master
of St. John's College, Cambridge. He was admitted to Lincoln's Inn, Aug. 19,
1587. The bequests of his books will be read with interest.
The original will is much decayed.

in full hope and expectation of eternall blisse, to sowle and body,. in the worlde to come. Before and above all thinges I desier that my debtes may be well and trulye paied to the uttermost farthinge ; it is the last expence that ever I shall putt my parentes unto. Then I bequeathe to Mr. Donell and Mr. Rose, prisoners and preachers,. 40s., to be equally divided betwene them. Out of my farme in Sedgefeild, 20 nobles to the poore of the same parishe. I give, as. tokens of remembrance, to my most deare and entirely beloved father, my ringe, with the armes of the Swiftes, my note-book of divinitie in folio and little Englishe Bible. To my most deare and welbeloved mother, my golde ringe, with seaven turky stones, and to every of my sisters an angell of golde. To Mr. Coys,[1] my deare and faithfull frend, all my paper bookes and writinges of divinitye, undisposed of to others. To Mr. Woolveredge of Lincolne's Inne, my *Lindwood*. To Mr. Collins, his chamber fellowe, *Eusebius Storye* in English. To Mr. John Meede, *Swinburne on Willes*. To Mr. Robert Hale, *Minsinger upon Justinianus Institutes* and my noted tearmes of the lawe. To Mr. Charles Haworth, my *Tremellius Bible*. To my neighbour, Mr. James Whitehall, the register of writtes. To Mr. Thomas Barnehere, nowe in Barbarye, *Eusebius Cosmopolitanus Tenos* [*sic*] Greke and Latine (whiche I had of him), my *Rastell's Abridgement of Statutes*, and Mr. Bradford's *Meditations*. To Mr. Rand of Guilford, *Alexander Benedictus* his booke of phisick. To Mr. Lever of Belstede in Suffolke, litle *Ortilius* Mappes. To Mr. Oliver of St. Helins, *Bilson against the Papistes*. To Mr. Brigges of Gresham college, Youdin's fower mappes, which I hadde of him, and *Sadeles Workes*. To Mr. Allanson of Cambridge, in St. Johns, *Hassemmterus Historia Jesuitica* [*sic*]. To Mr. Chope, at Mr. Coys his house, *Darandi Rationale Divinorum*. To Mr. Grame of Childer-dith, *Calvine's Epistles*. To Mr. Christopher Ridley of East Smith-feilde, whom I appointe the overseer of this my will and to inventorie my bookes and other goodes, about London, and to deliver them as aforesaid, to him I bequeathe the watche, which I had of him, my tuffe taffite jerkin, my silke stokkins, *Rastell's Abridgement of Statutes*, and my little English *Testament*. To Stephen Hegge, my true friend and brother, all, or soe many as myne executores shall think meate, of my bookes of the civil and common lawes, also *Plowden's Commentaries*, dyvers reportes and *Abridgementes of Booke* and Fitzharbart, *Magia Naturalis of Baptista Porta* and little *Tullyeus Offices* gilt with golde. To Thomas Kinge of Durham, *Dr. Ragnoldes Conference with Hart*. To Besse Walton a French crowne and to Robert Hegge [2] half an angell. To my servant, Richard Rothwell, my beddinge lynnen, and apparell, savinge my barester's gowne, with velvet face, and other apparell of velvet, sattan and

---

[1] William Coys of London was admitted to Lincoln's Inn, April 5, 1578.

[2] Stephen Hegge, notary public, married Anne, daughter of Chancellor Swift and sister of the testator. His son, Robert Hegge, was the author of the ' Legend of St. Cuthbert.'

grogram, also to him my *Palton Abridgment, Pagninus Bible, Kitchin's Parkins'* ould *Natura Brevium,* and *Doctor and Student,* or soo many of these thinges as myne executores shall thinke meate. My reportes and paper-bookes of lawe I bequeathe to Stephen Hegge. The residue of all my goodes, leases, etc., I frely give to my moste lovinge and kinde parentes Mr. and Mrs. Swift of Durham, to be given at there discretion to my loveinge sisters, whiche parentes of myne I make full executores. My flesh shall rest in hope. [Pr. April 11, 1600.]

INVENTORY. Sept. 15, 1599. His lease of Sedgefeild mylne and 3 ox-ganges of lande, 40*l*. His best barister gowne, 6*l*. 13*s*. 4*d*. His best velvet jerken, 4*l*. A tufted velvet jerken, 53*s*. 4*d*. His best saten dublet, 46*s*. 8*d*. His worste saten dublet, 30*s*. A greene clothe jerken, 20*s*. 3 olde gownes, 3*l*. 6*s*. 8*d*. 2 clokes, 4*l*. 13*s*. 4*d*. Hose and dublett, new, of silke rashe, 5*l*. Hose and dublettes, 2 of silke rashe, 4*l*. Bewgle breaches of velvet, 3*l*. 6*s*. 8*d*. Velvet breaches, plaine, 40*s*. His ridinge geare, viz., sadle, bridle, sworde, dager, etc., 53*s*. 4*d*. His beddinge, viz., 1 fetherbedd, bolster, pillowe, blanketts, 2 coverlettes and 1 coveringe, 6*l*. 13*s*. 4*d*. 3 paires of stockinges, 33*s*. 4*d*. 2 gold ringes, 3*l*. 13*s*. 4*d*. 1 olde mare and 3 fillies, 5*l*. 8*s*. His bookes, 13*l*. 6*s*. 8*d*. Barister gownes, two, 53*s*. 4*d*. His watch, 4*l*. 10*s*.

Summa totalis, 121*l*. 1*s*. 4*d*.

WILL OF JOHN SPENCER.

March 20, 1599/1600. John Spencer of Langton in the countie of Durham, bachelor. My bodie to be buried in the churchyard of Gainfordd near to my father.[1] I give to my brother, Cuthbert Spencer, all my waines, coopes, ploughs and all other things what-soever to the same belonginge—with such furniture as their is in the house to serve the Quene. Alsoe I give to my brother in lawe Christofer Sigdwicke one half acre of wheat and one half acre of oatts in lewe of his good love toward my mothere and the rest of my brethren and sisters. Alsoe I give unto my sister Anne one branded white lisked stirk. And for my farme and whole right theirof I doe give and bequeath for three years beginninge at Michaellmas next after the dait of thees presents unto the full end and tearme of three yeares next ensowinge—savinge one close called Mallican close which was granted to paie Christofer Sigwick[2] his wifes porcone both by my father and me—unto my well beloved mother, Margaret Spencer, and Percivell Spencer during the tearme aforesaid yf my mothere keepe her wedowe and yf she marie within the said tearme of three years then I will that it all redound unto Percivell Spencer

---

[1] 1600, March 28. Jhon Spencer buried. *Gainford Register.*

[2] 1595/6, ... Christofer Sigswick and Elizabeth Spencer mar. *Ibid.*

for and duringe soe longe as the tearme is unexpired. And furthere yf yt please God to call before Michaelmas then I will that unto that tyme that the comoditie that should be myne shall redound and come unto my brother Henrie, Anne, Katherine Spencer with all comodities whatsoever shall come of the said farme. And else I give to the said Henrie, Anne, Katherine Spencer all my other goods of what nature or propertie soever they bee moveable or unmoveable whom I maike my sole executors of this my last will and testament; made the 20th daie of March, 1599/1600; in the presence of William Garth, Christofer Sidgwick and Cuthbert Stodart.

INVENTORY praysed by Cuthbert Stodart, Christofer Sidgwick, John Taylor, John Card.

Imprimis: His apparrell, 30s. Three oxen, 7l. 5s. Two stirks, 53s. 4d. Five acres of hard corne, 5l. Six acres and a halfe of oats, 3l.

Summa, 19l. 8s. 4d.

WILL OF WILLIAM RIDDELL.

Aug. 27, 1600. William Riddell of Newcastle, marchant, and alderman.[1] My body to be buried in St. Nicholas church. To Barbara, my wife, my howses and my twelft parte of the grande leas of the cole mynes of Whicham, and after her death to Peter, my son. To my said wife, the third parte of the leas of the cole mynes in Gaitshead for her life and then to William and George, my sons. To my said wife, my five salt pannes at Sheales, and then to Michell, John and Robert, my sons, one each and the other two to Alice, my daughter. To my son, Thomas Riddell and Elizabeth, his wife, one old ryall each. To William and Ann Riddel, their children and the child his wife is with, 5l. each. To Peter Riddell, my brother, and Elienor, his wife, and to his children, an angell each. To Henrie Laws' children, 6l. among them. To William, Jane and Barbara, children of Anthony Laws, 40s. and 20s. and 20 nobles which my sister Marie gave them, which was dewe unto her by Raph Richerdsonn his will. To my cossyne, George Dente, one angell. To the poore of this towne, 10l. To my daughter Alice, towards hir mariage, 100l. To Mr. Henrie Anderson and Mr. Thomas Calverley, my brethren in law, one angell each. To Mr. William Jenisonn, now maior of Newcastell, Mr. Nicholas Tempest, my brother in law, and Mr. John Calverley and my sister Calverley, an old angell each. To Mr. Pearsonn, precher of this towne, 20s. To Mr. Allansonne, the precher, and Mr. Cooke, the scoolemaister, an angell each. The rest to my wife and children. Witnesses, William Morton, Archdeacon of Northumberland, Thomas Ridell, Nycholas Tempest. [Pr. Feb. 6.]

[1] This will illustrates and proves two generations of the pedigree of Riddell of Swinburn Castle printed in the new *History of Northumberland*, vol. iv. p. 284.

INVENTORY OF SIR WILLIAM HILTON OF HILTON, KNIGHT.

An INVENTARIE of all the goods and chattels whereof Sir William Hilton, late of Hilton,[1] knight, dyed possessed of, and apprised by Richard Midleton of Tunstall, Galfride Lawsonne of Gateshead, John Whitfield of Great Osworth, gentleman, and John King of the citie of Duresme, notarie publique, the 7th of October, Anno Domini 1600.

AT HILTON:—One olde table and a little forme of firdaile, 16s. Three side cupboordes, 20s. One olde picture, 20d. *The read chamber:* Four peecs of olde hangings, 40s. A litle liverie cupborde of ffirre, 3s. 3d. *The greene chamber:* One litle cupboord, 3s. 4d. An old case of a paire of virginals, 2s. 6d. Olde hangings their, 6s. 8d. One litle cupboorde, 20d. *In the parlour:* One olde longe table with a grene clothe, 16s. One square table and an olde clothe, 5s. One highe side cupboorde and an olde clothe, 8s. Three litle formes of ffirdaile, 2s. One paire of olde virginalls, 10s. An old chaire, 2s. 6d. 18 old buffet stooles, 7s. One litle lyverie cupboorde, 2s. Foure tables with armes, 6s. 8d. *In the low gallerie:* A litell square table and an olde candlesticke, 8s. An olde skreene, 6d. *In the ladie chamber:* On pulke, 3s. 4d. One side cupboord of ashe, 2s. One broken iron chymney, 2s. 6d. *In the nurcery:* One longe-setle bedd, 4s. One olde iron chymney, 5s. One fetherbed broke their, 10s. *In the low checquer:* On chiste, 6s. 8d. One olde trunk, 5s. One side table with boxes, 5s. One litle table, 4s. One side cupboord of ffirre for glasses, 2s. One pare of tongues and a porre, 12d. One planne deske, 2s. The wainescott in that chamber, 16s. 8d. *In the highe chequer:* One litle bedstead, 4s. One litle side table, 20d. One olde iron chymney, 3s. 4d. *In the kitchin:* One beef pott, 6s. One ffornace for beef, 10s. One laver, 7d. *In the towre:* Fowr corsletts with ther furniture, without weapons. Certaine hay, 26s. 8d.

A portall in the greate chamber at Hilton. All the wainescott and glasse at Hilton house. Foure pieces of olde hangings in the great chamber. An olde binge and an old cupborde in the butterie. Two leads for saltinge of beeves in the larder house ; and brewleade, maskefatte cooler, guilefatt, two troughes in the brewhouse. A great iron chymney, with the appurtenances in the kitchin ; a ffornace for beef their. A portall in the chequer chamber. A great presse that stood in the wardropp. The kitchin boordes and all the tables and formes in the hall apprized to and soulde for ye some of 30l.

AT NEWCASTELL :—*In the great chamber:* One table, 4s. One longe-settell of ffirre, 3s. A ffirre boorde of tressell, 8d. One litle stoole, 6d. One portall, 10s. Four barres of iron for a chymney, 12d. *In the bedd chamber:* Three litell cupbordes, 6s. 8d. One chare of firre, 18d. One close stoole of ffirre, 12d. One buffet

[1] For a pedigree of Hilton of Hilton, see Surtees, *Durham*, vol. ii. pp. 26, 27.

stoole, 8d. A poore and four litell barres of iron, 20d. Two portalles, 13s. 4d. *The inner chamber within the bedde chamber:* One litell bedstedde, 3s. 4d. Three barres of iron, 12d. *In the studie:* Three stooles, 2s. 6d. *In the hall:* Two litle tables, 3s. One forme, 12d. *In the great butterie:* One large gantrie and a planke, 2s. 6d. A litle gantrie and a planke, 18d. A graven armour with an head piece, being an armor of proof. 5l. A white armor, 26s. 8d. *In the chamber over the hall:* A bedstedde, a stoole, a forme and three barres of iron for a chymney, 6s. 8d. *In the kitchin:* Two dressinge boords, 2s. *In the litle butterie:* One old chist, a pare of litle gantrees and a litle swall, 16d. *In the stable:* Two racks and two maingers, 2s.

Sommā totalis, 54l. 7s. 2d. Out of which some to be deducted for funeral expences and other necessarie things as followeth: first for the buriall of the corpes of the said deceased, 30s. For blackes bestowed upon the wyddow, frendes and servantes of the said deceased, 13l. 6s. 8d. For a mortuaire, 10s. For and about the obtaining of administracion, 23s. 4d. For making up the inventaries and the charges of the prisers, the goods being in several places, 20s. *Somma,* 17l. 10s. *Somma declaro,* 36l. 17s. 2d.

WILL OF EDMUND WILSON.

Mar. 9, 1600/1. Edmonde Wilson of the Loinenge-heade in Teasdell. To be buried in the church of Midleton betwexte the founte wher my father was buried. Margaret my wife to have her wedowe righte of all my lands, etc. To Rabecca my daughter, one browne cowe. To Edmonde Bainbrigge my nephewe [*sic*], one of the sonnes of my said daughter, one graye mare to be let rune for foele till my nephewes, Thomas, George and William Bainbrigge have everie of them a foell of the same. To Francis Bainbrigge, my nephewe, one younge graye mare. To my nephewes, Thomas, George, Edmonde, Franses and William Bainbrigge, my said daughter's sonnes, 7l. among them when they come of age. To my neces [*sic*] Phillis and Rabecca Bainbrigge, my daughter's daughters, 10l. To Edmonde Bainbrigge, my nephew, all my lands, cornefeelds, etc., of Midleton in Teasdale, which, amongst other things, was boughte of Ninion Menvell, laite of Sledwiche, esquier, commonlie called 'Menvell's Lands,' and one messuage or tenement in the mide sid in the weste feild of Midleton of the yearlie rent of 22s. 2d. called the weste ferme. The reste to Thomas Bainbrigge my son in law and Rebacca, his wife, my daughter, my executors. Witnesses, Jacob Haneley, Christopher Bainbrigge, Henry Bainbrigge.

Postcriptum. To my nece, Catherin Haneley, one whye calfe and two gimmer lambes. To my nece, Phillis Bainbrigge, one grete cupporde and one stande bedde. To my nece, Rebecka Bainbrigge, one cowe and a calf. [Confirmed Sept. 21, 1602.]

INVENTORY Oct. 18, 1602.

WILL OF HENRY BRAKENBURY.

Nov. 6, 1601. I, Henry Brackenbury of Osmondcroft,[1] in the counttie of Durham, esquire, being at the makeinge hereof of sounde and perfect remembrance, whereof I give God hartie thancks, perceiveing th' incertainty of this liffe and not knoweinge howe suddenly God may call me from the same, willinge to dispose those lands and goods which God hath bestowed upon me as well for the advauncement of my howse and continuance of the same in my owne bloude, as also for the better education, maintainance and preferment of my children and there children, doe make this my last will and testament in manner and forme followeinge. I give and bequeath to Anne Brackenbury, my loveinge wyffe, all that my mannor or capitall messuage and tenement of Osmondcroft, aforesaide, with all lands, etc., thereto belonginge, with all goods, etc., upon the same, to have the same dureinge hir liffe naturall. I give unto my daughter, Anne Hutton, one yearely pencion of 10*l*. of lawfull Englisshe money out of my lands and tenements and hereditaments in Sellaby dureinge hir widdowe heade, and for the space of one whole yeare after the day of hir marriage, if she shall marrie, togither with sufficient habitation for hir and hir familie within my mansione howse at Selleby, or in the capitall mansion howse at Alwent, to dwell in dureinge hir widdowheade. I give unto Richard Hutton, the eldest sonne of my saide daughter, Anne, one yearely pencion of 10*l*. out of my said lands, etc., in Sellaby and elsewhere untill such time as he shall accomplishe the aige of twentie and one yeares. I give unto Tymothie Hutton, the seconde sonne of my said daughter Anne, one yearely pencion of 10*l*. out of my said lands in Sellaby, etc., dureinge the terme of his liffe naturall. I give unto Francis Hutton, the thirde sonne of my said daughter Anne, one yearelie pencion of 10*l*. to be paide to him out of my said lands, etc., in Sellaby and elsewhere duringe his liffe naturall. I will and hereby authorise my said doughter, Anne Hutton, and hir said three sonnes, Richard, Tymothy and Francis, and everie of them for non-payment of the severall pencions and annuities aforesaide, to everie of them given and bequeathed as aforesaid within the space of twenty daies next after anie of the severall feasts at which the same ought to be paied, shall lawfully enter into my said lands, etc., in Sellaby or elsewhere and distraine. To the end that my beloved sonne and heire, Francis Brackenbury, may the better and more willinglie see this my will performed, which hereby I will and charge him to doe, as my trust is in him, I doe give unto him my said sonne, Francis Brackenbury (all the former gifts, annuities and legacies first deducted), all that my mannor or lordshipp of Selleby, Osmondecroft, etc., with all other

---

[1] This will adds many details to the pedigree of Brackenbury of Sellaby, entered at Flower's *Visitation of Durham* in 1575. The testator was buried at Gainford, April 4, 1602.

my lands, etc., within the countie of Durham, my messuage, etc.,
called Westlopshowse, my rectory or parsonage of Martone, with
th' appurtenances in the couuntie of Yorke, with all my goods, furniture
and howsholde stuffe at Selleby aforesaid, dureinge his liffe naturall,
and, after his decease, to the heires of his body to be lawfully
begotten. And for default of such issue, to my said daughter, Anne
Hutton, full and sole sister to my said sonne Francis, and to th'eires
of hir body lawfully begotten, and for default of such issue, then to
the right heires of me the said Henry Brakenbury. I doe further
give to my beloved freind, John Cradock, vicar of Gaineford, outt of
my said lands, 13s. 4d. yearely dureinge his liffe, with one gowne of
blacke broad cloathe, one faire silke tippet, with one hatt and one
cappe. I give unto my nephewe, Lancelot Hilton, 40s. I give
to eche of my howsholde servaunts, one yeares waiges over
and besides what shalbe due to every of them at the day of my
deathe. And my will is that my executors shall pay all my said
legacies, funerall expences and debts out of my said lands and goods
at Selleby. I doe hereby make my beloved children, Francis
Brackenbury and Anne Hutton, aforesaid, executors of this my will,
requireinge them hereby to execute the same in every pointt
according to the trewe meaneinge thereof, etc.

Codicil. April 3, 1602. Henry Brakenbury, esquire, did
expresse and declare these wordes followinge to be parte of his
last will and testament and to be annexed unto the same as parte
thereof, *vidzt.*, that all such annuityes which he had formerly given
out of his mannor of Sellabye unto any person or personnes whatsoever in and by his said last will and testament should be voyde and
of none effect. And that in leiw thereof he did give unto the two
youngest children of Anne Hutton, *vidzt*, Tymothie and Francis, the
sume of 100*l.* to be paied unto the said Anne, by his said executors,
within one yeare next after his decease, and the said Francis
Brakenbury and John Cradock, clerk, to be sufficient securitie to be
entered by the said Anne for the repayment thereof unto the said
children at their severall aige of twenty and one yeares. Witnesses
hereof that this is trew, Anne Brakenbury, John Wickliffe, Elizabeth
Bannester and Elizabeth Spencer, wedow.

WILL OF CUTHBERT BATES.[1]

Jan. 23, 1601/2. Cuthbert Baites of Hallywell, in the county of
Northumberland, gentleman, whole of bodie, etc. My bodie to be
buried in the chappell of Earsddenn. I give unto my wife, Elizabethe
Baites, all my goods and chattels and debts upon condition that the

---

[1] An exhaustive pedigree of the family of Bates of Halliwell, in the parochial
chapelry of Earsdon, may be found in the eighth volume of the new *History of
Northumberland*. The testator was buried at Earsdon, Feb. 4, 1602/3.

said Elizabeth shall pay unto my sonne, Cuthbert Baites, when he shall attain 21 years, the summe of 100*l.* for his child's porcon. She shall likewise pay unto my daughter, Isabella Baites, when she attains 21 years, or marriage, the sum of 100*l.* and unto each of my two othere daughters, Dorothie Baites and Katherine Baites, one hundred marks. She shall likewise paie unto my baise daughter Margarett fourty marks. I will that as soone and when the said Elizabeth Baites, my wife, shall be assured and maried to any other man, that then Thomas Redhead of Trewhit shall have the custodie of my sone Cuthbert Baites during his minority, with his porcon of one hundred pounds. My will is that Mr. John Salkeld and Katherine, his wife, shall have my daughter Katherine Baites and her porconn and Richard Romaine of Newcastle-upon-Tyne, tanner, shall have my daughter Dorothie Baites, together with her porcon. I will that my said wife shall have the bringing upp of my daughter Isabella Baites. I give unto my wife, Elizabeth Baites, for the use of my sone Cuthbert Baites, one freehold in North Seaton during his minority. I give unto my sonnes, Thomas Baites and Cuthbert Baites, all my armer and artilerie equally. I will that these parcells conteyned in the note here enclosed and subscribed with my owne hand shall remaine and be in my house at Hallywell for heirloimes. I do make overseers of this my will the worshipfull my verie good friendes Mr. John Fenwick of Wallington and Mr. Anthonie Feltonne. I give unto Mr. John Fenwick aforesaid my sommeringe place in the hie lands called the Reyseat and Redpeth during the minorie [*sic*] of my heir. I have made a lease to my brother, Thomas Ogle, of all my lands in Hallywell for the term of eleven years, to the intent that the profitt thereof may be imployed for the uppbringing of my children. I will that Thomas Baites, my kinsman, sadler, shall everie yeare have a bowell of hard corne. I make my youngest daughter, Katherine Baites, executor. Witnesses, Thomas Houndley, Thomas Ogle, Myles Baites and Parcivall Smith.

Pr. June 1, 1605, by Elizabeth Baites, the widow, on behalf of his daughter, Katherine Baites, the sole executrix (then a minor).

Feb. 19, 1602/3. INVENTORY of all the goods and chattels movable and unmovable belonging unto Cuthbert Bates of Hallywell:—

Imprimis: In the clossett: 20 books, a form, and a cheste, 20*s.* *In the parler:* A stand-bedde, one hurle-bedde, a trunke, 12 payre of lynne sheats, 12 pyllowes, one chyste, 5 table cloathes, 4 coopperd cloathes, 3 dussen napkens, 3 lynne towels, 5*l.* 11*s.* *In the hall:* Two tables, 2 formes, a chayre, a dresser, and iron chymney, 40*s.* *In the west chamber:* A stand-bedde with courtings and a long chyste, 13*s.* 4*d.* *In the mydle chamber:* Two stand-bedds, with courtings, one hurle-bedde, a chyste, and a presser, 20*s.* *In the buttre:* One coopborde, 2 chysts and a malt toube, 10*s.* *In the brew-hoose:* A maskinge toobe, 3 worte toobes, 3 beare barrels, 3 stands and a table 6*s.* *In the lardner:* Beaffe toobes and other necessares, 5*s.*

In the brew-hoose lofte: 1 table, 1 olde bedstead and 1 olde coopbord, 6*s.* 8*d.*, two morters, 3*s.* 4*d.*, 8 stone of lymite [*sic*], 40*s.* *In the kytchinge:* A payre of irone racks, a porre, 2 payre of tonges, two fryinge pannes, 4 speatts, 4 crooks, 4 brasse potts, 2 caldrens, 2 kettels, 4 pannes, 4 candlesteaks, 16 peases of pewther vessell and 4 washinge toobbes, 38*s.* 8*d.*

A longe swoord, a shorte swoord, a gylted dagre, 11 staves, 4 goones, 2 pystalls, 2 steall capps, 2 jackes, 2 preavye coates, 2 payre of plate brytches, 2 payre of plate sleaves, 2 payre of plate stokens, 6*l.* 13*s.* 4*d.* 3 feather bedds, 2 matresses, 2 roogs, 12 coverletts, 8 happings, 6 payre of blanketts, 2 carpetts, 10 payre of coarse sheattes, 6 quisshens, 2 chamber potts, 7*l.* 10*s.* 12 yards of howswyfe cloathes, 30*s.* Narowe cloathes for courtings to bedde, 7*s.* In ewes 3 penns, 1 toope with saide ewes, 21*l.* In hogges, 9*l.* 9*s.* 20 kyne with 11 calves, 32*l.* 4 stottes, 4*l.* 14 younge stirkes and whyes, 9*l.* 6*s.* 8*d.* 24 oxene, 48*l.* 1 lytle nagge, 30*s.* 13 yokes for oxen, 9 irone sommes, 3 bolts and 3 sheakles, 20*s.* 6 plowes, 9*s.* 3 coultrs and 3 soks, 7*s.* 6*d.* 3 longe wannes, 2 shorte wannes, 2 irone harrowes and a stead, 3*l.* 6*s.* 8*d.* Hard corne in the howse and in the stackeyard, 46 booles, 16*l.* 2*s.* Hard corne sowen in the ground, 40 booles, 48*l.* Otts sowen, 42*l.* 2 sewes, 2 hoggs, 1 boare and 4 lyttle shotts, 29*s.*

Summ totall : 269*l.* 14*s.* 2*d.*

WILL OF JOHN WILSON.

April 20, 1602. John Wilson. To be buried in Midleton churchyard. To my eldest son, John Wilson, my right, etc., in my tenement, etc., at the Loneinge-head, and my gavelocke, my beste swoorde and dagger and my gray meare. To Peter, my son, my house and garth at the head of hoode. The rest to Peter, Alice and Elizabeth, my children. Whereas my brother in lawe, Edmonde Bainebrigge, did give me all his goods and tenement for the longer liver of him and his wife, after whose deceases the foresayd tenement to returne to his next heir, and I promised to give them meate, drinke and clotheing for their lives payinge yearely to them 10*s.* yearly. I will that 4 men indifferently chosen shall order the matter. Supervisors, Thomas Bainebrigge and John Neweby, to each of them, 7*s.* 6*d.* To the children of my sonne in lawe, William Lynd, viz., Thomas and Rebecca Lynd, a gymber lambe each. [Pr. Oct. 3, 1603.]

WILL OF THOMAS BECKHAM.

Sept. 27, 1602. Thomas Beckham of Barwike, burges, to be buryed in Barwicke church yard. To my wife, Jane, all my lands in Barwicke and elsewhere for 18 yeares, and if she be with childe with a sonne, I give him the hall howse and the kychine, with the haye loft and the great stable and the great garden. To my daughter, Margaret Beckham, after the 18 years, the chamber over the hall in the foreside of the strete and the litell garden, the courte-yard. To my wife, the shope with both the chambers joyninge to it, at, above and benethe, and the lytel stable and the seller both joyninge together, and a garden which is at the upper end of the great garden. To Margaret, my daughter, tow lytell copes. Overseers, Thomas Walker, and George Ferginson. Witnesses, Thomas Walker, Fowlke Mason, William Cooper, George Higginson, John Shotton. [Pr. Sept. 29, 1603.]

INVENTORY 10*l.* 16*s.* 10*d.*

WILL OF MARMADUKE CHAPMAN.

Dec. 12, 1602. Marmaduke Chapman of Billingham, yeoman.[1] To be buried in Billingham church. To the poore, 10*s.* To my sonne in lawe, Raiphe Trotter and Yssabell, my daughter, his wiffe, 30*l.* To my sonne in lawe, John Lawe, and Jane, my daughter, his wife, 10*l.* To each of my foresaid sonns in law, 10*s.* To each of Raiphe Trotter's children, 6*s.* 8*d.* To Robert Lawe, my daughter Jayne's sonne, 10*s.* To my godson, Marmaduke Chapman, 40*s.* and all my landes, tenements, etc., in Ryhopp and Sunderland-nigh-the-sea. To my daughter in lawe, Anne Chapman, widow, 20*s.*, and to her children, Thomas, John and Annesse Chapman, 10*s.* each. To Dorothy Hall, daughter of my son in lawe, Francis Hall, 10*s.* To my brother in lawe, Robert Jackson and to my sister, Frances, now his wife, 40*s.* and to each of their children an ewe and a lambe. To John Nevelson's 4 children an ewe and a lamb each. To George Fewler, one whie. To Richard Johnson of Durham, 5*s.* I give and bequith towards the repayring of Billingham church, 3*s.* 4*d.*, and towards the repairing of Billingham bridge, 6*s.* 8*d.* To Edward Lackenbye, 2*s.* 6*d.* To each of my servants, 12*d.* To Thomas Chapman, son of my nephew, Thomas Chapman, 5*s.* To George Moore, 3*s.* 4*d.* To William Smith, clarke, vicar of Billingham, 3*s.* 4*d.* The rest to Robert Chapman, my son, whom I make my sole executor. Supervisors, Charles Redclyfe of Tunstall, gentleman, and my cosen, Robert Farrowe . . . . th'elder, of Fishborne, 10*s.* to each.

Monye disburst by Robert Chapman at his buriall and since.—*Imprimis:* To the vicair and clerke and ringers, 2*s.* 8*d.* To the poore, 37*s.* 4*d.* To wedow Meynell for 14 meise of peope [*sic*], 26*s.* 4*d.* To Raiph Conyers for 12 meise, 22*s.* 6*d.* For the dinners of the

[1] In 1577 Marmaduke Chapman of Billingham, yeoman, took a conveyance of property in the Low Street, Sunderland, from his cousins, Elizabeth and Margaret, daughters and co-heirs of John Richardson of Durham, dyer. This property was conveyed in 1616 by Marmaduke Chapman of Norton, son and heir of John Chapman, son and heir of Marmaduke Chapman, to William Potts of Sunderland and Mary, his wife. *Ex inf.* Mr. Reginald Peacock.

praisers of the goods upon Tuesdaie at Raiph Conyers his house, 2*s* 8*d*. For their dinners at Peart's house, 3*s*. Law expences, etc. *Suma,* 10*l*. 8*s*. 6*d*.

INVENTORY. Jan. 17, 1603/4. *Imprimis:* 12 oxen, 33*l*. 28 ewes, 30 hogges, 4 tuppes, 17*l*. 4 steires, 7*l*. 6*s*. 8*d*. 9 horses, maires and 5 fooles, 20*l*. 6*s*. 8*d*. 6 kyne, 12*l*. 14*s*. All the corne in the staggarth and barne, etc., 30*l*. All the haye, 13*l*. 13*s*. 4*d*. Corne in George Fewler's staggarthe, 21*l*. 10*s*. Haye there, 3*l*. 13*s*. 4*d*. A stand bed in the parler with 1 coverlett, blacke and yellowe, with courtins of vallence, 48*s*. 3 bacon fletches, 18*s*. One corslett, 1 hedpece, 1 jacke, 30*s*. All his apparrell, 2 swords, 2 daggers, 5*l*. 2 steile cottes and steile cap, 1 bowe, 1 shaffe of arrowes, 11*s*. His owne chest, 3 sylver spones, 2 sylver ringes, 1 gold ringe; 2*s*. 6*d*. in gold; 4*s*. 11*d*. in money; his baggs, 38*s*. Paynted clothes about the halhouse, 12*d*. His owne horse and his saddell, 4*l*. All the yeres to come on George Fewler's farmhold, 50*l*. Whett and rye sowen on bothe fermholds, 38*l*. The wydowe's bedde, 40*s*.

Sum, 405*l*. 9*s*. 8*d*.

186

INDEX OF WILLS AND INVENTORIES

IN

VOLUME III.

A

ALLAN, JOHN, 1564, W., 28.
ALLISON, JOHN, 1586, W., 116.
ANDERSON, ALICE, 1583, W., 105.
ANDERSON, BERTRAM, 1571, W., 58.
ANDERSON, GILES, 1581, W.I., 88.
ANDERSON, JAMES, 1565, W., 138 n.
ANDERSON, JANET, 1587, W., 138.
AYNSLEY, JANE, 1582, W., 96.
AYRE, STEPHEN, 1586, I., 118.
AYTON, HENRY, 1581, W., 89.

B

BARROW, THOMAS, 1582, W., 95.
BARTON, CHRISTOPHER, 1592, W., 153.
BATES, CUTHBERT, 1602, W.I., 181.
BATES, WILLIAM, 1587, W., 119.
BAYLES, RICHARD, 1574, W., 71.
BAYNE, RICHARD, 1565, I., 30.
BECKHAM, THOMAS, 1602, W., 183.
BELL, THOMAS, 1584, W., 105.
BELL, WILLIAM, 1583, W., 103.
BENNETT, ISABEL, 1553, W., 10.
BERTRAM, THOMAS, 1544, W., 3.
BEST, ROBERT, 1569, W., 48.
BEWICK, EDWARD, 1587, W.I., 125.
BEWICK, PETER, 1587, W., 132.
BEWICK, WILLIAM, 1551, W., 8.
BIDDICK, ROBERT, 1544, W., 1.
BIRKENHEAD, ROBERT, 1571, W., 57.
BLAKISTON, RALPH, 1591, W., 149.
BLAKISTON, ROGER, 1570, I., 49.
BLENKINSOP, ROLAND, 1571, W., 62.
BLENKINSOP, WILLIAM, 1583, W., 102.
BLOUNT, CUTHBERT, 1559, W., 19.
BLYTHMAN, EDWARD, 1567, W., 57 n.
BLYTHMAN, NICHOLAS, 1571, W., 57.

BOURN, GEORGE, 1592, W.I., 154.
BOWDON, JASPER, 1589, W., 148.
BOWES, ROBERT, 1580, W., 84.
BRACKENBURY, HENRY, 1601, W., 180.
BRACKENBURY, MARTIN, 1574, W., 69.
BRADFORD, ANTHONY, 1584, W., 108.
BRASS, ROGER, 1587, W., 123.
BRIMLEY, JAMES, 1587, I., 131.
BROWN, JOHN, 1583, W., 101.
BROWN, ROBERT, 1587, I., 122.
BURDON, WILLIAM, 1587, W., 125.
BURLINSON, GEORGE, 1578, W., 80.
BURRELL, CUTHBERT, 1563, W., 27.
BURRELL, JOHN, 1597, I., 166.
BURRELL, WILLIAM, 1582, W., 96.

C

CARR, HUMPHREY, 1559, W., 20.
CARR, NICHOLAS, 1545, W., 4.
CARTER, WILLIAM, 1573, W., 68.
CATTERICK, RALPH, 1581, W., 86.
CATTERICK, RALPH, 1591, 86 n., 150.
CHAMBER, STEPHEN, 1587, W.I., 130.
CHAPMAN, MARMADUKE, 1602, W.I., 184.
CHARLTON, GAWEN, 1584, W., 105.
CHAYTOR, THOMAS, 1575, W., 74.
CLARK, HUGH, 1581, W., 89.
CLARK, NICHOLAS, 1573, W., 68.
CLARK, ROLAND, 1572, W., 64.
CLAXTON, RICHARD, 1598, W., 168.
CLAXTON, ROBERT, 1578, W., 79.
CLEOBURN, JOHN, 1599, W., 173.
CLIFF, RICHARD, 1582, W., 97.
COLE, RALPH, 1584, W., 40.
COLLINGWOOD, CUTHBERT, 1599, W., 171.
COLLINGWOOD, EDWARD, 1587, W., 130.

T

TEMPEST, THOMAS, 1569, I., 48.
THURSBY, CUTHBERT, 1574, W., 70.
TOBIE, THOMAS, 1585, W., 116.
TONGE, GEORGE, 1593, W., 157.
TOPIAS, GEORGE, 1583, W., 100.
TROLLOPE, ANTHONY, 1567, W.I., 37.
TURPIN, MARTIN, 1554, W., 11.

W

WARDLE, JOHN, 1581, W., 89.
WARDLE, THOMAS, 1581, W., 90 n.
WALL, JOHN, 1565, W., 31.
WARRENER, ELIZABETH, 1585, W., 114.
WATSON, JOHN, 1547, W., 5.
WATSON, JOHN, 1580, W., 84.
WELLBURY, JOHN, 1585, W., 87 n.

WELLBURY, SIMON, 1581, W., 87.
WHITFIELD, HUGH, 1576, W., 74.
WHITFIELD, THOMAS, 1578, W., 74 n.
WIDDRINGTON, JAMES, 1596, W., 161.
WILKINSON, ISABELLA, 1559, W., 18.
WILKINSON, MATTHEW, 1582, W.I., 92.
WILKINSON, THOMAS, 1588, W., 144.
WILSON, EDMUND, 1601, W., 179.
WILSON, JOHN, 1602, W., 183.
WOLDHAVE, CHRISTOPHER, 1584, W., 107.
WOLDHAVE, JOHN, 1566, W., 35.
WOODIFIELD, RICHARD, 1568, W., 40.
WOODIFIELD, WILLIAM, 1568, W., 40 n.
WOUMPHREY, THOMAS, 1585, W., 115.
WRAY, THOMAS, 1577, W., 79.
WREN, WILLIAM, 1570, I., 51.
WYVELL, SAMPSON, 1568, W., 40.

INDEX OF NAMES.*

* For the purpose of this index the names have been largely modernized, and no distinction has been attempted between the male and female names of Francis or Frances.

B

Bainbridge, Christopher, 179; Edmund, 179, 183; Frances, 44, 179; George, 179; Henry, 179; Margaret, 17; Phillis, 179; Rebecca, 179; Thomas, 179, 183; William, 77, 179.
Bailes (Bayles), Ann, 71; Elizabeth, 71; Henry, 51; John, 71; Ralph, 51; Richard, 71, 163; William, 71.
Bailey, Godfrey, 44.
Bailif (Balif), Alice, 8.
Baird, George, 165.
Baker (Bayker) Jane, 163; Richard, 119; Valentine, 64; Mrs., 62.
Baliol, John, king of Scotland, 77 n.
Bamford, James, 152.
Banks, Edward, 35.
Bannister, Elizabeth, 181; Lawrence, 121; Richard, 121.
Barber, Robert, 39.
Barbone, James, 58.
Barker, Edward, 130; George, 125; Jean, 148; Mr., 114.
Barloe, Richard, 158.
Barnes, Ralph, 82.
Barnhere, Thomas, 175.
Barras, Anthony, 49, 120.
Barrell (?Burrell), Richard, 51.
Barrow, Thomas, 95.
Barton, Anthony, 21, 141, 144; Brian, 153; Christopher, 21, 153; Ralph, 70.
Basnett, Alex., 16.
Baston, Sir Henry, 34.
Bates (Baites), Agnes, 36; Barbara, 119; Blease, 119; Catherine, 182; Cuthbert, 181, 182; Dorothy, 182; Elizabeth, 181, 182; George, 119; Isabella, 182; Margaret, 182; Miles, 182; Thomas, 182; William, 119.
Bateman (Baitman), Jane, 19; John, 19; Margaret, 121.
Bateson (Betsonn), Margaret, 167.
Batmanson, Marmaduke, 86.
Baxter, Christopher, 60; Nicholas, 8, 26.
Bayley, William, 61.
Bayne, Richard, 30.
Beadnel (Bednell, etc.), James, 9; William, 9; Mrs., 9.
Beck, John, 36.
Beckham, Jane, 183; Margaret, 184; Thomas, 183.
Bedall, Mark, 29.
Bee, George, 15.
Beere, William, 74.

Belamy, James, 29.
Bell, Agnes, 45, 103; Allison, 147; Christopher, 105, 106; Elizabeth, 105, 106, 151; George, 105, 106; Isabel, 71; Janet, 105, 106; John, 71, 54, 101, 105, 106; Mabel, 82; Margaret, 103; Richard, 3, 72; Robert, 26, 27, 103; Roger, 72; Thomas, 103, 105, 106; William, 103.
Bellasis (Bellasye), Sir William, 76; Lady, 76; Mr., 75 n.
Bellerbe, John, 45.
Bellingham (Billingham), Cuthbert, 135; John, 48.
Bennet, Isabel, 10; Margaret, 10 n.; William, 10 n., 44; Dr., 30.
Benson (Benison), Richard, 9; Robert, 133; Thomas, 37, 62, 73.
Bertram (Bartram), Edward, 125; George, 3; Thomas, 3; William, 3.
Best, Alison, 48; Margaret, 48; Martin, 48; Peter, 48; Robert, 48; Thomas, 48.
Bethoun, Elizabeth, 149.
Bettleston, Robert, 50.
Bewick, Agnes, 46, 125; Annes, 132; Andrew, 46, 126, 132; Barbara, 107, 132; Bertram, 9; Cuthbert, 8, 9, 172; Christopher, 46, 106; Edward, 125, 126; Eleanor, 46, 47; Elizabeth, 46, 47, 107, 132, 172 n.; Gillian, 46; Janet, 9; John, 9; Margaret, 132, 172; Percival, 8, 9; Peter (Piers), 8, 9, 107, 132; Robert, 46, 172; Thomas, 9; William, 8.
Biddick (Bedyke, etc.), Annes, 68; Maud, 1; Robert, etc., 1, 2; William, 1; Mr., 68.
Biggin, Margaret, 168; Mary, 168.
Bilton, Richard, 43; William, 142, 143.
Binks, John, 173.
Bird, Anthony, 59; Mark, 60.
Birkenhead, Anthony, 58; Dorothy, 57; George, 58; Gerard, 58; John, 58; Margaret, 58; Robert, 57; William, 58.
Blackburn (Blakeburn), Anne, 90.
Blackdene (Blaikden), Margery, 162; Thomas, 45.
Blackett, Thomas, 58.
Blackman, Edmund, 57.
Blakiston (Blaxton, etc.), Adam, 150; Anthony, 48; Humphrey, 44; John, 149, 150; Mary, 163; Ralph, 149; Robert, 163; Roger, 49; William, 49 n.

Camber, Magdalen, 4.
Cammont, John, 105; Mabel, 105.
Cardnell, Richard, 167.
Cardwell, William, 127.
Carey, Capt., 153.
Carnaby, Anthony, 61, 62; Cuthbert, 33; David, 61, 95; Dorothy, 33; Hector, 118; John, 33, 113; Lancelot, 155; Marion, 7; Odnell, 7; Raynold (Sir Reginald), 33, 146.
Carr (Carre), Alison, 4; Christopher, 20; Cuthbert, 20, 36, 63; Edward, 171; Elizabeth, 171; George, 4, 9, 63, 105, 152; Gerard, 135; Humphrey, 20; Isabel, 4, 20; James, 61; Jane, 4, 16; John, 9, 16, 20, 73, 97, 114, 126; Lancelot, 62; Margery, 20; Nicholas, 4, 48; Oswald, 37, 93, 94; Rebecca, 63; Richard, 73; Robert, 4, 20, 63, 113; Roger, 4; William, 4, 20, 61, 62.
Carter, Eleanor, 85; George, 28, 48; Henry, 28; John, 69; Margery, 69; Marmaduke, 28, 69; Peter, 68, 69; Wiliam, 56, 68.
Carvill, Robert, 91.
Case, Captain, 91.
Casson, Ann, 92.
Cassop, Anthony, 51.
Catterick (Katherick), Alison, 86 n., 150; John, 86 n., 150; Lawrence, 174; Margaret, 86 n., 150; Nicholas, 86; Ralph, 86, 150; Richard, 86 n., 150; William, 86.
Cay, John, 44. See Kay.
Chambers (Chamber), Alison, 130; Ann, 114; Catherine, 130; Elizabeth, 130; John, 130; Leonard, 130; Stephen, 130; Thomas, 121; William, 92.
Chapman, Ann, 184; Annas, 184; George, 37; John, 37, 161, 162, 184; Lancelot, 37, 52; Marion, 60; Marmaduke, 184; Matthew, 103; Robert, 184; Thomas, 184.
Charlton, Edward, 105; Elizabeth, 105; Gawen, 105; John, 105.
Chaytor (Chaitor, etc.), Agnes, 19; Christopher, 15, 19, 21, 32, 62, 81, 85, 94; Cuthbert, 74, 148; Elizabeth, 19; John, 3, 19; Margaret, 19; Nicholas, 74; Oswald and Oswin, 74, 148; Peter, 3; Thomas, 74; Mr., 36.
Cherteseye, Benet, 61.
Chilton, Agnes, 89; Janet, 89; Robert, 89; William, 89, 90.
Chope, Mr., 175.

Clapham (Clapam), John, 22.
Clark (Clerk), Agnes, 36; Christy, 146; Ellen, 146; Hugh, 89; John, 111; Marion, 89; Nicholas, 68; Robert, 111; Roger, 64; Roland, 64; Thomas, 89, 91, 108; William, 28, 31.
Clarkson (Clerkson), George, 66 n.; Henry, 171; John, 171.
Clavering, Grace, 148; Margaret, 97 n.; Ralph, 97 n.
Claxton, Allison, 168 n.; Ammonde, 79; Anne, 58; Anthony, 90; Christopher, 168; Cuthbert, 78; Dean, 18; Elizabeth, 22; George, 22, 67 n.; Gerard, 168; Humphrey, 168; Jane, 22; John, 22, 79, 168; Lancelot, 168; Lyones, 14; Margaret and Margery, 22, 79; Richard, 79, 168; Robert, 79, 168; Roger, 79; Thomas, 34, 168; William, 16, 58, 168; Mr., 86.
Clayton, widow, 54.
Cleborne (Clibbron, Cleoburn), Henry, 173; John, 173; Richard, 173; Thomas, 61; William, 173; Dame, 90.
Clesby, John, 86.
Clewes, Christopher, 155.
Cliffe, Eleanor, 97; John, 97; Richard, 97.
Clifton, Robert, 123.
Clopton, John, 82, 93, 94.
Clough, Alice, 154; George, 154; John, 80.
Cockfield, Christopher, 65; Henry, 166, 167; John, 65.
Cocks, William, 47.
Coise (Coys), Ralph, 111; William, 175 n.
Cole, James, 110; Jane, 110, 111; Nicholas, 110; Ralph, 110; Richard, 110; Robert, 110; Thomas, 110.
Colling (Collins), Ralph, 50; Thomas, 112; Mr., 175.
Collingson, Richard, 68.
Collingwood (Colynwood), Alexander, 149; Catherine, 149; Cuthbert, 95, 171; Dorothy, 171; Edward, 92, 130; Eleanor, 84; Elizabeth, 130, 171; Henry, 149, 161, 165, 171; Humphrey, 34; Janet, 149, 171; John, 10, 84, 119, 130, 149; Margaret, 84, 149, 165; Matthew, 171; Ralph, 13, 32, 95 n., 125, 149; Robert, 4, 149, 171; Roland, 165; Thomas, 84, 149, 161; Thomasine, 149; William, 130.

13

194

Colman, Anthony, 153.
Colmore, Clement, 145 n.
Coltman (Cowtman), Ralph, 17, 39;
Richard, 62.
Compton (Cowton), Ralph, 51;
Thomas, 51.
Constable, Michael, 23 n., 170;
William, 170.
Conyers, Anne, 34 n., 35; Christopher, 74; Cicely, 35; Edward, 35,
66 n.; Eleanor, 35; Elizabeth, 74;
Frances, 35; George (Sir George),
34, 35, 39; James, 35; John, 35;
Lancelot, 135; Margaret, 35;
Mary, 35; Ralph, 35, 184, 185;
Richard, 35, 87, 120; Robert, 34,
35, 58; Roger, 34; Thomas, 34;
William, 34, 35; Mr., 106; Mrs.,
87.
Cook (Coke), Anthony, 134, 135;
Christopher, 46, 47; Eleanor, 46,
134; Elizabeth, 46, 78; George,
45, 46, 134, 135; Henry, 100;
Jane, 134; John, 46, 47, 72, 78,
120; Margaret and Margery, 78,
134; Robert, 77, 78; Simon, 134;
Thomas, 78, 100, 143; William,
47; Mr., 74, 177; Mrs., 78.
Cookson (Coocheson), William, 20,
47.
Cooper, Wiliam, 184.
Coperthwait (Coperwhote), Matthew,
81.
Corby, Thomas, 98.
Cordell, Sir William, 27 n.
Cordmane, Edward, 160.
Corker, Dorothy, 58.
Cornforth, Robert, 135; Thomas, 72.
Cotes, William, 132.
Cotesworth (Cotterworth, Cotesforth,
etc.), George, 55; Richard, 44.
Cotton, Thomas, 88.
Couler, Robert, 54.
Coulson (Cowston, Cowson), Edward, 96; Janet, 146; John, 146;
Thomas, 146.
Coulthard (Coltard) Jane, 55.
Coward, Robert, 82.
Cowdon, James, 147.
Cowley, Margaret, 85; William, 85.
Cowper, Bartholomew, 89; Robert,
89.
Cowpland, Nicholas, 121, 122, 131.
Cowson, Janet, 146; John, 146;
Thomas, 146.
Cox (Cocks), Ralph, 103; William,
47.
Coxon (Cokson, Cocsone), Allison,
115; Charles, 115; Cicely, 115;
Clement, 113; Elizabeth, 115;

Henry, 115; Michael, 115;
Nicholas, 75 n., 115; Robert, 115.
Coys, William, 175. See Coise.
Cradock, John, 101, 181.
Craggs (Crage), Alexander, 107, 146;
Alice, 107; Anne, 23 n.; Gilbert,
11; Ralph, 45; Robert, 107;
Mr., 23 n.
Crakehall (Craycall), Elizabeth, 50,
51.
Cramer, Agnes, 10; Robert, 10.
Cramlington, Agnes, 8; Elizabeth,
8; Lamwell, 8; Lancelot, 8;
Thomas, 8.
Crane, Agnes, 96, Barbara, 97; Elizabeth, 96, 97; Jane, 97; John, 96;
Margaret, 97; Mary, 97;
Nicholas, 97; Thomas, 96.
Craster, Alice, 165; Barbara, 165;
Bartholomew, 82; Edmund, 165;
Eleanor, 165; Jane, 82; John,
82, 165; Lewis, 82; Margaret, 14,
82; Thomas, 13, 165; William,
14, 82.
Crathorn (Crawthorn, etc.), John,
86; Matthew, 23 n.; Mr., 18, 37.
Crawford, Christopher, 97, 98;
George, 98; Richard, 28, 97, 98;
Robert, 98.
Cresswell (Criswell), Catherine,
19 n.; Edward, 114; Robert,
19 n.
Croft, James, 19; Lady, 20.
Crook, John, 37.
Crosby, John, 32; (—), 44.
Crow (Craw, etc.), Edward, 52; John,
52; Ralph, 36; Thomas, 117.
Cumin (Comyn), Francis, 108;
Simon, 94.
Cunningham (Connyngham), George,
9.
Curry, Matthew, 74.
Curwen, Dorothy, 122; Eleanor, 90;
Nicholas, 121; Richard, 122;
Mrs., 90.
Cuthbert, George, 31; Janet, 31;
(—), 53.
Cutter, John, 96.

D

Dacre, Lord, 11; Lady Elizabeth, 11;
John, 11; Leonard, 11; Parson, 11; Sir Thomas, 11; Lord,
11.
Daglish (Dagleis), Matthew, 114.
Dale (Dayle, etc.), Anthony, 56, 57;
Christopher, 52, 53; George,
100; James, 56; Janet, 56;
Margaret, 56.

Dalton, Agnes, 36; Dorothy, 24;
Elizabeth, 23 n.; Frances, 24;
John, 36; Ralph, 14, 23 n.;
Robert, 23, 24, 39.
Daniel (Danyell), Robert, 134, 149.
Darling, Christobel, 72.
Darneton, Robert, 40 n.
Davell, George, 59.
Davis, John, 160.
Davison, Edward, 3; George, 86;
Thomas, 36.
Davey, Edward, 160; John, 160;
Robert, 160; William, 160.
Dawheth, David, 119.
Dawney, Anne, 34 n.; John, 34, 35.
Dawson, Anthony, 51; Henry, 144;
Hugh, 144; Isabel, 135; Jane,
68; Margaret, 144; Peter, 27;
Ranold, 50; Robert, 51; Thomas,
55, 144.
Deanham, Thomas, 143.
Dearham, Baldwin, 163; John, 163;
Richard, 163; Robert, 163;
Thomas, 162 n.
Delahay (Dallayhay), Henry, 9;
Oswald, 107.
Delaval, George, 36; Oswald, 36;
Sir John, 169 n.
Denman, Agnes, 79; Nicholas, 79.
Denninge, Christopher; 155.
Dennison, John, 29.
Dent, Ann, 152; Christopher, 112;
George, 177; John, 44; Robert,
152; William, 8, 26.
Denton, Henry, 163.
Dickinson (Dixhinson, etc.), Eleanor,
47; Margery, 46, 47; William,
4, 46, 47.
Diggles, Leonard, 126.
Dinsdale, Thomas, 44.
Dixon (Dickson), Anthony, 51; Mar-
garet, 45; Robert, 142; Thomas,
54, 154.
Dobinson, Henry, 51; William, 51.
Dobson, Agnes, 56; Bartholomew,
132; Christopher, 52; Janet, 57;
John, 56, 57, 132; Reginald,
132; Richard, 57; Thomas, 100;
William, 132.
Dodds (Doddes, etc.), George, 28;
James, 146, Janet, 84; Thomas,
160; Mr., 28.
Dodshon, Roger, 160.
Dodsworth, George, 86.
Donkin, Elizabeth, 112; John, 112;
William, 112.
Donell, Mr., 175.
Dossye, Annes, 140; Francis, 140;
Isabel, 140; John, 140; Thomas,
140.

Douglas (Duglas), Humphrey, 83.
Dowthwaite (Dowghtwhett, etc.),
John, 54; Robert, 54.
Duckett, Anthony, 51; Christopher,
173; Roger, 51.
Dunn (Don, Donne, Down), Agnes,
4, 99; Anthony, 100; Bridget,
99; Christopher, 120, 163;
Dorothy, 99; Elizabeth, 92, 99,
120; George, 30; James, 120;
John, 131; Ralph, 129; Richard,
160; Thomas, 71.
Durham, Dean and Chapter, 23 n.;
My Lord, 14; Richard, 158.
Dymoke, Margery, 156 n.; Sir Ed-
ward, 156 n.

E

Easterby, Thomas, 100.
Eden, Agnes, 10; Edward, 148;
Henry, 36; Robert, 23 n., 148,
155; William, 125.
Edgar, Thomas, 124.
Edward, Richard, 54.
Eggleston, Christopher, 30; Mar-
garet, 30; Richard, 30; Stephen,
30; Thomas, 30; William, 30.
Eland, Christopher, 111; Richard,
44.
Elder, Isabel, 96.
Ellener (Ellyner), Dorothy, 68; Ed-
mund, 68; Robert, 68.
Ellikar, Edward, 32, 34; John, 32,
95; Robert, 32; Thomas, 32;
William, 32.
Ellis, Anthony, 147; John, 147;
Margaret, 147; Robert, 147.
Ellison (Elyson), Andrew, 90; Ann,
91; Cuthbert, 4, 20, 91; George,
90; Humphrey, 114; Isabel, 91;
John, 15, 16, 91; Margaret, 90;
Stephen, 90.
Elmer, Christopher, 46, 47; Thomas,
47.
Elrington, Agnes, 73; Constance, 73;
Elizabeth, 62, 146; George, 73;
Janet, 73; John, 72, 73; Marion,
73; Martin, 73; Robert, 72, 146;
Simon, 61; William, 73.
Elstob (Elstobbe), Ann, 111, 112;
Anthony, 127; Eleanor, 111;
Henry, 111, 112; James, 111, 112;
John, 111, 112; Richard, 111;
Thomas, 111.
Elwood, James, 119.
Elwyn, William, 98.
Emmerson (Emerson), Agnes, 31;
Arthur, 55; Margaret, 31; Ralph,
58; Robert, 31, 131.

R

Rackett, Addelia, 140, 141; Anthony, 21; Catherine, 140; Cuthbert, 21, 140, 141; Elizabeth, 21, 140; George, 21, 140; John, 21, 140; Margaret, 140; Robert, 21, William, 21.

Radcliffe (Ratcliffe, etc.), Anthony, 62; Charles, 184; Cuthbert, 62; Frances, 102; George (Sir George), 102, 106; Mr., 114.

Raisley, Stephen, 107.

Ramshaw (Rampshawe), Hugh, 54.

Rand, Elizabeth, 112 n.; Fortune, 112; James, 112; John, 112; Margaret (Margery), 112; Ralph, 112, 130; Richard, 30, 36, 112; Robert, 130; Thomas, 130; William, 112; Mr., 175.

Rashell, —, 167.

Raw, Christopher, 124; Elizabeth, 4, 124; John, 4; Robert, 124; Roger, 4, 46, 124; William, 124, 125; Mr., 124; Mrs., 20. See Rea.

Raymes, George, 113, 114.

Raynton, Cuthbert, 109.

Rea (Rey, etc.), James, 37, 106; Thomas, 36, 85, 105; William, 36.

Read (Reed, Reid, Rede), Anne, 6, 113, 127, 128; Clement, 167; Elizabeth, 128; Gawen, 119; George, 6; Gerard, 167, 168; Isabel, 126; Janet, 6; Joan, 6; John, 6, 125, 127, 128; Margaret, 6; Richard, 6, 63; Rowland, 128; Thomas, 11 n., 81, 125; Walter, 6; William, 6, 118.

Readman, George, 23, 24; Mr., 58.

Redhead (Readhead), Janet (Jane), 45, 114; John, 45, 91; Thomas, 182.

Redshaw (Readshaw), Robert, 30; Thomas, 62.

Rennoldson (Ranoldson, Reynardson), Alison, 99; Anthony, 135; Janet, 99; John, 99.

Reveley, Clement, 88; Custance, 104; Eleanor, 88; Fortune, 88; Isabel, 88; Janet, 88; John, 96; Michael, 88; Thomas, 83, 88; William, 88.

Richardson (Richeson, etc.), Elizabeth, 184 n.; John, 28, 129, 143, 184 n.; Margaret, 184 n.; Ralph, 177; Richard, 135; Robert, 39, 160; Thomas, 60; William, 74.

Riddell (Ridell), Alice, 177; Ann, 177; Barbara, 167 n., 177; Catherine, 15; Edmund, 51; Eleanor, 15, 177; Elizabeth, 15, 177; George, 177; Henry, 167, 168; John, 177; Mary, 15, 177; Michael, 177; Peter, 15, 16, 177; Robert, 177; Thomas, 15, 16, 177; William, 15, 16, 167 n., 168 n., 177.

Ridley, Alexander, 96, 108, 109; Clement, 108; Cuthbert, 108; Christobel, 109; Christopher, 175; Dorothy, 108; Edward, 108; Elizabeth, 134, 135; Frances, 108; Gilbert, 108; Jane, 108; John, 108, 109, 119, 141; Nicholas, 96, 97, 108; Thomas, 96; William, 96, 108, 146.

Ripley (Rypley), Leonard, 51.

Rippes, John, 162, 163; Thomazine, 162, 163.

Rippon, John, 106; Robert, 106; William, 106.

Robinson, (Robeson, etc.), Agnes, 99; Anne, 121; Barbara, 14; Cicely, 14; Christopher, 28, 48, 131; Edward, 64; Elizabeth (Besse), 121; George, 14, 121; Henry, 54; Janet, 64; John, 52, 60, 102, 128, 131; Margaret (Margery), 65, 121, 165; Peter, 55; Robert, 94, 99; Susan, 102; Thomas, 43, 51, 52, 62, 65, 73; William, 14, 35, 105, 142.

Robson, Agnes (Annes), 108, 158; Robert, 57; William, 146.

Rochester, Agnes, 152; George, 151, 152; Henry, 152; Isabel, 96; James, 152; Janet (Jane), 96, 152; Robert, 96; Thomas, 152; William, 152.

Rogerly (Rogerlie), Cuthbert, 5; George, 5.

Rokeby (Rokesbye, Ruksbee), Cuthbert, 10; Elizabeth, 10; James, 10; John, 10, 110; Lawrence, 10, 46; Robert, 10; Mrs., 46.

Romaine, Richard, 182.

Rose, Mr., 175.

Rotheropp, Henry, 153.

Rothwell, Richard, 175.

Rounsenforth, Anthony, 157.

Routledge (Rutless, etc.), Andrew, 71; John, 161.

Rowlandson (Rolandson), Thomas, 29.

Rowth, John, 142.

Rumforth, Anthony, 137.

Russell, John, 96; Ursula, 96.

Rutherford (Ruddesforth, etc.), Barbara, 158; Gawen, 95; Grace, 95; John, 95; Margaret, 95; Thomas, 83, 95.

Rutter, Anthony, 28; Christopher, 28; Mrs., 129.

INDEX OF PLACES.

14

E

Eachwick, 82.
Earsdon (Earsddenn), 181.
Easington, 30, 74.
Edinburgh, 147.
Edmondsley, 18.
Edmundbyers, 62, 73.
Egglescliffe, 2, 3.
Eggleston, 81.
Eglingham, 160, 161.
Elbing, 167, 168.
Elrington, 72, 146.
Elswick, 35, 36, 146.
Elton, 38.
Embleton, 6, 68, 165.
'Eracowe,' 34.
Esh, 2 n., 17, 18, 39, 76, 148.
Eslington, 149 n.
Espershields (Hespershealls), 61, 72.
Ewart (Eworth), 32.

F

Fallowfield (Fallofeelde), 33.
Farneton-hall, 169.
Fawley, 92.
Felkington, 32.
Felton, 8, 16 n.
Fenham, 9.
Ferry-on-the-Hill, 40 n., 128, 129, 133, 134.
Fishburn (Fysheburn, etc.), 40, 89, 184.
Flanders, 79.
Flass, 148 n.
Flatworth, 158 n., 159.
Ford, 169.
Fourstones (Fowrestones), 33.
Framlington, 161.
'Fugfild,' 26.

G

Gainford (Gaynfourthe, etc.), 27, 48, 54, 69, 97, 98 n., 101, 122, 126, 166 n., 173, 176, 181.
Gallow Hill, 121.
'Gambleston,' 161.
'Garsdayle,' 41.
Gateshead, 19, 20, 30, 36, 45, 57 n., 59, 60, 75, 79, 94, 110, 112, 145 n., 161, 162, 170, 172, 177, 178; church, 57 n., 75; St. Edmund's chapel, 19, 79; Trinity chantry, 75.
Gibside (Gybsyde), 49.
Girsby, 34.
'Gordym,' 23.
Gosforth, 10.

Gresham College, 175.
Grindon, 25.
Guildford, 175.
Gunnerton, 33.
'Gyll-feilde' ('Gildfelde'), 81, 115.

H

Hackforth, 40 n., 42.
Haggerston, 88.
Halifax, 145.
Hallington (Halleden), 162.
Hallywell, 181, 182.
Halton, 34.
Haltwhistle, 97 n.
Hamburgh (Hambrowgh), 60.
Hardwick, 44.
'Hareham,' 30.
Harperley, 34, 35.
Harraton (Harradon), 37 n., 71, 75 n.
Hart (Herte), 19, 55, 87, 131.
Hartburn, 162.
Hartlepool, 98, 131.
Haswell, 30, 59.
Haughton, 14. (See Houghton.)
Hawkwell, 4.
'Hawletrasse,' 122.
Hawthorn, 74, 99.
Haydon (Haydon Bridge), 11, 73, 118, 146.
Headlam, 27, 28, 97, 127, 166, 167.
Healey (Temple Healey), 161 n.
Hearonhill, 96.
Heaton (Heghton), 8, 101.
Hebburn, 148, 153.
Heddon (Heddon-on-the-Wall, East Heddon, West Heddon), 10 n., 16, 70 n., 82, 113.
Hedleyhope, 7 n., 18, 75.
Heighington, 16, 17, 38, 40, 64, 69, 129, 142, 157 n.
Hesleyside (Hesslesyd), 105.
Hesledon (Hessledone), 68, 87, 99, 100.
Hetherycleugh (Hedrycloughe), 55.
Hetton in the Hole, 25, 131.
Hexham, 16, 33, 146.
Hilton, 37 n., 77, 137, 169 n., 178.
Hindon (Hyendon), 173.
Holliwell (Hallywell), 181, 182.
Hollingside, 157 n.
Holm, 24.
Holmeside (Holmesyde, etc.), 17, 39.
Holy Island, 5.
Hoppen, 66.
Horden, 74.
Hornby, 34.
Horsley in Weardale, 55.
Horton, 158 n., 159.